CFA Institute®
CFA Program

AF633491

ETHICAL AND PROFESSIONAL STANDARDS

CFA® Program Curriculum

2025 • LEVEL III CORE • VOLUME 5

WILEY

ISBN 978-1-961409-46-0 (paper)
ISBN 978-1-961409-58-3 (ebook)
May 2024

SKYA5C42C83-183D-4724-9F0A-AAF73E4374F1_032324

Please visit our website at
www.WileyGlobalFinance.com.

WILEY

CONTENTS

How to Use the CFA Program Curriculum

The CFA® Program exams measure your mastery of the core knowledge, skills, and abilities required to succeed as an investment professional. These core competencies are the basis for the Candidate Body of Knowledge (CBOK™). The CBOK consists of four components:

- A broad outline that lists the major CFA Program topic areas (www.cfainstitute.org/programs/cfa/curriculum/cbok/cbok)
- Topic area weights that indicate the relative exam weightings of the top-level topic areas (www.cfainstitute.org/en/programs/cfa/curriculum)
- Learning outcome statements (LOS) that advise candidates about the specific knowledge, skills, and abilities they should acquire from curriculum content covering a topic area: LOS are provided at the beginning of each block of related content and the specific lesson that covers them. We encourage you to review the information about the LOS on our website (www.cfainstitute.org/programs/cfa/curriculum/study-sessions), including the descriptions of LOS "command words" on the candidate resources page at www.cfainstitute.org/-/media/documents/support/programs/cfa-and-cipm-los-command-words.ashx.
- The CFA Program curriculum that candidates receive access to upon exam registration

Therefore, the key to your success on the CFA exams is studying and understanding the CBOK. You can learn more about the CBOK on our website: www.cfainstitute.org/programs/cfa/curriculum/cbok.

The curriculum, including the practice questions, is the basis for all exam questions. The curriculum is selected or developed specifically to provide candidates with the knowledge, skills, and abilities reflected in the CBOK.

CFA INSTITUTE LEARNING ECOSYSTEM (LES)

Your exam registration fee includes access to the CFA Institute Learning Ecosystem (LES). This digital learning platform provides access, even offline, to all the curriculum content and practice questions. The LES is organized as a series of learning modules consisting of short online lessons and associated practice questions. This tool is your source for all study materials, including practice questions and mock exams. The LES is the primary method by which CFA Institute delivers your curriculum experience. Here, candidates will find additional practice questions to test their knowledge. Some questions in the LES provide a unique interactive experience.

DESIGNING YOUR PERSONAL STUDY PROGRAM

An orderly, systematic approach to exam preparation is critical. You should dedicate a consistent block of time every week to reading and studying. Review the LOS both before and after you study curriculum content to ensure you can demonstrate the knowledge, skills, and abilities described by the LOS and the assigned reading. Use the LOS as a self-check to track your progress and highlight areas of weakness for later review.

Successful candidates report an average of more than 300 hours preparing for each exam. Your preparation time will vary based on your prior education and experience, and you will likely spend more time on some topics than on others.

ERRATA

The curriculum development process is rigorous and involves multiple rounds of reviews by content experts. Despite our efforts to produce a curriculum that is free of errors, in some instances, we must make corrections. Curriculum errata are periodically updated and posted by exam level and test date on the Curriculum Errata webpage (www.cfainstitute.org/en/programs/submit-errata). If you believe you have found an error in the curriculum, you can submit your concerns through our curriculum errata reporting process found at the bottom of the Curriculum Errata webpage.

OTHER FEEDBACK

Please send any comments or suggestions to info@cfainstitute.org, and we will review your feedback thoughtfully.

Ethical and Professional Standards

LEARNING MODULE

1

Code of Ethics and Standards of Professional Conduct

LEARNING OUTCOMES	
Mastery	*The candidate should be able to:*
□	describe the structure of the CFA Institute Professional Conduct Program and the disciplinary review process for the enforcement of the CFA Institute Code of Ethics and Standards of Professional Conduct
□	explain the ethical responsibilities required by the Code and Standards, including the subsections of each standard

PREFACE 1

□	describe the structure of the CFA Institute Professional Conduct Program and the disciplinary review process for the enforcement of the CFA Institute Code of Ethics and Standards of Professional Conduct
□	explain the ethical responsibilities required by the Code and Standards, including the subsections of each standard

The *Standards of Practice Handbook* (*Handbook*) provides guidance to the people who grapple with real ethical dilemmas in the investment profession on a daily basis; the *Handbook* addresses the professional intersection where theory meets practice and where the concept of ethical behavior crosses from the abstract to the concrete. The *Handbook* is intended for a diverse and global audience: CFA Institute members navigating ambiguous ethical situations; supervisors and direct/indirect reports determining the nature of their responsibilities to each other, to existing and potential clients, and to the broader financial markets; and candidates preparing for the Chartered Financial Analyst (CFA) examinations.

Events in global financial markets test the ethical mettle of financial market participants, including CFA Institute members and candidates. The standards taught in the CFA Program and by which CFA Institute members and candidates must abide represent timeless ethical principles and professional conduct for all market conditions.

Through adherence to these standards, which continue to serve as the model for ethical behavior in the investment profession globally, each market participant does his or her part to improve the integrity and efficient operations of the financial markets.

The *Handbook* provides guidance for understanding the interconnectedness of the aspirational and practical principles and provisions of the Code of Ethics and Standards of Professional Conduct (Code and Standards). The Code contains high-level aspirational ethical principles that drive members and candidates to create a positive and reputable investment profession. The Standards contain practical ethical principles of conduct that members and candidates must follow to achieve the broader industry expectations. However, applying the principles individually may not capture the complexity of ethical requirements related to the investment industry. The Code and Standards should be viewed and interpreted as an interwoven tapestry of ethical requirements. Through members' and candidates' adherence to these principles as a whole, the integrity of and trust in the capital markets are improved.

Evolution of the CFA Institute Code of Ethics and Standards of Professional Conduct

The Code and Standards are regularly reviewed and updated so that they remain effective and continue to represent the highest ethical standards in the global investment industry. CFA Institute strongly believes that revisions of the Code and Standards are undertaken not for cosmetic purposes but to add value by addressing legitimate concerns and improving comprehension. In 2023, the CFA Institute Board of Governors approved revisions to the Code and Standards that are fully described below.

Changes to the Code and Standards have far-reaching implications for the CFA Institute membership, the CFA Program, and the investment industry as a whole. CFA Institute members and candidates are *required* to adhere to the Code and Standards. In addition, the Code and Standards are often adopted, in whole or in part, by firms and regulatory authorities. Their relevance goes well beyond CFA Institute members and candidates.

Standards of Practice Handbook

The periodic revisions of the *Standards of Practice Handbook* have come in conjunction with updates of the Code and Standards. The *Handbook* is the fundamental element of the ethics education effort of CFA Institute and the primary resource for guidance in interpreting and implementing the Code and Standards. The *Handbook* seeks to educate members and candidates on how to apply the Code and Standards to their professional lives and thereby benefit their clients, employers, and the investing public in general. The *Handbook* explains the purpose of the Code and Standards and how they apply in a variety of situations. The sections discuss and amplify each standard and suggest procedures for compliance.

Examples in the "Application of the Standard" sections are meant to illustrate how the standard applies to hypothetical but factual situations. The names contained in the examples are fictional and are not meant to refer to any actual person or entity. Unless otherwise stated (e.g., one or more people specifically identified), individuals in each example are subject to the requirements of the Code and Standards. Because factual circumstances vary so widely and often involve gray areas, the explanatory material and examples are not intended to be all inclusive. Many examples set forth in the application sections involve standards that have legal counterparts; *members are strongly urged to discuss with their supervisors and legal and compliance departments the content of the Code and Standards and the members' general obligations under the Code and Standards.*

CFA Institute recognizes that the presence of any set of ethical standards may create a false sense of security unless the documents are fully understood, enforced, and made a meaningful part of everyday professional activities. The *Handbook* is intended to provide a useful frame of reference that outlines ethical professional conduct for the organization's members and candidates. The *Handbook* cannot cover every contingency or circumstance however, and it does not attempt to do so. The development and interpretation of the Code and Standards are evolving processes; the Code and Standards will be subject to continuing refinement.

Summary of the 2023 Revisions to the Code and Standards

In 2023, the CFA Institute Board of Governors revised the Standards of Professional Conduct in three areas, resulting in the inclusion of one new standard and revisions to two existing standards. The following is a summary of the changes:

1. Within Standard I: Professionalism, the Board approved a new standard requiring members to act with and maintain the competence necessary to fulfill their professional responsibilities, so reinforcing the principle set forth in the Code of Ethics.
2. Within Standard V: Investment Analysis, Recommendations, and Actions, the Board revised Standard V(B) Communication with Clients and Prospective Clients to require disclosures about the nature of the services provided by members and candidates and the costs to the client associated with those services.
3. Within Standard VI Conflicts of Interest, the Board changed the name of Standard VI(A) to "Standard VI(A) Avoid or Disclose Conflicts" and revised the standard to require members and candidates to either avoid conflicts of interest or disclose those conflicts. Previously there was no mention of avoiding conflicts of interest in the standard.

New guidance and examples have been added to the *Handbook* to fully explain these new requirements.

New and Revised Standards of Professional Conduct

Competence Standard

I. PROFESSIONALISM

E. Competence

Members and Candidates must:

1. Act with and maintain the competence necessary to fulfill their professional responsibilities.

Given the diverse range of professional services engaged in by members and candidates, the knowledge, skills, and abilities necessary to successfully fulfill their role will vary according to the nature of their professional duties. Over time, a member's role may expand, requiring new or different knowledge, skills, and abilities. Members will develop and refine their skills and abilities throughout their professional careers. Requiring members and candidates to act with and maintain appropriate levels of competence will help ensure they provide a high standard of professional service for their clients and employers.

Currently, the Code of Ethics requires members and candidates to "act with integrity, competence, and diligence" and to "maintain and improve their professional competence and strive to improve the competence of other investment professionals." This new standard is consistent with and directly supports the requirements of the Code of Ethics. Standard I(E) makes these requirements of the Code of Ethics more explicit and emphasizes the need for members and candidates to continuously maintain or improve the competence required by their professional position.

The skills and abilities necessary for members and candidates to successfully fulfill their role vary according to the nature and complexity of their professional duties. As a result, there will be different criteria for competence for different members. An examination of the facts and circumstances of each member or candidate will dictate their expected conduct under this standard.

Finally, Standard I(E) does not require members and candidates to engage in any specific program of professional development or continuing education. There are a variety of ways members and candidates can demonstrate and maintain competence when engaging in their professional responsibilities.

Disclosure of Nature of Services and Costs to Client

V. INVESTMENT ANALYSIS, RECOMMENDATIONS, AND ACTIONS

B. Communication with Clients and Prospective Clients

Members and Candidates must:

1. Disclose to clients and prospective clients the nature of the services provided, along with information about the costs to the client associated with those services.

A fundamental goal of the Code and Standards is to protect client interests and allow clients to make fully informed decisions about their investments and financial well-being. Providing clients with information about the nature of the services they can expect from investment professionals and the financial impact they can expect from those services is critical to achieving this goal. The disclosures required by this new standard will permit clients to make informed decisions as to whether to engage with the member or candidate and his or her firm.

Standard V(B) Communication with Clients and Prospective Clients also requires members to disclose the basic format and general principles of the investment processes they use to analyze investments, select securities, and construct portfolios and to promptly disclose any material changes to these processes. The associated financial impact is an important part of the investment process but, until now, was not explicitly addressed as part of this disclosure. The revision to Standard V(B) fills this gap.

Revised Standard Relating to Conflicts

VI. CONFLICTS OF INTEREST

A. Avoid or Disclose Conflicts

Members and Candidates must:

1. Avoid or make full and fair disclosure of all matters that could reasonably be expected to impair their independence and objectivity and interfere with respective duties to their clients, prospective clients, and employer.

2. Ensure that such disclosures are prominent, are delivered in plain language, and communicate the relevant information effectively.

Standard VI(A) has always required members and candidates to disclose conflicts, but previously, the language of the standard made no mention of avoiding conflicts. Nevertheless, the guidance for Standard VI: Conflicts of Interest has long stated that best practice is to avoid conflicts or the appearance of conflicts. Including the option to avoid versus simply disclosing conflicts in the language of the standard emphasizes that members and candidates should avoid conflicts of interest whenever reasonably possible. While avoiding conflicts altogether is preferred, often in the investment industry it may not be reasonable for members and candidates to avoid a conflict or the perception of a conflict. When it is not reasonable for members and candidates to avoid a conflict, Standard VI(A) continues to require clear and complete disclosure of the conflict.

CFA Institute Professional Conduct Program

All CFA Institute members and candidates enrolled in the CFA Program are required to comply with the Code and Standards. The CFA Institute Board of Governors maintains oversight and responsibility for the Professional Conduct Program (PCP), which, in conjunction with the Disciplinary Review Committee (DRC), is responsible for enforcement of the Code and Standards. The DRC is a volunteer committee of CFA charterholders who serve on panels to review conduct and partner with Professional Conduct staff to establish and review professional conduct policies. The CFA Institute Bylaws and Rules of Procedure for Professional Conduct (Rules of Procedure) form the basic structure for enforcing the Code and Standards. The Professional Conduct division is also responsible for enforcing testing policies of other CFA Institute education programs, as well as the professional conduct of Certificate in Investment Performance Measurement (CIPM) certificants.

Professional Conduct inquiries come from a number of sources. First, members and candidates must self-disclose on the annual Professional Conduct Statement all matters that question their professional conduct, such as involvement in civil litigation or a criminal investigation or being the subject of a written complaint. Second, written complaints received by Professional Conduct staff can bring about an investigation. Third, CFA Institute staff may become aware of questionable conduct by a member or candidate through the media, regulatory notices, or another public source. Fourth, candidate conduct is monitored by proctors who complete reports on candidates suspected to have violated testing rules on exam day. Lastly, CFA Institute may also conduct analyses of scores and exam materials after the exam, as well as monitor online and social media to detect disclosure of confidential exam information.

When an inquiry is initiated, the Professional Conduct staff conducts an investigation that may include requesting a written explanation from the member or candidate; interviewing the member or candidate, complaining parties, and third parties; and collecting documents and records relevant to the investigation. Upon reviewing the material obtained during the investigation, the Professional Conduct staff may conclude the inquiry with no disciplinary sanction, issue a cautionary letter, or continue proceedings to discipline the member or candidate. If the Professional Conduct staff believes a violation of the Code and Standards or testing policies has occurred, the member or candidate has the opportunity to reject or accept any charges and the proposed sanctions.

If the member or candidate does not accept the charges and proposed sanction, the matter is referred to a panel composed of DRC members. Panels review materials and presentations from Professional Conduct staff and from the member or candidate. The panel's task is to determine whether a violation of the Code and Standards or testing policies occurred and, if so, what sanction should be imposed.

Sanctions imposed by CFA Institute may have significant consequences; they include public censure, suspension of membership and use of the CFA designation, and revocation of the CFA charter. Candidates enrolled in the CFA Program who have violated the Code and Standards or testing policies may be suspended or prohibited from further participation in the CFA Program.

Adoption of the Code and Standards

The Code and Standards apply to individual members of CFA Institute and candidates in the CFA Program. CFA Institute does encourage firms to adopt the Code and Standards, however, as part of their code of ethics. Those who claim compliance should fully understand the requirements of each of the principles of the Code and Standards.

Once a party—nonmember or firm—ensures its code of ethics meets the principles of the Code and Standards, that party should make the following statement whenever claiming compliance:

> [Insert name of party] claims compliance with the CFA Institute Code of Ethics and Standards of Professional Conduct. This claim has not been verified by CFA Institute.

CFA Institute welcomes public acknowledgement, when appropriate, that firms are complying with the CFA Institute Code of Ethics and Standards of Professional Conduct. For firms that would like to distribute the Code and Standards to clients and potential clients, attractive one-page copies of the Code and Standards, including translations, are available on the CFA Institute website (www.cfainstitute.org).

CFA Institute has also published the Asset Manager Code, which is designed, in part, to help asset managers comply with regulations mandating codes of ethics for investment advisers. Whereas the Code and Standards are aimed at individual investment professionals who are members of CFA Institute or candidates in the CFA Program, the Asset Manager Code applies to firms. The Asset Manager Code provides specific, practical guidelines for asset managers in six areas: loyalty to clients, the investment process, trading, compliance, performance, and disclosure. The Asset Manager Code and the appropriate steps to acknowledge compliance can be found on the CFA Institute website (www.cfainstitute.org).

Acknowledgments

CFA Institute is a not-for-profit organization that is heavily dependent on the expertise and intellectual contributions of member volunteers. Members devote their time because they share a mutual interest in the organization's mission to promote and achieve ethical practice in the investment profession. CFA Institute owes much to the volunteers' abundant generosity and energy in extending ethical integrity.

The CFA Institute Standards of Practice Council (SPC), a group consisting of CFA charterholder volunteers from many different countries, is charged with maintaining and interpreting the Code and Standards and ensuring that they are effective. The SPC draws its membership from a broad spectrum of organizations in the securities field, including brokers, investment advisers, banks, and insurance companies.

The SPC continually evaluates the Code and Standards, as well as the guidance in the *Handbook*, to ensure that they are

- representative of high standards of professional conduct,
- relevant to the changing nature of the investment profession,
- globally applicable,
- sufficiently comprehensive, practical, and specific,
- enforceable, and
- testable for the CFA Program.

Over the years, many volunteer members of the SPC have spent countless hours reviewing and discussing revisions to the Code and Standards and updates to the guidance that make up the *Handbook*. CFA Institute would like to thank all the current and former members of the SPC who generously donated their time and energy to this effort.

2 ETHICS AND THE INVESTMENT INDUSTRY

Society ultimately benefits from efficient markets where capital can freely flow to the most productive or innovative destination. Well-functioning capital markets efficiently match those needing capital with those seeking to invest their assets in revenue-generating ventures. In order for capital markets to be efficient, investors must be able to trust that the markets are fair and transparent and offer them the opportunity to be rewarded for the risk they choose to take. Laws, regulations, and enforcement play a vital role but are insufficient alone to guarantee fair and transparent markets. The markets depend on an ethical foundation to guide participants' judgment and behavior. CFA Institute maintains and promotes the Code of Ethics and Standards of Professional Conduct in order to create a culture of ethics for the ultimate benefit of society.

Why Ethics Matters

Ethics can be defined as a set of moral principles or rules of conduct that provide guidance for our behavior when it affects others. Widely acknowledged fundamental ethical principles include honesty, fairness, diligence, and care and respect for others. Ethical conduct follows those principles and balances self-interest with both the direct and the indirect consequences of that behavior for other people.

Not only does unethical behavior by individuals have serious personal consequences—ranging from job loss and reputational damage to fines and even jail—but unethical conduct from market participants, investment professionals, and those who service investors can damage investor trust and thereby impair the sustainability of the global capital markets as a whole. Unfortunately, there seems to be an unending parade of stories bringing to light accounting frauds and manipulations, Ponzi schemes, insider-trading scandals, and other misdeeds. Not surprisingly, this has led to erosion in public confidence in investment professionals. Empirical evidence from numerous surveys documents the low standing in the eyes of the investing public of banks and financial services firms—the very institutions that are entrusted with the economic well-being and retirement security of society.

Governments and regulators have historically tried to combat misconduct in the industry through regulatory reform, with various levels of success. Global capital markets are highly regulated to protect investors and other market participants.

However, compliance with regulation alone is insufficient to fully earn investor trust. Individuals and firms must develop a "culture of integrity" that permeates all levels of operations and promotes the ethical principles of stewardship of investor assets and working in the best interests of clients, above and beyond strict compliance with the law. A strong ethical culture that helps honest, ethical people engage in ethical behavior will foster the trust of investors, lead to robust global capital markets, and ultimately benefit society. That is why ethics matters.

Ethics, Society, and the Capital Markets

CFA Institute includes the concept "for the ultimate benefit of society" as part of its mission. The premise is that we want to live in a socially, politically, and financially stable society that fosters individual well-being and welfare of the public. A key ingredient for this goal is global capital markets that facilitate the efficient allocation of resources so that the available capital finds its way to places where it most benefits that society. These investments are then used to produce goods and services, to fund innovation and jobs, and to promote improvements in standards of living. Indeed, such a function serves the interests of the society. Efficient capital markets, in turn, provide a host of benefits to those providing the investment capital. Investors are provided the opportunity to transfer and transform risk because the capital markets serve as an information exchange, create investment products, provide liquidity, and limit transaction costs.

However, a well-functioning and efficient capital market system is dependent on trust of the participants. If investors believe that capital market participants—investment professionals and firms—cannot be trusted with their financial assets or that the capital markets are unfair such that only insiders can be successful, they will be unlikely to invest or, at the very least, will require a higher risk premium. Decreased investment capital can reduce innovation and job creation and hurt the economy and society as a whole. Reduced trust in capital markets can also result in a less vibrant, if not smaller, investment industry.

Ethics for a global investment industry should be universal and ultimately support trust and integrity above acceptable local or regional customs and culture. Universal ethics for a global industry strongly supports the efficiency, values, and mission of the industry as a whole. Different countries may be at different stages of development in establishing standards of practice, but the end goal must be to achieve rules, regulations, and standards that support and promote fundamental ethical principles on a global basis.

Capital Market Sustainability and the Actions of One

Individuals and firms also have to look at the indirect impacts of their actions on the broader investment community. The increasingly interconnected nature of global finance brings to the fore an added consideration of market sustainability that was, perhaps, less appreciated in years past. In addition to committing to the highest levels of ethical behavior, today's investment professionals and their employers should consider the long-term health of the market as a whole.

Apparently isolated and unrelated decisions, however innocuous when considered on an individual basis, in aggregate can precipitate a market crisis. In an interconnected global economy and marketplace, each participant should strive to be aware of how his or her actions or the products he or she distributes may have an impact on capital market participants in other regions or countries.

Investment professionals should consider how their investment decision-making processes affect the global financial markets in the broader context of how they apply their ethical and professional obligations. Those in positions of authority have a special responsibility to consider the broader context of market sustainability in their development and approval of corporate policies, particularly those involving risk management and product development. In addition, corporate compensation strategies should not encourage otherwise ethically sound individuals to engage in unethical or questionable conduct for financial gain. Ethics, sustainability, and properly functioning capital markets are components of the same concept of protecting the best interests of all. To always place the interests of clients ahead of both investment professionals' own interests and those of their employer remains a key ethos.

The Relationship between Ethics and Regulations

Some equate ethical behavior with legal behavior: If you are following the law, you must be acting appropriately. Ethical principles, like laws and regulations, prescribe appropriate constraints on our natural tendency to pursue self-interest that could harm the interests of others. Laws and regulations often attempt to guide people toward ethical behavior, but they do not cover all unethical behavior. Ethical behavior is often distinguished from legal conduct by describing legal behavior as what is required and ethical behavior as conduct that is morally correct. Ethical principles go beyond that which is legally sufficient and encompass what is the right thing to do.

Given many regulators' lack of sufficient resources to enforce well-conceived rules and regulations, relying on a regulatory framework to lead the charge in establishing ethical behavior has its challenges. Therefore, reliance on compliance with laws and regulation alone is insufficient to ensure ethical behavior of investment professionals or to create a truly ethical culture in the industry.

Inevitably, some individuals will succeed at circumventing the regulatory rules for their personal gain. Only the application of strong ethical principles, at both the individual level and the firm level, will limit abuses. Knowing the rules or regulations to apply in a particular situation, although important, may not be sufficient to ensure ethical conduct. Individuals must be able both to recognize areas that are prone to ethical pitfalls and to identify and process those circumstances and influences that can impair ethical judgment.

Applying an Ethical Framework

Laws, regulations, professional standards, and codes of ethics can guide ethical behavior, but individual judgment is a critical ingredient in making principled choices and engaging in appropriate conduct. When faced with an ethical dilemma, individuals must have a well-developed set of principles; otherwise, their thought processes can lead to, at best, equivocation and indecision and, at worst, fraudulent conduct and destruction of the public trust. Establishing an ethical framework for an internal thought process prior to deciding to act is a crucial step in engaging in ethical conduct.

Most investment professionals are used to making decisions from a business (profit/loss) outlook. But given the importance of ethical behavior in carrying out professional responsibilities, it is critical to also analyze decisions and potential conduct from an ethical perspective. Utilizing a framework for ethical decision making will help investment professionals effectively examine their conduct in the context of conflicting interests common to their professional obligations (e.g., researching and gathering information, developing investment recommendations, and managing money for others). Such a framework will allow investment professionals to analyze their conduct in a way that meets high standards of ethical behavior.

An ethical decision-making framework can come in many forms but should provide investment professionals with a tool for following the principles of the firm's code of ethics. Through analyzing the particular circumstances of each decision, investment professionals are able to determine the best course of action to fulfill their responsibilities in an ethical manner.

Commitment to Ethics by Firms

A firm's code of ethics risks becoming a largely ignored, dusty compilation if it is not truly integrated into the fabric of the business. The ability to relate an ethical decision-making framework to a firm's code of ethics allows investment professionals to bring the aspirations and principles of the code of ethics to life—transforming it from a compliance exercise to something that is at the heart of a firm's culture.

An investment professional's natural desire to "do the right thing" must be reinforced by building a culture of integrity in the workplace. Development, maintenance, and demonstration of a strong culture of integrity within the firm by senior management may be the single most important factor in promoting ethical behavior among the firm's employees. Adopting a code of ethics that clearly lays out the ethical principles that guide the thought processes and conduct the firm expects from its employees is a critical first step. But a code of ethics, while necessary, is insufficient.

Simply nurturing an inclination to do right is no match for the multitude of daily decisions that investment managers make. We need to exercise ethical decision-making skills to develop the muscle memory necessary for fundamentally ethical people to make good decisions despite the reality of conflicts of interest. Just as coaching and practice transform our natural ability to run across a field into the technique and endurance required to run a race, teaching, reinforcing, and practicing ethical decision-making skills prepare us to confront the hard issues effectively. It is good for business, individuals, firms, the industry, and the markets, as well as society as a whole, to engage in the investment management profession in a highly ethical manner.

Ethical Commitment of CFA Institute

An important goal of CFA Institute is to ensure that the organization and its members and candidates develop, promote, and follow the highest ethical standards in the investment industry. The CFA Institute Code of Ethics (Code) and Standards of Professional Conduct (Standards) are the foundation supporting the organization's quest to uphold the industry's highest standards of individual and corporate practice and to help serve the greater good. The Code is a set of principles that define the overarching conduct CFA Institute expects from its members and CFA Program candidates. The Code works in tandem with the Standards, which outline professional conduct that constitutes fair and ethical business practices.

For more than 60 years, CFA Institute members and candidates have been required to abide by the organization's Code and Standards. Periodically, CFA Institute has revised and updated its Code and Standards to ensure that they remain relevant to the changing nature of the investment profession and representative of the highest standard of professional conduct. Within the *Standards of PracticeHandbook*, CFA Institute addresses ethical principles for the profession, including individual professionalism; responsibilities to capital markets, clients, and employers; ethics involved in investment analysis, recommendations, and actions; and possible conflicts of interest. Although the investment world has become a far more complex place since the first publication of the *Standards of Practice Handbook*, distinguishing right from wrong remains the paramount principle of the Code and Standards.

New challenges will continually arise for members and candidates in applying the Code and Standards because many decisions are not unambiguously right or wrong. The dilemma exists because the choice between right and wrong is not always clear. Even well-intentioned investment professionals can find themselves in circumstances that may tempt them to cut corners. Situational influences can overpower the best of intentions.

CFA Institute has made a significant commitment to providing members and candidates with the resources to extend and deepen their understanding of how to appropriately apply the principles of the Code and Standards. The product offerings from CFA Institute offer a wealth of material. Through publications, conferences, webcasts, and podcasts, the ethical challenges of investment professionals are brought to light. Archived issues of these items are available on the CFA Institute website (www.cfainstitute.org).

By reviewing these resources and discussing with their peers, market participants can further enhance their abilities to apply an effective ethical decision-making framework. In time, this should promote the trust of clients, investors, and market participants.

Markets function to an important extent on trust. Investment professionals should remain mindful of the long-term health of financial markets and incorporate this concern for the market's sustainability in their investment decision making. CFA Institute and the Standards of Practice Council hope the *Handbook* will assist and guide investment professionals in meeting the ethical demands of the highly interconnected global capital markets for the ultimate benefit of society.

CFA INSTITUTE CODE OF ETHICS AND STANDARDS OF PROFESSIONAL CONDUCT 3

Preamble

The CFA Institute Code of Ethics and Standards of Professional Conduct are fundamental to the values of CFA Institute and essential to achieving its mission to continue to lead the investment profession globally by promoting the highest standards of ethics, education, and professional excellence for the ultimate benefit of society. High ethical standards are critical to maintaining the public's trust in financial markets and in the investment profession. Since their creation in the 1960s, the Code and Standards have promoted the integrity of CFA Institute members and served as a model for measuring the ethics of investment professionals globally, regardless of job function, cultural differences, or local laws and regulations. All CFA Institute members (including holders of the Chartered Financial Analyst [CFA] designation) and CFA candidates have the personal responsibility to embrace and uphold the provisions of the Code and Standards and are encouraged to notify their employer of this responsibility. Violations may result in disciplinary sanctions by CFA Institute. Sanctions can include revocation of membership, revocation of candidacy in the CFA Program, and revocation of the right to use the CFA designation.

The Code of Ethics

Members of CFA Institute (including CFA charterholders) and candidates for the CFA designation ("Members and Candidates") must:

- Act with integrity, competence, diligence, and respect and in an ethical manner with the public, clients, prospective clients, employers, employees, colleagues in the investment profession, and other participants in the global capital markets.
- Place the integrity of the investment profession and the interests of clients above their own personal interests.
- Use reasonable care and exercise independent professional judgment when conducting investment analysis, making investment recommendations, taking investment actions, and engaging in other professional activities.

- Practice and encourage others to practice in a professional and ethical manner that will reflect credit on themselves and the profession.
- Promote the integrity and viability of the global capital markets for the ultimate benefit of society.
- Maintain and improve their professional competence and strive to maintain and improve the competence of other investment professionals.

Standards of Professional Conduct

i. PROFESSIONALISM

A. Knowledge of the Law

Members and Candidates must understand and comply with all applicable laws, rules, and regulations (including the CFA Institute Code of Ethics and Standards of Professional Conduct) of any government, regulatory organization, licensing agency, or professional association governing their professional activities. In the event of conflict, Members and Candidates must comply with the more strict law, rule, or regulation. Members and Candidates must not knowingly participate or assist in and must dissociate from any violation of such laws, rules, or regulations.

B. Independence and Objectivity

Members and Candidates must use reasonable care and judgment to achieve and maintain independence and objectivity in their professional activities. Members and Candidates must not offer, solicit, or accept any gift, benefit, compensation, or consideration that reasonably could be expected to compromise their own or another's independence and objectivity.

C. Misrepresentation

Members and Candidates must not knowingly make any misrepresentations relating to investment analysis, recommendations, actions, or other professional activities.

D. Misconduct

Members and Candidates must not engage in any professional conduct involving dishonesty, fraud, or deceit or commit any act that reflects adversely on their professional reputation, integrity, or competence.

E. Competence

Members and Candidates must act with and maintain the competence necessary to fulfill their professional responsibilities.

ii. INTEGRITY OF CAPITAL MARKETS

A. Material Nonpublic Information

Members and Candidates who possess material nonpublic information that could affect the value of an investment must not act or cause others to act on the information.

B. Market Manipulation

Members and Candidates must not engage in practices that distort prices or artificially inflate trading volume with the intent to mislead market participants.

iii. DUTIES TO CLIENTS

A. Loyalty, Prudence, and Care

Members and Candidates have a duty of loyalty to their clients and must act with reasonable care and exercise prudent judgment. Members and Candidates must act for the benefit of their clients and place their clients' interests before their employer's or their own interests.

B. Fair Dealing

Members and Candidates must deal fairly and objectively with all clients when providing investment analysis, making investment recommendations, taking investment action, or engaging in other professional activities.

C. Suitability

1. When Members and Candidates are in an advisory relationship with a client, they must:

   a. Make a reasonable inquiry into a client's or prospective client's investment experience, risk and return objectives, and financial constraints prior to making any investment recommendation or taking investment action and must reassess and update this information regularly.

   b. Determine that an investment is suitable to the client's financial situation and consistent with the client's written objectives, mandates, and constraints before making an investment recommendation or taking investment action.

   c. Judge the suitability of investments in the context of the client's total portfolio.

2. When Members and Candidates are responsible for managing a portfolio to a specific mandate, strategy, or style, they must make only investment recommendations or take only investment actions that are consistent with the stated objectives and constraints of the portfolio.

D. Performance Presentation

When communicating investment performance information, Members and Candidates must make reasonable efforts to ensure that it is fair, accurate, and complete.

E. Preservation of Confidentiality

Members and Candidates must keep information about current, former, and prospective clients confidential unless:

1. The information concerns illegal activities on the part of the client or prospective client,

2. Disclosure is required by law, or

3. The client or prospective client permits disclosure of the information.

iv. DUTIES TO EMPLOYERS

A. Loyalty

In matters related to their employment, Members and Candidates must act for the benefit of their employer and not deprive their employer of the advantage of their skills and abilities, divulge confidential information, or otherwise cause harm to their employer.

B. Additional Compensation Arrangements

Members and Candidates must not accept gifts, benefits, compensation, or consideration that competes with or might reasonably be expected to create a conflict of interest with their employer's interest unless they obtain written consent from all parties involved.

C. Responsibilities of Supervisors

Members and Candidates must make reasonable efforts to ensure that anyone subject to their supervision or authority complies with applicable laws, rules, regulations, and the Code and Standards.

V. INVESTMENT ANALYSIS, RECOMMENDATIONS, AND ACTIONS

A. Diligence and Reasonable Basis

Members and Candidates must:

1. Exercise diligence, independence, and thoroughness in analyzing investments, making investment recommendations, and taking investment actions.

2. Have a reasonable and adequate basis, supported by appropriate research and investigation, for any investment analysis, recommendation, or action.

B. Communication with Clients and Prospective Clients

Members and Candidates must:

1. Disclose to clients and prospective clients the nature of the services provided, along with information about the costs to the client associated with those services.

2. Disclose to clients and prospective clients the basic format and general principles of the investment processes they use to analyze investments, select securities, and construct portfolios and must promptly disclose any changes that might materially affect those processes.

3. Disclose to clients and prospective clients significant limitations and risks associated with the investment process.

4. Use reasonable judgment in identifying which factors are important to their investment analyses, recommendations, or actions and include those factors in communications with clients and prospective clients.

5. Distinguish between fact and opinion in the presentation of investment analysis and recommendations.

C. Record Retention

Members and Candidates must develop and maintain appropriate records to support their investment analyses, recommendations, actions, and other investment-related communications with clients and prospective clients.

vi. CONFLICTS OF INTEREST

A. Avoid or Disclose Conflicts

Members and Candidates must avoid or make full and fair disclosure of all matters that could reasonably be expected to impair their independence and objectivity and interfere with respective duties to their clients, prospective clients, and employer. Members and Candidates must ensure that such disclosures are prominent, are delivered in plain language, and communicate the relevant information effectively.

B. Priority of Transactions

Investment transactions for clients and employers must have priority over investment transactions in which a Member or Candidate is the beneficial owner.

C. Referral Fees

Members and Candidates must disclose to their employer, clients, and prospective clients, as appropriate, any compensation, consideration, or benefit received from or paid to others for the recommendation of products or services.

vii. RESPONSIBILITIES AS A CFA INSTITUTE MEMBER OR CFA CANDIDATE

A. Conduct as Participants in CFA Institute Programs

Members and Candidates must not engage in any conduct that compromises the reputation or integrity of CFA Institute or the CFA designation or the integrity, validity, or security of CFA Institute programs.

B. Reference to CFA Institute, the CFA Designation, and the CFA Program

When referring to CFA Institute, CFA Institute membership, the CFA designation, or candidacy in the CFA Program, Members and Candidates must not misrepresent or exaggerate the meaning or implications of membership in CFA Institute, holding the CFA designation, or candidacy in the CFA Program.

PRACTICE PROBLEMS

1. Which of the following statements *best* describes an aspect of the Professional Conduct Program process?
   - **A.** Inquiries are not initiated in response to information provided by the media.
   - **B.** Investigations result in Disciplinary Review Committee panels for each case.
   - **C.** Investigations may include requesting a written explanation from the member or candidate.

2. A current Code of Ethics principle reads in full, "Promote the integrity:
   - **A.** and viability of the global capital markets."
   - **B.** of and uphold the rules governing capital markets."
   - **C.** and viability of the global capital markets for the ultimate benefit of society."

3. Which of the following is correct with regard to the Standards of Professional Conduct?
   - **A.** They require supervisors to focus only on the detection and prevention of violations.
   - **B.** They set ethical conduct requirements for members and candidates that have remained unchanged since their creation.
   - **C.** They address the risks and limitations of recommendations being made to clients.

4. Which of the following statements *best* describes an aspect of the Standards of Professional Conduct? Members and candidates are required to:
   - **A.** ensure a portfolio mandate is suitable for all investors.
   - **B.** promptly disclose changes that might materially affect investment processes.
   - **C.** have a reasonable and adequate basis for decisions about client confidentiality.

5. A CFA Institute member or candidate violates Standard II(A) Material Nonpublic Information by:
   - **A.** conducting price distortion practices.
   - **B.** inappropriately causing others to act.
   - **C.** inadequately maintaining investment records.

6. Standard III(C) Suitability requires members and candidates in an advisory relationship with a client to:
   - **A.** place their client's interests before their own interests.
   - **B.** consider investments in the context of the client's total portfolio.
   - **C.** not knowingly make misrepresentations relating to recommendations.

7. Standard III: Duties to Clients states that members and candidates must:
   - **A.** document client financial constraints after an initial investment action.
   - **B.** maintain an equal balance of interests owed to their clients and employers.
   - **C.** deal fairly and objectively with all clients when engaging in professional activities.

8. Standard IV: Duties to Employers states that members and candidates must not:
   - **A.** accept any gifts that might compromise their independence and objectivity.
   - **B.** deprive their employer of their skills and abilities as related to their employment.
   - **C.** accept compensation competing with their employer's interest without the written consent of their employer only.

9. Standard V: Investment Analysis, Recommendations, and Actions states that members and candidates must:
   - **A.** find an investment suitable for their client before making a recommendation.
   - **B.** make reasonable efforts to ensure that performance presentation is fair, accurate, and complete.
   - **C.** distinguish between fact and opinion in the presentation of investment analysis and recommendations.

10. Standard VII: Responsibilities as a CFA Institute Member or CFA Candidate explicitly states a requirement regarding:
    - **A.** loyalty.
    - **B.** responsibility of supervisors.
    - **C.** reference to the CFA Program.

SOLUTIONS

1. C is correct. When an inquiry is initiated, the Professional Conduct staff conducts an investigation that may include requesting a written explanation from the member or candidate.

   A is incorrect because Professional Conduct inquiries can be initiated in response to information provided by the media. CFA Institute staff may become aware of questionable conduct by a member or candidate through the media, regulatory notices, or other public sources.

   B is incorrect because although the Disciplinary Review Committee (DRC) is responsible for enforcement of the Code and Standards in conjunction with the Professional Conduct Program (PCP), only in the event that a member or candidate does not accept the charges and proposed sanction is the matter referred to a panel composed of DRC members.

2. C is correct. One of the principles in the Code of Ethics reflects the role that the capital markets have in society as a whole.

   A is incorrect because it is incomplete, missing the additional language to reflect the role that the capital markets have in society as a whole.

   B is incorrect because the principle as written in the Code of Ethics reflects the role of the capital markets in society as a whole.

3. C is correct. Given the constant development of new and exotic financial instruments and strategies, the standard regarding communicating with clients includes an implicit requirement to disclose to clients the risks and limitations of recommendations being made to clients.

   A is incorrect because the standard for members and candidates with supervision or authority over others within their firms stresses broader compliance expectations beyond the detection and prevention aspects of violations.

   B is incorrect because the standards have evolved over time to remain representative of the highest standards of professional conduct and relevant to the changing nature of the investment profession.

4. B is correct. The Standards of Professional Conduct require members and candidates to promptly disclose any changes that might materially affect investment processes.

   A is incorrect because under Standard III(C) Suitability, when members and candidates are responsible for managing a portfolio according to a specific mandate, they must take only investment actions that are consistent with the stated objectives of the portfolio and not be concerned with whether the mandate is suitable for all investors.

   C is incorrect because under Standard III(E) Preservation of Confidentiality, members and candidates must keep information about current clients confidential unless the information concerns illegal activities on the part of the client, disclosure is required by law, or the client permits disclosure. No decisions on confidentiality are required, with the "reasonable and adequate basis" criterion related to Standard V(A) Diligence and Reasonable Basis.

5. B is correct. Under Standard II(A) Material Nonpublic Information, members who possess material nonpublic information that could affect the value of an investment must not cause others to act on the information.

   A is incorrect because price distortion is mentioned in Standard II(B) Market Manipulation, not Standard II(A) Material Nonpublic Information.

C is incorrect because the maintenance of appropriate records to support investment analyses is noted in Standard V(C) Record Retention, not Standard II(A) Material Nonpublic Information.

6. B is correct. Standard III(C) Suitability states that when members and candidates are in an advisory relationship with a client, they must judge the suitability of investments in the context of the client's total portfolio.

   A is incorrect because this requirement is addressed under Standard III(A) Loyalty, Prudence, and Care, not Standard III(C) Suitability.

   C is incorrect because this requirement is addressed under Standard I(C) Misrepresentation, not Standard III(C) Suitability.

7. C is correct. Under Standard III(B) Fair Dealing, members and candidates must deal fairly and objectively with all clients when providing investment analysis, making investment recommendations, taking investment action, or engaging in other professional activities.

   A is incorrect because under Standard III(C) Suitability, members and candidates in an advisory relationship must make a reasonable inquiry into a client's financial constraints prior to (not after) taking investment action and must reassess and update this regularly.

   B is incorrect because under Standard III(A) Loyalty, Prudence, and Care, members and candidates must act for the benefit of their clients and place their clients' interests before (not maintain an equal balance with) their employer's or their own interests.

8. B is correct. Standard IV(A) Loyalty states that members and candidates cannot deprive their employer of the advantage of their skills and abilities in matters related to their employment.

   A is incorrect because accepting gifts that might compromise a member's or candidate's independence and objectivity is addressed by Standard I: Professionalism, not Standard IV: Duties to Employers.

   C is incorrect because Standard IV(B) Additional Compensation Arrangements permits members and candidates to accept compensation that competes with their employer's interest if they obtain written consent from all parties involved.

9. C is correct. Standard V(B) Communication with Clients and Prospective Clients states that members and candidates must distinguish between fact and opinion in the presentation of investment analysis and recommendations.

   A is incorrect because this standard is discussed in Standard III: Duties to Clients.

   B is incorrect because performance presentation is discussed in Standard III: Duties to Clients.

10. C is correct. Standard VII(B) Reference to CFA Institute, the CFA Designation, and the CFA Program explicitly states the appropriate manner to make reference to CFA Institute, CFA Institute membership, the CFA designation, or candidacy in the CFA Program.

    A is incorrect because Standard VII: Responsibilities as a CFA Institute Member or CFA Candidate does not refer to loyalty. Loyalty is addressed in two other standards, Standard III(A) Loyalty, Prudence, and Care and as part of Standard IV: Duties to Employers.

    B is incorrect because Standard VII does not refer to the responsibility of supervisors. The responsibility of supervisors is addressed in Standard IV(C) Responsibility of Supervisors.

LEARNING MODULE

2

Guidance for Standards I–VII

LEARNING OUTCOMES	
Mastery	*The candidate should be able to:*
☐	demonstrate a thorough knowledge of the CFA Institute Code of Ethics and Standards of Professional Conduct by interpreting the Code and Standards in various situations involving issues of professional integrity
☐	recommend practices and procedures designed to prevent violations of the Code and Standards

STANDARD I: PROFESSIONALISM

1

☐	demonstrate a thorough knowledge of the CFA Institute Code of Ethics and Standards of Professional Conduct by interpreting the Code and Standards in various situations involving issues of professional integrity
☐	recommend practices and procedures designed to prevent violations of the Code and Standards

Standard I(A) Knowledge of the Law

Members and Candidates must understand and comply with all applicable laws, rules, and regulations (including the CFA Institute Code of Ethics and Standards of Professional Conduct) of any government, regulatory organization, licensing agency, or professional association governing their professional activities. In the event of conflict, Members and Candidates must comply with the more strict law, rule, or regulation. Members and Candidates must not knowingly participate or assist in and must dissociate from any violation of such laws, rules, or regulations.

Guidance

Highlights:

- *Relationship between the Code and Standards and Applicable Law*
- *Participation in or Association with Violations by Others*
- *Investment Products and Applicable Laws*

Members and candidates must understand the applicable laws and regulations of the countries and jurisdictions where they engage in professional activities. These activities may include, but are not limited to, trading of securities or other financial instruments, providing investment advice, conducting research, or performing other investment services. On the basis of their reasonable and good faith understanding, members and candidates must comply with the laws and regulations that directly govern their professional activities and resulting outcomes and that protect the interests of the clients.

When questions arise, members and candidates should know their firm's policies and procedures for accessing compliance guidance. This standard does not require members and candidates to become experts, however, in compliance. Additionally, members and candidates are not required to have detailed knowledge of or be experts on all the laws that could potentially govern their activities.

During times of changing regulations, members and candidates must remain vigilant in maintaining their knowledge of the requirements for their professional activities. New financial products and processes, along with uncovered ethical missteps, create an environment for recurring and potentially wide-ranging regulatory changes. Members and candidates are also continually provided improved and enhanced methods of communicating with both clients and potential clients, such as mobile applications and web-based social networking platforms. As new local, regional, and global requirements are updated to address these and other changes, members, candidates, and their firms must adjust their procedures and practices to remain in compliance.

Relationship between the Code and Standards and Applicable Law

Some members or candidates may live, work, or provide investment services to clients living in a country that has no law or regulation governing a particular action or that has laws or regulations that differ from the requirements of the Code and Standards. When applicable law and the Code and Standards require different conduct, members and candidates must follow the more strict of the applicable law or the Code and Standards.

"Applicable law" is the law that governs the member's or candidate's conduct. Which law applies will depend on the particular facts and circumstances of each case. The "more strict" law or regulation is the law or regulation that imposes greater restrictions on the action of the member or candidate or calls for the member or candidate to exert a greater degree of action that protects the interests of investors. For example, applicable law or regulation may not require members and candidates to disclose referral fees received from or paid to others for the recommendation of investment products or services. Because the Code and Standards impose this obligation, however, members and candidates must disclose the existence of such fees.

Members and candidates must adhere to the following principles:

- Members and candidates must comply with applicable laws or regulations related to their professional activities.
- Members and candidates must not engage in conduct that constitutes a violation of the Code and Standards, even though it may otherwise be legal.

- In the absence of any applicable law or regulation or when the Code and Standards impose a higher degree of responsibility than applicable laws and regulations, members and candidates must adhere to the Code and Standards. Applications of these principles are outlined in Exhibit 1.

The applicable laws governing the responsibilities of a member or candidate should be viewed as the minimal threshold of acceptable actions. When members and candidates take actions that exceed the minimal requirements, they further support the conduct required of Standard I(A).

CFA Institute members are obligated to abide by the CFA Institute Articles of Incorporation, Bylaws, Code of Ethics, Standards of Professional Conduct, Rules of Procedure, Membership Agreement, and other applicable rules promulgated by CFA Institute, all as amended periodically. CFA candidates who are not members must also abide by these documents (except for the Membership Agreement) as well as rules and regulations related to the administration of the CFA® exam, the Candidate Responsibility Statement, and the Candidate Pledge.

Participation in or Association with Violations by Others

Members and candidates are responsible for violations in which they *knowingly* participate or assist. Although members and candidates are presumed to have knowledge of all applicable laws, rules, and regulations, CFA Institute acknowledges that members may not recognize violations if they are not aware of all the facts giving rise to the violations. Standard I(A) applies when members and candidates know or should know that their conduct may contribute to a violation of applicable laws, rules, or regulations or the Code and Standards.

If a member or candidate has reasonable grounds to believe that imminent or ongoing client or employer activities are illegal or unethical, the member or candidate must dissociate, or separate, from the activity. In extreme cases, dissociation may require a member or candidate to leave his or her employment. Members and candidates may take the following intermediate steps to dissociate from ethical violations of others when direct discussions with the person or persons committing the violation are unsuccessful. The first step should be to attempt to stop the behavior by bringing it to the attention of the employer through a supervisor or the firm's compliance department. If this attempt is unsuccessful, then members and candidates have a responsibility to step away and dissociate from the activity. Dissociation practices will differ on the basis of the member's or candidate's role in the investment industry. It may include removing one's name from written reports or recommendations, asking for a different assignment, or refusing to accept a new client or continue to advise a current client. Inaction combined with continuing association with those involved in illegal or unethical conduct may be construed as participation or assistance in the illegal or unethical conduct.

CFA Institute strongly encourages members and candidates to report potential violations of the Code and Standards committed by fellow members and candidates. Although a failure to report is less likely to be construed as a violation than a failure to dissociate from unethical conduct, the impact of inactivity on the integrity of capital markets can be significant. Although the Code and Standards do not compel members and candidates to report violations to their governmental or regulatory organizations unless such disclosure is mandatory under applicable law (voluntary reporting is often referred to as whistleblowing), such disclosure may be prudent under certain circumstances. Members and candidates should consult their legal and compliance advisers for guidance.

Additionally, CFA Institute encourages members, nonmembers, clients, and the investing public to report violations of the Code and Standards by CFA Institute members or CFA candidates by submitting a complaint in writing to the CFA Institute Professional Conduct Program via e-mail (pcprogram@cfainstitute.org) or the CFA Institute website (www.cfainstitute.org).

Investment Products and Applicable Laws

Members and candidates involved in creating or maintaining investment services or investment products or packages of securities and/or derivatives should be mindful of where these products or packages will be sold as well as their places of origination. The applicable laws and regulations of the countries or regions of origination and expected sale should be understood by those responsible for the supervision of the services or creation and maintenance of the products or packages. Members or candidates should make reasonable efforts to review whether associated firms that are distributing products or services developed by their employing firm also abide by the laws and regulations of the countries and regions of distribution. Members and candidates should undertake the necessary due diligence when transacting cross-border business to understand the multiple applicable laws and regulations in order to protect the reputation of their firm and themselves.

Given the complexity that can arise with business transactions in today's market, there may be some uncertainty surrounding which laws or regulations are considered applicable when activities are being conducted in multiple jurisdictions. Members and candidates should seek the appropriate guidance, potentially including the firm's compliance or legal departments and legal counsel outside the organization, to gain a reasonable understanding of their responsibilities and how to implement them appropriately.

Exhibit 1: Global Application of the Code and Standards

Members and candidates who practice in multiple jurisdictions may be subject to varied securities laws and regulations. If applicable law is stricter than the requirements of the Code and Standards, members and candidates must adhere to applicable law; otherwise, they must adhere to the Code and Standards. The following chart provides illustrations involving a member who may be subject to the securities laws and regulations of three different types of countries:

NS: country with no securities laws or regulations

LS: country with *less* strict securities laws and regulations than the Code and Standards

MS: country with *more* strict securities laws and regulations than the Code and Standards

Applicable Law	Duties	Explanation
Member resides in NS country, does business in LS country; LS law applies.	Member must adhere to the Code and Standards.	Because applicable law is less strict than the Code and Standards, the member must adhere to the Code and Standards.
Member resides in NS country, does business in MS country; MS law applies.	Member must adhere to the law of MS country.	Because applicable law is stricter than the Code and Standards, member must adhere to the more strict applicable law.
Member resides in LS country, does business in NS country; LS law applies.	Member must adhere to the Code and Standards.	Because applicable law is less strict than the Code and Standards, member must adhere to the Code and Standards.
Member resides in LS country, does business in MS country; MS law applies.	Member must adhere to the law of MS country.	Because applicable law is stricter than the Code and Standards, member must adhere to the more strict applicable law.
Member resides in LS country, does business in NS country; LS law applies, but it states that law of locality where business is conducted governs.	Member must adhere to the Code and Standards.	Because applicable law states that the law of the locality where the business is conducted governs and there is no local law, the member must adhere to the Code and Standards.
Member resides in LS country, does business in MS country; LS law applies, but it states that law of locality where business is conducted governs.	Member must adhere to the law of MS country.	Because applicable law of the locality where the business is conducted governs and local law is stricter than the Code and Standards, member must adhere to the more strict applicable law.
Member resides in MS country, does business in LS country; MS law applies.	Member must adhere to the law of MS country.	Because applicable law is stricter than the Code and Standards, member must adhere to the more strict applicable law.
Member resides in MS country, does business in LS country; MS law applies, but it states that law of locality where business is conducted governs.	Member must adhere to the Code and Standards.	Because applicable law states that the law of the locality where the business is conducted governs and local law is less strict than the Code and Standards, member must adhere to the Code and Standards.

Applicable Law	Duties	Explanation
Member resides in MS country, does business in LS country with a client who is a citizen of LS country; MS law applies, but it states that the law of the client's home country governs.	Member must adhere to the Code and Standards.	Because applicable law states that the law of the client's home country governs (which is less strict than the Code and Standards), member must adhere to the Code and Standards.
Member resides in MS country, does business in LS country with a client who is a citizen of MS country; MS law applies, but it states that the law of the client's home country governs.	Member must adhere to the law of MS country.	Because applicable law states that the law of the client's home country governs and the law of the client's home country is stricter than the Code and Standards, the member must adhere to the more strict applicable law.

2 STANDARD I(A): RECOMMENDED PROCEDURES

Members and Candidates

Suggested methods by which members and candidates can acquire and maintain understanding of applicable laws, rules, and regulations include the following:

- *Stay informed*: Members and candidates should establish or encourage their employers to establish a procedure by which employees are regularly informed about changes in applicable laws, rules, regulations, and case law. In many instances, the employer's compliance department or legal counsel can provide such information in the form of memorandums distributed to employees in the organization. Also, participation in an internal or external continuing education program is a practical method of staying current.
- *Review procedures*: Members and candidates should review, or encourage their employers to review, the firm's written compliance procedures on a regular basis to ensure that the procedures reflect current law and provide adequate guidance to employees about what is permissible conduct under the law and/or the Code and Standards. Recommended compliance procedures for specific items of the Code and Standards are discussed in this *Handbook* in the "Guidance" sections associated with each standard.
- *Maintain current files*: Members and candidates should maintain or encourage their employers to maintain readily accessible current reference copies of applicable statutes, rules, regulations, and important cases.

Distribution Area Laws

Members and candidates should make reasonable efforts to understand the applicable laws—both country and regional—for the countries and regions where their investment products are developed and are most likely to be distributed to clients.

Legal Counsel

When in doubt about the appropriate action to undertake, it is recommended that a member or candidate seek the advice of compliance personnel or legal counsel concerning legal requirements. If a potential violation is being committed by a fellow employee, it may also be prudent for the member or candidate to seek the advice of the firm's compliance department or legal counsel.

Dissociation

When dissociating from an activity that violates the Code and Standards, members and candidates should document the violation and urge their firms to attempt to persuade the perpetrator(s) to cease such conduct. To dissociate from the conduct, a member or candidate may have to resign his or her employment.

Firms

The formality and complexity of compliance procedures for firms depend on the nature and size of the organization and the nature of its investment operations. Members and candidates should encourage their firms to consider the following policies and procedures to support the principles of Standard I(A):

- *Develop and/or adopt a code of ethics*: The ethical culture of an organization starts at the top. Members and candidates should encourage their supervisors or managers to adopt a code of ethics. Adhering to a code of ethics facilitates solutions when people face ethical dilemmas and can prevent the need for employees to resort to a "whistleblowing" solution publicly alleging concealed misconduct. CFA Institute has published the *Asset Manager Code of Professional Conduct*, which firms may adopt or use as the basis for their codes (visit www.cfainstitute.org).
- *Provide information on applicable laws*: Pertinent information that highlights applicable laws and regulations might be distributed to employees or made available in a central location. Information sources might include primary information developed by the relevant government, governmental agencies, regulatory organizations, licensing agencies, and professional associations (e.g., from their websites); law firm memorandums or newsletters; and association memorandums or publications (e.g., *CFA Institute Magazine*).
- *Establish procedures for reporting violations*: Firms might provide written protocols for reporting suspected violations of laws, regulations, or company policies.

3 STANDARD I(A): APPLICATION OF THE STANDARD

Example 1 (Notification of Known Violations):

Michael Allen works for a brokerage firm and is responsible for an underwriting of securities. A company official gives Allen information indicating that the financial statements Allen filed with the regulator overstate the issuer's earnings. Allen seeks the advice of the brokerage firm's general counsel, who states that it would be difficult for the regulator to prove that Allen has been involved in any wrongdoing.

> *Comment*: Although it is recommended that members and candidates seek the advice of legal counsel, the reliance on such advice does not absolve a member or candidate from the requirement to comply with the law or regulation. Allen should report this situation to his supervisor, seek an independent legal opinion, and determine whether the regulator should be notified of the error.

Example 2 (Dissociating from a Violation):

Lawrence Brown's employer, an investment banking firm, is the principal underwriter for an issue of convertible debentures by the Courtney Company. Brown discovers that the Courtney Company has concealed severe third-quarter losses in its foreign operations. The preliminary prospectus has already been distributed.

> *Comment*: Knowing that the preliminary prospectus is misleading, Brown should report his findings to the appropriate supervisory persons in his firm. If the matter is not remedied and Brown's employer does not dissociate from the underwriting, Brown should sever all his connections with the underwriting. Brown should also seek legal advice to determine whether additional reporting or other action should be taken.

Example 3 (Dissociating from a Violation):

Kamisha Washington's firm advertises its past performance record by showing the 10-year return of a composite of its client accounts. Washington discovers, however, that the composite omits the performance of accounts that have left the firm during the 10-year period, whereas the description of the composite indicates the inclusion of all firm accounts. This omission has led to an inflated performance figure. Washington is asked to use promotional material that includes the erroneous performance number when soliciting business for the firm.

> *Comment*: Misrepresenting performance is a violation of the Code and Standards. Although she did not calculate the performance herself, Washington would be assisting in violating Standard I(A) if she were to use the inflated performance number when soliciting clients. She must dissociate herself from the activity. If discussing the misleading number with the person responsible is not an option for correcting the problem, she can bring the situation to the attention of her supervisor or the compliance department at her firm. If her firm is unwilling to recalculate performance, she must refrain from using the misleading promotional material and should

notify the firm of her reasons. If the firm insists that she use the material, she should consider whether her obligation to dissociate from the activity requires her to seek other employment.

Example 4 (Following the Highest Requirements):

James Collins is an investment analyst for a major Wall Street brokerage firm. He works in a developing country with a rapidly modernizing economy and a growing capital market. Local securities laws are minimal—in form and content—and include no punitive prohibitions against insider trading.

> *Comment*: Collins must abide by the requirements of the Code and Standards, which might be more strict than the rules of the developing country. He should be aware of the risks that a small market and the absence of a fairly regulated flow of information to the market represent to his ability to obtain information and make timely judgments. He should include this factor in formulating his advice to clients. In handling material nonpublic information that accidentally comes into his possession, he must follow Standard II(A) Material Nonpublic Information.

Example 5 (Following the Highest Requirements):

Laura Jameson works for a multinational investment adviser based in the United States. Jameson lives and works as a registered investment adviser in the tiny, but wealthy, island nation of Karramba. Karramba's securities laws state that no investment adviser registered and working in that country can participate in initial public offerings (IPOs) for the adviser's personal account. Jameson, believing that, as a US citizen working for a US-based company, she should comply only with US law, has ignored this Karrambian law. In addition, Jameson believes that as a charterholder, as long as she adheres to the Code and Standards requirement that she disclose her participation in any IPO to her employer and clients when such ownership creates a conflict of interest, she is meeting the highest ethical requirements.

> *Comment*: Jameson is in violation of Standard I(A). As a registered investment adviser in Karramba, Jameson is prevented by Karrambian securities law from participating in IPOs regardless of the law of her home country. In addition, because the law of the country where she is working is stricter than the Code and Standards, she must follow the stricter requirements of the local law rather than the requirements of the Code and Standards.

Example 6 (Laws and Regulations Based on Religious Tenets):

Amanda Janney is employed as a fixed-income portfolio manager for a large international firm. She is on a team within her firm that is responsible for creating and managing a fixed-income hedge fund to be sold throughout the firm's distribution centers to high-net-worth clients. Her firm receives expressions of interest from potential clients from the Middle East who are seeking investments that comply with Islamic law. The marketing and promotional materials for the fixed-income hedge fund do not specify whether or not the fund is a suitable investment for an investor seeking compliance with Islamic law. Because the fund is being distributed globally, Janney is concerned about the reputation of the fund and the firm and believes disclosure of whether or not the fund complies with Islamic law could help minimize potential mistakes with placing this investment.

Comment: As the financial market continues to become globalized, members and candidates will need to be aware of the differences between cultural and religious laws and requirements as well as the different governmental laws and regulations. Janney and the firm could be proactive in their efforts to acknowledge areas where the new fund may not be suitable for clients.

Example 7 (Reporting Potential Unethical Actions):

Krista Blume is a junior portfolio manager for high-net-worth portfolios at a large global investment manager. She observes a number of new portfolios and relationships coming from a country in Europe where the firm did not have previous business and is told that a broker in that country is responsible for this new business. At a meeting on allocation of research resources to third-party research firms, Blume notes that this broker has been added to the list and is allocated payments for research. However, she knows the portfolios do not invest in securities in the broker's country, and she has not seen any research come from this broker. Blume asks her supervisor about the name being on the list and is told that someone in marketing is receiving the research and that the name being on the list is OK. She believes that what may be going on is that the broker is being paid for new business through the inappropriate research payments, and she wishes to dissociate from the misconduct.

Comment: Blume should follow the firm's policies and procedures for reporting potential unethical activity, which may include discussions with her supervisor or someone in a designated compliance department. She should communicate her concerns appropriately while advocating for disclosure between the new broker relationship and the research payments.

Example 8 (Failure to Maintain Knowledge of the Law):

Colleen White is excited to use new technology to communicate with clients and potential clients. She recently began posting investment information, including performance reports and investment opinions and recommendations, to her Facebook page. In addition, she sends out brief announcements, opinions, and thoughts via her X account (for example, "Prospects for future growth of XYZ company look good! #makingmoney4U"). Prior to White's use of these social media platforms, the local regulator had issued new requirements and guidance governing online electronic communication. White's communications appear to conflict with the recent regulatory announcements.

Comment: White is in violation of Standard I(A) because her communications do not comply with the existing guidance and regulation governing use of social media. White must be aware of the evolving legal requirements pertaining to new and dynamic areas of the financial services industry that are applicable to her. She should seek guidance from appropriate, knowledgeable, and reliable sources, such as her firm's compliance department, external service providers, or outside counsel, unless she diligently follows legal and regulatory trends affecting her professional responsibilities.

STANDARD I(B) INDEPENDENCE AND OBJECTIVITY

4

> Members and Candidates must use reasonable care and judgment to achieve and maintain independence and objectivity in their professional activities. Members and Candidates must not offer, solicit, or accept any gift, benefit, compensation, or consideration that reasonably could be expected to compromise their own or another's independence and objectivity.

Guidance

Highlights:

- *Buy-Side Clients*
- *Fund Manager and Custodial Relationships*
- *Investment Banking Relationships*
- *Performance Measurement and Attribution*
- *Public Companies*
- *Credit Rating Agency Opinions*
- *Influence during the Manager Selection/Procurement Process*
- *Issuer-Paid Research*
- *Travel Funding*

Standard I(B) states the responsibility of CFA Institute members and candidates in the CFA Program to maintain independence and objectivity so that their clients will have the benefit of their work and opinions unaffected by any potential conflict of interest or other circumstance adversely affecting their judgment. Every member and candidate should endeavor to avoid situations that could cause or be perceived to cause a loss of independence or objectivity in recommending investments or taking investment action.

External sources may try to influence the investment process by offering analysts and portfolio managers a variety of benefits. Corporations may seek expanded research coverage, issuers and underwriters may wish to promote new securities offerings, brokers may want to increase commission business, and independent rating agencies may be influenced by the company requesting the rating. Benefits may include gifts, invitations to lavish functions, tickets, favors, or job referrals. One type of benefit is the allocation of shares in oversubscribed IPOs to investment managers for their personal accounts. This practice affords managers the opportunity to make quick profits that may not be available to their clients. Such a practice is prohibited under Standard I(B). Modest gifts and entertainment are acceptable, but special care must be taken by members and candidates to resist subtle and not-so-subtle pressures to act in conflict with the interests of their clients. Best practice dictates that members and candidates reject any offer of gift or entertainment that could be expected to threaten their independence and objectivity.

Receiving a gift, benefit, or consideration from a *client* can be distinguished from gifts given by entities seeking to influence a member or candidate to the detriment of other clients. In a client relationship, the client has already entered some type of compensation arrangement with the member, candidate, or his or her firm. A gift from a client could be considered supplementary compensation. The potential for obtaining influence to the detriment of other clients, although present, is not as great as in situations where no compensation arrangement exists. When possible, prior to accepting "bonuses" or gifts from clients, members and candidates should disclose to their employers such benefits offered by clients. If notification is not possible prior to acceptance, members and candidates must disclose to their employer benefits previously accepted from clients. Disclosure allows the employer of a member or candidate to make an independent determination about the extent to which the gift may affect the member's or candidate's independence and objectivity.

Members and candidates may also come under pressure from their own firms to, for example, issue favorable research reports or recommendations for certain companies with potential or continuing business relationships with the firm. The situation may be aggravated if an executive of the company sits on the bank or investment firm's board and attempts to interfere in investment decision making. Members and candidates acting in a sales or marketing capacity must be especially mindful of their objectivity in promoting appropriate investments for their clients.

Left unmanaged, pressures that threaten independence place research analysts in a difficult position and may jeopardize their ability to act independently and objectively. One of the ways that research analysts have coped with these pressures in the past is to use subtle and ambiguous language in their recommendations or to temper the tone of their research reports. Such subtleties are lost on some investors, however, who reasonably expect research reports and recommendations to be straightforward and transparent and to communicate clearly an analyst's views based on unbiased analysis and independent judgment.

Members and candidates are personally responsible for maintaining independence and objectivity when preparing research reports, making investment recommendations, and taking investment action on behalf of clients. Recommendations must convey the member's or candidate's true opinions, free of bias from internal or external pressures, and be stated in clear and unambiguous language.

Members and candidates also should be aware that some of their professional or social activities within CFA Institute or its member societies may subtly threaten their independence or objectivity. When seeking corporate financial support for conventions, seminars, or even weekly society luncheons, the members or candidates responsible for the activities should evaluate both the actual effect of such solicitations on their independence and whether their objectivity might be perceived to be compromised in the eyes of their clients.

Buy-Side Clients

One source of pressure on sell-side analysts is buy-side clients. Institutional clients are traditionally the primary users of sell-side research, either directly or with soft dollar brokerage. Portfolio managers may have significant positions in the security of a company under review. A rating downgrade may adversely affect the portfolio's performance, particularly in the short term, because the sensitivity of stock prices to ratings changes has increased in recent years. A downgrade may also affect the manager's compensation, which is usually tied to portfolio performance. Moreover, portfolio performance is subject to media and public scrutiny, which may affect the manager's professional reputation. Consequently, some portfolio managers implicitly or explicitly support sell-side ratings inflation.

Portfolio managers have a responsibility to respect and foster the intellectual honesty of sell-side research. Therefore, it is improper for portfolio managers to threaten or engage in retaliatory practices, such as reporting sell-side analysts to the covered company in order to instigate negative corporate reactions. Although most portfolio managers do not engage in such practices, the perception by the research analyst that a reprisal is possible may cause concern and make it difficult for the analyst to maintain independence and objectivity.

Fund Manager and Custodial Relationships

Research analysts are not the only people who must be concerned with maintaining their independence. Members and candidates who are responsible for hiring and retaining outside managers and third-party custodians should not accepts gifts, entertainment, or travel funding that may be perceived as impairing their decisions. The use of secondary fund managers has evolved into a common practice to manage specific asset allocations. The use of third-party custodians is common practice for independent investment advisory firms and helps them with trading capabilities and reporting requirements. Primary and secondary fund managers, as well as third-party custodians, often arrange educational and marketing events to inform others about their business strategies, investment process, or custodial services. Members and candidates must review the merits of each offer individually in determining whether they may attend yet maintain their independence.

Investment Banking Relationships

Some sell-side firms may exert pressure on their analysts to issue favorable research reports on current or prospective investment banking clients. For many of these firms, income from investment banking has become increasingly important to overall firm profitability because brokerage income has declined as a result of price competition. Consequently, firms offering investment banking services work hard to develop and maintain relationships with investment banking clients and prospects. These companies are often covered by the firm's research analysts because companies often select their investment banks on the basis of the reputation of their research analysts, the quality of their work, and their standing in the industry.

In some countries, research analysts frequently work closely with their investment banking colleagues to help evaluate prospective investment banking clients. In other countries, because of past abuses in managing the obvious conflicts of interest, regulators have established clear rules prohibiting the interaction of these groups. Although collaboration between research analysts and investment banking colleagues may benefit the firm and enhance market efficiency (e.g., by allowing firms to assess risks more accurately and make better pricing assumptions), it requires firms to carefully balance the conflicts of interest inherent in the collaboration. Having analysts work with investment bankers is appropriate only when the conflicts are adequately and effectively managed and disclosed. Firm managers have a responsibility to provide an environment in which analysts are neither coerced nor enticed into issuing research that does not reflect their true opinions. Firms should require public disclosure of actual conflicts of interest to investors.

Members, candidates, and their firms must adopt and follow perceived best practices in maintaining independence and objectivity in the corporate culture and protecting analysts from undue pressure by their investment banking colleagues. The "firewalls" traditionally built between these two functions must be managed to minimize conflicts of interest; indeed, enhanced firewall policies may go as far as prohibiting all communications between these groups. A key element of an enhanced firewall is separate reporting structures for personnel on the research side and personnel on the investment banking side. For example, investment banking personnel should not have any authority to approve, disapprove, or make changes to research reports or recommendations. Another element should be a compensation arrangement that minimizes the pressures on research analysts and rewards objectivity and accuracy. Compensation arrangements should not link analyst remuneration directly to investment banking assignments in which the analyst may participate as a team member. Firms should also regularly review their policies and procedures to determine whether analysts are adequately safeguarded and to improve the transparency of disclosures relating to conflicts of interest. The highest level of transparency is achieved when disclosures are prominent and specific rather than marginalized and generic.

Performance Measurement and Attribution

Members and candidates working within a firm's investment performance measurement department may also be presented with situations that challenge their independence and objectivity. As performance analysts, their analyses may reveal instances where managers may appear to have strayed from their mandate. Additionally, the performance analyst may receive requests to alter the construction of composite indexes owing to negative results for a selected account or fund. The member or candidate must not allow internal or external influences to affect their independence and objectivity as they faithfully complete their performance calculation and analysis-related responsibilities.

Public Companies

Analysts may be pressured to issue favorable reports and recommendations by the companies they follow. Not every stock is a "buy," and not every research report is favorable—for many reasons, including the cyclical nature of many business activities and market fluctuations. For instance, a "good company" does not always translate into a "good stock" rating if the current stock price is fully valued. In making an investment recommendation, the analyst is responsible for anticipating, interpreting, and assessing a company's prospects and stock price performance in a factual manner. Many company managers, however, believe that their company's stock is undervalued, and these managers may find it difficult to accept critical research reports or ratings downgrades. Company managers' compensation may also be dependent on stock performance.

Due diligence in financial research and analysis involves gathering information from a wide variety of sources, including public disclosure documents (such as proxy statements, annual reports, and other regulatory filings) and also company management and investor-relations personnel, suppliers, customers, competitors, and other relevant sources. Research analysts may justifiably fear that companies will limit their ability to conduct thorough research by denying analysts who have "negative" views direct access to company managers and/or barring them from conference calls and other communication venues. Retaliatory practices include companies bringing legal action against analysts personally and/or their firms to seek monetary damages for the economic effects of negative reports and recommendations. Although few companies engage in such behavior, the perception that a reprisal is possible is a reasonable concern for analysts. This concern may make it difficult for them to conduct the comprehensive research needed to make objective recommendations. For further information and guidance, members and candidates should refer to the CFA Institute publication *Best Practice Guidelines Governing Analyst/Corporate Issuer Relations* (www.cfainstitute.org).

Credit Rating Agency Opinions

Credit rating agencies provide a service by grading the fixed-income products offered by companies. Analysts face challenges related to incentives and compensation schemes that may be tied to the final rating and successful placement of the product. Members and candidates employed at rating agencies should ensure that procedures and processes at the agencies prevent undue influences from a sponsoring company during the analysis. Members and candidates should abide by their agencies' and the industry's standards of conduct regarding the analytical process and the distribution of their reports.

The work of credit rating agencies also raises concerns similar to those inherent in investment banking relationships. Analysts may face pressure to issue ratings at a specific level because of other services the agency offers companies—namely, advising on the development of structured products. The rating agencies need to develop the necessary firewalls and protections to allow the independent operations of their different business lines.

When using information provided by credit rating agencies, members and candidates should be mindful of the potential conflicts of interest. And because of the potential conflicts, members and candidates may need to independently validate the rating granted.

Influence during the Manager Selection/Procurement Process

Members and candidates may find themselves on either side of the manager selection process. An individual may be on the hiring side as a representative of a pension organization or an investment committee member of an endowment or a charitable organization. Additionally, other members may be representing their organizations in attempts to earn new investment allocation mandates. The responsibility of members and candidates to maintain their independence and objectivity extends to the hiring or firing of those who provide business services beyond investment management.

When serving in a hiring capacity, members and candidates should not solicit gifts, contributions, or other compensation that may affect their independence and objectivity. Solicitations do not have to benefit members and candidates personally to conflict with Standard I(B). Requesting contributions to a favorite charity or political organization may also be perceived as an attempt to influence the decision-making process. Additionally, members and candidates serving in a hiring capacity should refuse gifts, donations, and other offered compensation that may be perceived to influence their decision-making process.

When working to earn a new investment allocation, members and candidates should not offer gifts, contributions, or other compensation to influence the decision of the hiring representative. The offering of these items with the intent to impair the independence and objectivity of another person would not comply with Standard I(B). Such prohibited actions may include offering donations to a charitable organization or political candidate referred by the hiring representative.

A clear example of improperly influencing hiring representatives was displayed in the "pay-to-play" scandal involving government-sponsored pension funds in the United States. Managers looking to gain lucrative allocations from the large funds made requested donations to the political campaigns of individuals directly responsible for the hiring decisions. This scandal and other similar events have led to new laws requiring additional reporting concerning political contributions and bans on hiring—or hiring delays for—managers that made campaign contributions to representatives associated with the decision-making process.

Issuer-Paid Research

In light of the recent reduction of sell-side research coverage, many companies, seeking to increase visibility both in the financial markets and with potential investors, have hired analysts to produce research reports analyzing their companies. These reports bridge the gap created by the lack of coverage and can be an effective method of communicating with investors.

Issuer-paid research conducted by independent analysts, however, is fraught with potential conflicts. Depending on how the research is written and distributed, investors may be misled into believing that the research is from an independent source when, in reality, it has been paid for by the subject company.

Members and candidates must adhere to strict standards of conduct that govern how the research is to be conducted and what disclosures must be made in the report. Analysts must engage in thorough, independent, and unbiased analysis and must fully disclose potential conflicts of interest, including the nature of their compensation. Otherwise, analysts risk misleading investors.

Investors need clear, credible, and thorough information about companies, and they need research based on independent thought. At a minimum, issuer-paid research should include a thorough analysis of the company's financial statements based on publicly disclosed information, benchmarking within a peer group, and industry analysis. Analysts must exercise diligence, independence, and thoroughness in conducting their research in an objective manner. Analysts must distinguish between fact and opinion in their reports. Conclusions must have a reasonable and adequate basis and must be supported by appropriate research.

Independent analysts must also strictly limit the type of compensation that they accept for conducting issuer-paid research. Otherwise, the content and conclusions of the reports could reasonably be expected to be determined or affected by compensation from the sponsoring companies. Compensation that might influence the research report could be direct, such as payment based on the conclusions of the report, or indirect, such as stock warrants or other equity instruments that could increase in value on the basis of positive coverage in the report. In such instances, the independent analyst has an incentive to avoid including negative information or making negative conclusions. Best practice is for independent analysts, prior to writing their reports, to negotiate only a flat fee for their work that is not linked to their conclusions or recommendations.

Travel Funding

The benefits related to accepting paid travel extend beyond the cost savings to the member or candidate and his firm, such as the chance to talk exclusively with the executives of a company or learning more about the investment options provided by an investment organization. Acceptance also comes with potential concerns; for example, members and candidates may be influenced by these discussions when flying on a corporate or chartered jet or attending sponsored conferences where many expenses, including airfare and lodging, are covered. To avoid the appearance of compromising their independence and objectivity, best practice dictates that members and candidates always use commercial transportation at their expense or at the expense of their firm rather than accept paid travel arrangements from an outside company. Should commercial transportation be unavailable, members and candidates may accept modestly arranged travel to participate in appropriate information-gathering events, such as a property tour.

5 STANDARD I(B): RECOMMENDED PROCEDURES

Members and candidates should adhere to the following practices and should encourage their firms to establish procedures to avoid violations of Standard I(B):

- *Protect the integrity of opinions*: Members, candidates, and their firms should establish policies stating that every research report concerning the securities of a corporate client should reflect the unbiased opinion of the analyst. Firms should also design compensation systems that protect the integrity of the investment decision process by maintaining the independence and objectivity of analysts.
- *Create a restricted list*: If the firm is unwilling to permit dissemination of adverse opinions about a corporate client, members and candidates should encourage the firm to remove the controversial company from the research universe and put it on a restricted list so that the firm disseminates only factual information about the company.

- *Restrict special cost arrangements*: When attending meetings at an issuer's headquarters, members and candidates should pay for commercial transportation and hotel charges. No corporate issuer should reimburse members or candidates for air transportation. Members and candidates should encourage issuers to limit the use of corporate aircraft to situations in which commercial transportation is not available or in which efficient movement could not otherwise be arranged. Members and candidates should take particular care that when frequent meetings are held between an individual issuer and an individual member or candidate, the issuer should not always host the member or candidate.
- *Limit gifts*: Members and candidates must limit the acceptance of gratuities and/or gifts to token items. Standard I(B) does not preclude customary, ordinary business-related entertainment as long as its purpose is not to influence or reward members or candidates. Firms should consider a strict value limit for acceptable gifts that is based on the local or regional customs and should address whether the limit is per gift or an aggregate annual value.
- *Restrict investments*: Members and candidates should encourage their investment firms to develop formal policies related to employee purchases of equity or equity-related IPOs. Firms should require prior approval for employee participation in IPOs, with prompt disclosure of investment actions taken following the offering. Strict limits should be imposed on investment personnel acquiring securities in private placements.
- *Review procedures*: Members and candidates should encourage their firms to implement effective supervisory and review procedures to ensure that analysts and portfolio managers comply with policies relating to their personal investment activities.
- *Independence policy*: Members, candidates, and their firms should establish a formal written policy on the independence and objectivity of research and implement reporting structures and review procedures to ensure that research analysts do not report to and are not supervised or controlled by any department of the firm that could compromise the independence of the analyst. More detailed recommendations related to a firm's policies regarding research objectivity are set forth in the CFA Institute statement *Research Objectivity Standards* (www.cfainstitute.org).
- *Appointed officer*: Firms should appoint a senior officer with oversight responsibilities for compliance with the firm's code of ethics and all regulations concerning its business. Firms should provide every employee with the procedures and policies for reporting potentially unethical behavior, violations of regulations, or other activities that may harm the firm's reputation.

STANDARD I(B): APPLICATION OF THE STANDARD

6

Example 1 (Travel Expenses):

Steven Taylor, a mining analyst with Bronson Brokers, is invited by Precision Metals to join a group of his peers in a tour of mining facilities in several western US states. The company arranges for chartered group flights from site to site and for accommodations in Spartan Motels, the only chain with accommodations near the mines, for three nights. Taylor allows Precision Metals to pick up his tab, as do the other analysts, with one exception—John Adams, an employee of a large trust company who insists on following his company's policy and paying for his hotel room himself.

> *Comment*: The policy of the company where Adams works complies closely with Standard I(B) by avoiding even the appearance of a conflict of interest, but Taylor and the other analysts were not necessarily violating Standard I(B). In general, when allowing companies to pay for travel and/or accommodations in these circumstances, members and candidates must use their judgment. They must be on guard that such arrangements not impinge on a member's or candidate's independence and objectivity. In this example, the trip was strictly for business and Taylor was not accepting irrelevant or lavish hospitality. The itinerary required chartered flights, for which analysts were not expected to pay. The accommodations were modest. These arrangements are not unusual and did not violate Standard I(B) as long as Taylor's independence and objectivity were not compromised. In the final analysis, members and candidates should consider both whether they can remain objective and whether their integrity might be perceived by their clients to have been compromised.

Example 2 (Research Independence):

Susan Dillon, an analyst in the corporate finance department of an investment services firm, is making a presentation to a potential new business client that includes the promise that her firm will provide full research coverage of the potential client.

> *Comment*: Dillon may agree to provide research coverage, but she must not commit her firm's research department to providing a favorable recommendation. The firm's recommendation (favorable, neutral, or unfavorable) must be based on an independent and objective investigation and analysis of the company and its securities.

Example 3 (Research Independence and Intrafirm Pressure):

Walter Fritz is an equity analyst with Hilton Brokerage who covers the mining industry. He has concluded that the stock of Metals & Mining is overpriced at its current level, but he is concerned that a negative research report will hurt the good relationship between Metals & Mining and the investment banking division of his firm. In fact, a senior manager of Hilton Brokerage has just sent him a copy of a proposal his firm has made to Metals & Mining to underwrite a debt offering. Fritz needs to produce a report right away and is concerned about issuing a less-than-favorable rating.

> *Comment*: Fritz's analysis of Metals & Mining must be objective and based solely on consideration of company fundamentals. Any pressure from other divisions of his firm is inappropriate. This conflict could have been eliminated if, in anticipation of the offering, Hilton Brokerage had placed Metals & Mining on a restricted list for its sales force.

Example 4 (Research Independence and Issuer Relationship Pressure):

As in Example 3, Walter Fritz has concluded that Metals & Mining stock is overvalued at its current level, but he is concerned that a negative research report might jeopardize a close rapport that he has nurtured over the years with Metals & Mining's CEO, chief finance officer, and investment relations officer. Fritz is concerned that a negative report might result also in management retaliation—for instance, cutting him off from participating in conference calls when a quarterly earnings release is made, denying him the ability to ask questions on such calls, and/or denying him access to top management for arranging group meetings between Hilton Brokerage clients and top Metals & Mining managers.

> *Comment*: As in Example 3, Fritz's analysis must be objective and based solely on consideration of company fundamentals. Any pressure from Metals & Mining is inappropriate. Fritz should reinforce the integrity of his conclusions by stressing that his investment recommendation is based on relative valuation, which may include qualitative issues with respect to Metals & Mining's management.

Example 5 (Research Independence and Sales Pressure):

As support for the sales effort of her corporate bond department, Lindsey Warner offers credit guidance to purchasers of fixed-income securities. Her compensation is closely linked to the performance of the corporate bond department. Near the quarter's end, Warner's firm has a large inventory position in the bonds of Milton, Ltd., and has been unable to sell the bonds because of Milton's recent announcement of an operating problem. Salespeople have asked her to contact large clients to push the bonds.

> *Comment*: Unethical sales practices create significant potential violations of the Code and Standards. Warner's opinion of the Milton bonds must not be affected by internal pressure or compensation. In this case, Warner must refuse to push the Milton bonds unless she is able to justify that the market price has already adjusted for the operating problem.

Example 6 (Research Independence and Prior Coverage):

Jill Jorund is a securities analyst following airline stocks and a rising star at her firm. Her boss has been carrying a "buy" recommendation on International Airlines and asks Jorund to take over coverage of that airline. He tells Jorund that under no circumstances should the prevailing buy recommendation be changed.

> *Comment*: Jorund must be independent and objective in her analysis of International Airlines. If she believes that her boss's instructions have compromised her, she has two options: She can tell her boss that she cannot cover the company under these constraints, or she can take over coverage of the company, reach her own independent conclusions, and if they conflict with her boss's opinion, share the conclusions with her boss or other supervisors in the firm so that they can make appropriate recommendations. Jorund must issue only recommendations that reflect her independent and objective opinion.

Example 7 (Gifts and Entertainment from Related Party):

Edward Grant directs a large amount of his commission business to a New York–based brokerage house. In appreciation for all the business, the brokerage house gives Grant two tickets to the World Cup in South Africa, two nights at a nearby resort, several meals, and transportation via limousine to the game. Grant fails to disclose receiving this package to his supervisor.

> *Comment*: Grant has violated Standard I(B) because accepting these substantial gifts may impede his independence and objectivity. Every member and candidate should endeavor to avoid situations that might cause or be perceived to cause a loss of independence or objectivity in recommending investments or taking investment action. By accepting the trip, Grant has opened himself up to the accusation that he may give the broker favored treatment in return.

Example 8 (Gifts and Entertainment from Client):

Theresa Green manages the portfolio of Ian Knowlden, a client of Tisbury Investments. Green achieves an annual return for Knowlden that is consistently better than that of the benchmark she and the client previously agreed to. As a reward, Knowlden offers Green two tickets to Wimbledon and the use of Knowlden's flat in London for a week. Green discloses this gift to her supervisor at Tisbury.

> *Comment*: Green is in compliance with Standard I(B) because she disclosed the gift from one of her clients in accordance with the firm's policies. Members and candidates may accept bonuses or gifts from clients as long as they disclose them to their employer because gifts in a client relationship are deemed less likely to affect a member's or candidate's objectivity and independence than gifts in other situations. Disclosure is required, however, so that supervisors can monitor such situations to guard against employees favoring a gift-giving client to the detriment of other fee-paying clients (such as by allocating a greater proportion of IPO stock to the gift-giving client's portfolio).
>
> Best practices for monitoring include comparing the transaction costs of the Knowlden account with the costs of other accounts managed by Green and other similar accounts within Tisbury. The supervisor could also compare the performance returns with the returns of other clients with the same mandate. This comparison will assist in determining whether a pattern of favoritism by Green is disadvantaging other Tisbury clients or the possibility that this favoritism could affect her future behavior.

Example 9 (Travel Expenses from External Manager):

Tom Wayne is the investment manager of the Franklin City Employees Pension Plan. He recently completed a successful search for a firm to manage the foreign equity allocation of the plan's diversified portfolio. He followed the plan's standard procedure of seeking presentations from a number of qualified firms and recommended that his board select Penguin Advisors because of its experience, well-defined investment strategy, and performance record. The firm claims compliance with the Global Investment Performance Standards (GIPS®) and has been verified. Following the selection of Penguin, a reporter from the *Franklin City Record* calls to ask if there was any connection between this action and the fact that Penguin was one of the sponsors of an "investment fact-finding trip to Asia" that Wayne made earlier in the year. The trip was one of several conducted by the Pension Investment Academy, which had arranged the itinerary of meetings with economic, government, and corporate officials in major cities in several Asian countries. The Pension Investment Academy obtains support for the cost of these trips from a number of investment managers, including Penguin Advisors; the Academy then pays the travel expenses of the various pension plan managers on the trip and provides all meals and accommodations. The president of Penguin Advisors was also one of the travelers on the trip.

> *Comment*: Although Wayne can probably put to good use the knowledge he gained from the trip in selecting portfolio managers and in other areas of managing the pension plan, his recommendation of Penguin Advisors may be tainted by the possible conflict incurred when he participated in a trip partly paid for by Penguin Advisors and when he was in the daily company of the president of Penguin Advisors. To avoid violating Standard I(B), Wayne's basic expenses for travel and accommodations should have been paid by his employer or the pension plan; contact with the president of Penguin Advisors should have been limited to informational or educational events only; and the trip, the organizer, and the sponsor should have been made a matter of public record. Even if his actions were not in violation of Standard I(B), Wayne should have been sensitive to the public perception of the trip when reported in the newspaper and the extent to which the subjective elements of his decision might have been affected by the familiarity that the daily contact of such a trip would encourage. This advantage would probably not be shared by firms competing with Penguin Advisors.

Example 10 (Research Independence and Compensation Arrangements):

Javier Herrero recently left his job as a research analyst for a large investment adviser. While looking for a new position, he was hired by an investor-relations firm to write a research report on one of its clients, a small educational software company. The investor-relations firm hopes to generate investor interest in the technology company. The firm will pay Herrero a flat fee plus a bonus if any new investors buy stock in the company as a result of Herrero's report.

> *Comment*: If Herrero accepts this payment arrangement, he will be in violation of Standard I(B) because the compensation arrangement can reasonably be expected to compromise his independence and objectivity. Herrero will receive a bonus for attracting investors, which provides an incentive to draft a positive report regardless of the facts and to ignore or play down any negative information about the company. Herrero should accept only a flat fee that is not tied to the conclusions or recommendations of the report. Issuer-paid research that is objective and unbiased can be done under the right circumstances as long as the analyst takes steps to maintain his or her objectivity and includes in the report proper disclosures regarding potential conflicts of interest.

Example 11 (Recommendation Objectivity and Service Fees):

Two years ago, Bob Wade, trust manager for Central Midas Bank, was approached by Western Funds about promoting its family of funds, with special interest in the service-fee class of funds. To entice Central to promote this class, Western Funds offered to pay the bank a service fee of 0.25%. Without disclosing the fee being offered to the bank, Wade asked one of the investment managers to review Western's funds to determine whether they were suitable for clients of Central Midas Bank. The manager completed the normal due diligence review and determined that the new funds were fairly valued in the market with fee structures on a par with competitors. Wade decided to accept Western's offer and instructed the team of portfolio managers to exclusively promote these funds and the service-fee class to clients seeking to invest new funds or transfer from their current investments.

Now, two years later, the funds managed by Western begin to underperform their peers. Wade is counting on the fees to reach his profitability targets and continues to push these funds as acceptable investments for Central's clients.

> *Comment*: Wade is violating Standard I(B) because the fee arrangement has affected the objectivity of his recommendations. Wade is relying on the fee as a component of the department's profitability and is unwilling to offer other products that may affect the fees received.
>
> See also Standard VI(A) Disclosure of Conflicts.

Example 12 (Recommendation Objectivity):

Bob Thompson has been doing research for the portfolio manager of the fixed-income department. His assignment is to do sensitivity analysis on securitized subprime mortgages. He has discussed with the manager possible scenarios to use to calculate expected returns. A key assumption in such calculations is housing price appreciation (HPA) because it drives "prepays" (prepayments of mortgages) and losses. Thompson is concerned with the significant appreciation experienced over the previous five years as a result of the increased availability of funds from subprime mortgages. Thompson insists that the analysis should include a scenario run with –10% for Year 1, –5% for Year 2, and then (to project a worst-case scenario) 0% for Years 3 through 5. The manager replies that these assumptions are too dire because there has never been a time in their available database when HPA was negative.

Thompson conducts his research to better understand the risks inherent in these securities and evaluates these securities in the worst-case scenario, an unlikely but possible environment. Based on the results of the enhanced scenarios, Thompson does not recommend the purchase of the securitization. Against the general market trends, the manager follows Thompson's recommendation and does not invest. The following year, the housing market collapses. In avoiding the subprime investments, the manager's portfolio outperforms its peer group that year.

> *Comment*: Thompson's actions in running the worst-case scenario against the protests of the portfolio manager are in alignment with the principles of Standard I(B). Thompson did not allow his research to be pressured by the general trends of the market or the manager's desire to limit the research to historical norms.
>
> See also Standard V(A) Diligence and Reasonable Basis.

Example 13 (Influencing Manager Selection Decisions):

Adrian Mandel, CFA, is a senior portfolio manager for ZZYY Capital Management who oversees a team of investment professionals who manage labor union pension funds. A few years ago, ZZYY sought to win a competitive asset manager search to manage a significant allocation of the pension fund of the United Doughnut and Pretzel Bakers Union (UDPBU). UDPBU's investment board is chaired by a recognized key decision maker and long-time leader of the union, Ernesto Gomez. To improve ZZYY's chances of winning the competition, Mandel made significant monetary contributions to Gomez's union reelection campaign fund. Even after ZZYY was hired as a primary manager of the pension, Mandel believed that his firm's position was not secure. Mandel continued to contribute to Gomez's reelection campaign chest as well as to entertain lavishly the union leader and his family at top restaurants on a regular basis. All of Mandel's outlays were routinely handled as marketing expenses reimbursed by ZZYY's expense accounts and were disclosed to his senior management as being instrumental in maintaining a strong close relationship with an important client.

> *Comment*: Mandel not only offered but actually gave monetary gifts, benefits, and other considerations that reasonably could be expected to compromise Gomez's objectivity. Therefore, Mandel was in violation of Standard I(B).

Example 14 (Influencing Manager Selection Decisions):

Adrian Mandel, CFA, had heard about the manager search competition for the UDPBU Pension Fund through a broker/dealer contact. The contact told him that a well-known retired professional golfer, Bobby "The Bear" Finlay, who had become a licensed broker/dealer serving as a pension consultant, was orchestrating the UDPBU manager search. Finlay had gained celebrity status with several labor union pension fund boards by entertaining their respective board members and regaling them with colorful stories of fellow pro golfers' antics in clubhouses around the world. Mandel decided to improve ZZYY's chances of being invited to participate in the search competition by befriending Finlay to curry his favor. Knowing Finlay's love of entertainment, Mandel wined and dined Finlay at high-profile bistros where Finlay could glow in the fan recognition lavished on him by all the other patrons. Mandel's endeavors paid off handsomely when Finlay recommended to the UDPBU board that ZZYY be entered as one of three finalist asset management firms in its search.

> *Comment*: Similar to Example 13, Mandel lavished gifts, benefits, and other considerations in the form of expensive entertainment that could reasonably be expected to influence the consultant to recommend the hiring of his firm. Therefore, Mandel was in violation of Standard I(B).

Example 15 (Fund Manager Relationships):

Amie Scott is a performance analyst within her firm with responsibilities for analyzing the performance of external managers. While completing her quarterly analysis, Scott notices a change in one manager's reported composite construction. The change concealed the bad performance of a particularly large account by placing that account into a new residual composite. This change allowed the manager to remain at the top of the list of manager performance. Scott knows her firm has a large allocation to this manager, and the fund's manager is a close personal friend of the CEO. She needs to deliver her final report but is concerned with pointing out the composite change.

> *Comment*: Scott would be in violation of Standard I(B) if she did not disclose the change in her final report. The analysis of managers' performance should not be influenced by personal relationships or the size of the allocation to the outside managers. By not including the change, Scott would not be providing an independent analysis of the performance metrics for her firm.

Example 16 (Intrafirm Pressure):

Jill Stein is head of performance measurement for her firm. During the last quarter, many members of the organization's research department were removed because of the poor quality of their recommendations. The subpar research caused one larger account holder to experience significant underperformance, which resulted in the client withdrawing his money after the end of the quarter. The head of sales requests that Stein remove this account from the firm's performance composite because the performance decline can be attributed to the departed research team and not the client's adviser.

> *Comment*: Pressure from other internal departments can create situations that cause a member or candidate to violate the Code and Standards. Stein must maintain her independence and objectivity and refuse to exclude specific accounts from the firm's performance composites to which they belong. As long as the client invested under a strategy similar to that of the defined composite, it cannot be excluded because of the poor stock selections that led to the underperformance and asset withdrawal.

7 STANDARD I(C) MISREPRESENTATION

- [ ] demonstrate a thorough knowledge of the CFA Institute Code of Ethics and Standards of Professional Conduct by interpreting the Code and Standards in various situations involving issues of professional integrity
- [ ] recommend practices and procedures designed to prevent violations of the Code and Standards

Members and Candidates must not knowingly make any misrepresentations relating to investment analysis, recommendations, actions, or other professional activities.

Guidance

Highlights:

- *Impact on Investment Practice*
- *Performance Reporting*
- *Social Media*
- *Omissions*
- *Plagiarism*
- *Work Completed for Employer*

Trust is the foundation of the investment profession. Investors must be able to rely on the statements and information provided to them by those with whom the investors have trusted their financial well-being. Investment professionals who make false or misleading statements not only harm investors but also reduce the level of investor confidence in the investment profession and threaten the integrity of capital markets as a whole.

A misrepresentation is any untrue statement or omission of a fact or any statement that is otherwise false or misleading. A member or candidate must not knowingly omit or misrepresent information or give a false impression of a firm, organization, or security in the member's or candidate's oral representations, advertising (whether in the press or through brochures), electronic communications, or written materials (whether publicly disseminated or not). In this context, "knowingly" means that the member or candidate either knows or should have known that the misrepresentation was being made or that omitted information could alter the investment decision-making process.

Written materials include, but are not limited to, research reports, underwriting documents, company financial reports, market letters, newspaper columns, and books. Electronic communications include, but are not limited to, internet communications, webpages, mobile applications, and e-mails. Members and candidates who use webpages should regularly monitor materials posted on these sites to ensure that they contain current information. Members and candidates should also ensure that all reasonable precautions have been taken to protect the site's integrity and security and that the site does not misrepresent any information and does provide full disclosure.

Standard I(C) prohibits members and candidates from guaranteeing clients any specific return on volatile investments. Most investments contain some element of risk that makes their return inherently unpredictable. For such investments, guaranteeing either a particular rate of return or preservation of investment capital (e.g., "I can guarantee that you will earn 8% on equities this year" or "I can guarantee that you will not lose money on this investment") is misleading to investors. Standard I(C) does not prohibit members and candidates from providing clients with information on investment products that have guarantees built into the structure of the products themselves or for which an institution has agreed to cover any losses.

Impact on Investment Practice

Members and candidates must not misrepresent any aspect of their practice, including (but not limited to) their qualifications or credentials, the qualifications or services provided by their firm, their performance record and the record of their firm, and the characteristics of an investment. Any misrepresentation made by a member or candidate relating to the member's or candidate's professional activities is a breach of this standard.

Members and candidates should exercise care and diligence when incorporating third-party information. Misrepresentations resulting from the use of the credit ratings, research, testimonials, or marketing materials of outside parties become the responsibility of the investment professional when it affects that professional's business practices.

Investing through outside managers continues to expand as an acceptable method of investing in areas outside a firm's core competencies. Members and candidates must disclose their intended use of external managers and must not represent those managers' investment practices as their own. Although the level of involvement of outside managers may change over time, appropriate disclosures by members and candidates are important in avoiding misrepresentations, especially if the primary activity is to invest directly with a single external manager. Standard V(B)–Communication with Clients and Prospective Clients discusses in further detail communicating the firm's investment practices.

Performance Reporting

The performance benchmark selection process is another area where misrepresentations may occur. Members and candidates may misrepresent the success of their performance record through presenting benchmarks that are not comparable to their strategies. Further, clients can be misled if the benchmark's results are not reported on a basis comparable to that of the fund's or client's results. Best practice is selecting the most appropriate available benchmark from a universe of available options. The transparent presentation of appropriate performance benchmarks is an important aspect in providing clients with information that is useful in making investment decisions.

However, Standard I(C) does not require that a benchmark always be provided in order to comply. Some investment strategies may not lend themselves to displaying an appropriate benchmark because of the complexity or diversity of the investments included. Furthermore, some investment strategies may use reference indexes that do not reflect the opportunity set of the invested assets—for example, a hedge fund comparing its performance with a "cash plus" basis. When such a benchmark is used, members and candidates should make reasonable efforts to ensure that they disclose the reasons behind the use of this reference index to avoid misrepresentations of their performance. Members and candidates should discuss with clients on a continuous basis the appropriate benchmark to be used for performance evaluations and related fee calculations.

Reporting misrepresentations may also occur when valuations for illiquid or non-traded securities are available from more than one source. When different options are available, members and candidates may be tempted to switch providers to obtain higher security valuations. The process of shopping for values may misrepresent a security's worth, lead to misinformed decisions to sell or hold an investment, and result in overcharging clients advisory fees.

Members and candidates should take reasonable steps to provide accurate and reliable security pricing information to clients on a consistent basis. Changing pricing providers should not be based solely on the justification that the new provider reports a higher current value of a security. Consistency in the reported information will improve the perception of the valuation process for illiquid securities. Clients will likely have additional confidence that they were able to make an informed decision about continuing to hold these securities in their portfolios.

Social Media

The advancement of online discussion forums and communication platforms, commonly referred to as "social media," is placing additional responsibilities on members and candidates. When communicating through social media channels, members and candidates should provide only the same information they are allowed to distribute to clients and potential clients through other traditional forms of communication. The online or interactive aspects of social media do not remove the need to be open and honest about the information being distributed.

Along with understanding and following existing and newly developing rules and regulations regarding the allowed use of social media, members and candidates should also ensure that all communications in this format adhere to the requirements of the Code and Standards. The perceived anonymity granted through these platforms may entice individuals to misrepresent their qualifications or abilities or those of their employer. Actions undertaken through social media that knowingly misrepresent investment recommendations or professional activities are considered a violation of Standard I(C).

Omissions

The omission of a fact or outcome can be misleading, especially given the growing use of models and technical analysis processes. Many members and candidates rely on such models and processes to scan for new investment opportunities, to develop investment vehicles, and to produce investment recommendations and ratings. When inputs are knowingly omitted, the resulting outcomes may provide misleading information to those who rely on it for making investment decisions. Additionally, the outcomes from models shall not be presented as fact because they represent the expected results based on the inputs and analysis process incorporated.

Omissions in the performance measurement and attribution process can also misrepresent a manager's performance and skill. Members and candidates should encourage their firms to develop strict policies for composite development to prevent cherry picking—situations in which selected accounts are presented as representative of the firm's abilities. The omission of any accounts appropriate for the defined composite may misrepresent to clients the success of the manager's implementation of its strategy.

Plagiarism

Standard I(C) also prohibits plagiarism in the preparation of material for distribution to employers, associates, clients, prospects, or the general public. Plagiarism is defined as copying or using in substantially the same form materials prepared by others without acknowledging the source of the material or identifying the author and publisher of such material. Members and candidates must not copy (or represent as their own) original ideas or material without permission and must acknowledge and identify the source of ideas or material that is not their own.

The investment profession uses a myriad of financial, economic, and statistical data in the investment decision-making process. Through various publications and presentations, the investment professional is constantly exposed to the work of others and to the temptation to use that work without proper acknowledgment.

Misrepresentation through plagiarism in investment management can take various forms. The simplest and most flagrant example is to take a research report or study done by another firm or person, change the names, and release the material as one's own original analysis. This action is a clear violation of Standard I(C). Other practices include (1) using excerpts from articles or reports prepared by others either verbatim or with only slight changes in wording without acknowledgment, (2) citing specific quotations as attributable to "leading analysts" and "investment experts" without naming the specific references, (3) presenting statistical estimates of forecasts prepared by others and identifying the sources but without including the qualifying statements or caveats that may have been used, (4) using charts and graphs without stating their sources, and (5) copying proprietary computerized spreadsheets or algorithms without seeking the cooperation or authorization of their creators.

In the case of distributing third-party, outsourced research, members and candidates may use and distribute such reports as long as they do not represent themselves as the report's authors. Indeed, the member or candidate may add value for the client by sifting through research and repackaging it for clients. In such cases, clients should be fully informed that they are paying for the ability of the member or candidate to find the best research from a wide variety of sources. Members and candidates must not misrepresent their abilities, the extent of their expertise, or the extent of their work in a way that would mislead their clients or prospective clients. Members and candidates should disclose whether the research being presented to clients comes from another source—from either within or outside the member's or candidate's firm. This allows clients to understand who has the expertise behind the report or whether the work is being done by the analyst, other members of the firm, or an outside party.

Standard I(C) also applies to plagiarism in oral communications, such as through group meetings; visits with associates, clients, and customers; use of audio/video media (which is rapidly increasing); and telecommunications, including electronic data transfer and the outright copying of electronic media.

One of the most egregious practices in violation of this standard is the preparation of research reports based on multiple sources of information without acknowledging the sources. Examples of information from such sources include ideas, statistical compilations, and forecasts combined to give the appearance of original work. Although there is no monopoly on ideas, members and candidates must give credit where it is clearly due. Analysts should not use undocumented forecasts, earnings projections, asset values, and so on. Sources must be revealed to bring the responsibility directly back to the author of the report or the firm involved.

Work Completed for Employer

The preceding paragraphs address actions that would constitute a violation of Standard I(C). In some situations, however, members or candidates may use research conducted or models developed by others within the same firm without committing a violation. The most common example relates to the situation in which one (or more) of the original analysts is no longer with the firm. Research and models developed while employed by a firm are the property of the firm. The firm retains the right to continue using the work completed after a member or candidate has left the organization. The firm may issue future reports without providing attribution to the prior analysts. A member or candidate cannot, however, reissue a previously released report solely under his or her name.

8 STANDARD I(C): RECOMMENDED PROCEDURES

Factual Presentations

Members and candidates can prevent unintentional misrepresentations of their qualifications or the services they or their firms provide if each member and candidate understands the limit of the firm's or individual's capabilities and the need to be accurate and complete in presentations. Firms can provide guidance for employees who make written or oral presentations to clients or potential clients by providing a written list of the firm's available services and a description of the firm's qualifications. This list should suggest ways of describing the firm's services, qualifications, and compensation that are both accurate and suitable for client or customer presentations. Firms can also help prevent misrepresentation by specifically designating which employees are authorized to speak on behalf of the firm. Regardless of whether the firm provides guidance, members and candidates should make certain that they understand the services the firm can perform and its qualifications.

Qualification Summary

In addition, to ensure accurate presentations to clients, each member and candidate should prepare a summary of his or her own qualifications and experience and a list of the services the member or candidate is capable of performing. Firms can assist member and candidate compliance by periodically reviewing employee correspondence and documents that contain representations of individual or firm qualifications.

Verify Outside Information

When providing information to clients from a third party, members and candidates share a responsibility for the accuracy of the marketing and distribution materials that pertain to the third party's capabilities, services, and products. Misrepresentation by third parties can damage the member's or candidate's reputation, the reputation of the firm, and the integrity of the capital markets. Members and candidates should encourage their employers to develop procedures for verifying information of third-party firms.

Maintain Webpages

Members and candidates who publish a webpage should regularly monitor materials posted on the site to ensure that the site contains current information. Members and candidates should also ensure that all reasonable precautions have been taken to protect the site's integrity, confidentiality, and security and that the site does not misrepresent any information and provides full disclosure.

Plagiarism Policy

To avoid plagiarism in preparing research reports or conclusions of analysis, members and candidates should take the following steps:

- *Maintain copies*: Keep copies of all research reports, articles containing research ideas, material with new statistical methodologies, and other materials that were relied on in preparing the research report.
- *Attribute quotations*: Attribute to their sources any direct quotations, including projections, tables, statistics, model/product ideas, and new methodologies prepared by persons other than recognized financial and statistical reporting services or similar sources.
- *Attribute summaries*: Attribute to their sources any paraphrases or summaries of material prepared by others. For example, to support his analysis of Brown Company's competitive position, the author of a research report on Brown might summarize another analyst's report on Brown's chief competitor, but the author of the Brown report must acknowledge in his own report the reliance on the other analyst's report.

STANDARD I(C): APPLICATION OF THE STANDARD 9

Example 1 (Disclosure of Issuer-Paid Research):

Anthony McGuire is an issuer-paid analyst hired by publicly traded companies to electronically promote their stocks. McGuire creates a website that promotes his research efforts as a seemingly independent analyst. McGuire posts a profile and a strong buy recommendation for each company on the website indicating that the stock is expected to increase in value. He does not disclose the contractual relationships with the companies he covers on his website, in the research reports he issues, or in the statements he makes about the companies in internet chat rooms.

> *Comment*: McGuire has violated Standard I(C) because the website is misleading to potential investors. Even if the recommendations are valid and supported with thorough research, his omissions regarding the true relationship between himself and the companies he covers constitute a misrepresentation. McGuire has also violated Standard VI(A)–Disclosure of Conflicts by not disclosing the existence of an arrangement with the companies through which he receives compensation in exchange for his services.

Example 2 (Correction of Unintentional Errors):

Hijan Yao is responsible for the creation and distribution of the marketing materials for his firm, which claims compliance with the GIPS standards. Yao creates and distributes a presentation of performance by the firm's Asian equity composite that states the composite has ¥350 billion in assets. In fact, the composite has only ¥35 billion in assets, and the higher figure on the presentation is a result of a typographical error. Nevertheless, the erroneous material is distributed to a number of clients before Yao catches the mistake.

> *Comment*: Once the error is discovered, Yao must take steps to cease distribution of the incorrect material and correct the error by informing those who have received the erroneous information. Because Yao did not knowingly make the misrepresentation, however, he did not violate Standard I(C). Because his firm claims compliance with the GIPS standards, it must also comply with the GIPS Guidance Statement on Error Correction in relation to the error.

Example 3 (Noncorrection of Known Errors):

Syed Muhammad is the president of an investment management firm. The promotional material for the firm, created by the firm's marketing department, incorrectly claims that Muhammad has an advanced degree in finance from a prestigious business school in addition to the CFA designation. Although Muhammad attended the school for a short period of time, he did not receive a degree. Over the years, Muhammad and others in the firm have distributed this material to numerous prospective clients and consultants.

> *Comment*: Even though Muhammad may not have been directly responsible for the misrepresentation of his credentials in the firm's promotional material, he used this material numerous times over an extended period and should have known of the misrepresentation. Thus, Muhammad has violated Standard I(C).

Example 4 (Plagiarism):

Cindy Grant, a research analyst for a Canadian brokerage firm, has specialized in the Canadian mining industry for the past 10 years. She recently read an extensive research report on Jefferson Mining, Ltd., by Jeremy Barton, another analyst. Barton provided extensive statistics on the mineral reserves, production capacity, selling rates, and marketing factors affecting Jefferson's operations. He also noted that initial drilling results on a new ore body, which had not been made public, might show the existence of mineral zones that could increase the life of Jefferson's main mines, but Barton cited no specific data as to the initial drilling results. Grant called an officer of Jefferson, who gave her the initial drilling results over the telephone. The data indicated that the expected life of the main mines would be tripled. Grant added these statistics to Barton's report and circulated it within her firm as her own report.

> *Comment*: Grant plagiarized Barton's report by reproducing large parts of it in her own report without acknowledgment.

Example 5 (Misrepresentation of Information):

When Ricki Marks sells mortgage-backed derivatives called "interest-only strips" (IOs) to public pension plan clients, she describes them as "guaranteed by the US government." Purchasers of the IOs are entitled only to the interest stream generated by the mortgages, however, not the notional principal itself. One particular municipality's investment policies and local law require that securities purchased by its public pension plans be guaranteed by the US government. Although the underlying mortgages are guaranteed, neither the investor's investment nor the interest stream on the IOs is guaranteed. When interest rates decline, causing an increase in prepayment of mortgages, interest payments to the IOs' investors decline, and these investors lose a portion of their investment.

> *Comment*: Marks violated Standard I(C) by misrepresenting the terms and character of the investment.

Example 6 (Potential Information Misrepresentation):

Khalouck Abdrabbo manages the investments of several high-net-worth individuals in the United States who are approaching retirement. Abdrabbo advises these individuals that a portion of their investments be moved from equity to bank-sponsored certificates of deposit and money market accounts so that the principal will be "guaranteed" up to a certain amount. The interest is not guaranteed.

> *Comment*: Although there is risk that the institution offering the certificates of deposits and money market accounts could go bankrupt, in the United States, these accounts are insured by the US government through the Federal Deposit Insurance Corporation. Therefore, using the term "guaranteed" in this context is not inappropriate as long as the amount is within the government-insured limit. Abdrabbo should explain these facts to the clients.

Example 7 (Plagiarism):

Steve Swanson is a senior analyst in the investment research department of Ballard and Company. Apex Corporation has asked Ballard to assist in acquiring the majority ownership of stock in the Campbell Company, a financial consulting firm, and to prepare a report recommending that stockholders of Campbell agree to the acquisition. Another investment firm, Davis and Company, had already prepared a report for Apex analyzing both Apex and Campbell and recommending an exchange ratio. Apex has given the Davis report to Ballard officers, who have passed it on to Swanson. Swanson reviews the Davis report and other available material on Apex and Campbell. From his analysis, he concludes that the common stocks of Campbell and Apex represent good value at their current prices; he believes, however, that the Davis report does not consider all the factors a Campbell stockholder would need to know to make a decision. Swanson reports his conclusions to the partner in charge, who tells him to "use the Davis report, change a few words, sign your name, and get it out."

> *Comment*: If Swanson does as requested, he will violate Standard I(C). He could refer to those portions of the Davis report that he agrees with if he identifies Davis as the source; he could then add his own analysis and conclusions to the report before signing and distributing it.

Example 8 (Plagiarism):

Claude Browning, a quantitative analyst for Double Alpha, Inc., returns from a seminar in great excitement. At that seminar, Jack Jorrely, a well-known quantitative analyst at a national brokerage firm, discussed one of his new models in great detail, and Browning is intrigued by the new concepts. He proceeds to test the model, making some minor mechanical changes but retaining the concepts, until he produces some very positive results. Browning quickly announces to his supervisors at Double Alpha that he has discovered a new model and that clients and prospective clients should be informed of this positive finding as ongoing proof of Double Alpha's continuing innovation and ability to add value.

> *Comment*: Although Browning tested Jorrely's model on his own and even slightly modified it, he must still acknowledge the original source of the idea. Browning can certainly take credit for the final, practical results; he can also support his conclusions with his own test. The credit for the innovative thinking, however, must be awarded to Jorrely.

Example 9 (Plagiarism):

Fernando Zubia would like to include in his firm's marketing materials some "plain-language" descriptions of various concepts, such as the price-to-earnings (P/E) multiple and why standard deviation is used as a measure of risk. The descriptions come from other sources, but Zubia wishes to use them without reference to the original authors. Would this use of material be a violation of Standard I(C)?

> *Comment*: Copying verbatim any material without acknowledgement, including plain-language descriptions of the P/E multiple and standard deviation, violates Standard I(C). Even though these concepts are general, best practice would be for Zubia to describe them in his own words or cite the sources from which the descriptions are quoted. Members and candidates would be violating Standard I(C) if they either were responsible for creating marketing materials without attribution or knowingly use plagiarized materials.

Example 10 (Plagiarism):

Through a mainstream media outlet, Erika Schneider learns about a study that she would like to cite in her research. Should she cite both the mainstream intermediary source as well as the author of the study itself when using that information?

> *Comment*: In all instances, a member or candidate must cite the actual source of the information. Best practice for Schneider would be to obtain the information directly from the author and review it before citing it in a report. In that case, Schneider would not need to report how she found out about the information. For example, suppose Schneider read in the *Financial Times* about a study issued by CFA Institute; best practice for Schneider would be to obtain a copy of the study from CFA Institute, review it, and then cite it in her report. If she does not use any interpretation of the report from the *Financial Times* and the newspaper does not add value to the report itself, the newspaper is merely a conduit of the original information and does not need to be cited. If she does not obtain the report and review the information, Schneider runs the risk of relying on second-hand information that may misstate facts. If, for example, the *Financial Times* erroneously reported some information from the original CFA Institute

study and Schneider copied that erroneous information without acknowledging CFA Institute, she could be the object of complaints. Best practice would be either to obtain the complete study from its original author and cite only that author or to use the information provided by the intermediary and cite both sources.

Example 11 (Misrepresentation of Information):

Paul Ostrowski runs a two-person investment management firm. Ostrowski's firm subscribes to a service from a large investment research firm that provides research reports that can be repackaged by smaller firms for those firms' clients. Ostrowski's firm distributes these reports to clients as its own work.

Comment: Ostrowski can rely on third-party research that has a reasonable and adequate basis, but he cannot imply that he is the author of such research. If he does, Ostrowski is misrepresenting the extent of his work in a way that misleads the firm's clients or prospective clients.

Example 12 (Misrepresentation of Information):

Tom Stafford is part of a team within Appleton Investment Management responsible for managing a pool of assets for Open Air Bank, which distributes structured securities to offshore clients. He becomes aware that Open Air is promoting the structured securities as a much less risky investment than the investment management policy followed by him and the team to manage the original pool of assets. Also, Open Air has procured an independent rating for the pool that significantly overstates the quality of the investments. Stafford communicates his concerns to his supervisor, who responds that Open Air owns the product and is responsible for all marketing and distribution. Stafford's supervisor goes on to say that the product is outside of the US regulatory regime that Appleton follows and that all risks of the product are disclosed at the bottom of page 184 of the prospectus.

Comment: As a member of the investment team, Stafford is qualified to recognize the degree of accuracy of the materials that characterize the portfolio, and he is correct to be worried about Appleton's responsibility for a misrepresentation of the risks. Thus, he should continue to pursue the issue of Open Air's inaccurate promotion of the portfolio according to the firm's policies and procedures.

The Code and Standards stress protecting the reputation of the firm and the sustainability and integrity of the capital markets. Misrepresenting the quality and risks associated with the investment pool may lead to negative consequences for others well beyond the direct investors.

Example 13 (Avoiding a Misrepresentation):

Trina Smith is a fixed-income portfolio manager at a pension fund. She has observed that the market for highly structured mortgages is the focus of salespeople she meets and that these products represent a significant number of trading opportunities. In discussions about this topic with her team, Smith learns that calculating yields on changing cash flows within the deal structure requires very specialized vendor software. After more research, they find out that each deal is unique and that deals can have more than a dozen layers and changing cash flow priorities. Smith comes to the conclusion that, because of the complexity of these securities, the team cannot effectively distinguish between potentially good and bad investment options. To avoid misrepresenting their understanding, the team decides that the highly structured mortgage segment of the securitized market should not become part of the core of the fund's portfolio; they will allow some of the less complex securities to be part of the core.

> *Comment*: Smith is in compliance with Standard I(C) by not investing in securities that she and her team cannot effectively understand. Because she is not able to describe the risk and return profile of the securities to the pension fund beneficiaries and trustees, she appropriately limits the fund's exposure to this sector.

Example 14 (Misrepresenting Composite Construction):

Robert Palmer is head of performance for a fund manager. When asked to provide performance numbers to fund rating agencies, he avoids mentioning that the fund manager is quite liberal in composite construction. The reason accounts are included/excluded is not fully explained. The performance values reported to the rating agencies for the composites, although accurate for the accounts shown each period, may not present a true representation of the fund manager's ability.

> *Comment*: "Cherry picking" accounts to include in either published reports or information provided to rating agencies conflicts with Standard I(C). Moving accounts into or out of a composite to influence the overall performance results materially misrepresents the reported values over time. Palmer should work with his firm to strengthen its reporting practices concerning composite construction to avoid misrepresenting the firm's track record or the quality of the information being provided.

Example 15 (Presenting Out-of-Date Information):

David Finch is a sales director at a commercial bank, where he directs the bank's client advisers in the sale of third-party mutual funds. Each quarter, he holds a division-wide training session where he provides fact sheets on investment funds the bank is allowed to offer to clients. These fact sheets, which can be redistributed to potential clients, are created by the fund firms and contain information about the funds, including investment strategy and target distribution rates.

Finch knows that some of the fact sheets are out of date; for example, one long-only fund approved the use of significant leverage last quarter as a method to enhance returns. He continues to provide the sheets to the sales team without updates because the bank has no control over the marketing material released by the mutual fund firms.

> *Comment*: Finch is violating Standard I(C) by providing information that misrepresents aspects of the funds. By not providing the sales team and, ultimately, the clients with the updated information, he is misrepresenting the potential risks associated with the funds with outdated fact sheets. Finch can instruct the sales team to clarify the deficiencies in the fact sheets with clients and ensure they have the most recent fund prospectus document before accepting orders for investing in any fund.

Example 16 (Overemphasis of Firm Results):

Bob Anderson is chief compliance officer for Optima Asset Management Company, a firm currently offering eight funds to clients. Seven of the eight had 10-year returns below the median for their respective sectors. Anderson approves a recent advertisement, which includes this statement: "Optima Asset Management is achieving excellent returns for its investors. The Optima Emerging Markets Equity fund, for example, has 10-year returns that exceed the sector median by more than 10%."

> *Comment*: From the information provided it is difficult to determine whether a violation has occurred as long as the sector outperformance is correct. Anderson may be attempting to mislead potential clients by citing the performance of the sole fund that achieved such results. Past performance is often used to demonstrate a firm's skill and abilities in comparison to funds in the same sectors.
>
> However, if all the funds outperformed their respective benchmarks, then Anderson's assertion that the company "is achieving excellent returns" may be factual. Funds may exhibit positive returns for investors, exceed benchmarks, and yet have returns below the median in their sectors.
>
> Members and candidates need to ensure that their marketing efforts do not include statements that misrepresent their skills and abilities to remain compliant with Standard I(C). Unless the returns of a single fund reflect the performance of a firm as a whole, the use of a singular fund for performance comparisons should be avoided.

STANDARD I(D) MISCONDUCT

10

- [ ] demonstrate a thorough knowledge of the CFA Institute Code of Ethics and Standards of Professional Conduct by interpreting the Code and Standards in various situations involving issues of professional integrity
- [ ] recommend practices and procedures designed to prevent violations of the Code and Standards

Members and Candidates must not engage in any professional conduct involving dishonesty, fraud, or deceit or commit any act that reflects adversely on their professional reputation, integrity, or competence.

Guidance

Whereas Standard I(A) addresses the obligation of members and candidates to comply with applicable law that governs their professional activities, Standard I(D) addresses *all* conduct that reflects poorly on the professional integrity, good reputation, or competence of members and candidates. Any act that involves lying, cheating, stealing, or other dishonest conduct is a violation of this standard if the offense reflects adversely on a member's or candidate's professional activities. Although CFA Institute discourages any sort of unethical behavior by members and candidates, the Code and Standards are primarily aimed at conduct and actions related to a member's or candidate's professional life.

Conduct that damages trustworthiness or competence may include behavior that, although not illegal, nevertheless negatively affects a member's or candidate's ability to perform his or her responsibilities. For example, abusing alcohol during business hours might constitute a violation of this standard because it could have a detrimental effect on the member's or candidate's ability to fulfill his or her professional responsibilities. Personal bankruptcy may not reflect on the integrity or trustworthiness of the person declaring bankruptcy, but if the circumstances of the bankruptcy involve fraudulent or deceitful business conduct, the bankruptcy may be a violation of this standard.

In some cases, the absence of appropriate conduct or the lack of sufficient effort may be a violation of Standard I(D). The integrity of the investment profession is built on trust. A member or candidate—whether an investment banker, rating or research analyst, or portfolio manager—is expected to conduct the necessary due diligence to properly understand the nature and risks of an investment before making an investment recommendation. By not taking these steps and, instead, relying on someone else in the process to perform them, members or candidates may violate the trust their clients have placed in them. This loss of trust may have a significant impact on the reputation of the member or candidate and the operations of the financial market as a whole.

Individuals may attempt to abuse the CFA Institute Professional Conduct Program by actively seeking CFA Institute enforcement of the Code and Standards, and Standard I(D) in particular, as a method of settling personal, political, or other disputes unrelated to professional ethics. CFA Institute is aware of this issue, and appropriate disciplinary policies, procedures, and enforcement mechanisms are in place to address misuse of the Code and Standards and the Professional Conduct Program in this way.

11 STANDARD I(D): RECOMMENDED PROCEDURES

In addition to ensuring that their own behavior is consistent with Standard I(D), to prevent general misconduct, members and candidates should encourage their firms to adopt the following policies and procedures to support the principles of Standard I(D):

- *Code of ethics*: Develop and/or adopt a code of ethics to which every employee must subscribe, and make clear that any personal behavior that reflects poorly on the individual involved, the institution as a whole, or the investment industry will not be tolerated.
- *List of violations*: Disseminate to all employees a list of potential violations and associated disciplinary sanctions, up to and including dismissal from the firm.
- *Employee references*: Check references of potential employees to ensure that they are of good character and not ineligible to work in the investment industry because of past infractions of the law.

12 STANDARD I(D): APPLICATION OF THE STANDARD

Example 1 (Professionalism and Competence):

Simon Sasserman is a trust investment officer at a bank in a small affluent town. He enjoys lunching every day with friends at the country club, where his clients have observed him having numerous drinks. Back at work after lunch, he clearly is intoxicated while making investment decisions. His colleagues make a point of handling any business with Sasserman in the morning because they distrust his judgment after lunch.

Comment: Sasserman's excessive drinking at lunch and subsequent intoxication at work constitute a violation of Standard I(D) because this conduct has raised questions about his professionalism and competence. His behavior reflects poorly on him, his employer, and the investment industry.

Example 2 (Fraud and Deceit):

Howard Hoffman, a security analyst at ATZ Brothers, Inc., a large brokerage house, submits reimbursement forms over a two-year period to ATZ's self-funded health insurance program for more than two dozen bills, most of which have been altered to increase the amount due. An investigation by the firm's director of employee benefits uncovers the inappropriate conduct. ATZ subsequently terminates Hoffman's employment and notifies CFA Institute.

Comment: Hoffman violated Standard I(D) because he engaged in intentional conduct involving fraud and deceit in the workplace that adversely reflected on his integrity.

Example 3 (Fraud and Deceit):

Jody Brink, an analyst covering the automotive industry, volunteers much of her spare time to local charities. The board of one of the charitable institutions decides to buy five new vans to deliver hot lunches to low-income elderly people. Brink offers to donate her time to handle purchasing agreements. To pay a long-standing debt to a friend who operates an automobile dealership—and to compensate herself for her trouble—she agrees to a price 20% higher than normal and splits the surcharge with her friend. The director of the charity ultimately discovers the scheme and tells Brink that her services, donated or otherwise, are no longer required.

Comment: Brink engaged in conduct involving dishonesty, fraud, and misrepresentation and has violated Standard I(D).

Example 4 (Personal Actions and Integrity):

Carmen Garcia manages a mutual fund dedicated to socially responsible investing. She is also an environmental activist. As the result of her participation in nonviolent protests, Garcia has been arrested on numerous occasions for trespassing on the property of a large petrochemical plant that is accused of damaging the environment.

Comment: Generally, Standard I(D) is not meant to cover legal transgressions resulting from acts of civil disobedience in support of personal beliefs because such conduct does not reflect poorly on the member's or candidate's professional reputation, integrity, or competence.

Example 5 (Professional Misconduct):

Meredith Rasmussen works on a buy-side trading desk of an investment management firm and concentrates on in-house trades for a hedge fund subsidiary managed by a team at the investment management firm. The hedge fund has been very successful and is marketed globally by the firm. From her experience as the trader for much of the activity of the fund, Rasmussen has become quite knowledgeable about the hedge fund's strategy, tactics, and performance. When a distinct break in the market occurs and many of the securities involved in the hedge fund's strategy decline markedly in value, Rasmussen observes that the reported performance of the hedge fund does not reflect this decline. In her experience, the lack of effect is a very unlikely occurrence. She approaches the head of trading about her concern and is told that she should not ask any questions and that the fund is big and successful and is not her concern. She is fairly sure something is not right, so she contacts the compliance officer, who also tells her to stay away from the issue of the hedge fund's reporting.

Comment: Rasmussen has clearly come across an error in policies, procedures, and compliance practices within the firm's operations. According to the firm's procedures for reporting potentially unethical activity, she should pursue the issue by gathering some proof of her reason for doubt. Should all internal communications within the firm not satisfy her concerns, Rasmussen should consider reporting the potential unethical activity to the appropriate regulator.

See also Standard IV(A) for guidance on whistleblowing and Standard IV(C) for the duties of a supervisor.

13 STANDARD I(E) COMPETENCE

- ☐ demonstrate a thorough knowledge of the CFA Institute Code of Ethics and Standards of Professional Conduct by interpreting the Code and Standards in various situations involving issues of professional integrity
- ☐ recommend practices and procedures designed to prevent violations of the Code and Standards

Members and Candidates must act with and maintain the competence necessary to fulfill their professional responsibilities.

Guidance

Standard I(E) requires members and candidates to act with and maintain appropriate knowledge, skills, and diligence when they carry out their professional responsibilities so that they provide a high standard of professional service for their clients and employers. The Code of Ethics requires members and candidates to "act with integrity, competence, and diligence" and to "maintain and improve their professional competence and strive to improve the competence of other investment professionals." Standard I(E) directly supports these requirements of the Code of Ethics.

Given the diverse range of professional services members and candidates engage in, the knowledge, skills, and abilities necessary to successfully fulfill their roles will vary according to the nature of their professional duties. Determining what conduct specifically constitutes competence will differ for each role and will depend on the facts and circumstances applicable to each member or candidate.

While the specific conduct that leads to competence may be different for each member or candidate, the underlying principle of competence is straightforward. To be competent in your role and meet your duties under this standard means having sufficient knowledge, skills, and abilities suitable for a professional to work in that specific role with success. These attributes govern the expertise, experience, and accomplishments that professionals need to perform at the highest level.

- Knowledge is the body of information applied directly to the performance of a function and how effectively it is applied.
- Skills are capabilities to perform a role-specific act or function to complete specific tasks and achieve professional goals.
- Abilities are capabilities and attitudes that support behaviors that result in observable outcomes.

While competence allows members and candidates the opportunity to undertake an activity successfully, lack of competence cannot necessarily be determined by an unsuccessful or a negative outcome. Many competent investment professionals have experienced failure or loss in their professional lives. For example, a competent investment manager may not always make profitable investment decisions. A competent securities analyst may not accurately predict the future prospects of an investment, despite diligent and thorough analysis.

Competence is not limited to an examination of the education level of a member or candidate. A highly educated investment consultant may not have the experience to undertake consulting activities in an unfamiliar area of practice. An accounting professional supremely competent in providing financial statement audits may not be competent in assessing compliance with performance presentation standards, such as the GIPS standards. Or an investment consultant hired to conduct a search for an investment manager focused on sustainable investing may not have the skills needed to competently evaluate managers with that focus.

Over time, the professional responsibilities of members and candidates may change or expand, requiring new or different knowledge, skills, and abilities. Members and candidates will develop and refine their skills and abilities as their careers progress. Standard I(E) imposes the duty to not simply achieve but also maintain competence, emphasizing the need for members to continuously maintain or improve the competence required of their professional position. Although Standard I(E) contemplates ongoing professional development to maintain proficiency and competence, this standard does not mandate participation in a particular continuing education program or professional development plan. Members and candidates can attain and maintain the competence needed to fulfill their professional responsibilities in a variety of ways.

STANDARD I(E): RECOMMENDED PROCEDURES

14

To achieve and maintain competence, members and candidates should consider the following activities:

- Regularly engaging in a professional development or continuing education program
- Studying for or earning professional certifications or designations
- Attending conferences, seminars, or webinars
- Regularly participating in training offered by their employer
- Diligently engaging in informal continuing education or self-study, such as through outside reading of subject matter articles, treatises, and publications
- Participating in expert groups or organizations

- Becoming proficient with any new skill or knowledge, as necessary, when their professional responsibilities change

15 STANDARD I(E): APPLICATION OF THE STANDARD

Example 1 (Maintaining Competence):

Michelle Lee runs a geopolitical consulting firm where she analyzes international political, social, and economic issues and developments to produce research reports for her clients, many of which are investment management firms. Lee has been closely monitoring news regarding a new multinational trade deal that has the potential to significantly boost commercial activity among countries in a certain region of the world. As soon as the trade deal was officially ratified and announced, she quickly downloaded a copy of the agreement and read it to understand its terms and impact. She also consulted with experts in the field to obtain their opinions on the impacts of the trade deal and confirm her understanding of its terms and implications.

> *Comment*: Lee satisfied the requirement of Standard I(E). Lee was able to write a knowledgeable and informative research report for her clients by keeping abreast of developments in her field through news reports, consulting with experts, and studying the trade deal itself to ensure that her knowledge was up to date.

Example 2 (Improving Competence):

Chris Choe is the director of research at a large sell-side firm. Several of Choe's clients have asked her to incorporate environmental, social, and governance (ESG) ratings into the research reports the firm produces. Until now, the firm's research reports have been based only on traditional quantitative metrics. Choe hires an experienced ESG analyst for her team, and she requires all research analysts, including herself, to attend ESG-focused seminars and obtain an ESG investment specialist certificate. In due time, Choe and her team begin to incorporate ESG considerations into their research reports.

> *Comment*: Choe extended her competence in her field by educating herself on new considerations relevant to her industry and by hiring someone with ESG expertise to fill a knowledge and skills gap before she and her team incorporated ESG considerations into the firm's research reports. As such, Choe satisfied the requirement of Standard I(E).

Example 3 (Change in Role):

Gerhardt Glusker is a regulatory attorney for a hedge fund who sought to transition to a sales role after impressing senior management with his strong business acumen. There is a licensing requirement involving an examination that an individual must first pass before being qualified to serve in a sales function. Among other things, the examination covers technical rules and regulations designed to ensure fairness when dealing with clients and prospects. Glusker was not familiar with these rules and regulations because he was never asked to provide guidance on them as a regulatory attorney. Glusker did not learn the materials or study for the examination and instead relied on his industry knowledge to receive a passing score.

> *Comment*: Glusker failed to satisfy the requirement of Standard I(E). He did receive a passing score on a licensing examination, but passing the examination, by itself, is not adequate to demonstrate competency. Glusker's failure to learn the applicable rules and regulations relating to fairness when dealing with clients and prospects means that he does not possess the required knowledge to serve in his new role, despite passing the licensing examination.

Example 4 (Supervisory Responsibility):

Linda Evans is one member of a five-person team of analysts at a boutique research firm providing independent research to buy-side firms. Evans primarily covers the energy and transportation sectors. Evans's boss leaves the firm to return to academia. Firm management promotes Evans to director of research and hires two junior analysts to replace her. Evans now has supervisory responsibility for four analysts and is responsible for all research produced by the firm. Prior to her promotion date, Evans spends a great deal of time and effort getting up to speed on the research projects of the firm that she was not involved in. Although she has never directly managed others in the past, Evans does not spend any time becoming familiar with effectively managing employees, leading teams, or compliance requirements relating to subordinates.

> *Comment:* Evans's new position demands competence in other skills, abilities, and knowledge beyond those needed for her previous position. Evans must ensure she extends her competence to cover all responsibilities of her new role. She also must now obtain the skills and knowledge needed for fulfilling her supervisory responsibility of the other analysts. This could include attending conferences or taking professional development courses on management, earning compliance credentials, and internal training on supervisory responsibility.

Example 5 (Choosing Investments):

Kwame Mifune is a financial planner for over 150 retail investors. Based on the investment objectives, financial circumstances, and risk tolerance of 40 of his clients, he suggests they purchase life insurance products from Vouchsafe Insurance Company. Mifune researched Vouchsafe and recommended it because it has a high credit rating, strong financials, and a decade-long history of providing affordable, safe insurance products. Within 18 months, as the result of previously unknown financial impropriety and fraud by the company's chief financial officer, Vouchsafe goes bankrupt and the insurance contracts for thousands of policyholders become worthless. Mifune's clients claim that he was incompetent in recommending the Vouchsafe policies.

> *Comment*: Assuming that Mifune's research of Vouchsafe was thorough and appropriate, his failure to uncover the fraudulent practices of the company he recommended, which had misled the investment industry as whole, does not, by itself, indicate that Mifune is an incompetent financial planner.

Example 6 (Understanding New Investment Products):

Alex Halsey is a portfolio manager for a number of high-net-worth individuals. Several of his clients are impressed by the significant gains in a short time frame that they believe can be achieved by investing in cryptocurrency. They urge Halsey to include cryptocurrency products as part of their portfolios. Although Halsey is generally aware of cryptocurrency and has read several articles about the cryptocurrency investment trend in reputable newspapers, Halsey is unfamiliar with the nature of the asset or the difference between the many cryptocurrency products. Not wanting to seem out of touch with current developments in the market, lose clients, or miss out on a hot market trend by delaying an investment decision until he completes research into the asset, Halsey purchases a cryptocurrency product that has been heavily promoted through social media and online advertising for several of his clients.

> *Comment*: Given his limited knowledge, Halsey is not competent to invest in cryptocurrency for his clients. By hastily investing in cryptocurrency products without understanding the nature of the investment or the suitability of the investment for his clients, Halsey has violated Standard I(E).

16 STANDARD II: INTEGRITY OF CAPITAL MARKETS

- ☐ demonstrate a thorough knowledge of the CFA Institute Code of Ethics and Standards of Professional Conduct by interpreting the Code and Standards in various situations involving issues of professional integrity
- ☐ recommend practices and procedures designed to prevent violations of the Code and Standards

Standard II(A) Material Nonpublic Information

Members and Candidates who possess material nonpublic information that could affect the value of an investment must not act or cause others to act on the information.

Guidance

Highlights:

- *What Is "Material" Information?*
- *What Constitutes "Nonpublic" Information?*
- *Mosaic Theory*
- *Social Media*
- *Using Industry Experts*
- *Investment Research Reports*

Trading or inducing others to trade on material nonpublic information erodes confidence in capital markets, institutions, and investment professionals by supporting the idea that those with inside information and special access can take unfair advantage of the general investing public. Although trading on inside information may lead to short-term profits, in the long run, individuals and the profession as a whole suffer from such trading. These actions have caused and will continue to cause investors to avoid capital markets because the markets are perceived to be "rigged" in favor of the knowledgeable insider. When the investing public avoids capital markets, the markets and capital allocation become less efficient and less supportive of strong and vibrant economies. Standard II(A) promotes and maintains a high level of confidence in market integrity, which is one of the foundations of the investment profession.

The prohibition on using this information goes beyond the direct buying and selling of individual securities or bonds. Members and candidates must not use material nonpublic information to influence their investment actions related to derivatives (e.g., swaps or option contracts), mutual funds, or other alternative investments. *Any* trading based on material nonpublic information constitutes a violation of Standard II(A). The expansion of financial products and the increasing interconnectivity of financial markets globally have resulted in new potential opportunities for trading on material nonpublic information.

What Is "Material" Information?

Information is "material" if its disclosure would probably have an impact on the price of a security or if reasonable investors would want to know the information before making an investment decision. In other words, information is material if it would significantly alter the total mix of information currently available about a security in such a way that the price of the security would be affected.

The specificity of the information, the extent of its difference from public information, its nature, and its reliability are key factors in determining whether a particular piece of information fits the definition of material. For example, material information may include, but is not limited to, information on the following:

- earnings;
- mergers, acquisitions, tender offers, or joint ventures;
- changes in assets or asset quality;
- innovative products, processes, or discoveries (e.g., new product trials or research efforts);
- new licenses, patents, registered trademarks, or regulatory approval/rejection of a product;
- developments regarding customers or suppliers (e.g., the acquisition or loss of a contract);
- changes in management;
- change in auditor notification or the fact that the issuer may no longer rely on an auditor's report or qualified opinion;
- events regarding the issuer's securities (e.g., defaults on senior securities, calls of securities for redemption, repurchase plans, stock splits, changes in dividends, changes to the rights of security holders, and public or private sales of additional securities);
- bankruptcies;
- significant legal disputes;
- government reports of economic trends (employment, housing starts, currency information, etc.);
- orders for large trades before they are executed; and

- new or changing equity or debt ratings issued by a third party (e.g., sell-side recommendations and credit ratings).

In addition to the substance and specificity of the information, the source or relative reliability of the information also determines materiality. The less reliable a source, the less likely the information provided would be considered material. For example, factual information from a corporate insider regarding a significant new contract for a company is likely to be material, whereas an assumption based on speculation by a competitor about the same contract is likely to be less reliable and, therefore, not material. Additionally, information about trials of a new drug, product, or service under development from qualified personnel involved in the trials is likely to be material, whereas educated conjecture by subject experts not connected to the trials is unlikely to be material.

Also, the more ambiguous the effect of the information on price, the less material that information is considered. If it is unclear whether and to what extent the information will affect the price of a security, the information may not be considered material. The passage of time may also render information that was once important immaterial.

What Constitutes "Nonpublic" Information?

Information is "nonpublic" until it has been disseminated or is available to the marketplace in general (as opposed to a select group of investors). "Disseminated" can be defined as "made known." For example, a company report of profits that is posted on the internet and distributed widely through a press release or accompanied by a filing has been effectively disseminated to the marketplace. Members and candidates must have a reasonable expectation that people have received the information before it can be considered public. It is not necessary, however, to wait for the slowest method of delivery. Once the information is disseminated to the market, it is public information that is no longer covered by this standard.

Members and candidates must be particularly aware of information that is selectively disclosed by corporations to a small group of investors, analysts, or other market participants. Information that is made available to analysts remains nonpublic until it is made available to investors in general. Corporations that disclose information on a limited basis create the potential for insider-trading violations.

Issues of selective disclosure often arise when a corporate insider provides material information to analysts in a briefing or conference call before that information is released to the public. Analysts must be aware that a disclosure made to a room full of analysts does not necessarily make the disclosed information "public." Analysts should also be alert to the possibility that they are selectively receiving material nonpublic information when a company provides them with guidance or interpretation of such publicly available information as financial statements or regulatory filings.

A member or candidate may use insider information provided legitimately by the source company for the specific purpose of conducting due diligence according to the business agreement between the parties for such activities as mergers, loan underwriting, credit ratings, and offering engagements. In such instances, the investment professional would not be considered in violation of Standard II(A) by using the material information. However, the use of insider information provided by the source company for other purposes, especially to trade or entice others to trade the securities of the firm, conflicts with this standard.

Mosaic Theory

A financial analyst gathers and interprets large quantities of information from many sources. The analyst may use significant conclusions derived from the analysis of public and nonmaterial nonpublic information as the basis for investment recommendations and decisions even if those conclusions would have been material inside information had they been communicated directly to the analyst by a company. Under the "mosaic theory," financial analysts are free to act on this collection, or mosaic, of information without risking violation.

The practice of financial analysis depends on the free flow of information. For the fair and efficient operation of the capital markets, analysts and investors must have the greatest amount of information possible to facilitate making well-informed investment decisions about how and where to invest capital. Accurate, timely, and intelligible communication is essential if analysts and investors are to obtain the data needed to make informed decisions about how and where to invest capital. These disclosures must go beyond the information mandated by the reporting requirements of the securities laws and should include specific business information about items used to guide a company's future growth, such as new products, capital projects, and the competitive environment. Analysts seek and use such information to compare and contrast investment alternatives.

Much of the information used by analysts comes directly from companies. Analysts often receive such information through contacts with corporate insiders, especially investor-relations staff and financial officers. Information may be disseminated in the form of press releases, through oral presentations by company executives in analysts' meetings or conference calls, or during analysts' visits to company premises. In seeking to develop the most accurate and complete picture of a company, analysts should also reach beyond contacts with companies themselves and collect information from other sources, such as customers, contractors, suppliers, and the companies' competitors.

Analysts are in the business of formulating opinions and insights that are not obvious to the general investing public about the attractiveness of particular securities. In the course of their work, analysts actively seek out corporate information not generally known to the market for the express purpose of analyzing that information, forming an opinion on its significance, and informing their clients, who can be expected to trade on the basis of the recommendation. Analysts' initiatives to discover and analyze information and communicate their findings to their clients significantly enhance market efficiency, thus benefiting all investors (see *Dirks v. Securities and Exchange Commission*). Accordingly, violations of Standard II(A) will *not* result when a perceptive analyst reaches a conclusion about a corporate action or event through an analysis of public information and items of nonmaterial nonpublic information.

Investment professionals should note, however, that although analysts are free to use mosaic information in their research reports, they should save and document all their research [see Standard V(C) Record Retention]. Evidence of the analyst's knowledge of public and nonmaterial nonpublic information about a corporation strengthens the assertion that the analyst reached his or her conclusions solely through appropriate methods rather than through the use of material nonpublic information.

Social Media

The continuing advancement in technology allows members, candidates, and the industry at large to exchange information at rates not previously available. It is important for investment professionals to understand the implications of using information from the internet and social media platforms because all such information may not actually be considered public.

Some social media platforms require membership in specific groups in order to access the published content. Members and candidates participating in groups with membership limitations should verify that material information obtained from these sources can also be accessed from a source that would be considered available to the public (e.g., company filings, webpages, and press releases).

Members and candidates may use social media platforms to communicate with clients or investors without conflicting with this standard. As long as the information reaches all clients or is open to the investing public, the use of these platforms would be comparable with other traditional forms of communications, such as e-mails and press releases. Members and candidates, as required by Standard I(A), should also complete all appropriate regulatory filings related to information distributed through social media platforms.

Using Industry Experts

The increased demand for insights for understanding the complexities of some industries has led to an expansion of engagement with outside experts. As the level of engagement increased, new businesses formed to connect analysts and investors with individuals who have specialized knowledge of their industry (e.g., technology or pharmaceuticals). These networks offer investors the opportunity to reach beyond their usual business circles to speak with experts regarding economic conditions, industry trends, and technical issues relating to specific products and services.

Members and candidates may provide compensation to individuals for their insights without violating this standard. However, members and candidates are ultimately responsible for ensuring that they are not requesting or acting on confidential information received from external experts, which is in violation of security regulations and laws or duties to others. As the recent string of insider-trading cases displayed, some experts are willing to provide confidential and protected information for the right incentive.

Firms connecting experts with members or candidates often require both parties to sign agreements concerning the disclosure of material nonpublic information. Even with the protections from such compliance practices, if an expert provides material nonpublic information, members and candidates would be prohibited from taking investment actions on the associated firm until the information became publicly known to the market.

Investment Research Reports

When a particularly well-known or respected analyst issues a report or makes changes to his or her recommendation, that information alone may have an effect on the market and thus may be considered material. Theoretically, under Standard II(A), such a report would have to be made public at the time it was distributed to clients. The analyst is not a company insider, however, and does not have access to inside information. Presumably, the analyst created the report from information available to the public (mosaic theory) and by using his or her expertise to interpret the information. The analyst's hard work, paid for by the client, generated the conclusions.

Simply because the public in general would find the conclusions material does not require that the analyst make his or her work public. Investors who are not clients of the analyst can either do the work themselves or become clients of the analyst to gain access to the analyst's expertise.

17 STANDARD II(A): RECOMMENDED PROCEDURES

Achieve Public Dissemination

If a member or candidate determines that information is material, the member or candidate should make reasonable efforts to achieve public dissemination of the information. These efforts usually entail encouraging the issuing company to make the information public. If public dissemination is not possible, the member or candidate must communicate the information only to the designated supervisory and compliance personnel within the member's or candidate's firm and must not take investment action or alter current investment recommendations on the basis of the information. Moreover, members and candidates must not knowingly engage in any conduct that may induce company insiders to privately disclose material nonpublic information.

Adopt Compliance Procedures

Members and candidates should encourage their firms to adopt compliance procedures to prevent the misuse of material nonpublic information. Particularly important is improving compliance in such areas as the review of employee and proprietary trading, the review of investment recommendations, documentation of firm procedures, and the supervision of interdepartmental communications in multiservice firms. Compliance procedures should suit the particular characteristics of a firm, including its size and the nature of its business.

Members and candidates are encouraged to inform their supervisor and compliance personnel of suspected inappropriate use of material nonpublic information as the basis for security trading activities or recommendations being made within their firm.

Adopt Disclosure Procedures

Members and candidates should encourage their firms to develop and follow disclosure policies designed to ensure that information is disseminated to the marketplace in an equitable manner. For example, analysts from small firms should receive the same information and attention from a company as analysts from large firms receive. Similarly, companies should not provide certain information to buy-side analysts but not to sell-side analysts, or vice versa. Furthermore, a company should not discriminate among analysts in the provision of information or "blackball" particular analysts who have given negative reports on the company in the past.

Within investment and research firms, members and candidates should encourage the development of and compliance with procedures for distributing new and updated investment opinions to clients. Recommendations of this nature may represent material market-moving information that needs to be communicated to all clients fairly.

Issue Press Releases

Companies should consider issuing press releases prior to analyst meetings and conference calls and scripting those meetings and calls to decrease the chance that further information will be disclosed. If material nonpublic information is disclosed for the first time in an analyst meeting or call, the company should promptly issue a press release or otherwise make the information publicly available.

Firewall Elements

An information barrier commonly referred to as a "firewall" is the most widely used approach for preventing the communication of material nonpublic information within firms. It restricts the flow of confidential information to those who need to know the information to perform their jobs effectively. The minimum elements of such a system include, but are not limited to, the following:

- substantial control of relevant interdepartmental communications, preferably through a clearance area within the firm in either the compliance or legal department;
- review of employee trading through the maintenance of "watch," "restricted," and "rumor" lists;

- documentation of the procedures designed to limit the flow of information between departments and of the actions taken to enforce those procedures; and
- heightened review or restriction of proprietary trading while a firm is in possession of material nonpublic information.

Appropriate Interdepartmental Communications

Although documentation requirements must, for practical reasons, take into account the differences between the activities of small firms and those of large, multiservice firms, firms of all sizes and types benefit by improving the documentation of their internal enforcement of firewall procedures. Therefore, even at small firms, procedures concerning interdepartmental communication, the review of trading activity, and the investigation of possible violations should be compiled and formalized.

Physical Separation of Departments

As a practical matter, to the greatest extent possible, firms should consider the physical separation of departments and files to prevent the communication of sensitive information that should not be shared. For example, the investment banking and corporate finance areas of a brokerage firm should be separated from the sales and research departments, and a bank's commercial lending department should be segregated from its trust and research departments.

Prevention of Personnel Overlap

There should be no overlap of personnel between the investment banking and corporate finance areas of a brokerage firm and the sales and research departments or between a bank's commercial lending department and its trust and research departments. For a firewall to be effective in a multiservice firm, an employee should be on only one side of the firewall at any time. Inside knowledge may not be limited to information about a specific offering or the current financial condition of a company. Analysts may be exposed to much information about the company, including new product developments or future budget projections that clearly constitute inside knowledge and thus preclude the analyst from returning to his or her research function. For example, an analyst who follows a particular company may provide limited assistance to the investment bankers under carefully controlled circumstances when the firm's investment banking department is involved in a deal with the company. That analyst must then be treated as though he or she were an investment banker; the analyst must remain on the investment banking side of the wall until any information he or she learns is publicly disclosed. In short, the analyst cannot use any information learned in the course of the project for research purposes and cannot share that information with colleagues in the research department.

A Reporting System

A primary objective of an effective firewall procedure is to establish a reporting system in which authorized people review and approve communications between departments. If an employee behind a firewall believes that he or she needs to share confidential information with someone on the other side of the wall, the employee should consult a designated compliance officer to determine whether sharing the information is necessary and how much information should be shared. If the sharing is necessary, the compliance officer should coordinate the process of "looking over the wall" so that the necessary information will be shared and the integrity of the procedure will be maintained.

A single supervisor or compliance officer should have the specific authority and responsibility of deciding whether information is material and whether it is sufficiently public to be used as the basis for investment decisions. Ideally, the supervisor or compliance officer responsible for communicating information to a firm's research or brokerage area would not be a member of that area.

Personal Trading Limitations

Firms should consider restrictions or prohibitions on personal trading by employees and should carefully monitor both proprietary trading and personal trading by employees. Firms should require employees to make periodic reports (to the extent that such reporting is not already required by securities laws) of their own transactions and transactions made for the benefit of family members. Securities should be placed on a restricted list when a firm has or may have material nonpublic information. The broad distribution of a restricted list often triggers the sort of trading the list was developed to avoid. Therefore, a watch list shown to only the few people responsible for compliance should be used to monitor transactions in specified securities. The use of a watch list in combination with a restricted list is an increasingly common means of ensuring effective control of personal trading.

Record Maintenance

Multiservice firms should maintain written records of the communications between various departments. Firms should place a high priority on training and should consider instituting comprehensive training programs, particularly for employees in sensitive areas.

Proprietary Trading Procedures

Procedures concerning the restriction or review of a firm's proprietary trading while the firm possesses material nonpublic information will necessarily depend on the types of proprietary trading in which the firm may engage. A prohibition on all types of proprietary activity when a firm comes into possession of material nonpublic information is *not* appropriate. For example, when a firm acts as a market maker, a prohibition on proprietary trading may be counterproductive to the goals of maintaining the confidentiality of information and market liquidity. This concern is particularly important in the relationships between small, regional broker/dealers and small issuers. In many situations, a firm will take a small issuer public with the understanding that the firm will continue to be a market maker in the stock. In such instances, a withdrawal by the firm from market-making activities would be a clear tip to outsiders. Firms that continue market-making activity while in the possession of material nonpublic information should, however, instruct their market makers to remain passive with respect to the market—that is, to take only the contra side of unsolicited customer trades.

In risk-arbitrage trading, the case for a trading prohibition is more compelling than it is in the case of market making. The impetus for arbitrage trading is neither passive nor reactive, and the potential for illegal profits is greater than in market making. The most prudent course for firms is to suspend arbitrage activity when a security is placed on the watch list. Those firms that continue arbitrage activity face a high hurdle in proving the adequacy of their internal procedures for preventing trading on material nonpublic information and must demonstrate a stringent review and documentation of firm trades.

Communication to All Employees

Members and candidates should encourage their employers to circulate written compliance policies and guidelines to all employees. Policies and guidelines should be used in conjunction with training programs aimed at enabling employees to recognize material nonpublic information. Such information is not always clearly identifiable.

Employees must be given sufficient training to either make an informed decision or to realize they need to consult a supervisor or compliance officer before engaging in questionable transactions. Appropriate policies reinforce that using material nonpublic information is illegal in many countries. Such trading activities based on material nonpublic information undermine the integrity of the individual, the firm, and the capital markets.

18 STANDARD II(A): APPLICATION OF THE STANDARD

Example 1 (Acting on Nonpublic Information):

Frank Barnes, the president and controlling shareholder of the SmartTown clothing chain, decides to accept a tender offer and sell the family business at a price almost double the market price of its shares. He describes this decision to his sister (SmartTown's treasurer), who conveys it to her daughter (who owns no stock in the family company at present), who tells her husband, Staple. Staple, however, tells his stockbroker, Alex Halsey, who immediately buys SmartTown stock for himself.

> *Comment*: The information regarding the pending sale is both material and nonpublic. Staple has violated Standard II(A) by communicating the inside information to his broker. Halsey also has violated the standard by buying the shares on the basis of material nonpublic information.

Example 2 (Controlling Nonpublic Information):

Samuel Peter, an analyst with Scotland and Pierce Incorporated, is assisting his firm with a secondary offering for Bright Ideas Lamp Company. Peter participates, via telephone conference call, in a meeting with Scotland and Pierce investment banking employees and Bright Ideas' CEO. Peter is advised that the company's earnings projections for the next year have significantly dropped. Throughout the telephone conference call, several Scotland and Pierce salespeople and portfolio managers walk in and out of Peter's office, where the telephone call is taking place. As a result, they are aware of the drop in projected earnings for Bright Ideas. Before the conference call is concluded, the salespeople trade the stock of the company on behalf of the firm's clients and other firm personnel trade the stock in a firm proprietary account and in employees' personal accounts.

> *Comment*: Peter has violated Standard II(A) because he failed to prevent the transfer and misuse of material nonpublic information to others in his firm. Peter's firm should have adopted information barriers to prevent the communication of nonpublic information between departments of the firm. The salespeople and portfolio managers who traded on the information have also violated Standard II(A) by trading on inside information.

Example 3 (Selective Disclosure of Material Information):

Elizabeth Levenson is based in Hanoi and covers the Vietnamese market for her firm, which is based in Singapore. She is invited, together with the other 10 largest shareholders of a manufacturing company, to meet the finance director of that company. During the meeting, the finance director states that the company expects its workforce to strike next Friday, which will cripple productivity and distribution. Can Levenson use this information as a basis to change her rating on the company from "buy" to "sell"?

> *Comment*: Levenson must first determine whether the material information is public. According to Standard II(A), if the company has not made this information public (a small group forum does not qualify as a method of public dissemination), she cannot use the information.

Example 4 (Determining Materiality):

Leah Fechtman is trying to decide whether to hold or sell shares of an oil-and-gas exploration company that she owns in several of the funds she manages. Although the company has underperformed the index for some time already, the trends in the industry sector signal that companies of this type might become takeover targets. While she is considering her decision, her doctor, who casually follows the markets, mentions that she thinks that the company in question will soon be bought out by a large multinational conglomerate and that it would be a good idea to buy the stock right now. After talking to various investment professionals and checking their opinions on the company as well as checking industry trends, Fechtman decides the next day to accumulate more stock in the oil-and-gas exploration company.

> *Comment*: Although information on an expected takeover bid may be of the type that is generally material and nonpublic, in this case, the source of information is unreliable, so the information cannot be considered material. Therefore, Fechtman is not prohibited from trading the stock on the basis of this information.

Example 5 (Applying the Mosaic Theory):

Jagdish Teja is a buy-side analyst covering the furniture industry. Looking for an attractive company to recommend as a buy, he analyzes several furniture makers by studying their financial reports and visiting their operations. He also talks to some designers and retailers to find out which furniture styles are trendy and popular. Although none of the companies that he analyzes are a clear buy, he discovers that one of them, Swan Furniture Company (SFC), may be in financial trouble. SFC's extravagant new designs have been introduced at substantial cost. Even though these designs initially attracted attention, the public is now buying more conservative furniture from other makers. Based on this information and on a profit-and-loss analysis, Teja believes that SFC's next-quarter earnings will drop substantially. He issues a sell recommendation for SFC. Immediately after receiving that recommendation, investment managers start reducing the SFC stock in their portfolios.

> *Comment*: Information on quarterly earnings data is material and nonpublic. Teja arrived at his conclusion about the earnings drop on the basis of public information and pieces of nonmaterial nonpublic information (such as opinions of designers and retailers). Therefore, trading based on Teja's correct conclusion is not prohibited by Standard II(A).

Example 6 (Applying the Mosaic Theory):

Roger Clement is a senior financial analyst who specializes in the European automobile sector at Rivoli Capital. Because he has been repeatedly nominated by many leading industry magazines and newsletters as a "best analyst" for the automobile industry, he is widely regarded as an authority on the sector. After speaking with representatives of Turgot Chariots—a European auto manufacturer with sales primarily in South Korea—and after conducting interviews with salespeople, labor leaders, his firm's South Korean currency analysts, and banking officials, Clement analyzed Turgot Chariots and concluded that (1) its newly introduced model will probably not meet sales expectations, (2) its corporate restructuring strategy may well face serious opposition from unions, (3) the depreciation of the South Korean won should lead to pressure on margins for the industry in general and Turgot's market segment in particular, and (4) banks could take a tougher-than-expected stance in the upcoming round of credit renegotiations with the company. For these reasons, he changes his conclusion about the company from "market outperform" to "market underperform." Clement retains the support material used to reach his conclusion in case questions later arise.

> *Comment*: To reach a conclusion about the value of the company, Clement has pieced together a number of nonmaterial or public bits of information that affect Turgot Chariots. Therefore, under the mosaic theory, Clement has not violated Standard II(A) in drafting the report.

Example 7 (Analyst Recommendations as Material Nonpublic Information):

The next day, Clement is preparing to be interviewed on a global financial news television program where he will discuss his changed recommendation on Turgot Chariots for the first time in public. While preparing for the program, he mentions to the show's producers and Mary Zito, the journalist who will be interviewing him, the information he will be discussing. Just prior to going on the air, Zito sells her holdings in Turgot Chariots. She also phones her father with the information because she knows that he and other family members have investments in Turgot Chariots.

> *Comment*: When Zito receives advance notice of Clement's change of opinion, she knows it will have a material impact on the stock price, even if she is not totally aware of Clement's underlying reasoning. She is not a client of Clement but obtains early access to the material nonpublic information prior to publication. Her trades are thus based on material nonpublic information and violate Standard II(A).
>
> Zito further violates the Standard by relaying the information to her father. It would not matter if he or any other family member traded; the act of providing the information violates Standard II(A). The fact that the information is provided to a family member does not absolve someone of the prohibition of using or communicating material nonpublic information.

Example 8 (Acting on Nonpublic Information):

Ashton Kellogg is a retired investment professional who manages his own portfolio. He owns shares in National Savings, a large local bank. A close friend and golfing buddy, John Mayfield, is a senior executive at National. National has seen its stock price drop considerably, and the news and outlook are not good. In a conversation about the economy and the banking industry on the golf course, Mayfield relays the information that National will surprise the investment community in a few days when it announces excellent earnings for the quarter. Kellogg is pleasantly surprised by this information, and thinking that Mayfield, as a senior executive, knows the law and would not disclose inside information, he doubles his position in the bank. Subsequently, National announces that it had good operating earnings but had to set aside reserves for anticipated significant losses on its loan portfolio. The combined news causes the stock to go down 60%.

> *Comment*: Even though Kellogg believes that Mayfield would not break the law by disclosing inside information and money was lost on the purchase, Kellogg should not have purchased additional shares of National. It is the member's or candidate's responsibility to make sure, before executing investment actions, that comments about earnings are not material nonpublic information. Kellogg has violated Standard II(A).

Example 9 (Mosaic Theory):

John Doll is a research analyst for a hedge fund that also sells its research to a select group of paying-client investment firms. Doll's focus is medical technology companies and products, and he has been in the business long enough and has been successful enough to build up a very credible network of friends and experts in the business. Doll has been working on a major research report recommending Boyce Health, a medical device manufacturer. He recently ran into an old acquaintance at a wedding who is a senior executive at Boyce, and Doll asked about the business. Doll was drawn to a statement that the executive, who has responsibilities in the new products area, made about a product: "I would not get too excited about the medium-term prospects; we have a lot of work to do first." Doll incorporated this and other information about the new Boyce product in his long-term recommendation of Boyce.

> *Comment*: Doll's conversation with the senior executive is part of the mosaic of information used in recommending Boyce. When holding discussions with a firm executive, Doll would need to guard against soliciting or obtaining material nonpublic information. Before issuing the report, the executive's statement about the continuing development of the product would need to be weighed against the other known public facts to determine whether it would be considered material.

Example 10 (Materiality Determination):

Larry Nadler, a trader for a mutual fund, gets a text message from another firm's trader, whom he has known for years. The message indicates a software company is going to report strong earnings when the firm publicly announces in two days. Nadler has a buy order from a portfolio manager within his firm to purchase several hundred thousand shares of the stock. Nadler is aggressive in placing the portfolio manager's order and completes the purchases by the following morning, a day ahead of the firm's planned earnings announcement.

> *Comment*: There are often rumors and whisper numbers before a release of any kind. The text message from the other trader would most likely be considered market noise. Unless Nadler knew that the trader had an ongoing business relationship with the public firm, he had no reason to suspect he was receiving material nonpublic information that would prevent him from completing the trading request of the portfolio manager.

Example 11 (Using an Expert Network):

Mary McCoy is the senior drug analyst at a mutual fund. Her firm hires a service that connects her to experts in the treatment of cancer. Through various phone conversations, McCoy enhances her understanding of the latest therapies for successful treatment. This information is critical to Mary making informed recommendations of the companies producing these drugs.

> *Comment*: McCoy is appropriately using the expert networks to enhance her evaluation process. She has neither asked for nor received information that may be considered material and nonpublic, such as preliminary trial results. McCoy is allowed to seek advice from professionals within the industry that she follows.

Example 12 (Using an Expert Network):

Tom Watson is a research analyst working for a hedge fund. To stay informed, Watson relies on outside experts for information on such industries as technology and pharmaceuticals, where new advancements occur frequently. The meetings with the industry experts often are arranged through networks or placement agents that have specific policies and procedures in place to deter the exchange of material nonpublic information.

Watson arranges a call to discuss future prospects for one of the fund's existing technology company holdings, a company that was testing a new semiconductor product. The scientist leading the tests indicates his disappointment with the performance of the new semiconductor. Following the call, Watson relays the insights he received to others at the fund. The fund sells its current position in the company and buys many put options because the market is anticipating the success of the new semiconductor and the share price reflects the market's optimism.

> *Comment*: Watson has violated Standard II(A) by passing along material nonpublic information concerning the ongoing product tests, which the fund used to trade in the securities and options of the related company. Watson cannot simply rely on the agreements signed by individuals who participate in expert networks that state that he has not received information that would prohibit his trading activity. He must make his own determination whether information he received through these arrangements reaches a materiality threshold that would affect his trading abilities.

19 STANDARD II(B) MARKET MANIPULATION

- ☐ demonstrate a thorough knowledge of the CFA Institute Code of Ethics and Standards of Professional Conduct by interpreting the Code and Standards in various situations involving issues of professional integrity
- ☐ recommend practices and procedures designed to prevent violations of the Code and Standards

Members and Candidates must not engage in practices that distort prices or artificially inflate trading volume with the intent to mislead market participants.

Guidance

Highlights:

- *Information-Based Manipulation*
- *Transaction-Based Manipulation*

Standard II(B) requires that members and candidates uphold market integrity by prohibiting market manipulation. Market manipulation includes practices that distort security prices or trading volume with the intent to deceive people or entities that rely on information in the market. Market manipulation damages the interests of all investors by disrupting the smooth functioning of financial markets and lowering investor confidence.

Market manipulation may lead to a lack of trust in the fairness of the capital markets, resulting in higher risk premiums and reduced investor participation. A reduction in the efficiency of a local capital market may negatively affect the growth and economic health of the country and may also influence the operations of the globally interconnected capital markets. Although market manipulation may be less likely to occur in mature financial markets than in emerging markets, cross-border investing increasingly exposes all global investors to the potential for such practices.

Market manipulation includes (1) the dissemination of false or misleading information and (2) transactions that deceive or would be likely to mislead market participants by distorting the price-setting mechanism of financial instruments. The development of new products and technologies increases the incentives, means, and opportunities for market manipulation. Additionally, the increasing complexity and sophistication of the technologies used for communicating with market participants have created new avenues for manipulation.

Information-Based Manipulation

Information-based manipulation includes, but is not limited to, spreading false rumors to induce trading by others. For example, members and candidates must refrain from "pumping up" the price of an investment by issuing misleading positive information or overly optimistic projections of a security's worth only to later "dump" the investment (i.e., sell it) once the price, fueled by the misleading information's effect on other market participants, reaches an artificially high level.

Transaction-Based Manipulation

Transaction-based manipulation involves instances where a member or candidate knew or should have known that his or her actions could affect the pricing of a security. This type of manipulation includes, but is not limited to, the following:

- transactions that artificially affect prices or volume to give the impression of activity or price movement in a financial instrument, which represent a diversion from the expectations of a fair and efficient market, and
- securing a controlling, dominant position in a financial instrument to exploit and manipulate the price of a related derivative and/or the underlying asset.

Standard II(B) is not intended to preclude transactions undertaken on legitimate trading strategies based on perceived market inefficiencies. The intent of the action is critical to determining whether it is a violation of this standard.

20 STANDARD II(B): APPLICATION OF THE STANDARD

Example 1 (Independent Analysis and Company Promotion):

The principal owner of Financial Information Services (FIS) entered into an agreement with two microcap companies to promote the companies' stock in exchange for stock and cash compensation. The principal owner caused FIS to disseminate e-mails, design and maintain several websites, and distribute an online investment newsletter—all of which recommended investment in the two companies. The systematic publication of purportedly independent analyses and recommendations containing inaccurate and highly promotional and speculative statements increased public investment in the companies and led to dramatically higher stock prices.

> *Comment*: The principal owner of FIS violated Standard II(B) by using inaccurate reporting and misleading information under the guise of independent analysis to artificially increase the stock price of the companies. Furthermore, the principal owner violated Standard V(A) Diligence and Reasonable Basis by not having a reasonable and adequate basis for recommending the two companies and violated Standard VI(A) Disclosure of Conflicts by not disclosing to investors the compensation agreements (which constituted a conflict of interest).

Example 2 (Personal Trading Practices and Price):

John Gray is a private investor in Belgium who bought a large position several years ago in Fame Pharmaceuticals, a German small-cap security with limited average trading volume. He has now decided to significantly reduce his holdings owing to the poor price performance. Gray is worried that the low trading volume for the stock may cause the price to decline further as he attempts to sell his large position.

Gray devises a plan to divide his holdings into multiple accounts in different brokerage firms and private banks in the names of family members, friends, and even a private religious institution. He then creates a rumor campaign on various blogs and social media outlets promoting the company.

Gray begins to buy and sell the stock using the accounts in hopes of raising the trading volume and the price. He conducts the trades through multiple brokers, selling slightly larger positions than he bought on a tactical schedule, and over time, he is able to reduce his holding as desired without negatively affecting the sale price.

> *Comment*: John violated Standard II(B) by fraudulently creating the appearance that there was a greater investor interest in the stock through the online rumors. Additionally, through his trading strategy, he created the appearance that there was greater liquidity in the stock than actually existed. He was able to manipulate the price through both misinformation and trading practices.

Example 3 (Creating Artificial Price Volatility):

Matthew Murphy is an analyst at Divisadero Securities & Co., which has a significant number of hedge funds among its most important brokerage clients. Some of the hedge funds hold short positions on Wirewolf Semiconductor. Two trading days before the publication of a quarter-end report, Murphy alerts his sales force that he is about to issue a research report on Wirewolf that will include the following opinions:

- quarterly revenues are likely to fall short of management's guidance,
- earnings will be as much as 5 cents per share (or more than 10%) below consensus, and
- Wirewolf's highly respected chief financial officer may be about to join another company.

Knowing that Wirewolf has already entered its declared quarter-end "quiet period" before reporting earnings (and thus would be reluctant to respond to rumors), Murphy times the release of his research report specifically to sensationalize the negative aspects of the message in order to create significant downward pressure on Wirewolf's stock—to the distinct advantage of Divisadero's hedge fund clients. The report's conclusions are based on speculation, not on fact. The next day, the research report is broadcast to all of Divisadero's clients and to the usual newswire services.

Before Wirewolf's investor-relations department can assess the damage on the final trading day of the quarter and refute Murphy's report, its stock opens trading sharply lower, allowing Divisadero's clients to cover their short positions at substantial gains.

> *Comment*: Murphy violated Standard II(B) by aiming to create artificial price volatility designed to have a material impact on the price of an issuer's stock. Moreover, by lacking an adequate basis for the recommendation, Murphy also violated Standard V(A) Diligence and Reasonable Basis.

Example 4 (Personal Trading and Volume):

Rajesh Sekar manages two funds—an equity fund and a balanced fund—whose equity components are supposed to be managed in accordance with the same model. According to that model, the funds' holdings in stock of Digital Design Inc. (DD) are excessive. Reduction of the DD holdings would not be easy, however, because the stock has low liquidity in the stock market. Sekar decides to start trading larger portions of DD stock back and forth between his two funds to slowly increase the price; he believes market participants will see growing volume and increasing price and become interested in the stock. If other investors are willing to buy the DD stock because of such interest, then Sekar will be able to get rid of at least some of his overweight position without inducing price decreases. In this way, the whole transaction will be for the benefit of fund participants, even if additional brokers' commissions are incurred.

> *Comment*: Sekar's plan would be beneficial for his funds' participants but is based on artificial distortion of both trading volume and the price of the DD stock and thus constitutes a violation of Standard II(B).

Example 5 ("Pump-Priming" Strategy):

ACME Futures Exchange is launching a new bond futures contract. To convince investors, traders, arbitrageurs, hedgers, and so on, to use its contract, the exchange attempts to demonstrate that it has the best liquidity. To do so, it enters into agreements with members in which they commit to a substantial minimum trading volume on the new contract over a specific period in exchange for substantial reductions of their regular commissions.

> *Comment*: The formal liquidity of a market is determined by the obligations set on market makers, but the actual liquidity of a market is better estimated by the actual trading volume and bid–ask spreads. Attempts to mislead participants about the actual liquidity of the market constitute a violation of Standard II(B). In this example, investors have been intentionally misled to believe they chose the most liquid instrument for some specific purpose, but they could eventually see the actual liquidity of the contract significantly reduced after the term of the agreement expires. If the ACME Futures Exchange fully discloses its agreement with members to boost transactions over some initial launch period, it will not violate Standard II(B). ACME's intent is not to harm investors but, on the contrary, to give them a better service. For that purpose, it may engage in a liquidity-pumping strategy, but the strategy must be disclosed.

Example 6 (Creating Artificial Price Volatility):

Emily Gordon, an analyst of household products companies, is employed by a research boutique, Picador & Co. Based on information that she has gathered during a trip through Latin America, she believes that Hygene, Inc., a major marketer of personal care products, has generated better-than-expected sales from its new product initiatives in South America. After modestly boosting her projections for revenue and for gross profit margin in her worksheet models for Hygene, Gordon estimates that her earnings projection of US$2.00 per diluted share for the current year may be as much as 5% too low. She contacts the chief financial officer (CFO) of Hygene to try to gain confirmation of her findings from her trip and to get some feedback regarding her revised models. The CFO declines to comment and reiterates management's most recent guidance of US$1.95–US$2.05 for the year.

Gordon decides to try to force a comment from the company by telling Picador & Co. clients who follow a momentum investment style that consensus earnings projections for Hygene are much too low; she explains that she is considering raising her published estimate by an ambitious US$0.15 to US$2.15 per share. She believes that when word of an unrealistically high earnings projection filters back to Hygene's investor-relations department, the company will feel compelled to update its earnings guidance. Meanwhile, Gordon hopes that she is at least correct with respect to the earnings direction and that she will help clients who act on her insights to profit from a quick gain by trading on her advice.

> *Comment*: By exaggerating her earnings projections in order to try to fuel a quick gain in Hygene's stock price, Gordon is in violation of Standard II(B). Furthermore, by virtue of previewing her intentions of revising upward her earnings projections to only a select group of clients, she is in violation of Standard III(B) Fair Dealing. However, it would have been acceptable for Gordon to write a report that

- framed her earnings projection in a range of possible outcomes,
- outlined clearly the assumptions used in her Hygene models that took into consideration the findings from her trip through Latin America, and
- was distributed to all Picador & Co. clients in an equitable manner.

Example 7 (Pump and Dump Strategy):

In an effort to pump up the price of his holdings in Moosehead & Belfast Railroad Company, Steve Weinberg logs on to several investor chat rooms on the internet to start rumors that the company is about to expand its rail network in anticipation of receiving a large contract for shipping lumber.

> *Comment*: Weinberg has violated Standard II(B) by disseminating false information about Moosehead & Belfast with the intent to mislead market participants.

Example 8 (Manipulating Model Inputs):

Bill Mandeville supervises a structured financing team for Superior Investment Bank. His responsibilities include packaging new structured investment products and managing Superior's relationship with relevant rating agencies. To achieve the best rating possible, Mandeville uses mostly positive scenarios as model inputs—scenarios that reflect minimal downside risk in the assets underlying the structured products. The resulting output statistics in the rating request and underwriting prospectus support the idea that the new structured products have minimal potential downside risk. Additionally, Mandeville's compensation from Superior is partially based on both the level of the rating assigned and the successful sale of new structured investment products but does not have a link to the long-term performance of the instruments.

Mandeville is extremely successful and leads Superior as the top originator of structured investment products for the next two years. In the third year, the economy experiences difficulties and the values of the assets underlying structured products significantly decline. The subsequent defaults lead to major turmoil in the capital markets, the demise of Superior Investment Bank, and the loss of Mandeville's employment.

> *Comment*: Mandeville manipulates the inputs of a model to minimize associated risk to achieve higher ratings. His understanding of structured products allows him to skillfully decide which inputs to include in support of the desired rating and price. This information manipulation for short-term gain, which is in violation of Standard II(B), ultimately causes significant damage to many parties and the capital markets as a whole. Mandeville should have realized that promoting a rating and price with inaccurate information could cause not only a loss of price confidence in the particular structured product but also a loss of investor trust in the system. Such loss of confidence affects the ability of the capital markets to operate efficiently.

Example 9 (Information Manipulation):

Allen King is a performance analyst for Torrey Investment Funds. King believes that the portfolio manager for the firm's small- and microcap equity fund dislikes him because the manager never offers him tickets to the local baseball team's games but does offer tickets to other employees. To incite a potential regulatory review of the manager, King creates user profiles on several online forums under the portfolio manager's name and starts rumors about potential mergers for several of the smaller companies in the portfolio. As the prices of these companies' stocks increase, the portfolio manager sells the position, which leads to an investigation by the regulator as King desired.

> *Comment*: King has violated Standard II(B) even though he did not personally profit from the market's reaction to the rumor. In posting the false information, King misleads others into believing the companies were likely

to be acquired. Although his intent was to create trouble for the portfolio manager, his actions clearly manipulated the factual information that was available to the market.

21 STANDARD III: DUTIES TO CLIENTS

- ☐ demonstrate a thorough knowledge of the CFA Institute Code of Ethics and Standards of Professional Conduct by interpreting the Code and Standards in various situations involving issues of professional integrity
- ☐ recommend practices and procedures designed to prevent violations of the Code and Standards

Standard III(A) Loyalty, Prudence, and Care

Members and Candidates have a duty of loyalty to their clients and must act with reasonable care and exercise prudent judgment. Members and Candidates must act for the benefit of their clients and place their clients' interests before their employer's or their own interests.

Guidance

Highlights:

- *Understanding the Application of Loyalty, Prudence, and Care*
- *Identifying the Actual Investment Client*
- *Developing the Client's Portfolio*
- *Soft Commission Policies*
- *Proxy Voting Policies*

Standard III(A) clarifies that client interests are paramount. A member's or candidate's responsibility to a client includes a duty of loyalty and a duty to exercise reasonable care. Investment actions must be carried out for the sole benefit of the client and in a manner the member or candidate believes, given the known facts and circumstances, to be in the best interest of the client. Members and candidates must exercise the same level of prudence, judgment, and care that they would apply in the management and disposition of their own interests in similar circumstances.

Prudence requires caution and discretion. The exercise of prudence by investment professionals requires that they act with the care, skill, and diligence that a reasonable person acting in a like capacity and familiar with such matters would use. In the context of managing a client's portfolio, prudence requires following the investment parameters set forth by the client and balancing risk and return. Acting with care requires members and candidates to act in a prudent and judicious manner in avoiding harm to clients.

Standard III(A) sets minimum expectations for members and candidates when fulfilling their responsibilities to their clients. Regulatory and legal requirements for such duties can vary across the investment industry depending on a variety of factors, including job function of the investment professional, the existence of an adviser/client relationship, and the nature of the recommendations being offered. From the perspective of the end user of financial services, these different standards can be arcane and confusing, leaving investors unsure of what level of service to expect from investment professionals they employ. The single standard of conduct described in Standard III(A) benefits investors by establishing a benchmark for the duties of loyalty, prudence, and care and clarifies that all CFA Institute members and candidates, regardless of job title, local laws, or cultural differences, are required to comply with these fundamental responsibilities. Investors hiring members or candidates who must adhere to the duty of loyalty, prudence, and care set forth in this standard can be confident that these responsibilities are a requirement regardless of any legally imposed fiduciary duties.

Standard III(A), however, is not a substitute for a member's or candidate's legal or regulatory obligations. As stated in Standard I(A), members and candidates must abide by the most strict requirements imposed on them by regulators or the Code and Standards, including any legally imposed fiduciary duty. Members and candidates must also be aware of whether they have "custody" or effective control of client assets. If so, a heightened level of responsibility arises. Members and candidates are considered to have custody if they have any direct or indirect access to client funds. Members and candidates must manage any pool of assets in their control in accordance with the terms of the governing documents (such as trust documents and investment management agreements), which are the primary determinant of the manager's powers and duties. Whenever their actions are contrary to provisions of those instruments or applicable law, members and candidates are at risk of violating Standard III(A).

Understanding the Application of Loyalty, Prudence, and Care

Standard III(A) establishes a minimum benchmark for the duties of loyalty, prudence, and care that are required of all members and candidates regardless of whether a legal fiduciary duty applies. Although fiduciary duty often encompasses the principles of loyalty, prudence, and care, Standard III(A) does not render all members and candidates fiduciaries. The responsibilities of members and candidates for fulfilling their obligations under this standard depend greatly on the nature of their professional responsibilities and the relationships they have with clients. The conduct of members and candidates may or may not rise to the level of being a fiduciary, depending on the type of client, whether the member or candidate is giving investment advice, and the many facts and circumstances surrounding a particular transaction or client relationship.

Fiduciary duties are often imposed by law or regulation when an individual or institution is charged with the duty of acting for the benefit of another party, such as managing investment assets. The duty required in fiduciary relationships exceeds what is acceptable in many other business relationships because a fiduciary is in an enhanced position of trust. Although members and candidates must comply with any legally imposed fiduciary duty, the Code and Standards neither impose such a legal responsibility nor require all members or candidates to act as fiduciaries. However, Standard III(A) requires members and candidates to work in the client's best interest no matter what the job function.

A member or candidate who does not provide advisory services to a client but who acts only as a trade execution professional must prudently work in the client's interest when completing requested trades. Acting in the client's best interest requires these professionals to use their skills and diligence to execute trades in the most favorable terms that can be achieved. Members and candidates operating in such positions must use care to operate within the parameters set by the client's trading instructions.

Members and candidates may also operate in a blended environment where they execute client trades and offer advice on a limited set of investment options. The extent of the advisory arrangement and limitations should be outlined in the agreement with the client at the outset of the relationship. For instance, members and candidates should inform clients that the advice provided will be limited to the propriety products of the firm and not include other products available on the market. Clients who want access to a wider range of investment products would have the information necessary to decide not to engage with members or candidates working under these restrictions.

Members and candidates operating in this blended context would comply with their obligations by recommending the allowable products that are consistent with the client's objectives and risk tolerance. They would exercise care through diligently aligning the client's needs with the attributes of the products being recommended. Members and candidates should place the client's interests first by disregarding any firm or personal interest in motivating a recommended transaction.

There is a large variety of professional relationships that members and candidates have with their clients. Standard III(A) requires them to fulfill the obligations outlined explicitly or implicitly in the client agreements to the best of their abilities and with loyalty, prudence, and care. Whether a member or candidate is structuring a new securitization transaction, completing a credit rating analysis, or leading a public company, he or she must work with prudence and care in delivering the agreed-on services.

Identifying the Actual Investment Client

The first step for members and candidates in fulfilling their duty of loyalty to clients is to determine the identity of the "client" to whom the duty of loyalty is owed. In the context of an investment manager managing the personal assets of an individual, the client is easily identified. When the manager is responsible for the portfolios of pension plans or trusts, however, the client is not the person or entity who hires the manager but, rather, the beneficiaries of the plan or trust. The duty of loyalty is owed to the ultimate beneficiaries.

In some situations, an actual client or group of beneficiaries may not exist. Members and candidates managing a fund to an index or an expected mandate owe the duty of loyalty, prudence, and care to invest in a manner consistent with the stated mandate. The decisions of a fund's manager, although benefiting all fund investors, do not have to be based on an individual investor's requirements and risk profile. Client loyalty and care for those investing in the fund are the responsibility of members and candidates who have an advisory relationship with those individuals.

Situations involving potential conflicts of interest with respect to responsibilities to clients may be extremely complex because they may involve a number of competing interests. The duty of loyalty, prudence, and care applies to a large number of persons in varying capacities, but the exact duties may differ in many respects in accord with the relationship with each client or each type of account in which the assets are managed. Members and candidates must not only put their obligations to clients first in all dealings but also endeavor to avoid all real or potential conflicts of interest.

Members and candidates with positions whose responsibilities do not include direct investment management also have "clients" that must be considered. Just as there are various types of advisory relationships, members and candidates must look at their roles and responsibilities when making a determination of who their clients are. Sometimes the client is easily identifiable; such is the case in the relationship between a company executive and the firm's public shareholders. At other times, the client may be the investing public as a whole, in which case the goals of independence and objectivity of research surpass the goal of loyalty to a single organization.

Developing the Client's Portfolio

The duty of loyalty, prudence, and care owed to the individual client is especially important because the professional investment manager typically possesses greater knowledge in the investment arena than the client does. This disparity places the individual client in a vulnerable position; the client must trust the manager. The manager in these situations should ensure that the client's objectives and expectations for the performance of the account are realistic and suitable to the client's circumstances and that the risks involved are appropriate. In most circumstances, recommended investment strategies should relate to the long-term objectives and circumstances of the client.

Particular care must be taken to detect whether the goals of the investment manager or the firm in conducting business, selling products, and executing security transactions potentially conflict with the best interests and objectives of the client. When members and candidates cannot avoid potential conflicts between their firm and clients' interests, they must provide clear and factual disclosures of the circumstances to the clients.

Members and candidates must follow any guidelines set by their clients for the management of their assets. Some clients, such as charitable organizations and pension plans, have strict investment policies that limit investment options to certain types or classes of investment or prohibit investment in certain securities. Other organizations have aggressive policies that do not prohibit investments by type but, instead, set criteria on the basis of the portfolio's total risk and return.

Investment decisions must be judged in the context of the total portfolio rather than by individual investment within the portfolio. The member's or candidate's duty is satisfied with respect to a particular investment if the individual has thoroughly considered the investment's place in the overall portfolio, the risk of loss and opportunity for gains, tax implications, and the diversification, liquidity, cash flow, and overall return requirements of the assets or the portion of the assets for which the manager is responsible.

Soft Commission Policies

An investment manager often has discretion over the selection of brokers executing transactions. Conflicts may arise when an investment manager uses client brokerage to purchase research services, a practice commonly called "soft dollars" or "soft commissions." A member or candidate who pays a higher brokerage commission than he or she would normally pay to allow for the purchase of goods or services, without corresponding benefit to the client, violates the duty of loyalty to the client.

From time to time, a client will direct a manager to use the client's brokerage to purchase goods or services for the client, a practice that is commonly called "directed brokerage." Because brokerage commission is an asset of the client and is used to benefit that client, not the manager, such a practice does not violate any duty of loyalty. However, a member or candidate is obligated to seek "best price" and "best execution" and be assured by the client that the goods or services purchased from the brokerage will benefit the account beneficiaries. "Best execution" refers to a trading process that seeks to maximize the value of the client's portfolio within the client's stated investment objectives and constraints. In addition, the member or candidate should disclose to the client that the client may not be getting best execution from the directed brokerage.

Proxy Voting Policies

The duty of loyalty, prudence, and care may apply in a number of situations facing the investment professional besides those related directly to investing assets.

Part of a member's or candidate's duty of loyalty includes voting proxies in an informed and responsible manner. Proxies have economic value to a client, and members and candidates must ensure that they properly safeguard and maximize this value. An investment manager who fails to vote, casts a vote without considering the impact of the question, or votes blindly with management on nonroutine governance issues (e.g., a change in company capitalization) may violate this standard. Voting of proxies is an integral part of the management of investments.

A cost–benefit analysis may show that voting all proxies may not benefit the client, so voting proxies may not be necessary in all instances. Members and candidates should disclose to clients their proxy voting policies.

22 STANDARD III(A): RECOMMENDED PROCEDURES

Regular Account Information

Members and candidates with control of client assets (1) should submit to each client, at least quarterly, an itemized statement showing the funds and securities in the custody or possession of the member or candidate plus all debits, credits, and transactions that occurred during the period, (2) should disclose to the client where the assets are to be maintained, as well as where or when they are moved, and (3) should separate the client's assets from any other party's assets, including the member's or candidate's own assets.

Client Approval

If a member or candidate is uncertain about the appropriate course of action with respect to a client, the member or candidate should consider what he or she would expect or demand if the member or candidate were the client. If in doubt, a member or candidate should disclose the questionable matter in writing to the client and obtain client approval.

Firm Policies

Members and candidates should address and encourage their firms to address the following topics when drafting the statements or manuals containing their policies and procedures regarding responsibilities to clients:

- *Follow all applicable rules and laws*: Members and candidates must follow all legal requirements and applicable provisions of the Code and Standards.
- *Establish the investment objectives of the client*: Make a reasonable inquiry into a client's investment experience, risk and return objectives, and financial constraints prior to making investment recommendations or taking investment actions.
- *Consider all the information when taking actions*: When taking investment actions, members and candidates must consider the appropriateness and suitability of the investment relative to (1) the client's needs and circumstances, (2) the investment's basic characteristics, and (3) the basic characteristics of the total portfolio.

- *Diversify*: Members and candidates should diversify investments to reduce the risk of loss, unless diversification is not consistent with plan guidelines or is contrary to the account objectives.
- *Carry out regular reviews*: Members and candidates should establish regular review schedules to ensure that the investments held in the account adhere to the terms of the governing documents.
- *Deal fairly with all clients with respect to investment actions*: Members and candidates must not favor some clients over others and should establish policies for allocating trades and disseminating investment recommendations.
- *Disclose conflicts of interest*: Members and candidates must disclose all actual and potential conflicts of interest so that clients can evaluate those conflicts.
- *Disclose compensation arrangements*: Members and candidates should make their clients aware of all forms of manager compensation.
- *Vote proxies*: In most cases, members and candidates should determine who is authorized to vote shares and vote proxies in the best interests of the clients and ultimate beneficiaries.
- *Maintain confidentiality*: Members and candidates must preserve the confidentiality of client information.
- *Seek best execution*: Unless directed by the client as ultimate beneficiary, members and candidates must seek best execution for their clients. (Best execution is defined in the preceding text.)
- *Place client interests first*: Members and candidates must serve the best interests of clients.

STANDARD III(A): APPLICATION OF THE STANDARD 23

Example 1 (Identifying the Client—Plan Participants):

First Country Bank serves as trustee for the Miller Company's pension plan. Miller is the target of a hostile takeover attempt by Newton, Inc. In attempting to ward off Newton, Miller's managers persuade Julian Wiley, an investment manager at First Country Bank, to purchase Miller common stock in the open market for the employee pension plan. Miller's officials indicate that such action would be favorably received and would probably result in other accounts being placed with the bank. Although Wiley believes the stock is overvalued and would not ordinarily buy it, he purchases the stock to support Miller's managers, to maintain Miller's good favor toward the bank, and to realize additional new business. The heavy stock purchases cause Miller's market price to rise to such a level that Newton retracts its takeover bid.

> *Comment*: Standard III(A) requires that a member or candidate, in evaluating a takeover bid, act prudently and solely in the interests of plan participants and beneficiaries. To meet this requirement, a member or candidate must carefully evaluate the long-term prospects of the company against the short-term prospects presented by the takeover offer and by the ability to invest elsewhere. In this instance, Wiley, acting on behalf of his employer, which was the trustee for a pension plan, clearly violated Standard III(A). He used the pension plan to perpetuate existing management, perhaps to the detriment of plan participants and the company's shareholders, and

to benefit himself. Wiley's responsibilities to the plan participants and beneficiaries should have taken precedence over any ties of his bank to corporate managers and over his self-interest. Wiley had a duty to examine the takeover offer on its own merits and to make an independent decision. The guiding principle is the appropriateness of the investment decision to the pension plan, not whether the decision benefited Wiley or the company that hired him.

Example 2 (Client Commission Practices):

JNI, a successful investment counseling firm, serves as investment manager for the pension plans of several large regionally based companies. Its trading activities generate a significant amount of commission-related business. JNI uses the brokerage and research services of many firms, but most of its trading activity is handled through a large brokerage company, Thompson, Inc., because the executives of the two firms have a close friendship. Thompson's commission structure is high in comparison with charges for similar brokerage services from other firms. JNI considers Thompson's research services and execution capabilities average. In exchange for JNI directing its brokerage to Thompson, Thompson absorbs a number of JNI overhead expenses, including those for rent.

> *Comment*: JNI executives are breaching their responsibilities by using client brokerage for services that do not benefit JNI clients and by not obtaining best price and best execution for their clients. Because JNI executives are not upholding their duty of loyalty, they are violating Standard III(A).

Example 3 (Brokerage Arrangements):

Charlotte Everett, a struggling independent investment adviser, serves as investment manager for the pension plans of several companies. One of her brokers, Scott Company, is close to consummating management agreements with prospective new clients whereby Everett would manage the new client accounts and trade the accounts exclusively through Scott. One of Everett's existing clients, Crayton Corporation, has directed Everett to place securities transactions for Crayton's account exclusively through Scott. But to induce Scott to exert efforts to send more new accounts to her, Everett also directs transactions to Scott from other clients without their knowledge.

> *Comment*: Everett has an obligation at all times to seek best price and best execution on all trades. Everett may direct new client trades exclusively through Scott Company as long as Everett receives best price and execution on the trades or receives a written statement from new clients that she is *not* to seek best price and execution and that they are aware of the consequence for their accounts. Everett may trade other accounts through Scott as a reward for directing clients to Everett only if the accounts receive best price and execution and the practice is disclosed to the accounts. Because Everett does not disclose the directed trading, Everett has violated Standard III(A).

Example 4 (Brokerage Arrangements):

Emilie Rome is a trust officer for Paget Trust Company. Rome's supervisor is responsible for reviewing Rome's trust account transactions and her monthly reports of personal stock transactions. Rome has been using Nathan Gray, a broker, almost exclusively for trust account brokerage transactions. When Gray makes a market in stocks, he has been giving Rome a lower price for personal purchases and a higher price for sales than he gives to Rome's trust accounts and other investors.

> *Comment*: Rome is violating her duty of loyalty to the bank's trust accounts by using Gray for brokerage transactions simply because Gray trades Rome's personal account on favorable terms. Rome is placing her own interests before those of her clients.

Example 5 (Client Commission Practices):

Lauren Parker, an analyst with Provo Advisors, covers South American equities for her firm. She likes to travel to the markets for which she is responsible and decides to go on a trip to Chile, Argentina, and Brazil. The trip is sponsored by SouthAM, Inc., a research firm with a small broker/dealer affiliate that uses the clearing facilities of a larger New York brokerage house. SouthAM specializes in arranging South American trips for analysts during which they can meet with central bank officials, government ministers, local economists, and senior executives of corporations. SouthAM accepts commission dollars at a ratio of 2 to 1 against the hard-dollar costs of the research fee for the trip. Parker is not sure that SouthAM's execution is competitive, but without informing her supervisor, she directs the trading desk at Provo to start giving commission business to SouthAM so she can take the trip. SouthAM has conveniently timed the briefing trip to coincide with the beginning of Carnival season, so Parker also decides to spend five days of vacation in Rio de Janeiro at the end of the trip. Parker uses commission dollars to pay for the five days of hotel expenses.

> *Comment*: Parker is violating Standard III(A) by not exercising her duty of loyalty to her clients. She should have determined whether the commissions charged by SouthAM are reasonable in relation to the benefit of the research provided by the trip. She also should have determined whether best execution and prices could be received from SouthAM. In addition, the five extra days are not part of the research effort because they do not assist in the investment decision making. Thus, the hotel expenses for the five days should not be paid for with client assets.

Example 6 (Excessive Trading):

Vida Knauss manages the portfolios of a number of high-net-worth individuals. A major part of her investment management fee is based on trading commissions. Knauss engages in extensive trading for each of her clients to ensure that she attains the minimum commission level set by her firm. Although the securities purchased and sold for the clients are appropriate and fall within the acceptable asset classes for the clients, the amount of trading for each account exceeds what is necessary to accomplish the client's investment objectives.

> *Comment*: Knauss has violated Standard III(A) because she is using the assets of her clients to benefit her firm and herself.

Example 7 (Managing Family Accounts):

Adam Dill recently joined New Investments Asset Managers. To assist Dill in building a book of clients, both his father and brother opened new fee-paying accounts. Dill followed all the firm's procedures in noting his relationships with these clients and in developing their investment policy statements.

After several years, the number of Dill's clients has grown, but he still manages the original accounts of his family members. An IPO is coming to market that is a suitable investment for many of his clients, including his brother. Dill does not receive the amount of stock he requested, so to avoid any appearance of a conflict of interest, he does not allocate any shares to his brother's account.

> *Comment:* Dill has violated Standard III(A) because he is not acting for the benefit of his brother's account as well as his other accounts. The brother's account is a regular fee-paying account comparable to the accounts of his other clients. By not allocating the shares proportionately across *all* accounts for which he thought the IPO was suitable, Dill is disadvantaging specific clients.
>
> Dill would have been correct in not allocating shares to his brother's account if that account was being managed outside the normal fee structure of the firm.

Example 8 (Identifying the Client):

Donna Hensley has been hired by a law firm to testify as an expert witness. Although the testimony is intended to represent impartial advice, she is concerned that her work may have negative consequences for the law firm. If the law firm is Hensley's client, how does she ensure that her testimony will not violate the required duty of loyalty, prudence, and care to one's client?

> *Comment:* In this situation, the law firm represents Hensley's employer and the aspect of "who is the client" is not well defined. When acting as an expert witness, Hensley is bound by the standard of independence and objectivity in the same manner as an independent research analyst would be bound. Hensley must not let the law firm influence the testimony she provides in the legal proceedings.

Example 9 (Identifying the Client):

Jon Miller is a mutual fund portfolio manager. The fund is focused on the global financial services sector. Wanda Spears is a private wealth manager in the same city as Miller and is a friend of Miller. At a local CFA Institute society meeting, Spears mentions to Miller that her new client is an investor in Miller's fund. She states that the two of them now share a responsibility to this client.

> *Comment:* Spears' statement is not totally correct. Because she provides the advisory services to her new client, she alone is bound by the duty of loyalty to this client. Miller's responsibility is to manage the fund according to the investment policy statement of the fund. His actions should not be influenced by the needs of any particular fund investor.

Example 10 (Client Loyalty):

After providing client account investment performance to the external-facing departments but prior to it being finalized for release to clients, Teresa Nguyen, an investment performance analyst, notices the reporting system missed a trade. Correcting the omission resulted in a large loss for a client that had previously placed the firm on "watch" for potential termination owing to underperformance in prior periods. Nguyen knows this news is unpleasant but informs the appropriate individuals that the report needs to be updated before releasing it to the client.

Comment: Nguyen's actions align with the requirements of Standard III(A). Even though the correction may lead to the firm's termination by the client, withholding information on errors would not be in the best interest of the client.

Example 11 (Execution-Only Responsibilities):

Baftija Sulejman recently became a candidate in the CFA Program. He is a broker who executes client-directed trades for several high-net-worth individuals. Sulejman does not provide any investment advice and only executes the trading decisions made by clients. He is concerned that the Code and Standards impose a fiduciary duty on him in his dealing with clients and sends an e-mail to the CFA Ethics Helpdesk (ethics@cfainstitute.org) to seek guidance on this issue.

Comment: In this instance, Sulejman serves in an execution-only capacity and his duty of loyalty, prudence, and care is centered on the skill and diligence used when executing trades—namely, by seeking best execution and making trades within the parameters set by the clients (instructions on quantity, price, timing, etc.). Acting in the best interests of the client dictates that trades are executed on the most favorable terms that can be achieved for the client. Given this job function, the requirements of the Code and Standards for loyalty, prudence, and care clearly do not impose a fiduciary duty.

STANDARD III(B) FAIR DEALING

24

- ☐ demonstrate a thorough knowledge of the CFA Institute Code of Ethics and Standards of Professional Conduct by interpreting the Code and Standards in various situations involving issues of professional integrity
- ☐ recommend practices and procedures designed to prevent violations of the Code and Standards

Members and Candidates must deal fairly and objectively with all clients when providing investment analysis, making investment recommendations, taking investment action, or engaging in other professional activities.

Guidance

Highlights:

- *Investment Recommendations*
- *Investment Action*

Standard III(B) requires members and candidates to treat all clients fairly when disseminating investment recommendations or making material changes to prior investment recommendations or when taking investment action with regard to general purchases, new issues, or secondary offerings. Only through the fair treatment of all parties can the investment management profession maintain the confidence of the investing public.

When an investment adviser has multiple clients, the potential exists for the adviser to favor one client over another. This favoritism may take various forms—from the quality and timing of services provided to the allocation of investment opportunities.

The term "fairly" implies that the member or candidate must take care not to discriminate against any clients when disseminating investment recommendations or taking investment action. Standard III(B) does not state "equally" because members and candidates could not possibly reach all clients at exactly the same time—whether by printed mail, telephone (including text messaging), computer (including internet updates and e-mail distribution), facsimile (fax), or wire. Each client has unique needs, investment criteria, and investment objectives, so not all investment opportunities are suitable for all clients. In addition, members and candidates may provide more personal, specialized, or in-depth service to clients who are willing to pay for premium services through higher management fees or higher levels of brokerage. Members and candidates may differentiate their services to clients, but different levels of service must not disadvantage or negatively affect clients. In addition, the different service levels should be disclosed to clients and prospective clients and should be available to everyone (i.e., different service levels should not be offered selectively).

Standard III(B) covers conduct in two broadly defined categories—investment recommendations and investment action.

Investment Recommendations

The first category of conduct involves members and candidates whose primary function is the preparation of investment recommendations to be disseminated either to the public or within a firm for the use of others in making investment decisions. This group includes members and candidates employed by investment counseling, advisory, or consulting firms as well as banks, brokerage firms, and insurance companies. The criterion is that the member's or candidate's primary responsibility is the preparation of recommendations to be acted on by others, including those in the member's or candidate's organization.

An investment recommendation is any opinion expressed by a member or candidate in regard to purchasing, selling, or holding a given security or other investment. The opinion may be disseminated to customers or clients through an initial detailed research report, through a brief update report, by addition to or deletion from a list of recommended securities, or simply by oral communication. A recommendation that is distributed to anyone outside the organization is considered a communication for general distribution under Standard III(B).

Standard III(B) addresses the manner in which investment recommendations or changes in prior recommendations are disseminated to clients. Each member or candidate is obligated to ensure that information is disseminated in such a manner that all clients have a fair opportunity to act on every recommendation. Communicating with all clients on a uniform basis presents practical problems for members and candidates because of differences in timing and methods of communication with various types of customers and clients. Members and candidates should encourage their firms to design an equitable system to prevent selective or discriminatory disclosure and should inform clients about what kind of communications they will receive.

The duty to clients imposed by Standard III(B) may be more critical when members or candidates change their recommendations than when they make initial recommendations. Material changes in a member's or candidate's prior investment recommendations because of subsequent research should be communicated to all current clients; particular care should be taken that the information reaches those clients who the member or candidate knows have acted on or been affected by the earlier advice. Clients who do not know that the member or candidate has changed a recommendation and who, therefore, place orders contrary to a current recommendation should be advised of the changed recommendation before the order is accepted.

Investment Action

The second category of conduct includes those members and candidates whose primary function is taking investment action (portfolio management) on the basis of recommendations prepared internally or received from external sources. Investment action, like investment recommendations, can affect market value. Consequently, Standard III(B) requires that members or candidates treat all clients fairly in light of their investment objectives and circumstances. For example, when making investments in new offerings or in secondary financings, members and candidates should distribute the issues to all customers for whom the investments are appropriate in a manner consistent with the policies of the firm for allocating blocks of stock. If the issue is oversubscribed, then the issue should be prorated to all subscribers. This action should be taken on a round-lot basis to avoid odd-lot distributions. In addition, if the issue is oversubscribed, members and candidates should forgo any sales to themselves or their immediate families in order to free up additional shares for clients. If the investment professional's family-member accounts are managed similarly to the accounts of other clients of the firm, however, the family-member accounts should not be excluded from buying such shares.

Members and candidates must make every effort to treat all individual and institutional clients in a fair and impartial manner. A member or candidate may have multiple relationships with an institution; for example, the member or candidate may be a corporate trustee, pension fund manager, manager of funds for individuals employed by the customer, loan originator, or creditor. A member or candidate must exercise care to treat all clients fairly.

Members and candidates should disclose to clients and prospective clients the documented allocation procedures they or their firms have in place and how the procedures would affect the client or prospect. The disclosure should be clear and complete so that the client can make an informed investment decision. Even when complete disclosure is made, however, members and candidates must put client interests ahead of their own. A member's or candidate's duty of fairness and loyalty to clients can never be overridden by client consent to patently unfair allocation procedures.

Treating clients fairly also means that members and candidates should not take advantage of their position in the industry to the detriment of clients. For instance, in the context of IPOs, members and candidates must make bona fide public distributions of "hot issue" securities (defined as securities of a public offering that are trading at a premium in the secondary market whenever such trading commences because of the great demand for the securities). Members and candidates are prohibited from withholding such securities for their own benefit and must not use such securities as a reward or incentive to gain benefit.

25 STANDARD III(B): RECOMMENDED PROCEDURES

Develop Firm Policies

Although Standard III(B) refers to a member's or candidate's responsibility to deal fairly and objectively with clients, members and candidates should also encourage their firms to establish compliance procedures requiring all employees who disseminate investment recommendations or take investment actions to treat customers and clients fairly. At the very least, a member or candidate should recommend appropriate procedures to management if none are in place. And the member or candidate should make management aware of possible violations of fair-dealing practices within the firm when they come to the attention of the member or candidate.

The extent of the formality and complexity of such compliance procedures depends on the nature and size of the organization and the type of securities involved. An investment adviser who is a sole proprietor and handles only discretionary accounts might not disseminate recommendations to the public, but that adviser should have formal written procedures to ensure that all clients receive fair investment action.

Good business practice dictates that initial recommendations be made available to all customers who indicate an interest. Although a member or candidate need not communicate a recommendation to all customers, the selection process by which customers receive information should be based on suitability and known interest, not on any preferred or favored status. A common practice to assure fair dealing is to communicate recommendations simultaneously within the firm and to customers.

Members and candidates should consider the following points when establishing fair-dealing compliance procedures:

- *Limit the number of people involved*: Members and candidates should make reasonable efforts to limit the number of people who are privy to the fact that a recommendation is going to be disseminated.
- *Shorten the time frame between decision and dissemination*: Members and candidates should make reasonable efforts to limit the amount of time that elapses between the decision to make an investment recommendation and the time the actual recommendation is disseminated. If a detailed institutional recommendation that might take two or three weeks to publish is in preparation, a short summary report including the conclusion might be published in advance. In an organization where both a research committee and an investment policy committee must approve a recommendation, the meetings should be held on the same day if possible. The process of reviewing reports and printing and mailing them, faxing them, or distributing them by e-mail necessarily involves the passage of time, sometimes long periods of time. In large firms with extensive review processes, the time factor is usually not within the control of the analyst who prepares the report. Thus, many firms and their analysts communicate to customers and firm personnel the new or changed recommendations by an update or "flash" report. The communication technique might be fax, e-mail, wire, or short written report.
- *Publish guidelines for pre-dissemination behavior*: Members and candidates should encourage firms to develop guidelines that prohibit personnel who have prior knowledge of an investment recommendation from discussing or taking any action on the pending recommendation.

- *Simultaneous dissemination*: Members and candidates should establish procedures for the timing of dissemination of investment recommendations so that all clients are treated fairly—that is, are informed at approximately the same time. For example, if a firm is going to announce a new recommendation, supervisory personnel should time the announcement to avoid placing any client or group of clients at an unfair advantage relative to other clients. A communication to all branch offices should be sent at the time of the general announcement. (When appropriate, the firm should accompany the announcement of a new recommendation with a statement that trading restrictions for the firm's employees are now in effect. The trading restrictions should stay in effect until the recommendation is widely distributed to all relevant clients.) Once this distribution has occurred, the member or candidate may follow up separately with individual clients, but members and candidates should not give favored clients advance information when such advance notification may disadvantage other clients.
- *Maintain a list of clients and their holdings*: Members and candidates should maintain a list of all clients and the securities or other investments each client holds in order to facilitate notification of customers or clients of a change in an investment recommendation. If a particular security or other investment is to be sold, such a list can be used to ensure that all holders are treated fairly in the liquidation of that particular investment.
- *Develop and document trade allocation procedures*: When formulating procedures for allocating trades, members and candidates should develop a set of guiding principles that ensure
    - fairness to advisory clients, both in priority of execution of orders and in the allocation of the price obtained in execution of block orders or trades,
    - timeliness and efficiency in the execution of orders, and
    - accuracy of the member's or candidate's records as to trade orders and client account positions.

With these principles in mind, members and candidates should develop or encourage their firm to develop written allocation procedures, with particular attention to procedures for block trades and new issues. Procedures to consider are as follows:

- requiring orders and modifications or cancellations of orders to be documented and time stamped;
- processing and executing orders on a first-in, first-out basis with consideration of bundling orders for efficiency as appropriate for the asset class or the security;
- developing a policy to address such issues as calculating execution prices and "partial fills" when trades are grouped, or in a block, for efficiency;
- giving all client accounts participating in a block trade the same execution price and charging the same commission;
- when the full amount of the block order is not executed, allocating partially executed orders among the participating client accounts pro rata on the basis of order size while not going below an established minimum lot size for some securities (e.g., bonds); and
- when allocating trades for new issues, obtaining advance indications of interest, allocating securities by client (rather than portfolio manager), and providing a method for calculating allocations.

Disclose Trade Allocation Procedures

Members and candidates should disclose to clients and prospective clients how they select accounts to participate in an order and how they determine the amount of securities each account will buy or sell. Trade allocation procedures must be fair and equitable, and disclosure of inequitable allocation methods does not relieve the member or candidate of this obligation.

Establish Systematic Account Review

Member and candidate supervisors should review each account on a regular basis to ensure that no client or customer is being given preferential treatment and that the investment actions taken for each account are suitable for each account's objectives. Because investments should be based on individual needs and circumstances, an investment manager may have good reasons for placing a given security or other investment in one account while selling it from another account and should fully document the reasons behind both sides of the transaction. Members and candidates should encourage firms to establish review procedures, however, to detect whether trading in one account is being used to benefit a favored client.

Disclose Levels of Service

Members and candidates should disclose to all clients whether the organization offers different levels of service to clients for the same fee or different fees. Different levels of service should not be offered to clients selectively.

26 STANDARD III(B): APPLICATION OF THE STANDARD

Example 1 (Selective Disclosure):

Bradley Ames, a well-known and respected analyst, follows the computer industry. In the course of his research, he finds that a small, relatively unknown company whose shares are traded over the counter has just signed significant contracts with some of the companies he follows. After a considerable amount of investigation, Ames decides to write a research report on the small company and recommend purchase of its shares. While the report is being reviewed by the company for factual accuracy, Ames schedules a luncheon with several of his best clients to discuss the company. At the luncheon, he mentions the purchase recommendation scheduled to be sent early the following week to all the firm's clients.

> *Comment*: Ames has violated Standard III(B) by disseminating the purchase recommendation to the clients with whom he has lunch a week before the recommendation is sent to all clients.

Example 2 (Fair Dealing between Funds):

Spencer Rivers, president of XYZ Corporation, moves his company's growth-oriented pension fund to a particular bank primarily because of the excellent investment performance achieved by the bank's commingled fund for the prior five-year period. Later, Rivers compares the results of his pension fund with those of the bank's commingled fund. He is startled to learn that, even though the two accounts have the same investment objectives and similar portfolios, his company's pension fund has significantly underperformed the bank's commingled fund. Questioning this result at his next meeting with the pension fund's manager, Rivers is told that, as a matter of policy, when a new security is placed on the recommended list, Morgan Jackson, the pension fund manager, first purchases the security for the commingled account and then purchases it on a pro rata basis for all other pension fund accounts. Similarly, when a sale is recommended, the security is sold first from the commingled account and then sold on a pro rata basis from all other accounts. Rivers also learns that if the bank cannot get enough shares (especially of hot issues) to be meaningful to all the accounts, its policy is to place the new issues only in the commingled account.

Seeing that Rivers is neither satisfied nor pleased by the explanation, Jackson quickly adds that nondiscretionary pension accounts and personal trust accounts have a lower priority on purchase and sale recommendations than discretionary pension fund accounts. Furthermore, Jackson states, the company's pension fund had the opportunity to invest up to 5% in the commingled fund.

> *Comment*: The bank's policy does not treat all customers fairly, and Jackson has violated her duty to her clients by giving priority to the growth-oriented commingled fund over all other funds and to discretionary accounts over nondiscretionary accounts. Jackson must execute orders on a systematic basis that is fair to all clients. In addition, trade allocation procedures should be disclosed to all clients when they become clients. Of course, in this case, disclosure of the bank's policy would not change the fact that the policy is unfair.

Example 3 (Fair Dealing and IPO Distribution):

Dominic Morris works for a small regional securities firm. His work consists of corporate finance activities and investing for institutional clients. Arena, Ltd., is planning to go public. The partners have secured rights to buy an arena football league franchise and are planning to use the funds from the issue to complete the purchase. Because arena football is the current rage, Morris believes he has a hot issue on his hands. He has quietly negotiated some options for himself for helping convince Arena to do the financing through his securities firm. When he seeks expressions of interest, the institutional buyers oversubscribe the issue. Morris, assuming that the institutions have the financial clout to drive the stock up, then fills all orders (including his own) and decreases the institutional blocks.

> *Comment*: Morris has violated Standard III(B) by not treating all customers fairly. He should not have taken any shares himself and should have prorated the shares offered among all clients. In addition, he should have disclosed to his firm and to his clients that he received options as part of the deal [see Standard VI(A) Disclosure of Conflicts].

Example 4 (Fair Dealing and Transaction Allocation):

Eleanor Preston, the chief investment officer of Porter Williams Investments (PWI), a medium-size money management firm, has been trying to retain a client, Colby Company. Management at Colby, which accounts for almost half of PWI's revenues, recently told Preston that if the performance of its account did not improve, it would find a new money manager. Shortly after this threat, Preston purchases mortgage-backed securities (MBSs) for several accounts, including Colby's. Preston is busy with a number of transactions that day, so she fails to allocate the trades immediately or write up the trade tickets. A few days later, when Preston is allocating trades, she notes that some of the MBSs have significantly increased in price and some have dropped. Preston decides to allocate the profitable trades to Colby and spread the losing trades among several other PWI accounts.

> *Comment*: Preston has violated Standard III(B) by failing to deal fairly with her clients in taking these investment actions. Preston should have allocated the trades prior to executing the orders, or she should have had a systematic approach to allocating the trades, such as pro rata, as soon as practical after they were executed. Among other things, Preston must disclose to the client that the adviser may act as broker for, receive commissions from, and have a potential conflict of interest regarding both parties in agency cross-transactions. After the disclosure, she should obtain from the client consent authorizing such transactions in advance.

Example 5 (Selective Disclosure):

Saunders Industrial Waste Management (SIWM) publicly indicates to analysts that it is comfortable with the somewhat disappointing earnings-per-share projection of US$1.16 for the quarter. Bernard Roberts, an analyst at Coffey Investments, is confident that SIWM management has understated the forecasted earnings so that the real announcement will cause an "upside surprise" and boost the price of SIWM stock. The "whisper number" (rumored) estimate based on extensive research and discussed among knowledgeable analysts is higher than US$1.16. Roberts repeats the US$1.16 figure in his research report to all Coffey clients but informally tells his large clients that he expects the earnings per share to be higher, making SIWM a good buy.

> *Comment*: By not sharing his opinion regarding the potential for a significant upside earnings surprise with all clients, Roberts is not treating all clients fairly and has violated Standard III(B).

Example 6 (Additional Services for Select Clients):

Jenpin Weng uses e-mail to issue a new recommendation to all his clients. He then calls his three largest institutional clients to discuss the recommendation in detail.

> *Comment*: Weng has not violated Standard III(B) because he widely disseminated the recommendation and provided the information to all his clients prior to discussing it with a select few. Weng's largest clients received additional personal service because they presumably pay higher fees or because they have a large amount of assets under Weng's management. If Weng had discussed the report with a select group of clients prior to distributing it to all his clients, he would have violated Standard III(B).

Example 7 (Minimum Lot Allocations):

Lynn Hampton is a well-respected private wealth manager in her community with a diversified client base. She determines that a new 10-year bond being offered by Healthy Pharmaceuticals is appropriate for five of her clients. Three clients request to purchase US$10,000 each, and the other two request US$50,000 each. The minimum lot size is established at US$5,000, and the issue is oversubscribed at the time of placement. Her firm's policy is that odd-lot allocations, especially those below the minimum, should be avoided because they may affect the liquidity of the security at the time of sale.

Hampton is informed she will receive only US$55,000 of the offering for all accounts. Hampton distributes the bond investments as follows: The three accounts that requested US$10,000 are allocated US$5,000 each, and the two accounts that requested US$50,000 are allocated US$20,000 each.

> *Comment*: Hampton has not violated Standard III(B), even though the distribution is not on a completely pro rata basis because of the required minimum lot size. With the total allocation being significantly below the amount requested, Hampton ensured that each client received at least the minimum lot size of the issue. This approach allowed the clients to efficiently sell the bond later if necessary.

Example 8 (Excessive Trading):

Ling Chan manages the accounts for many pension plans, including the plan of his father's employer. Chan developed similar but not identical investment policies for each client, so the investment portfolios are rarely the same. To minimize the cost to his father's pension plan, he intentionally trades more frequently in the accounts of other clients to ensure the required brokerage is incurred to continue receiving free research for use by all the pensions.

> *Comment*: Chan is violating Standard III(B) because his trading actions are disadvantaging his clients to enhance a relationship with a preferred client. All clients are benefiting from the research being provided and should incur their fair portion of the costs. This does not mean that additional trading should occur if a client has not paid an equal portion of the commission; trading should occur only as required by the strategy.

Example 9 (Limited Social Media Disclosures):

Mary Burdette was recently hired by Fundamental Investment Management (FIM) as a junior auto industry analyst. Burdette is expected to expand the social media presence of the firm because she is active with various networks, including Facebook, LinkedIn, and X. Although Burdette's supervisor, Joe Graf, has never used social media, he encourages Burdette to explore opportunities to increase FIM's online presence and ability to share content, communicate, and broadcast information to clients. In response to Graf's encouragement, Burdette is working on a proposal detailing the advantages of getting FIM onto X in addition to launching a company Facebook page.

As part of her auto industry research for FIM, Burdette is completing a report on the financial impact of Sun Drive Auto Ltd.'s new solar technology for compact automobiles. This research report will be her first for FIM, and she believes Sun Drive's technology could revolutionize the auto industry. In her excitement, Burdette sends a quick post to FIM X followers summarizing her "buy" recommendation for Sun Drive Auto stock.

> *Comment*: Burdette has violated Standard III(B) by sending an investment recommendation to a select group of contacts prior to distributing it to all clients. Burdette must make sure she has received the appropriate training about FIM's policies and procedures, including the appropriate business use of personal social media networks before engaging in such activities.
>
> See Standard IV(C) for guidance related to the duties of the supervisor.

Example 10 (Fair Dealing between Clients):

Paul Rove, performance analyst for Alpha-Beta Investment Management, is describing to the firm's chief investment officer (CIO) two new reports he would like to develop to assist the firm in meeting its obligations to treat clients fairly. Because many of the firm's clients have similar investment objectives and portfolios, Rove suggests a report detailing securities owned across several clients and the percentage of the portfolio the security represents. The second report would compare the monthly performance of portfolios with similar strategies. The outliers within each report would be submitted to the CIO for review.

> *Comment*: As a performance analyst, Rove likely has little direct contact with clients and thus has limited opportunity to treat clients differently. The recommended reports comply with Standard III(B) while helping the firm conduct after-the-fact reviews of how effectively the firm's advisers are dealing with their clients' portfolios. Reports that monitor the fair treatment of clients are an important oversight tool to ensure that clients are treated fairly.

27 STANDARD III(C) SUITABILITY

- ☐ demonstrate a thorough knowledge of the CFA Institute Code of Ethics and Standards of Professional Conduct by interpreting the Code and Standards in various situations involving issues of professional integrity
- ☐ recommend practices and procedures designed to prevent violations of the Code and Standards

1. When Members and Candidates are in an advisory relationship with a client, they must:
   a. Make a reasonable inquiry into a client's or prospective client's investment experience, risk and return objectives, and financial constraints prior to making any investment recommendation or taking investment action and must reassess and update this information regularly.
   b. Determine that an investment is suitable to the client's financial situation and consistent with the client's written objectives, mandates, and constraints before making an investment recommendation or taking investment action.
   c. Judge the suitability of investments in the context of the client's total portfolio.
2. When Members and Candidates are responsible for managing a portfolio to a specific mandate, strategy, or style, they must make only investment recommendations or take only investment actions that are consistent with the stated objectives and constraints of the portfolio.

Guidance

Highlights:

- *Developing an Investment Policy*
- *Understanding the Client's Risk Profile*
- *Updating an Investment Policy*
- *The Need for Diversification*
- *Addressing Unsolicited Trading Requests*
- *Managing to an Index or Mandate*

Standard III(C) requires that members and candidates who are in an investment advisory relationship with clients consider carefully the needs, circumstances, and objectives of the clients when determining the appropriateness and suitability of a given investment or course of investment action. An appropriate suitability determination will not, however, prevent some investments or investment actions from losing value.

In judging the suitability of a potential investment, the member or candidate should review many aspects of the client's knowledge, experience related to investing, and financial situation. These aspects include, but are not limited to, the risk profile of the investment as compared with the constraints of the client, the impact of the investment on the diversity of the portfolio, and whether the client has the means or net worth to assume the associated risk. The investment professional's determination of suitability should reflect only the investment recommendations or actions that a prudent person would be willing to undertake. Not every investment opportunity will be suitable for every portfolio, regardless of the potential return being offered.

The responsibilities of members and candidates to gather information and make a suitability analysis prior to making a recommendation or taking investment action fall on those members and candidates who provide investment advice in the course of an advisory relationship with a client. Other members and candidates may be simply executing specific instructions for retail clients when buying or selling securities, such as shares in mutual funds. These members and candidates and some others, such as sell-side analysts, may not have the opportunity to judge the suitability of a particular investment for the ultimate client.

Developing an Investment Policy

When an advisory relationship exists, members and candidates must gather client information at the inception of the relationship. Such information includes the client's financial circumstances, personal data (such as age and occupation) that are relevant to investment decisions, attitudes toward risk, and objectives in investing. This information should be incorporated into a written investment policy statement (IPS) that addresses the client's risk tolerance, return requirements, and all investment constraints (including time horizon, liquidity needs, tax concerns, legal and regulatory factors, and unique circumstances). Without identifying such client factors, members and candidates cannot judge whether a particular investment or strategy is suitable for a particular client. The IPS also should identify and describe the roles and responsibilities of the parties to the advisory relationship and investment process, as well as schedules for review and evaluation of the IPS. After formulating long-term capital market expectations, members and candidates can assist in developing an appropriate strategic asset allocation and investment program for the client, whether these are presented in separate documents or incorporated in the IPS or in appendices to the IPS.

Understanding the Client's Risk Profile

One of the most important factors to be considered in matching appropriateness and suitability of an investment with a client's needs and circumstances is measuring that client's tolerance for risk. The investment professional must consider the possibilities of rapidly changing investment environments and their likely impact on a client's holdings, both individual securities and the collective portfolio. The risk of many investment strategies can and should be analyzed and quantified in advance.

The use of synthetic investment vehicles and derivative investment products has introduced particular issues of risk. Members and candidates should pay careful attention to the leverage inherent in many of these vehicles or products when considering them for use in a client's investment program. Such leverage and limited liquidity, depending on the degree to which they are hedged, bear directly on the issue of suitability for the client.

Updating an Investment Policy

Updating the IPS should be repeated at least annually and also prior to material changes to any specific investment recommendations or decisions on behalf of the client. The effort to determine the needs and circumstances of each client is not a one-time occurrence. Investment recommendations or decisions are usually part of an ongoing process that takes into account the diversity and changing nature of portfolio and client characteristics. The passage of time is bound to produce changes that are important with respect to investment objectives.

For an individual client, important changes might include the number of dependents, personal tax status, health, liquidity needs, risk tolerance, amount of wealth beyond that represented in the portfolio, and extent to which compensation and other income provide for current income needs. With respect to an institutional client, such changes might relate to the magnitude of unfunded liabilities in a pension fund, the withdrawal privileges in an employee savings plan, or the distribution requirements of a charitable foundation. Without efforts to update information concerning client factors, one or more factors could change without the investment manager's knowledge.

Suitability review can be done most effectively when the client fully discloses his or her complete financial portfolio, including those portions not managed by the member or candidate. If clients withhold information about their financial portfolios, the suitability analysis conducted by members and candidates cannot be expected to be complete; it must be based on the information provided.

The Need for Diversification

The investment profession has long recognized that combining several different investments is likely to provide a more acceptable level of risk exposure than having all assets in a single investment. The unique characteristics (or risks) of an individual investment may become partially or entirely neutralized when it is combined with other individual investments within a portfolio. Some reasonable amount of diversification is thus the norm for many portfolios, especially those managed by individuals or institutions that have some degree of legal fiduciary responsibility.

An investment with high relative risk on its own may be a suitable investment in the context of the entire portfolio or when the client's stated objectives contemplate speculative or risky investments. The manager may be responsible for only a portion of the client's total portfolio, or the client may not have provided a full financial picture. Members and candidates can be responsible for assessing the suitability of an investment only on the basis of the information and criteria actually provided by the client.

Addressing Unsolicited Trading Requests

Members and candidates may receive requests from a client for trades that do not properly align with the risk and return objectives outlined in the client's investment policy statement. These transaction requests may be based on the client's individual biases or professional experience. Members and candidates will need to make reasonable efforts to balance their clients' trading requests with their responsibilities to follow the agreed-on investment policy statement.

In cases of unsolicited trade requests that a member or candidate knows are unsuitable for a client, the member or candidate should refrain from making the trade until he or she discusses the concerns with the client. The discussions and resulting actions may encompass a variety of scenarios depending on how the requested unsuitable investment relates to the client's full portfolio.

Many times, an unsolicited request may be expected to have only a minimum impact on the entire portfolio because the size of the requested trade is small or the trade would result in a limited change to the portfolio's risk profile. In discussing the trade, the member or candidate should focus on educating the investor on how the request deviates from the current policy statement. Following the discussion, the member or candidate may follow his or her firm's policies regarding the necessary client approval for executing unsuitable trades. At a minimum, the client should acknowledge the discussion and accept the conditions that make the recommendation unsuitable.

Should the unsolicited request be expected to have a material impact on the portfolio, the member or candidate should use this opportunity to update the investment policy statement. Doing so would allow the client to fully understand the potential effect of the requested trade on his or her current goals or risk levels.

Members and candidates may have some clients who decline to modify their policy statements while insisting an unsolicited trade be made. In such instances, members or candidates will need to evaluate the effectiveness of their services to the client. The options available to the members or candidates will depend on the services provided by their employer. Some firms may allow for the trade to be executed in a new unmanaged account. If alternative options are not available, members and candidates ultimately will need to determine whether they should continue the advisory arrangement with the client.

Managing to an Index or Mandate

Some members and candidates do not manage money for individuals but are responsible for managing a fund to an index or an expected mandate. The responsibility of these members and candidates is to invest in a manner consistent with the stated mandate. For example, a member or candidate who serves as the fund manager for a large-cap income fund would not be following the fund mandate by investing heavily in small-cap or start-up companies whose stock is speculative in nature. Members and candidates who manage pooled assets to a specific mandate are not responsible for determining the suitability of the *fund* as an investment for investors who may be purchasing shares in the fund. The responsibility for determining the suitability of an investment for clients can be conferred only on members and candidates who have an advisory relationship with clients.

28 STANDARD III(C): RECOMMENDED PROCEDURES

Investment Policy Statement

To fulfill the basic provisions of Standard III(C), a member or candidate should put the needs and circumstances of each client and the client's investment objectives into a written investment policy statement. In formulating an investment policy for the client, the member or candidate should take the following into consideration:

- client identification—(1) type and nature of client, (2) the existence of separate beneficiaries, and (3) approximate portion of total client assets that the member or candidate is managing;
- investor objectives—(1) return objectives (income, growth in principal, maintenance of purchasing power) and (2) risk tolerance (suitability, stability of values);
- investor constraints—(1) liquidity needs, (2) expected cash flows (patterns of additions and/or withdrawals), (3) investable funds (assets and liabilities or other commitments), (4) time horizon, (5) tax considerations, (6) regulatory and legal circumstances, (7) investor preferences, prohibitions, circumstances, and unique needs, and (8) proxy voting responsibilities and guidance; and
- performance measurement benchmarks.

Regular Updates

The investor's objectives and constraints should be maintained and reviewed periodically to reflect any changes in the client's circumstances. Members and candidates should regularly compare client constraints with capital market expectations to arrive at an appropriate asset allocation. Changes in either factor may result in a fundamental change in asset allocation. Annual review is reasonable unless business or other reasons, such as a major change in market conditions, dictate more frequent review. Members and candidates should document attempts to carry out such a review if circumstances prevent it.

Suitability Test Policies

With the increase in regulatory required suitability tests, members and candidates should encourage their firms to develop related policies and procedures. The procedures will differ according to the size of the firm and the scope of the services offered to its clients.

The test procedures should require the investment professional to look beyond the potential return of the investment and include the following:

- an analysis of the impact on the portfolio's diversification,
- a comparison of the investment risks with the client's assessed risk tolerance, and
- the fit of the investment with the required investment strategy.

STANDARD III(C): APPLICATION OF THE STANDARD

29

Example 1 (Investment Suitability—Risk Profile):

Caleb Smith, an investment adviser, has two clients: Larry Robertson, 60 years old, and Gabriel Lanai, 40 years old. Both clients earn roughly the same salary, but Robertson has a much higher risk tolerance because he has a large asset base. Robertson is willing to invest part of his assets very aggressively; Lanai wants only to achieve a steady rate of return with low volatility to pay for his children's education. Smith recommends investing 20% of both portfolios in zero-yield, small-cap, high-technology equity issues.

> *Comment*: In Robertson's case, the investment may be appropriate because of his financial circumstances and aggressive investment position, but this investment is not suitable for Lanai. Smith is violating Standard III(C) by applying Robertson's investment strategy to Lanai because the two clients' financial circumstances and objectives differ.

Example 2 (Investment Suitability—Entire Portfolio):

Jessica McDowell, an investment adviser, suggests to Brian Crosby, a risk-averse client, that covered call options be used in his equity portfolio. The purpose would be to enhance Crosby's income and partially offset any untimely depreciation in the portfolio's value should the stock market or other circumstances affect his holdings unfavorably. McDowell educates Crosby about all possible outcomes, including the risk of incurring an added tax liability if a stock rises in price and is called away and, conversely, the risk of his holdings losing protection on the downside if prices drop sharply.

> *Comment*: When determining suitability of an investment, the primary focus should be the characteristics of the client's entire portfolio, not the characteristics of single securities on an issue-by-issue basis. The basic characteristics of the entire portfolio will largely determine whether investment recommendations are taking client factors into account. Therefore, the most important aspects of a particular investment are those that will affect the characteristics of the total portfolio. In this case, McDowell properly considers the investment in the context of the entire portfolio and thoroughly explains the investment to the client.

Example 3 (IPS Updating):

In a regular meeting with client Seth Jones, the portfolio managers at Blue Chip Investment Advisors are careful to allow some time to review his current needs and circumstances. In doing so, they learn that some significant changes have recently taken place in his life. A wealthy uncle left Jones an inheritance that increased his net worth fourfold, to US$1 million.

> *Comment*: The inheritance has significantly increased Jones's ability (and possibly his willingness) to assume risk and has diminished the average yield required to meet his current income needs. Jones's financial circumstances have definitely changed, so Blue Chip managers must update Jones's investment policy statement to reflect how his investment objectives have changed. Accordingly, the Blue Chip portfolio managers should consider

a somewhat higher equity ratio for his portfolio than was called for by the previous circumstances, and the managers' specific common stock recommendations might be heavily tilted toward low-yield, growth-oriented issues.

Example 4 (Following an Investment Mandate):

Louis Perkowski manages a high-income mutual fund. He purchases zero-dividend stock in a financial services company because he believes the stock is undervalued and is in a potential growth industry, which makes it an attractive investment.

Comment: A zero-dividend stock does not seem to fit the mandate of the fund that Perkowski is managing. Unless Perkowski's investment fits within the mandate or is within the realm of allowable investments the fund has made clear in its disclosures, Perkowski has violated Standard III(C).

Example 5 (IPS Requirements and Limitations):

Max Gubler, chief investment officer of a property/casualty insurance subsidiary of a large financial conglomerate, wants to improve the diversification of the subsidiary's investment portfolio and increase its returns. The subsidiary's investment policy statement provides for highly liquid investments, such as large-cap equities and government, supranational, and corporate bonds with a minimum credit rating of AA and maturity of no more than five years. In a recent presentation, a venture capital group offered very attractive prospective returns on some of its private equity funds that provide seed capital to ventures. An exit strategy was already contemplated, but investors would have to observe a minimum three-year lockup period and a subsequent laddered exit option for a maximum of one-third of their shares per year. Gubler does not want to miss this opportunity. After extensive analysis, with the intent to optimize the return on the equity assets within the subsidiary's current portfolio, he invests 4% in this seed fund, leaving the portfolio's total equity exposure still well below its upper limit.

Comment: Gubler is violating Standard III(A) Loyalty, Prudence, and Care as well as Standard III(C). His new investment locks up part of the subsidiary's assets for at least three years and up to as many as five years and possibly beyond. The IPS requires investments in highly liquid investments and describes accepted asset classes; private equity investments with a lockup period certainly do not qualify. Even without a lockup period, an asset class with only an occasional, and thus implicitly illiquid, market may not be suitable for the portfolio. Although an IPS typically describes objectives and constraints in great detail, the manager must also make every effort to understand the client's business and circumstances. Doing so should enable the manager to recognize, understand, and discuss with the client other factors that may be or may become material in the investment management process.

Example 6 (Submanager and IPS Reviews):

Paul Ostrowski's investment management business has grown significantly over the past couple of years, and some clients want to diversify internationally. Ostrowski decides to find a submanager to handle the expected international investments. Because this will be his first subadviser, Ostrowski uses the CFA Institute model "request for proposal" to design a questionnaire for his search. By his deadline, he receives seven completed questionnaires from a variety of domestic and international firms trying to gain his business. Ostrowski reviews all the applications in detail and decides to select the firm that charges the lowest fees because doing so will have the least impact on his firm's bottom line.

> *Comment*: When selecting an external manager or subadviser, Ostrowski needs to ensure that the new manager's services are appropriate for his clients. This due diligence includes comparing the risk profile of the clients with the investment strategy of the manager. In basing the decision on the fee structure alone, Ostrowski may be violating Standard III(C).
>
> When clients ask to diversify into international products, it is an appropriate time to review and update the clients' IPSs. Ostrowski's review may determine that the risk of international investments modifies the risk profiles of the clients or does not represent an appropriate investment.
>
> See also Standard V(A) Diligence and Reasonable Basis for further discussion of the review process needed in selecting appropriate submanagers.

Example 7 (Investment Suitability—Risk Profile):

Samantha Snead, a portfolio manager for Thomas Investment Counsel, Inc., specializes in managing public retirement funds and defined benefit pension plan accounts, all of which have long-term investment objectives. A year ago, Snead's employer, in an attempt to motivate and retain key investment professionals, introduced a bonus compensation system that rewards portfolio managers on the basis of quarterly performance relative to their peers and to certain benchmark indexes. In an attempt to improve the short-term performance of her accounts, Snead changes her investment strategy and purchases several high-beta stocks for client portfolios. These purchases are seemingly contrary to the clients' investment policy statements. Following their purchase, an officer of Griffin Corporation, one of Snead's pension fund clients, asks why Griffin Corporation's portfolio seems to be dominated by high-beta stocks of companies that often appear among the most actively traded issues. No change in objective or strategy has been recommended by Snead during the year.

> *Comment*: Snead violated Standard III(C) by investing the clients' assets in high-beta stocks. These high-risk investments are contrary to the long-term risk profile established in the clients' IPSs. Snead has changed the investment strategy of the clients in an attempt to reap short-term rewards offered by her firm's new compensation arrangement, not in response to changes in clients' investment policy statements.
>
> See also Standard VI(A) Disclosure of Conflicts.

Example 8 (Investment Suitability):

Andre Shrub owns and operates Conduit, an investment advisory firm. Prior to opening Conduit, Shrub was an account manager with Elite Investment, a hedge fund managed by his good friend Adam Reed. To attract clients to a new Conduit fund, Shrub offers lower-than-normal management fees. He can do so because the fund consists of two top-performing funds managed by Reed. Given his personal friendship with Reed and the prior performance record of these two funds, Shrub believes this new fund is a winning combination for all parties. Clients quickly invest with Conduit to gain access to the Elite funds. No one is turned away because Conduit is seeking to expand its assets under management.

Comment: Shrub has violated Standard III(C) because the risk profile of the new fund may not be suitable for every client. As an investment adviser, Shrub needs to establish an investment policy statement for each client and recommend only investments that match each client's risk and return profile in the IPS. Shrub is required to act as more than a simple sales agent for Elite.

Although Shrub cannot disobey the direct request of a client to purchase a specific security, he should fully discuss the risks of a planned purchase and provide reasons why it might not be suitable for a client. This requirement may lead members and candidates to decline new customers if those customers' requested investment decisions are significantly out of line with their stated requirements.

See also Standard V(A) Diligence and Reasonable Basis.

30 STANDARD III(D) PERFORMANCE PRESENTATION

- [ ] demonstrate a thorough knowledge of the CFA Institute Code of Ethics and Standards of Professional Conduct by interpreting the Code and Standards in various situations involving issues of professional integrity
- [ ] recommend practices and procedures designed to prevent violations of the Code and Standards

When communicating investment performance information, Members and Candidates must make reasonable efforts to ensure that it is fair, accurate, and complete.

Guidance

Standard III(D) requires members and candidates to provide credible performance information to clients and prospective clients and to avoid misstating performance or misleading clients and prospective clients about the investment performance of members or candidates or their firms. This standard encourages full disclosure of investment performance data to clients and prospective clients.

Standard III(D) covers any practice that would lead to misrepresentation of a member's or candidate's performance record, whether the practice involves performance presentation or performance measurement. This standard prohibits misrepresentations of past performance or reasonably expected performance. A member or candidate must give a fair and complete presentation of performance information whenever communicating data with respect to the performance history of individual accounts, composites or groups of accounts, or composites of an analyst's or firm's performance results. Furthermore, members and candidates should not state or imply that clients will obtain or benefit from a rate of return that was generated in the past.

The requirements of this standard are not limited to members and candidates managing separate accounts. Whenever a member or candidate provides performance information for which the manager is claiming responsibility, such as for pooled funds, the history must be accurate. Research analysts promoting the success or accuracy of their recommendations must ensure that their claims are fair, accurate, and complete.

If the presentation is brief, the member or candidate must make available to clients and prospects, on request, the detailed information supporting that communication. Best practice dictates that brief presentations include a reference to the limited nature of the information provided.

STANDARD III(D): RECOMMENDED PROCEDURES

31

Apply the GIPS Standards

For members and candidates who are showing the performance history of the assets they manage, compliance with the GIPS standards is the best method to meet their obligations under Standard III(D). Members and candidates should encourage their firms to comply with the GIPS standards.

Compliance without Applying GIPS Standards

Members and candidates can also meet their obligations under Standard III(D) by

- considering the knowledge and sophistication of the audience to whom a performance presentation is addressed,
- presenting the performance of the weighted composite of similar portfolios rather than using a single representative account,
- including terminated accounts as part of performance history with a clear indication of when the accounts were terminated,
- including disclosures that fully explain the performance results being reported (for example, stating, when appropriate, that results are simulated when model results are used, clearly indicating when the performance record is that of a prior entity, or disclosing whether the performance is gross of fees, net of fees, or after tax), and
- maintaining the data and records used to calculate the performance being presented.

STANDARD III(D): APPLICATION OF THE STANDARD

32

Example 1 (Performance Calculation and Length of Time):

Kyle Taylor of Taylor Trust Company, noting the performance of Taylor's common trust fund for the past two years, states in a brochure sent to his potential clients, "You can expect steady 25% annual compound growth of the value of your investments over the year." Taylor Trust's common trust fund did increase at the rate of 25% per year for the past year, which mirrored the increase of the entire market. The fund has never averaged that growth for more than one year, however, and the average rate of growth of all of its trust accounts for five years is 5% per year.

> *Comment*: Taylor's brochure is in violation of Standard III(D). Taylor should have disclosed that the 25% growth occurred only in one year. Additionally, Taylor did not include client accounts other than those in the firm's common

trust fund. A general claim of firm performance should take into account the performance of all categories of accounts. Finally, by stating that clients can expect a steady 25% annual compound growth rate, Taylor is also violating Standard I(C) Misrepresentation, which prohibits assurances or guarantees regarding an investment.

Example 2 (Performance Calculation and Asset Weighting):

Anna Judd, a senior partner of Alexander Capital Management, circulates a performance report for the capital appreciation accounts for the years 1988 through 2004. The firm claims compliance with the GIPS standards. Returns are not calculated in accordance with the requirements of the GIPS standards, however, because the composites are not asset weighted.

Comment: Judd is in violation of Standard III(D). When claiming compliance with the GIPS standards, firms must meet *all* of the requirements, make mandatory disclosures, and meet any other requirements that apply to that firm's specific situation. Judd's violation is not from any misuse of the data but from a false claim of GIPS compliance.

Example 3 (Performance Presentation and Prior Fund/Employer):

Aaron McCoy is vice president and managing partner of the equity investment group of Mastermind Financial Advisors, a new business. Mastermind recruited McCoy because he had a proven six-year track record with G&P Financial. In developing Mastermind's advertising and marketing campaign, McCoy prepares an advertisement that includes the equity investment performance he achieved at G&P Financial. The advertisement for Mastermind does not identify the equity performance as being earned while at G&P. The advertisement is distributed to existing clients and prospective clients of Mastermind.

Comment: McCoy has violated Standard III(D) by distributing an advertisement that contains material misrepresentations about the historical performance of Mastermind. Standard III(D) requires that members and candidates make every reasonable effort to ensure that performance information is a fair, accurate, and complete representation of an individual's or firm's performance. As a general matter, this standard does not prohibit showing past performance of funds managed at a prior firm as part of a performance track record as long as showing that record is accompanied by appropriate disclosures about where the performance took place and the person's specific role in achieving that performance. If McCoy chooses to use his past performance from G&P in Mastermind's advertising, he should make full disclosure of the source of the historical performance.

Example 4 (Performance Presentation and Simulated Results):

Jed Davis has developed a mutual fund selection product based on historical information from the 1990–95 period. Davis tested his methodology by applying it retroactively to data from the 1996–2003 period, thus producing simulated performance results for those years. In January 2004, Davis's employer decided to offer the product and Davis began promoting it through trade journal advertisements and direct dissemination to clients. The advertisements included the performance results for the 1996–2003 period but did not indicate that the results were simulated.

> *Comment*: Davis violated Standard III(D) by failing to clearly identify simulated performance results. Standard III(D) prohibits members and candidates from making any statements that misrepresent the performance achieved by them or their firms and requires members and candidates to make every reasonable effort to ensure that performance information presented to clients is fair, accurate, and complete. Use of simulated results should be accompanied by full disclosure as to the source of the performance data, including the fact that the results from 1995 through 2003 were the result of applying the model retroactively to that time period.

Example 5 (Performance Calculation and Selected Accounts Only):

In a presentation prepared for prospective clients, William Kilmer shows the rates of return realized over a five-year period by a "composite" of his firm's discretionary accounts that have a "balanced" objective. This composite, however, consisted of only a few of the accounts that met the balanced criterion set by the firm, excluded accounts under a certain asset level without disclosing the fact of their exclusion, and included accounts that did not have the balanced mandate because those accounts would boost the investment results. In addition, to achieve better results, Kilmer manipulated the narrow range of accounts included in the composite by changing the accounts that made up the composite over time.

> *Comment*: Kilmer violated Standard III(D) by misrepresenting the facts in the promotional material sent to prospective clients, distorting his firm's performance record, and failing to include disclosures that would have clarified the presentation.

Example 6 (Performance Attribution Changes):

Art Purell is reviewing the quarterly performance attribution reports for distribution to clients. Purell works for an investment management firm with a bottom-up, fundamentals-driven investment process that seeks to add value through stock selection. The attribution methodology currently compares each stock with its sector. The attribution report indicates that the value added this quarter came from asset allocation and that stock selection contributed negatively to the calculated return.

Through running several different scenarios, Purell discovers that calculating attribution by comparing each stock with its industry and then rolling the effect to the sector level improves the appearance of the manager's stock selection activities. Because the firm defines the attribution terms and the results better reflect the stated strategy, Purell recommends that the client reports should use the revised methodology.

> *Comment*: Modifying the attribution methodology without proper notifications to clients would fail to meet the requirements of Standard III(D). Purell's recommendation is being done solely for the interest of the firm to improve its perceived ability to meet the stated investment strategy. Such changes are unfair to clients and obscure the facts regarding the firm's abilities.

Had Purell believed the new methodology offered improvements to the original model, then he would have needed to report the results of both calculations to the client. The report should also include the reasons why the new methodology is preferred, which would allow the client to make a meaningful comparison to prior results and provide a basis for comparing future attributions.

Example 7 (Performance Calculation Methodology Disclosure):

While developing a new reporting package for existing clients, Alisha Singh, a performance analyst, discovers that her company's new system automatically calculates both time-weighted and money-weighted returns. She asks the head of client services and retention which value would be preferred given that the firm has various investment strategies that include bonds, equities, securities without leverage, and alternatives. Singh is told not to label the return value so that the firm may show whichever value is greatest for the period.

Comment: Following these instructions would lead to Singh violating Standard III(D). In reporting inconsistent return values, Singh would not be providing complete information to the firm's clients. Full information is provided when clients have sufficient information to judge the performance generated by the firm.

Example 8 (Performance Calculation Methodology Disclosure):

Richmond Equity Investors manages a long–short equity fund in which clients can trade once a week (on Fridays). For transparency reasons, a daily net asset value of the fund is calculated by Richmond. The monthly fact sheets of the fund report month-to-date and year-to-date performance. Richmond publishes the performance based on the higher of the last trading day of the month (typically, not the last business day) or the last business day of the month as determined by Richmond. The fact sheet mentions only that the data are as of the end of the month, without giving the exact date. Maggie Clark, the investment performance analyst in charge of the calculations, is concerned about the frequent changes and asks her supervisor whether they are appropriate.

Comment: Clark's actions in questioning the changing performance metric comply with Standard III(D). She has shown concern that these changes are not presenting an accurate and complete picture of the performance generated.

STANDARD III(E) PRESERVATION OF CONFIDENTIALITY

33

- [ ] demonstrate a thorough knowledge of the CFA Institute Code of Ethics and Standards of Professional Conduct by interpreting the Code and Standards in various situations involving issues of professional integrity
- [ ] recommend practices and procedures designed to prevent violations of the Code and Standards

Members and Candidates must keep information about current, former, and prospective clients confidential unless:

1. The information concerns illegal activities on the part of the client;
2. Disclosure is required by law; or
3. The client or prospective client permits disclosure of the information.

Guidance

Highlights:

- *Status of Client*
- *Compliance with Laws*
- *Electronic Information and Security*
- *Professional Conduct Investigations by CFA Institute*

Standard III(E) requires that members and candidates preserve the confidentiality of information communicated to them by their clients, prospective clients, and former clients. This standard is applicable when (1) the member or candidate receives information because of his or her special ability to conduct a portion of the client's business or personal affairs and (2) the member or candidate receives information that arises from or is relevant to that portion of the client's business that is the subject of the special or confidential relationship. If disclosure of the information is required by law or the information concerns illegal activities by the client, however, the member or candidate may have an obligation to report the activities to the appropriate authorities.

Status of Client

This standard protects the confidentiality of client information even if the person or entity is no longer a client of the member or candidate. Therefore, members and candidates must continue to maintain the confidentiality of client records even after the client relationship has ended. If a client or former client expressly authorizes the member or candidate to disclose information, however, the member or candidate may follow the terms of the authorization and provide the information.

Compliance with Laws

As a general matter, members and candidates must comply with applicable law. If applicable law requires disclosure of client information in certain circumstances, members and candidates must comply with the law. Similarly, if applicable law requires members and candidates to maintain confidentiality, even if the information concerns illegal activities on the part of the client, members and candidates should not disclose such information. Additionally, applicable laws, such as inter-departmental communication restrictions within financial institutions, can impose limitations on information flow about a client within an entity that may lead to a violation of confidentiality. When in doubt, members and candidates should consult with their employer's compliance personnel or legal counsel before disclosing confidential information about clients.

Electronic Information and Security

Because of the ever-increasing volume of electronically stored information, members and candidates need to be particularly aware of possible accidental disclosures. Many employers have strict policies about how to electronically communicate sensitive client information and store client information on personal laptops, mobile devices, or portable disk/flash drives. In recent years, regulatory authorities have imposed stricter data security laws applying to the use of mobile remote digital communication, including the use of social media, that must be considered. Standard III(E) does not require members or candidates to become experts in information security technology, but they should have a thorough understanding of the policies of their employer. The size and operations of the firm will lead to differing policies for ensuring the security of confidential information maintained within the firm. Members and candidates should encourage their firm to conduct regular periodic training on confidentiality procedures for all firm personnel, including portfolio associates, receptionists, and other non-investment staff who have routine direct contact with clients and their records.

Professional Conduct Investigations by CFA Institute

The requirements of Standard III(E) are not intended to prevent members and candidates from cooperating with an investigation by the CFA Institute Professional Conduct Program (PCP). When permissible under applicable law, members and candidates shall consider the PCP an extension of themselves when requested to provide information about a client in support of a PCP investigation into their own conduct. Members and candidates are encouraged to cooperate with investigations into the conduct of others. Any information turned over to the PCP is kept in the strictest confidence. Members and candidates will not be considered in violation of this standard by forwarding confidential information to the PCP.

34 STANDARD III(E): RECOMMENDED PROCEDURES

The simplest, most conservative, and most effective way to comply with Standard III(E) is to avoid disclosing any information received from a client except to authorized fellow employees who are also working for the client. In some instances, however, a member or candidate may want to disclose information received from clients that is outside the scope of the confidential relationship and does not involve illegal activities. Before making such a disclosure, a member or candidate should ask the following:

- In what context was the information disclosed? If disclosed in a discussion of work being performed for the client, is the information relevant to the work?
- Is the information background material that, if disclosed, will enable the member or candidate to improve service to the client?

Members and candidates need to understand and follow their firm's electronic information communication and storage procedures. If the firm does not have procedures in place, members and candidates should encourage the development of procedures that appropriately reflect the firm's size and business operations.

Communicating with Clients

Technological changes are constantly enhancing the methods that are used to communicate with clients and prospective clients. Members and candidates should make reasonable efforts to ensure that firm-supported communication methods and compliance procedures follow practices designed for preventing accidental distribution of confidential information. Given the rate at which technology changes, a regular review of privacy protection measures is encouraged.

Members and candidates should be diligent in discussing with clients the appropriate methods for providing confidential information. It is important to convey to clients that not all firm-sponsored resources may be appropriate for such communications.

STANDARD III(E): APPLICATION OF THE STANDARD 35

Example 1 (Possessing Confidential Information):

Sarah Connor, a financial analyst employed by Johnson Investment Counselors, Inc., provides investment advice to the trustees of City Medical Center. The trustees have given her a number of internal reports concerning City Medical's needs for physical plant renovation and expansion. They have asked Connor to recommend investments that would generate capital appreciation in endowment funds to meet projected capital expenditures. Connor is approached by a local businessman, Thomas Kasey, who is considering a substantial contribution either to City Medical Center or to another local hospital. Kasey wants to find out the building plans of both institutions before making a decision, but he does not want to speak to the trustees.

> *Comment*: The trustees gave Connor the internal reports so she could advise them on how to manage their endowment funds. Because the information in the reports is clearly both confidential and within the scope of the confidential relationship, Standard III(E) requires that Connor refuse to divulge information to Kasey.

Example 2 (Disclosing Confidential Information):

Lynn Moody is an investment officer at the Lester Trust Company. She has an advisory customer who has talked to her about giving approximately US$50,000 to charity to reduce her income taxes. Moody is also treasurer of the Home for Indigent Widows (HIW), which is planning its annual giving campaign. HIW hopes to expand its list of prospects, particularly those capable of substantial gifts. Moody recommends that HIW's vice president for corporate gifts call on her customer and ask for a donation in the US$50,000 range.

> *Comment*: Even though the attempt to help the Home for Indigent Widows was well intended, Moody violated Standard III(E) by revealing confidential information about her client.

Example 3 (Disclosing Possible Illegal Activity):

Government officials approach Casey Samuel, the portfolio manager for Garcia Company's pension plan, to examine pension fund records. They tell her that Garcia's corporate tax returns are being audited and the pension fund is being reviewed. Two days earlier, Samuel had learned in a regular investment review with Garcia officers that potentially excessive and improper charges were being made to the pension plan by Garcia. Samuel consults her employer's general counsel and is advised that Garcia has probably violated tax and fiduciary regulations and laws.

> *Comment*: Samuel should inform her supervisor of these activities, and her employer should take steps, with Garcia, to remedy the violations. If that approach is not successful, Samuel and her employer should seek advice of legal counsel to determine the appropriate steps to be taken. Samuel may well have a duty to disclose the evidence she has of the continuing legal violations and to resign as asset manager for Garcia.

Example 4 (Disclosing Possible Illegal Activity):

David Bradford manages money for a family-owned real estate development corporation. He also manages the individual portfolios of several of the family members and officers of the corporation, including the chief financial officer (CFO). Based on the financial records of the corporation and some questionable practices of the CFO that Bradford has observed, Bradford believes that the CFO is embezzling money from the corporation and putting it into his personal investment account.

> *Comment*: Bradford should check with his firm's compliance department or appropriate legal counsel to determine whether applicable securities regulations require reporting the CFO's financial records.

Example 5 (Accidental Disclosure of Confidential Information):

Lynn Moody is an investment officer at the Lester Trust Company (LTC). She has stewardship of a significant number of individually managed taxable accounts. In addition to receiving quarterly written reports, about a dozen high-net-worth individuals have indicated to Moody a willingness to receive communications about overall economic and financial market outlooks directly from her by way of a social media platform. Under the direction of her firm's technology and compliance departments, she established a new group page on an existing social media platform specifically for her clients. In the instructions provided to clients, Moody asked them to "join" the group so they may be granted access to the posted content. The instructions also advised clients that all comments posted would be available to the public and thus the platform was not an appropriate method for communicating personal or confidential information.

Six months later, in early January, Moody posted LTC's year-end "Market Outlook." The report outlined a new asset allocation strategy that the firm is adding to its recommendations in the new year. Moody introduced the publication with a note informing her clients that she would be discussing the changes with them individually in their upcoming meetings.

One of Moody's clients responded directly on the group page that his family recently experienced a major change in their financial profile. The client described highly personal and confidential details of the event. Unfortunately, all clients that were part of the group were also able to read the detailed posting until Moody was able to have the comment removed.

Comment: Moody has taken reasonable steps for protecting the confidentiality of client information while using the social media platform. She provided instructions clarifying that all information posted to the site would be publicly viewable to all group members and warned against using this method for communicating confidential information. The accidental disclosure of confidential information by a client is not under Moody's control. Her actions to remove the information promptly once she became aware further align with Standard III(E).

In understanding the potential sensitivity clients express surrounding the confidentiality of personal information, this event highlights a need for further training. Moody might advocate for additional warnings or controls for clients when they consider using social media platforms for two-way communications.

STANDARD IV: DUTIES TO EMPLOYERS

36

- ☐ demonstrate a thorough knowledge of the CFA Institute Code of Ethics and Standards of Professional Conduct by interpreting the Code and Standards in various situations involving issues of professional integrity
- ☐ recommend practices and procedures designed to prevent violations of the Code and Standards

Standard IV(A) Loyalty

In matters related to their employment, Members and Candidates must act for the benefit of their employer and not deprive their employer of the advantage of their skills and abilities, divulge confidential information, or otherwise cause harm to their employer.

Guidance

Highlights:

- *Employer Responsibilities*
- *Independent Practice*
- *Leaving an Employer*
- *Use of Social Media*
- *Whistleblowing*
- *Nature of Employment*

Standard IV(A) requires members and candidates to protect the interests of their firm by refraining from any conduct that would injure the firm, deprive it of profit, or deprive it of the member's or candidate's skills and ability. Members and candidates must always place the interests of clients above the interests of their employer but should also consider the effects of their conduct on the sustainability and integrity of the employer firm. In matters related to their employment, members and candidates must not engage in conduct that harms the interests of their employer. Implicit in this standard is the obligation of members and candidates to comply with the policies and procedures established by their employers that govern the employer–employee relationship—to the extent that such policies and procedures do not conflict with applicable laws, rules, or regulations or the Code and Standards.

This standard is not meant to be a blanket requirement to place employer interests ahead of personal interests in all matters. The standard does not require members and candidates to subordinate important personal and family obligations to their work. Members and candidates should enter into a dialogue with their employer about balancing personal and employment obligations when personal matters may interfere with their work on a regular or significant basis.

Employer Responsibilities

The employer–employee relationship imposes duties and responsibilities on both parties. Employers must recognize the duties and responsibilities that they owe to their employees if they expect to have content and productive employees.

Members and candidates are encouraged to provide their employer with a copy of the Code and Standards. These materials will inform the employer of the responsibilities of a CFA Institute member or a candidate in the CFA Program. The Code and Standards also serve as a basis for questioning employer policies and practices that conflict with these responsibilities.

Employers are not obligated to adhere to the Code and Standards. In expecting to retain competent employees who are members and candidates, however, they should not develop conflicting policies and procedures. The employer is responsible for a positive working environment, which includes an ethical workplace. Senior management has the additional responsibility to devise compensation structures and incentive arrangements that do not encourage unethical behavior.

Independent Practice

Included in Standard IV(A) is the requirement that members and candidates abstain from independent competitive activity that could conflict with the interests of their employer. Although Standard IV(A) does not preclude members or candidates from entering into an independent business while still employed, members and candidates who plan to engage in independent practice for compensation must notify their employer and describe the types of services they will render to prospective independent clients, the expected duration of the services, and the compensation for the services. Members and candidates should not render services until they receive consent from their employer to all of the terms of the arrangement. "Practice" means any service that the employer currently makes available for remuneration. "Undertaking independent practice" means engaging in competitive business, as opposed to making preparations to begin such practice.

Leaving an Employer

When members and candidates are planning to leave their current employer, they must continue to act in the employer's best interest. They must not engage in any activities that would conflict with this duty until their resignation becomes effective. It is difficult to define specific guidelines for those members and candidates who are planning to compete with their employer as part of a new venture. The circumstances of each situation must be reviewed to distinguish permissible preparations from violations of duty. Activities that might constitute a violation, especially in combination, include the following:

- misappropriation of trade secrets,
- misuse of confidential information,
- solicitation of the employer's clients prior to cessation of employment,
- self-dealing (appropriating for one's own property a business opportunity or information belonging to one's employer), and
- misappropriation of clients or client lists.

A departing employee is generally free to make arrangements or preparations to go into a competitive business before terminating the relationship with his or her employer as long as such preparations do not breach the employee's duty of loyalty. A member or candidate who is contemplating seeking other employment must not contact existing clients or potential clients prior to leaving his or her employer for purposes of soliciting their business for the new employer. Once notice is provided to the employer of the intent to resign, the member or candidate must follow the employer's policies and procedures related to notifying clients of his or her planned departure. In addition, the member or candidate must not take records or files to a new employer without the written permission of the previous employer.

Once an employee has left the firm, the skills and experience that an employee obtained while employed are not "confidential" or "privileged" information. Similarly, simple knowledge of the names and existence of former clients is generally not confidential information unless deemed such by an agreement or by law. Standard IV(A) does not prohibit experience or knowledge gained at one employer from being used at another employer. Firm records or work performed on behalf of the firm that is stored in paper copy or electronically for the member's or candidate's convenience while employed, however, should be erased or returned to the employer unless the firm gives permission to keep those records after employment ends.

The standard does not prohibit former employees from contacting clients of their previous firm as long as the contact information does not come from the records of the former employer or violate an applicable "noncompete agreement." Members and candidates are free to use public information after departing to contact former clients without violating Standard IV(A) as long as there is no specific agreement not to do so.

Employers often require employees to sign noncompete agreements that preclude a departing employee from engaging in certain conduct. Members and candidates should take care to review the terms of any such agreement when leaving their employer to determine what, if any, conduct those agreements may prohibit.

In some markets, there are agreements between employers within an industry that outline information that departing employees are permitted to take upon resignation, such as the "Protocol for Broker Recruiting" in the United States. These agreements ease individuals' transition between firms that have agreed to follow the outlined procedures. Members and candidates who move between firms that sign such agreements may rely on the protections provided as long as they faithfully adhere to all the procedures outlined.

For example, under the agreement between many US brokers, individuals are allowed to take some general client contact information when departing. To be protected, a copy of the information the individual is taking must be provided to the local management team for review. Additionally, the specific client information may only be used by the departing employee and not others employed by the new firm.

Use of Social Media

The growth in various online networking platforms, such as LinkedIn, X, and Facebook (commonly referred to as social media platforms), is providing new opportunities and challenges for businesses. Members and candidates should understand and abide by all applicable firm policies and regulations as to the acceptable use of social media platforms to interact with clients and prospective clients. This is especially important when a member or candidate is planning to leave an employer.

Social media use makes determining how and when departure notification is delivered to clients more complex. Members and candidates may have developed profiles on these platforms that include connections with individuals who are clients of the firm, as well as individuals unrelated to their employer. Communications through social media platforms that potentially reach current clients should adhere to the employer's policies and procedures regarding notification of departing employees.

Social media connections with clients are also raising questions concerning the differences between public information and firm property. Specific accounts and user profiles of members and candidates may be created for solely professional reasons, including firm-approved accounts for client engagements. Such firm-approved business-related accounts would be considered part of the firm's assets, thus requiring members and candidates to transfer or delete the accounts as directed by their firm's policies and procedures. Best practice for members and candidates is to maintain separate accounts for their personal and professional social media activities. Members and candidates should discuss with their employers how profiles should be treated when a single account includes personal connections and also is used to conduct aspects of their professional activities.

Whistleblowing

A member's or candidate's personal interests, as well as the interests of his or her employer, are secondary to protecting the integrity of capital markets and the interests of clients. Therefore, circumstances may arise (e.g., when an employer is engaged in illegal or unethical activity) in which members and candidates must act contrary to their employer's interests in order to comply with their duties to the market and clients. In such instances, activities that would normally violate a member's or candidate's duty to his or her employer (such as contradicting employer instructions, violating certain policies and procedures, or preserving a record by copying employer records) may be justified. Such action would be permitted only if the intent is clearly aimed at protecting clients or the integrity of the market, not for personal gain.

Nature of Employment

A wide variety of business relationships exists within the investment industry. For instance, a member or candidate may be an employee or an independent contractor. Members and candidates must determine whether they are employees or independent contractors in order to determine the applicability of Standard IV(A). This issue will be decided largely by the degree of control exercised by the employing entity over the member or candidate. Factors determining control include whether the member's or candidate's hours, work location, and other parameters of the job are set; whether facilities are provided to the member or candidate; whether the member's or candidate's expenses are reimbursed; whether the member or candidate seeks work from other employers; and the number of clients or employers the member or candidate works for.

A member's or candidate's duties within an independent contractor relationship are governed by the oral or written agreement between the member and the client. Members and candidates should take care to define clearly the scope of their responsibilities and the expectations of each client within the context of each relationship. Once a member or candidate establishes a relationship with a client, the member or candidate has a duty to abide by the terms of the agreement.

STANDARD IV(A): RECOMMENDED PROCEDURES

37

Employers may establish codes of conduct and operating procedures for their employees to follow. Members and candidates should fully understand the policies to ensure that they are not in conflict with the Code and Standards. The following topics identify policies that members and candidates should encourage their firms to adopt if the policies are not currently in place.

Competition Policy

A member or candidate must understand any restrictions placed by the employer on offering similar services outside the firm while employed by the firm. The policy may outline the procedures for requesting approval to undertake the outside service or may be a strict prohibition of such service. If a member's or candidate's employer elects to have its employees sign a noncompete agreement as part of the employment agreement, the member or candidate should ensure that the details are clear and fully explained prior to signing the agreement.

Termination Policy

Members and candidates should clearly understand the termination policies of their employer. Termination policies should establish clear procedures regarding the resignation process, including addressing how the termination will be disclosed to clients and staff and whether updates posted through social media platforms will be allowed. The firm's policy may also outline the procedures for transferring ongoing research and account management responsibilities. Finally, the procedures should address agreements that allow departing employees to remove specific client-related information upon resignation.

Incident-Reporting Procedures

Members and candidates should be aware of their firm's policies related to whistleblowing and encourage their firm to adopt industry best practices in this area. Many firms are required by regulatory mandates to establish confidential and anonymous reporting procedures that allow employees to report potentially unethical and illegal activities in the firm.

Employee Classification

Members and candidates should understand their status within their employer firm. Firms are encouraged to adopt a standardized classification structure (e.g., part time, full time, outside contractor) for their employees and indicate how each of the firm's policies applies to each employee class.

38 STANDARD IV(A): APPLICATION OF THE STANDARD

- ☐ demonstrate a thorough knowledge of the CFA Institute Code of Ethics and Standards of Professional Conduct by interpreting the Code and Standards in various situations involving issues of professional integrity
- ☐ recommend practices and procedures designed to prevent violations of the Code and Standards

Example 1 (Soliciting Former Clients):

Samuel Magee manages pension accounts for Trust Assets, Inc., but has become frustrated with the working environment and has been offered a position with Fiduciary Management. Before resigning from Trust Assets, Magee asks four big accounts to leave that firm and open accounts with Fiduciary. Magee also persuades several prospective clients to sign agreements with Fiduciary Management. Magee had previously made presentations to these prospects on behalf of Trust Assets.

> *Comment*: Magee violated the employee–employer principle requiring him to act solely for his employer's benefit. Magee's duty is to Trust Assets as long as he is employed there. The solicitation of Trust Assets' current clients and prospective clients is unethical and violates Standard IV(A).

Example 2 (Former Employer's Documents and Files):

James Hightower has been employed by Jason Investment Management Corporation for 15 years. He began as an analyst but assumed increasing responsibilities and is now a senior portfolio manager and a member of the firm's investment policy committee. Hightower has decided to leave Jason Investment and start his own investment management business. He has been careful not to tell any of Jason's clients that he is leaving; he does not want to be accused of breaching his duty to Jason by soliciting Jason's clients before his departure. Hightower is planning to copy and take with him the following documents and information he developed or worked on while at Jason: (1) the client list, with addresses, telephone numbers, and other pertinent client information; (2) client account statements; (3) sample marketing presentations to prospective clients containing Jason's performance record; (4) Jason's recommended list of securities; (5) computer models to determine asset allocations for accounts with various objectives; (6) computer models for stock selection; and (7) personal computer spreadsheets for Hightower's major corporate recommendations, which he developed when he was an analyst.

> *Comment*: Except with the consent of their employer, departing members and candidates may not take employer property, which includes books, records, reports, and other materials, because taking such materials may interfere with their employer's business opportunities. Taking any employer records, even those the member or candidate prepared, violates Standard IV(A). Employer records include items stored in hard copy or any other medium (e.g., home computers, portable storage devices, cell phones).

Example 3 (Addressing Rumors):

Reuben Winston manages all-equity portfolios at Target Asset Management (TAM), a large, established investment counselor. Ten years previously, Philpott & Company, which manages a family of global bond mutual funds, acquired TAM in a diversification move. After the merger, the combined operations prospered in the fixed-income business but the equity management business at TAM languished. Lately, a few of the equity pension accounts that had been with TAM before the merger have terminated their relationships with TAM. One day, Winston finds on his voice mail the following message from a concerned client: "Hey! I just heard that Philpott is close to announcing the sale of your firm's equity management business to Rugged Life. What is going on?" Not being aware of any such deal, Winston and his associates are stunned. Their internal inquiries are met with denials from Philpott management, but the rumors persist. Feeling left in the dark, Winston contemplates leading an employee buyout of TAM's equity management business.

> *Comment*: An employee-led buyout of TAM's equity asset management business would be consistent with Standard IV(A) because it would rest on the permission of the employer and, ultimately, the clients. In this case, however, in which employees suspect the senior managers or principals are not truthful or forthcoming, Winston should consult legal counsel to determine appropriate action.

Example 4 (Ownership of Completed Prior Work):

Laura Clay, who is unemployed, wants part-time consulting work while seeking a full-time analyst position. During an interview at Bradley Associates, a large institutional asset manager, Clay is told that the firm has no immediate research openings but would be willing to pay her a flat fee to complete a study of the wireless communications industry within a given period of time. Clay would be allowed unlimited access to Bradley's research files and would be welcome to come to the offices and use whatever support facilities are available during normal working hours. Bradley's research director does not seek any exclusivity for Clay's output, and the two agree to the arrangement on a handshake. As Clay nears completion of the study, she is offered an analyst job in the research department of Winston & Company, a brokerage firm, and she is pondering submitting the draft of her wireless study for publication by Winston.

> *Comment*: Although she is under no written contractual obligation to Bradley, Clay has an obligation to let Bradley act on the output of her study before Winston & Company or Clay uses the information to their advantage. That is, unless Bradley gives permission to Clay and waives its rights to her wireless report, Clay would be in violation of Standard IV(A) if she were to immediately recommend to Winston the same transactions recommended in the report to Bradley. Furthermore, Clay must not take from Bradley any research file material or other property that she may have used.

Example 5 (Ownership of Completed Prior Work):

Emma Madeline, a recent college graduate and a candidate in the CFA Program, spends her summer as an unpaid intern at Murdoch and Lowell. The senior managers at Murdoch are attempting to bring the firm into compliance with the GIPS standards, and Madeline is assigned to assist in its efforts. Two months into her internship, Madeline applies for a job at McMillan & Company, which has plans to become GIPS compliant. Madeline accepts the job with McMillan. Before leaving Murdoch, she copies the firm's software that she helped develop because she believes this software will assist her in her new position.

Comment: Even though Madeline does not receive monetary compensation for her services at Murdoch, she has used firm resources in creating the software and is considered an employee because she receives compensation and benefits in the form of work experience and knowledge. By copying the software, Madeline violated Standard IV(A) because she misappropriated Murdoch's property without permission.

Example 6 (Soliciting Former Clients):

Dennis Elliot has hired Sam Chisolm, who previously worked for a competing firm. Chisolm left his former firm after 18 years of employment. When Chisolm begins working for Elliot, he wants to contact his former clients because he knows them well and is certain that many will follow him to his new employer. Is Chisolm in violation of Standard IV(A) if he contacts his former clients?

Comment: Because client records are the property of the firm, contacting former clients for any reason through the use of client lists or other information taken from a former employer without permission would be a violation of Standard IV(A). In addition, the nature and extent of the contact with former clients may be governed by the terms of any noncompete agreement signed by the employee and the former employer that covers contact with former clients after employment.

Simple knowledge of the names and existence of former clients is not confidential information, just as skills or experience that an employee obtains while employed are not "confidential" or "privileged" information. The Code and Standards do not impose a prohibition on the use of experience or knowledge gained at one employer from being used at another employer. The Code and Standards also do not prohibit former employees from contacting clients of their previous firm, in the absence of a noncompete agreement. Members and candidates are free to use public information about their former firm after departing to contact former clients without violating Standard IV(A).

In the absence of a noncompete agreement, as long as Chisolm maintains his duty of loyalty to his employer before joining Elliot's firm, does not take steps to solicit clients until he has left his former firm, and does not use material from his former employer without its permission after he has left, he is not in violation of the Code and Standards.

Example 7 (Starting a New Firm):

Geraldine Allen currently works at a registered investment company as an equity analyst. Without notice to her employer, she registers with government authorities to start an investment company that will compete with her employer, but she does not actively seek clients. Does registration of this competing company with the appropriate regulatory authorities constitute a violation of Standard IV(A)?

Comment: Allen's preparation for the new business by registering with the regulatory authorities does not conflict with the work for her employer if the preparations have been done on Allen's own time outside the office and if Allen will not be soliciting clients for the business or otherwise operating the new company until she has left her current employer.

Example 8 (Competing with Current Employer):

Several employees are planning to depart their current employer within a few weeks and have been careful to not engage in any activities that would conflict with their duty to their current employer. They have just learned that one of their employer's clients has undertaken a request for proposal (RFP) to review and possibly hire a new investment consultant. The RFP has been sent to the employer and all of its competitors. The group believes that the new entity to be formed would be qualified to respond to the RFP and be eligible for the business. The RFP submission period is likely to conclude before the employees' resignations are effective. Is it permissible for the group of departing employees to respond to the RFP for their anticipated new firm?

Comment: A group of employees responding to an RFP that their employer is also responding to would lead to direct competition between the employees and the employer. Such conduct violates Standard IV(A) unless the group of employees receives permission from their employer as well as the entity sending out the RFP.

Example 9 (Externally Compensated Assignments):

Alfonso Mota is a research analyst with Tyson Investments. He works part time as a mayor for his hometown, a position for which he receives compensation. Must Mota seek permission from Tyson to serve as mayor?

Comment: If Mota's mayoral duties are so extensive and time-consuming that they might detract from his ability to fulfill his responsibilities at Tyson, he should discuss his outside activities with his employer and come to a mutual agreement regarding how to manage his personal commitments with his responsibilities to his employer.

Example 10 (Soliciting Former Clients):

After leaving her employer, Shawna McQuillen establishes her own money management business. While with her former employer, she did not sign a noncompete agreement that would have prevented her from soliciting former clients. Upon her departure, she does not take any of her client lists or contact information and she clears her personal computer of any employer records, including client contact information. She obtains the phone numbers of her former clients through public records and contacts them to solicit their business.

Comment: McQuillen is not in violation of Standard IV(A) because she has not used information or records from her former employer and is not prevented by an agreement with her former employer from soliciting her former clients.

Example 11 (Whistleblowing Actions):

Meredith Rasmussen works on a buy-side trading desk and concentrates on in-house trades for a hedge fund subsidiary managed by a team at the investment management firm. The hedge fund has been very successful and is marketed globally by the firm. From her experience as the trader for much of the activity of the fund, Rasmussen has become quite knowledgeable about the hedge fund's strategy, tactics, and performance. When a distinct break in the market occurs, however, and many of the securities involved in the hedge fund's strategy decline markedly in value, Rasmussen observes that the reported performance of the hedge fund does not reflect this decline. In her experience, the lack of any effect is a very unlikely occurrence. She approaches the head of trading about her concern and is told that she should not ask any questions and that the fund is big and successful and is not her concern. She is fairly sure something is not right, so she contacts the compliance officer, who also tells her to stay away from the issue of this hedge fund's reporting.

> *Comment*: Rasmussen has clearly come upon an error in policies, procedures, and compliance practices in the firm's operations. Having been unsuccessful in finding a resolution with her supervisor and the compliance officer, Rasmussen should consult the firm's whistleblowing policy to determine the appropriate next step toward informing management of her concerns. The potentially unethical actions of the investment management division are appropriate grounds for further disclosure, so Rasmussen's whistleblowing would not represent a violation of Standard IV(A).
>
> See also Standard I(D) Misconduct and Standard IV(C) Responsibilities of Supervisors.

Example 12 (Soliciting Former Clients):

Angel Crome has been a private banker for YBSafe Bank for the past eight years. She has been very successful and built a considerable client portfolio during that time but is extremely frustrated by the recent loss of reputation by her current employer and subsequent client insecurity. A locally renowned headhunter contacted Crome a few days ago and offered her an interesting job with a competing private bank. This bank offers a substantial signing bonus for advisers with their own client portfolios. Crome figures that she can solicit at least 70% of her clients to follow her and gladly enters into the new employment contract.

> *Comment*: Crome may contact former clients upon termination of her employment with YBSafe Bank, but she is prohibited from using client records built by and kept with her in her capacity as an employee of YBSafe Bank. Client lists are proprietary information of her former employer and must not be used for her or her new employer's benefit. The use of written, electronic, or any other form of records other than publicly available information to contact her former clients at YBSafe Bank will be a violation of Standard IV(A).

Example 13 (Notification of Code and Standards):

Krista Smith is a relatively new assistant trader for the fixed-income desk of a major investment bank. She is on a team responsible for structuring collateralized debt obligations (CDOs) made up of securities in the inventory of the trading desk. At a meeting of the team, senior executives explain the opportunity to eventually separate the CDO into various risk-rated tranches to be sold to the clients of the firm. After the senior executives leave the meeting, the head trader announces various responsibilities of each member of the team and then says, "This is a good time to unload some of the junk we have been stuck with for a while and disguise it with ratings and a thick, unreadable prospectus, so don't be shy in putting this CDO together. Just kidding." Smith is worried by this remark and asks some of her colleagues what the head trader meant. They all respond that he was just kidding but that there is some truth in the remark because the CDO is seen by management as an opportunity to improve the quality of the securities in the firm's inventory.

Concerned about the ethical environment of the workplace, Smith decides to talk to her supervisor about her concerns and provides the head trader with a copy of the Code and Standards. Smith discusses the principle of placing the client above the interest of the firm and the possibility that the development of the new CDO will not adhere to this responsibility. The head trader assures Smith that the appropriate analysis will be conducted when determining the appropriate securities for collateral. Furthermore, the ratings are assigned by an independent firm and the prospectus will include full and factual disclosures. Smith is reassured by the meeting, but she also reviews the company's procedures and requirements for reporting potential violations of company policy and securities laws.

> *Comment*: Smith's review of the company policies and procedures for reporting violations allows her to be prepared to report through the appropriate whistleblower process if she decides that the CDO development process involves unethical actions by others. Smith's actions comply with the Code and Standards principles of placing the client's interests first and being loyal to her employer. In providing her supervisor with a copy of the Code and Standards, Smith is highlighting the high level of ethical conduct she is required to adhere to in her professional activities.

Example 14 (Leaving an Employer):

Laura Webb just left her position as portfolio analyst at Research Systems, Inc. (RSI). Her employment contract included a non-solicitation agreement that requires her to wait two years before soliciting RSI clients for any investment-related services. Upon leaving, Webb was informed that RSI would contact clients immediately about her departure and introduce her replacement.

While working at RSI, Webb connected with clients, other industry associates, and friends through her LinkedIn network. Her business and personal relationships were intermingled because she considered many of her clients to be personal friends. Realizing that her LinkedIn network would be a valuable resource for new employment opportunities, she updated her profile several days following her departure from RSI. LinkedIn automatically sent a notification to Webb's entire network that her employment status had been changed in her profile.

> *Comment*: Prior to her departure, Webb should have discussed any client information contained in her social media networks. By updating her LinkedIn profile after RSI notified clients and after her employment ended, she has appropriately placed her employer's interests ahead of her own personal interests. In addition, she has not violated the non-solicitation agreement with RSI, unless it prohibited any contact with clients during the two-year period.

Example 15 (Confidential Firm Information):

Sanjay Gupta is a research analyst at Naram Investment Management (NIM). NIM uses a team-based research process to develop recommendations on investment opportunities covered by the team members. Gupta, like others, provides commentary for NIM's clients through the company blog, which is posted weekly on the NIM password-protected website. According to NIM's policy, every contribution to the website must be approved by the company's compliance department before posting. Any opinions expressed on the website are disclosed as representing the perspective of NIM.

Gupta also writes a personal blog to share his experiences with friends and family. As with most blogs, Gupta's personal blog is widely available to interested readers through various internet search engines. Occasionally, when he disagrees with the team-based research opinions of NIM, Gupta uses his personal blog to express his own opinions as a counterpoint to the commentary posted on the NIM website. Gupta believes this provides his readers with a more complete perspective on these investment opportunities.

> *Comment*: Gupta is in violation of Standard IV(A) for disclosing confidential firm information through his personal blog. The recommendations on the firm's blog to clients are not freely available across the internet, but his personal blog post indirectly provides the firm's recommendations.
>
> Additionally, by posting research commentary on his personal blog, Gupta is using firm resources for his personal advantage. To comply with Standard IV(A), members and candidates must receive consent from their employer prior to using company resources.

39 STANDARD IV(B) ADDITIONAL COMPENSATION ARRANGEMENTS

> Members and Candidates must not accept gifts, benefits, compensation, or consideration that competes with or might reasonably be expected to create a conflict of interest with their employer's interest unless they obtain written consent from all parties involved.

Guidance

Standard IV(B) requires members and candidates to obtain permission from their employer before accepting compensation or other benefits from third parties for the services rendered to the employer or for any services that might create a conflict with their employer's interest. Compensation and benefits include direct compensation by the client and any indirect compensation or other benefits received from third parties. "Written consent" includes any form of communication that can be documented (for example, communication via e-mail that can be retrieved and documented).

Members and candidates must obtain permission for additional compensation/benefits because such arrangements may affect loyalties and objectivity and create potential conflicts of interest. Disclosure allows an employer to consider the outside arrangements when evaluating the actions and motivations of members and candidates.

Moreover, the employer is entitled to have full knowledge of all compensation/benefit arrangements so as to be able to assess the true cost of the services members or candidates are providing.

There may be instances in which a member or candidate is hired by an employer on a "part-time" basis. "Part-time" status applies to employees who do not commit the full number of hours required for a normal work week. Members and candidates should discuss possible limitations to their abilities to provide services that may be competitive with their employer during the negotiation and hiring process. The requirements of Standard IV(B) would be applicable to limitations identified at that time.

STANDARD IV(B): RECOMMENDED PROCEDURES 40

Members and candidates should make an immediate written report to their supervisor and compliance officer specifying any compensation they propose to receive for services in addition to the compensation or benefits received from their employer. The details of the report should be confirmed by the party offering the additional compensation, including performance incentives offered by clients. This written report should state the terms of any agreement under which a member or candidate will receive additional compensation; "terms" include the nature of the compensation, the approximate amount of compensation, and the duration of the agreement.

STANDARD IV(B): APPLICATION OF THE STANDARD 41

Example 1 (Notification of Client Bonus Compensation):

Geoff Whitman, a portfolio analyst for Adams Trust Company, manages the account of Carol Cochran, a client. Whitman is paid a salary by his employer, and Cochran pays the trust company a standard fee based on the market value of assets in her portfolio. Cochran proposes to Whitman that "any year that my portfolio achieves at least a 15% return before taxes, you and your wife can fly to Monaco at my expense and use my condominium during the third week of January." Whitman does not inform his employer of the arrangement and vacations in Monaco the following January as Cochran's guest.

> *Comment*: Whitman violated Standard IV(B) by failing to inform his employer in writing of this supplemental, contingent compensation arrangement. The nature of the arrangement could have resulted in partiality to Cochran's account, which could have detracted from Whitman's performance with respect to other accounts he handles for Adams Trust. Whitman must obtain the consent of his employer to accept such a supplemental benefit.

Example 2 (Notification of Outside Compensation):

Terry Jones sits on the board of directors of Exercise Unlimited, Inc. In return for his services on the board, Jones receives unlimited membership privileges for his family at all Exercise Unlimited facilities. Jones purchases Exercise Unlimited stock for the client accounts for which it is appropriate. Jones does not disclose this arrangement to his employer because he does not receive monetary compensation for his services to the board.

> *Comment*: Jones has violated Standard IV(B) by failing to disclose to his employer benefits received in exchange for his services on the board of directors. The nonmonetary compensation may create a conflict of interest in the same manner as being paid to serve as a director.

Example 3 (Prior Approval for Outside Compensation):

Jonathan Hollis is an analyst of oil-and-gas companies for Specialty Investment Management. He is currently recommending the purchase of ABC Oil Company shares and has published a long, well-thought-out research report to substantiate his recommendation. Several weeks after publishing the report, Hollis receives a call from the investor-relations office of ABC Oil saying that Thomas Andrews, CEO of the company, saw the report and really liked the analyst's grasp of the business and his company. The investor-relations officer invites Hollis to visit ABC Oil to discuss the industry further. ABC Oil offers to send a company plane to pick Hollis up and arrange for his accommodations while visiting. Hollis, after gaining the appropriate approvals, accepts the meeting with the CEO but declines the offered travel arrangements.

Several weeks later, Andrews and Hollis meet to discuss the oil business and Hollis's report. Following the meeting, Hollis joins Andrews and the investment relations officer for dinner at an upscale restaurant near ABC Oil's headquarters.

Upon returning to Specialty Investment Management, Hollis provides a full review of the meeting to the director of research, including a disclosure of the dinner attended.

> *Comment*: Hollis's actions did not violate Standard IV(B). Through gaining approval before accepting the meeting and declining the offered travel arrangements, Hollis sought to avoid any potential conflicts of interest between his company and ABC Oil. Because the location of the dinner was not available prior to arrival and Hollis notified his company of the dinner upon his return, accepting the dinner should not impair his objectivity. By disclosing the dinner, Hollis has enabled Specialty Investment Management to assess whether it has any impact on future reports and recommendations by Hollis related to ABC Oil.

42 STANDARD IV(C) RESPONSIBILITIES OF SUPERVISORS

- [ ] demonstrate a thorough knowledge of the CFA Institute Code of Ethics and Standards of Professional Conduct by interpreting the Code and Standards in various situations involving issues of professional integrity
- [ ] recommend practices and procedures designed to prevent violations of the Code and Standards

Members and Candidates must make reasonable efforts to ensure that anyone subject to their supervision or authority complies with applicable laws, rules, regulations, and the Code and Standards.

Guidance

Highlights:

- *System for Supervision*
- *Supervision Includes Detection*

Standard IV(C) states that members and candidates must promote actions by all employees under their supervision and authority to comply with applicable laws, rules, regulations, and firm policies and the Code and Standards.

Any investment professional who has employees subject to her or his control or influence—whether or not the employees are CFA Institute members, CFA charterholders, or candidates in the CFA Program—exercises supervisory responsibility. Members and candidates acting as supervisors must also have in-depth knowledge of the Code and Standards so that they can apply this knowledge in discharging their supervisory responsibilities.

The conduct that constitutes reasonable supervision in a particular case depends on the number of employees supervised and the work performed by those employees. Members and candidates with oversight responsibilities for large numbers of employees may not be able to personally evaluate the conduct of these employees on a continuing basis. These members and candidates may delegate supervisory duties to subordinates who directly oversee the other employees. A member's or candidate's responsibilities under Standard IV(C) include instructing those subordinates to whom supervision is delegated about methods to promote compliance, including preventing and detecting violations of laws, rules, regulations, firm policies, and the Code and Standards.

At a minimum, Standard IV(C) requires that members and candidates with supervisory responsibility make reasonable efforts to prevent and detect violations by ensuring the establishment of effective compliance systems. However, an effective compliance system goes beyond enacting a code of ethics, establishing policies and procedures to achieve compliance with the code and applicable law, and reviewing employee actions to determine whether they are following the rules.

To be effective supervisors, members and candidates should implement education and training programs on a recurring or regular basis for employees under their supervision. Such programs will assist the employees with meeting their professional obligations to practice in an ethical manner within the applicable legal system. Further, establishing incentives—monetary or otherwise—for employees not only to meet business goals but also to reward ethical behavior offers supervisors another way to assist employees in complying with their legal and ethical obligations.

Often, especially in large organizations, members and candidates may have supervisory responsibility but not the authority to establish or modify firm-wide compliance policies and procedures or incentive structures. Such limitations should not prevent a member or candidate from working with his or her own superiors and within the firm structure to develop and implement effective compliance tools, including but not limited to:

- a code of ethics,
- compliance policies and procedures,
- education and training programs,
- an incentive structure that rewards ethical conduct, and
- adoption of firm-wide best practice standards (e.g., the GIPS standards, the CFA Institute Asset Manager Code of Professional Conduct).

A member or candidate with supervisory responsibility should bring an inadequate compliance system to the attention of the firm's senior managers and recommend corrective action. If the member or candidate clearly cannot discharge supervisory responsibilities because of the absence of a compliance system or because of an inadequate compliance system, the member or candidate should decline in writing to accept supervisory responsibility until the firm adopts reasonable procedures to allow adequate exercise of supervisory responsibility.

System for Supervision

Members and candidates with supervisory responsibility must understand what constitutes an adequate compliance system for their firms and make reasonable efforts to see that appropriate compliance procedures are established, documented, communicated to covered personnel, and followed. "Adequate" procedures are those designed to meet industry standards, regulatory requirements, the requirements of the Code and Standards, and the circumstances of the firm. Once compliance procedures are established, the supervisor must also make reasonable efforts to ensure that the procedures are monitored and enforced.

To be effective, compliance procedures must be in place prior to the occurrence of a violation of the law or the Code and Standards. Although compliance procedures cannot be designed to anticipate every potential violation, they should be designed to anticipate the activities most likely to result in misconduct. Compliance programs must be appropriate for the size and nature of the organization. The member or candidate should review model compliance procedures or other industry programs to ensure that the firm's procedures meet the minimum industry standards.

Once a supervisor learns that an employee has violated or may have violated the law or the Code and Standards, the supervisor must promptly initiate an assessment to determine the extent of the wrongdoing. Relying on an employee's statements about the extent of the violation or assurances that the wrongdoing will not reoccur is not enough. Reporting the misconduct up the chain of command and warning the employee to cease the activity are also not enough. Pending the outcome of the investigation, a supervisor should take steps to ensure that the violation will not be repeated, such as placing limits on the employee's activities or increasing the monitoring of the employee's activities.

Supervision Includes Detection

Members and candidates with supervisory responsibility must also make reasonable efforts to detect violations of laws, rules, regulations, firm policies, and the Code and Standards. The supervisors exercise reasonable supervision by establishing and implementing written compliance procedures and ensuring that those procedures are followed through periodic review. If a member or candidate has adopted reasonable procedures and taken steps to institute an effective compliance program, then the member or candidate may not be in violation of Standard IV(C) if he or she does not detect violations that occur despite these efforts. The fact that violations do occur may indicate, however, that the compliance procedures are inadequate. In addition, in some cases, merely enacting such procedures may not be sufficient to fulfill the duty required by Standard IV(C). A member or candidate may be in violation of Standard IV(C) if he or she knows or should know that the procedures designed to promote compliance, including detecting and preventing violations, are not being followed.

STANDARD IV(C): RECOMMENDED PROCEDURES

43

Codes of Ethics or Compliance Procedures

Members and candidates are encouraged to recommend that their employers adopt a code of ethics. Adoption of a code of ethics is critical to establishing a strong ethical foundation for investment advisory firms and their employees. Codes of ethics formally emphasize and reinforce the client loyalty responsibilities of investment firm personnel, protect investing clients by deterring misconduct, and protect the firm's reputation for integrity.

There is a distinction, however, between codes of ethics and the specific policies and procedures needed to ensure compliance with the codes and with securities laws and regulations. Although both are important, codes of ethics should consist of fundamental, principle-based ethical and fiduciary concepts that are applicable to all of the firm's employees. In this way, firms can best convey to employees and clients the ethical ideals that investment advisers strive to achieve. These concepts need to be implemented, however, by detailed, firm-wide compliance policies and procedures. Compliance procedures assist the firm's personnel in fulfilling the responsibilities enumerated in the code of ethics and make probable that the ideals expressed in the code of ethics will be adhered to in the day-to-day operation of the firm.

Stand-alone codes of ethics should be written in plain language and should address general fiduciary concepts. They should be unencumbered by numerous detailed procedures. Codes presented in this way are the most effective in stressing to employees that they are in positions of trust and must act with integrity at all times. Mingling compliance procedures in the firm's code of ethics goes against the goal of reinforcing the ethical obligations of employees.

Separating the code of ethics from compliance procedures will also reduce, if not eliminate, the legal terminology and "boilerplate" language that can make the underlying ethical principles incomprehensible to the average person. Above all, to ensure the creation of a culture of ethics and integrity rather than one that merely focuses on following the rules, the principles in the code of ethics must be stated in a way that is accessible and understandable to everyone in the firm.

Members and candidates should encourage their employers to provide their codes of ethics to clients. In this case also, a simple, straightforward code of ethics will be best understood by clients. Unencumbered by the compliance procedures, the code of ethics will be effective in conveying that the firm is committed to conducting business in an ethical manner and in the best interests of the clients.

Adequate Compliance Procedures

A supervisor complies with Standard IV(C) by identifying situations in which legal violations or violations of the Code and Standards are likely to occur and by establishing and enforcing compliance procedures to prevent such violations. Adequate compliance procedures should

- be contained in a clearly written and accessible manual that is tailored to the firm's operations,
- be drafted so that the procedures are easy to understand,
- designate a compliance officer whose authority and responsibility are clearly defined and who has the necessary resources and authority to implement the firm's compliance procedures,
- describe the hierarchy of supervision and assign duties among supervisors,

- implement a system of checks and balances,
- outline the scope of the procedures,
- outline procedures to document the monitoring and testing of compliance procedures,
- outline permissible conduct, and
- delineate procedures for reporting violations and sanctions.

Once a compliance program is in place, a supervisor should

- disseminate the contents of the program to appropriate personnel,
- periodically update procedures to ensure that the measures are adequate under the law,
- continually educate personnel regarding the compliance procedures,
- issue periodic reminders of the procedures to appropriate personnel,
- incorporate a professional conduct evaluation as part of an employee's performance review,
- review the actions of employees to ensure compliance and identify violators, and
- take the necessary steps to enforce the procedures once a violation has occurred.

Once a violation is discovered, a supervisor should

- respond promptly,
- conduct a thorough investigation of the activities to determine the scope of the wrongdoing,
- increase supervision or place appropriate limitations on the wrongdoer pending the outcome of the investigation, and
- review procedures for potential changes necessary to prevent future violations from occurring.

Implementation of Compliance Education and Training

No amount of ethics education and awareness will deter someone determined to commit fraud for personal enrichment. But the vast majority of investment professionals strive to achieve personal success with dedicated service to their clients and employers.

Regular ethics and compliance training, in conjunction with adoption of a code of ethics, is critical to investment firms seeking to establish a strong culture of integrity and to provide an environment in which employees routinely engage in ethical conduct in compliance with the law. Training and education assist individuals in both recognizing areas that are prone to ethical and legal pitfalls and identifying those circumstances and influences that can impair ethical judgment.

By implementing educational programs, supervisors can train their subordinates to put into practice what the firm's code of ethics requires. Education helps employees make the link between legal and ethical conduct and the long-term success of the business; a strong culture of compliance signals to clients and potential clients that the firm has truly embraced ethical conduct as fundamental to the firm's mission to serve its clients.

Establish an Appropriate Incentive Structure

Even if individuals want to make the right choices and follow an ethical course of conduct and are aware of the obstacles that may trip them up, they can still be influenced to act improperly by a corporate culture that embraces a "succeed at all costs" mentality, stresses results regardless of the methods used to achieve those results, and does not reward ethical behavior. Supervisors can reinforce an individual's natural desire to "do the right thing" by building a culture of integrity in the workplace.

Supervisors and firms must look closely at their incentive structure to determine whether the structure encourages profits and returns at the expense of ethically appropriate conduct. Reward structures may turn a blind eye to how desired outcomes are achieved and encourage dysfunctional or counterproductive behavior. Only when compensation and incentives are firmly tied to client interests and *how* outcomes are achieved, rather than *how much* is generated for the firm, will employees work to achieve a culture of integrity.

STANDARD IV(C): APPLICATION OF THE STANDARD 44

Example 1 (Supervising Research Activities):

Jane Mattock, senior vice president and head of the research department of H&V, Inc., a regional brokerage firm, has decided to change her recommendation for Timber Products from buy to sell. In line with H&V's procedures, she orally advises certain other H&V executives of her proposed actions before the report is prepared for publication. As a result of Mattock's conversation with Dieter Frampton, one of the H&V executives accountable to Mattock, Frampton immediately sells Timber's stock from his own account and from certain discretionary client accounts. In addition, other personnel inform certain institutional customers of the changed recommendation before it is printed and disseminated to all H&V customers who have received previous Timber reports.

> *Comment*: Mattock has violated Standard IV(C) by failing to reasonably and adequately supervise the actions of those accountable to her. She did not prevent or establish reasonable procedures designed to prevent dissemination of or trading on the information by those who knew of her changed recommendation. She must ensure that her firm has procedures for reviewing or recording any trading in the stock of a corporation that has been the subject of an unpublished change in recommendation. Adequate procedures would have informed the subordinates of their duties and detected sales by Frampton and selected customers.

Example 2 (Supervising Research Activities):

Deion Miller is the research director for Jamestown Investment Programs. The portfolio managers have become critical of Miller and his staff because the Jamestown portfolios do not include any stock that has been the subject of a merger or tender offer. Georgia Ginn, a member of Miller's staff, tells Miller that she has been studying a local company, Excelsior, Inc., and recommends its purchase. Ginn adds that the company has been widely rumored to be the subject of a merger study by a well-known conglomerate and discussions between them are under way. At Miller's request, Ginn prepares a memo recommending the stock. Miller passes along Ginn's memo to the portfolio managers prior to leaving for vacation, and he notes that he has not reviewed the memo. As a result of the memo, the portfolio managers buy Excelsior stock immediately. The day Miller returns to the office, he learns that Ginn's only sources for the report were her brother, who is an acquisitions analyst with Acme Industries, the "well-known conglomerate," and that the merger discussions were planned but not held.

> *Comment*: Miller violated Standard IV(C) by not exercising reasonable supervision when he disseminated the memo without checking to ensure that Ginn had a reasonable and adequate basis for her recommendations and that Ginn was not relying on material nonpublic information.

Example 3 (Supervising Trading Activities):

David Edwards, a trainee trader at Wheeler & Company, a major national brokerage firm, assists a customer in paying for the securities of Highland, Inc., by using anticipated profits from the immediate sale of the same securities. Despite the fact that Highland is not on Wheeler's recommended list, a large volume of its stock is traded through Wheeler in this manner. Roberta Ann Mason is a Wheeler vice president responsible for supervising compliance with the securities laws in the trading department. Part of her compensation from Wheeler is based on commission revenues from the trading department. Although she notices the increased trading activity, she does nothing to investigate or halt it.

> *Comment*: Mason's failure to adequately review and investigate purchase orders in Highland stock executed by Edwards and her failure to supervise the trainee's activities violate Standard IV(C). Supervisors should be especially sensitive to actual or potential conflicts between their own self-interests and their supervisory responsibilities.

Example 4 (Supervising Trading Activities and Record Keeping):

Samantha Tabbing is senior vice president and portfolio manager for Crozet, Inc., a registered investment advisory and registered broker/dealer firm. She reports to Charles Henry, the president of Crozet. Crozet serves as the investment adviser and principal underwriter for ABC and XYZ public mutual funds. The two funds' prospectuses allow Crozet to trade financial futures for the funds for the limited purpose of hedging against market risks. Henry, extremely impressed by Tabbing's performance in the past two years, directs Tabbing to act as portfolio manager for the funds. For the benefit of its employees, Crozet has also organized the Crozet Employee Profit-Sharing Plan (CEPSP), a defined contribution retirement plan. Henry assigns Tabbing to manage 20% of the assets of CEPSP. Tabbing's investment objective for her portion of CEPSP's assets is aggressive growth. Unbeknownst to Henry, Tabbing frequently places S&P 500 Index purchase and sale orders for the funds and the CEPSP without providing the futures commission merchants (FCMs) who take the orders with any prior or simultaneous designation of the account for which the trade has been placed. Frequently, neither Tabbing nor anyone else at Crozet completes an internal trade ticket to record the time an order was placed or the specific account for which the order was intended. FCMs often designate a specific account only after the trade, when Tabbing provides such designation. Crozet has no written operating procedures or compliance manual concerning its futures trading, and its compliance department does not review such trading. After observing the market's movement, Tabbing assigns to CEPSP the S&P 500 positions with more favorable execution prices and assigns positions with less favorable execution prices to the funds.

Comment: Henry violated Standard IV(C) by failing to adequately supervise Tabbing with respect to her S&P 500 trading. Henry further violated Standard IV(C) by failing to establish record-keeping and reporting procedures to prevent or detect Tabbing's violations. Henry must make a reasonable effort to determine that adequate compliance procedures covering all employee trading activity are established, documented, communicated, and followed.

Example 5 (Accepting Responsibility):

Meredith Rasmussen works on a buy-side trading desk and concentrates on in-house trades for a hedge fund subsidiary managed by a team at the investment management firm. The hedge fund has been very successful and is marketed globally by the firm. From her experience as the trader for much of the activity of the fund, Rasmussen has become quite knowledgeable about the hedge fund's strategy, tactics, and performance. When a distinct break in the market occurs and many of the securities involved in the hedge fund's strategy decline markedly in value, however, Rasmussen observes that the reported performance of the hedge fund does not at all reflect this decline. From her experience, this lack of an effect is a very unlikely occurrence. She approaches the head of trading about her concern and is told that she should not ask any questions and that the fund is too big and successful and is not her concern. She is fairly sure something is not right, so she contacts the compliance officer and is again told to stay away from the hedge fund reporting issue.

Comment: Rasmussen has clearly come upon an error in policies, procedures, and compliance practices within the firm's operations. According to Standard IV(C), the supervisor and the compliance officer have the responsibility to review the concerns brought forth by Rasmussen. Supervisors have the responsibility of establishing and encouraging an ethical culture in the firm. The dismissal of Rasmussen's question violates Standard IV(C) and undermines the firm's ethical operations.

See also Standard I(D) Misconduct and, for guidance on whistleblowing, Standard IV(A) Loyalty.

Example 6 (Inadequate Procedures):

Brendan Witt, a former junior sell-side technology analyst, decided to return to school to earn an MBA. To keep his research skills and industry knowledge sharp, Witt accepted a position with On-line and Informed, an independent internet-based research company. The position requires the publication of a recommendation and report on a different company every month. Initially, Witt is a regular contributor of new research and a participant in the associated discussion boards that generally have positive comments on the technology sector. Over time, his ability to manage his educational requirements and his work requirements begin to conflict with one another. Knowing a recommendation is due the next day for On-line, Witt creates a report based on a few news articles and what the conventional wisdom of the markets has deemed the "hot" security of the day.

Comment: Allowing the report submitted by Witt to be posted highlights a lack of compliance procedures by the research firm. Witt's supervisor needs to work with the management of On-line to develop an appropriate review process to ensure that all contracted analysts comply with the requirements.

See also Standard V(A) Diligence and Reasonable Basis because it relates to Witt's responsibility for substantiating a recommendation.

Example 7 (Inadequate Supervision):

Michael Papis is the chief investment officer of his state's retirement fund. The fund has always used outside advisers for the real estate allocation, and this information is clearly presented in all fund communications. Thomas Nagle, a recognized sell-side research analyst and Papis's business school classmate, recently left the investment bank he worked for to start his own asset management firm, Accessible Real Estate. Nagle is trying to build his assets under management and contacts Papis about gaining some of the retirement fund's allocation. In the previous few years, the performance of the retirement fund's real estate investments was in line with the fund's benchmark but was not extraordinary. Papis decides to help out his old friend and also to seek better returns by moving the real estate allocation to Accessible. The only notice of the change in adviser appears in the next annual report in the listing of associated advisers.

> *Comment*: Papis's actions highlight the need for supervision and review at all levels in an organization. His responsibilities may include the selection of external advisers, but the decision to change advisers appears arbitrary. Members and candidates should ensure that their firm has appropriate policies and procedures in place to detect inappropriate actions, such as the action taken by Papis.
>
> See also Standard V(A) Diligence and Reasonable Basis, Standard V(B) Communication with Clients and Prospective Clients, and Standard VI(A) Disclosure of Conflicts.

Example 8 (Supervising Research Activities):

Mary Burdette was recently hired by Fundamental Investment Management (FIM) as a junior auto industry analyst. Burdette is expected to expand the social media presence of the firm because she is active with various networks, including Facebook, LinkedIn, and X. Although Burdette's supervisor, Joe Graf, has never used social media, he encourages Burdette to explore opportunities to increase FIM's online presence and ability to share content, communicate, and broadcast information to clients. In response to Graf's encouragement, Burdette is working on a proposal detailing the advantages of getting FIM onto X in addition to launching a company Facebook page.

As part of her auto industry research for FIM, Burdette is completing a report on the financial impact of Sun Drive Auto Ltd.'s new solar technology for compact automobiles. This research report will be her first for FIM, and she believes Sun Drive's technology could revolutionize the auto industry. In her excitement, Burdette sends a quick post to FIM X followers summarizing her "buy" recommendation for Sun Drive Auto stock.

> *Comment*: Graf has violated Standard IV(C) by failing to reasonably supervise Burdette with respect to the contents of her post. He did not establish reasonable procedures to prevent the unauthorized dissemination of company research through social media networks. Graf must make sure all employees receive regular training about FIM's policies and procedures, including the appropriate business use of personal social media networks.
>
> See Standard III(B) for additional guidance.

Example 9 (Supervising Research Activities):

Chen Wang leads the research department at YYRA Retirement Planning Specialists. Chen supervises a team of 10 analysts in a fast-paced and understaffed organization. He is responsible for coordinating the firm's approved process to review all reports before they are provided to the portfolio management team for use in rebalancing client portfolios.

One of Chen's direct reports, Huang Mei, covers the banking industry. Chen must submit the latest updates to the portfolio management team tomorrow morning. Huang has yet to submit her research report on ZYX Bank because she is uncomfortable providing a "buy" or "sell" opinion of ZYX on the basis of the completed analysis. Pressed for time and concerned that Chen will reject a "hold" recommendation, she researches various websites and blogs on the banking sector for whatever she can find on ZYX. One independent blogger provides a new interpretation of the recently reported data Huang has analyzed and concludes with a strong "sell" recommendation for ZYX. She is impressed by the originality and resourcefulness of this blogger's report.

Very late in the evening, Huang submits her report and "sell" recommendation to Chen without any reference to the independent blogger's report. Given the late time of the submission and the competence of Huang's prior work, Chen compiles this report with the recommendations from each of the other analysts and meets with the portfolio managers to discuss implementation.

> *Comment*: Chen has violated Standard IV(C) by neglecting to reasonably and adequately follow the firm's approved review process for Huang's research report. The delayed submission and the quality of prior work do not remove Chen's requirement to uphold the designated review process. A member or candidate with supervisory responsibility must make reasonable efforts to see that appropriate procedures are established, documented, communicated to covered personnel, and followed.

STANDARD V: INVESTMENT ANALYSIS, RECOMMENDATIONS, AND ACTIONS

45

- ☐ demonstrate a thorough knowledge of the CFA Institute Code of Ethics and Standards of Professional Conduct by interpreting the Code and Standards in various situations involving issues of professional integrity
- ☐ recommend practices and procedures designed to prevent violations of the Code and Standards

Standard V(A) Diligence and Reasonable Basis

Members and Candidates must:

1. Exercise diligence, independence, and thoroughness in analyzing investments, making investment recommendations, and taking investment actions.

2. Have a reasonable and adequate basis, supported by appropriate research and investigation, for any investment analysis, recommendation, or action.

Guidance

Highlights:

- *Defining Diligence and Reasonable Basis*
- *Using Secondary or Third-Party Research*
- *Using Quantitatively Oriented Research*
- *Developing Quantitatively Oriented Techniques*
- *Selecting External Advisers and Subadvisers*
- *Group Research and Decision Making*

The application of Standard V(A) depends on the investment philosophy the member, candidate, or firm is following, the role of the member or candidate in the investment decision-making process, and the support and resources provided by the member's or candidate's employer. These factors will dictate the nature of the diligence and thoroughness of the research and the level of investigation required by Standard V(A).

The requirements for issuing conclusions based on research will vary in relation to the member's or candidate's role in the investment decision-making process, but the member or candidate must make reasonable efforts to cover all pertinent issues when arriving at a recommendation. Members and candidates enhance transparency by providing or offering to provide supporting information to clients when recommending a purchase or sale or when changing a recommendation.

Defining Diligence and Reasonable Basis

Every investment decision is based on a set of facts known and understood at the time. Clients turn to members and candidates for advice and expect these advisers to have more information and knowledge than they do. This information and knowledge is the basis from which members and candidates apply their professional judgment in taking investment actions and making recommendations.

At a basic level, clients want assurance that members and candidates are putting forth the necessary effort to support the recommendations they are making. Communicating the level and thoroughness of the information reviewed before the member or candidate makes a judgment allows clients to understand the reasonableness of the recommended investment actions.

As with determining the suitability of an investment for the client, the necessary level of research and analysis will differ with the product, security, or service being offered. In providing an investment service, members and candidates typically use a variety of resources, including company reports, third-party research, and results from quantitative models. A reasonable basis is formed through a balance of these resources appropriate for the security or decision being analyzed.

The following list provides some, but definitely not all, examples of attributes to consider while forming the basis for a recommendation:

- global, regional, and country macroeconomic conditions,
- a company's operating and financial history,
- the industry's and sector's current conditions and the stage of the business cycle,

- a mutual fund's fee structure and management history,
- the output and potential limitations of quantitative models,
- the quality of the assets included in a securitization, and
- the appropriateness of selected peer-group comparisons.

Even though an investment recommendation may be well informed, downside risk remains for any investment. Members and candidates can base their decisions only on the information available at the time decisions are made. The steps taken in developing a diligent and reasonable recommendation should minimize unexpected downside events.

Using Secondary or Third-Party Research

If members and candidates rely on secondary or third-party research, they must make reasonable and diligent efforts to determine whether such research is sound. Secondary research is defined as research conducted by someone else in the member's or candidate's firm. Third-party research is research conducted by entities outside the member's or candidate's firm, such as a brokerage firm, bank, or research firm. If a member or candidate has reason to suspect that either secondary or third-party research or information comes from a source that lacks a sound basis, the member or candidate must not rely on that information.

Members and candidates should make reasonable enquiries into the source and accuracy of all data used in completing their investment analysis and recommendations. The sources of the information and data will influence the level of the review a member or candidate must undertake. Information and data taken from internet sources, such as personal blogs, independent research aggregation websites, or social media websites, likely require a greater level of review than information from more established research organizations.

Criteria that a member or candidate can use in forming an opinion on whether research is sound include the following:

- assumptions used,
- rigor of the analysis performed,
- date/timeliness of the research, and
- evaluation of the objectivity and independence of the recommendations.

A member or candidate may rely on others in his or her firm to determine whether secondary or third-party research is sound and use the information in good faith unless the member or candidate has reason to question its validity or the processes and procedures used by those responsible for the research. For example, a portfolio manager may not have a choice of a data source because the firm's senior managers conducted due diligence to determine which vendor would provide services; the member or candidate can use the information in good faith assuming the due diligence process was deemed adequate.

A member or candidate should verify that the firm has a policy about the timely and consistent review of approved research providers to ensure that the quality of the research continues to meet the necessary standards. If such a policy is not in place at the firm, the member or candidate should encourage the development and adoption of a formal review practice.

Using Quantitatively Oriented Research

Standard V(A) applies to the rapidly expanding use of quantitatively oriented research models and processes, such as computer-generated modeling, screening, and ranking of investment securities; the creation or valuation of derivative instruments; and quantitative portfolio construction techniques. These models and processes are being used for much more than the back testing of investment strategies, especially with continually advancing technology and techniques. The continued broad development of quantitative methods and models is an important part of capital market developments.

Members and candidates need to have an understanding of the parameters used in models and quantitative research that are incorporated into their investment recommendations. Although they are not required to become experts in every technical aspect of the models, they must understand the assumptions and limitations inherent in any model and how the results were used in the decision-making process.

The reliance on and potential limitations of financial models became clear through the investment crisis that unfolded in 2007 and 2008. In some cases, the financial models used to value specific securities and related derivative products did not adequately demonstrate the level of associated risks. Members and candidates should make reasonable efforts to test the output of investment models and other pre-programed analytical tools they use. Such validation should occur before incorporating the process into their methods, models, or analyses.

Although not every model can test for every factor or outcome, members and candidates should ensure that their analyses incorporate a broad range of assumptions sufficient to capture the underlying characteristics of investments. The omission from the analysis of potentially negative outcomes or of levels of risk outside the norm may misrepresent the true economic value of an investment. The possible scenarios for analysis should include factors that are likely to have a substantial influence on the investment value and may include extremely positive and negative scenarios.

Developing Quantitatively Oriented Techniques

Individuals who create new quantitative models and services must exhibit a higher level of diligence in reviewing new products than the individuals who ultimately use the analytical output. Members and candidates involved in the development and oversight of quantitatively oriented models, methods, and algorithms must understand the technical aspects of the products they provide to clients. A thorough testing of the model and resulting analysis should be completed prior to product distribution.

Members and candidates need to consider the source and time horizon of the data used as inputs in financial models. The information from many commercially available databases may not effectively incorporate both positive and negative market cycles. In the development of a recommendation, the member or candidate may need to test the models by using volatility and performance expectations that represent scenarios outside the observable databases. In reviewing the computer models or the resulting output, members and candidates need to pay particular attention to the assumptions used in the analysis and the rigor of the analysis to ensure that the model incorporates a wide range of possible input expectations, including negative market events.

Selecting External Advisers and Subadvisers

Financial instruments and asset allocation techniques continue to develop and evolve. This progression has led to the use of specialized managers to invest in specific asset classes or diversification strategies that complement a firm's in-house expertise. Standard V(A) applies to the level of review necessary in selecting an external adviser or subadviser to manage a specifically mandated allocation. Members and candidates must review managers as diligently as they review individual funds and securities.

Members and candidates who are directly involved with the use of external advisers need to ensure that their firms have standardized criteria for reviewing these selected external advisers and managers. Such criteria would include, but would not be limited to, the following:

- reviewing the adviser's established code of ethics,
- understanding the adviser's compliance and internal control procedures,

- assessing the quality of the published return information, and
- reviewing the adviser's investment process and adherence to its stated strategy.

Codes, standards, and guides to best practice published by CFA Institute provide members and candidates with examples of acceptable practices for external advisers and advice in selecting a new adviser. The following guides are available at the CFA Institute website (www.cfainstitute.org): Asset Manager Code of Professional Conduct, Global Investment Performance Standards, and Model Request for Proposal (for equity, credit, or real estate managers).

Group Research and Decision Making

Commonly, members and candidates are part of a group or team that is collectively responsible for producing investment analysis or research. The conclusions or recommendations of the group report represent the consensus of the group and are not necessarily the views of the member or candidate, even though the name of the member or candidate is included on the report. In some instances, a member or candidate will not agree with the view of the group. If, however, the member or candidate believes that the consensus opinion has a reasonable and adequate basis and is independent and objective, the member or candidate need not decline to be identified with the report. If the member or candidate is confident in the process, the member or candidate does not need to dissociate from the report even if it does not reflect his or her opinion.

STANDARD V(A): RECOMMENDED PROCEDURES 46

Members and candidates should encourage their firms to consider the following policies and procedures to support the principles of Standard V(A):

- Establish a policy requiring that research reports, credit ratings, and investment recommendations have a basis that can be substantiated as reasonable and adequate. An individual employee (a supervisory analyst) or a group of employees (a review committee) should be appointed to review and approve such items prior to external circulation to determine whether the criteria established in the policy have been met.
- Develop detailed, written guidance for analysts (research, investment, or credit), supervisory analysts, and review committees that establishes the due diligence procedures for judging whether a particular recommendation has a reasonable and adequate basis.
- Develop measurable criteria for assessing the quality of research, the reasonableness and adequacy of the basis for any recommendation or rating, and the accuracy of recommendations over time. In some cases, firms may consider implementing compensation arrangements that depend on these measurable criteria and that are applied consistently to all related analysts.
- Develop detailed, written guidance that establishes minimum levels of scenario testing of all computer-based models used in developing, rating, and evaluating financial instruments. The policy should contain criteria related to the breadth of the scenarios tested, the accuracy of the output over time, and the analysis of cash flow sensitivity to inputs.

- Develop measurable criteria for assessing outside providers, including the quality of information being provided, the reasonableness and adequacy of the provider's collection practices, and the accuracy of the information over time. The established policy should outline how often the provider's products are reviewed.
- Adopt a standardized set of criteria for evaluating the adequacy of external advisers. The policy should include how often and on what basis the allocation of funds to the adviser will be reviewed.

47 STANDARD V(A): APPLICATION OF THE STANDARD

- ☐ demonstrate a thorough knowledge of the CFA Institute Code of Ethics and Standards of Professional Conduct by interpreting the Code and Standards in various situations involving issues of professional integrity
- ☐ recommend practices and procedures designed to prevent violations of the Code and Standards

Example 1 (Sufficient Due Diligence):

Helen Hawke manages the corporate finance department of Sarkozi Securities, Ltd. The firm is anticipating that the government will soon close a tax loophole that currently allows oil-and-gas exploration companies to pass on drilling expenses to holders of a certain class of shares. Because market demand for this tax-advantaged class of stock is currently high, Sarkozi convinces several companies to undertake new equity financings at once, before the loophole closes. Time is of the essence, but Sarkozi lacks sufficient resources to conduct adequate research on all the prospective issuing companies. Hawke decides to estimate the IPO prices on the basis of the relative size of each company and to justify the pricing later when her staff has time.

> *Comment*: Sarkozi should have taken on only the work that it could adequately handle. By categorizing the issuers by general size, Hawke has bypassed researching all the other relevant aspects that should be considered when pricing new issues and thus has not performed sufficient due diligence. Such an omission can result in investors purchasing shares at prices that have no actual basis. Hawke has violated Standard V(A).

Example 2 (Sufficient Scenario Testing):

Babu Dhaliwal works for Heinrich Brokerage in the corporate finance group. He has just persuaded Feggans Resources, Ltd., to allow his firm to do a secondary equity financing at Feggans Resources' current stock price. Because the stock has been trading at higher multiples than similar companies with equivalent production, Dhaliwal presses the Feggans Resources managers to project what would be the maximum production they could achieve in an optimal scenario. Based on these numbers, he is able to justify the price his firm will be asking for the secondary issue. During a sales pitch to the brokers, Dhaliwal then uses these numbers as the base-case production levels that Feggans Resources will achieve.

Comment: When presenting information to the brokers, Dhaliwal should have given a range of production scenarios and the probability of Feggans Resources achieving each level. By giving the maximum production level as the likely level of production, he has misrepresented the chances of achieving that production level and seriously misled the brokers. Dhaliwal has violated Standard V(A).

Example 3 (Developing a Reasonable Basis):

Brendan Witt, a former junior sell-side technology analyst, decided to return to school to earn an MBA. To keep his research skills and industry knowledge sharp, Witt accepted a position with On-line and Informed, an independent internet-based research company. The position requires the publication of a recommendation and report on a different company every month. Initially, Witt is a regular contributor of new research and a participant in the associated discussion boards that generally have positive comments on the technology sector. Over time, his ability to manage his educational requirements and his work requirements begin to conflict with one another. Knowing a recommendation is due the next day for On-line, Witt creates a report based on a few news articles and what the conventional wisdom of the markets has deemed the "hot" security of the day.

Comment: Witt's knowledge of and exuberance for technology stocks, a few news articles, and the conventional wisdom of the markets do not constitute, without more information, a reasonable and adequate basis for a stock recommendation that is supported by appropriate research and investigation. Therefore, Witt has violated Standard V(A).

See also Standard IV(C) Responsibilities of Supervisors because it relates to the firm's inadequate procedures.

Example 4 (Timely Client Updates):

Kristen Chandler is an investment consultant in the London office of Dalton Securities, a major global investment consultant firm. One of her UK pension funds has decided to appoint a specialist US equity manager. Dalton's global manager of research relies on local consultants to cover managers within their regions and, after conducting thorough due diligence, puts their views and ratings in Dalton's manager database. Chandler accesses Dalton's global manager research database and conducts a screen of all US equity managers on the basis of a match with the client's desired philosophy/style, performance, and tracking-error targets. She selects the five managers that meet these criteria and puts them in a briefing report that is delivered to the client 10 days later. Between the time of Chandler's database search and the delivery of the report to the client, Chandler is told that Dalton has updated the database with the information that one of the firms that Chandler has recommended for consideration lost its chief investment officer, the head of its US equity research, and the majority of its portfolio managers on the US equity product—all of whom have left to establish their own firm. Chandler does not revise her report with this updated information.

Comment: Chandler has failed to satisfy the requirement of Standard V(A). Although Dalton updated the manager ratings to reflect the personnel turnover at one of the firms, Chandler did not update her report to reflect the new information.

Example 5 (Group Research Opinions):

Evelyn Mastakis is a junior analyst who has been asked by her firm to write a research report predicting the expected interest rate for residential mortgages over the next six months. Mastakis submits her report to the fixed-income investment committee of her firm for review, as required by firm procedures. Although some committee members support Mastakis's conclusion, the majority of the committee disagrees with her conclusion, and the report is significantly changed to indicate that interest rates are likely to increase more than originally predicted by Mastakis. Should Mastakis ask that her name be taken off the report when it is disseminated?

> *Comment*: The results of research are not always clear, and different people may have different opinions based on the same factual evidence. In this case, the committee may have valid reasons for issuing a report that differs from the analyst's original research. The firm can issue a report that is different from the original report of an analyst as long as there is a reasonable and adequate basis for its conclusions.
>
> Generally, analysts must write research reports that reflect their own opinion and can ask the firm not to put their name on reports that ultimately differ from that opinion. When the work is a group effort, however, not all members of the team may agree with all aspects of the report. Ultimately, members and candidates can ask to have their names removed from the report, but if they are satisfied that the process has produced results or conclusions that have a reasonable and adequate basis, members and candidates do not have to dissociate from the report even when they do not agree with its contents. If Mastakis is confident in the process, she does not need to dissociate from the report even if it does not reflect her opinion.

Example 6 (Reliance on Third-Party Research):

Gary McDermott runs a two-person investment management firm. McDermott's firm subscribes to a service from a large investment research firm that provides research reports. McDermott's firm makes investment recommendations on the basis of these reports.

> *Comment*: Members and candidates can rely on third-party research but must make reasonable and diligent efforts to determine that such research is sound. If McDermott undertakes due diligence efforts on a regular basis to ensure that the research produced by the large firm is objective and reasonably based, McDermott can rely on that research when making investment recommendations to clients.

Example 7 (Due Diligence in Submanager Selection):

Paul Ostrowski's business has grown significantly over the past couple of years, and some clients want to diversify internationally. Ostrowski decides to find a submanager to handle the expected international investments. Because this will be his first subadviser, Ostrowski uses the CFA Institute model "request for proposal" to design a questionnaire for his search. By his deadline, he receives seven completed questionnaires from a variety of domestic and international firms trying to gain his business. Ostrowski reviews all the applications in detail and decides to select the firm that charges the lowest fees because doing so will have the least impact on his firm's bottom line.

Comment: The selection of an external adviser or subadviser should be based on a full and complete review of the adviser's services, performance history, and cost structure. In basing the decision on the fee structure alone, Ostrowski may be violating Standard V(A).

See also Standard III(C) Suitability because it relates to the ability of the selected adviser to meet the needs of the clients.

Example 8 (Sufficient Due Diligence):

Michael Papis is the chief investment officer of his state's retirement fund. The fund has always used outside advisers for the real estate allocation, and this information is clearly presented in all fund communications. Thomas Nagle, a recognized sell-side research analyst and Papis's business school classmate, recently left the investment bank he worked for to start his own asset management firm, Accessible Real Estate. Nagle is trying to build his assets under management and contacts Papis about gaining some of the retirement fund's allocation. In the previous few years, the performance of the retirement fund's real estate investments was in line with the fund's benchmark but was not extraordinary. Papis decides to help out his old friend and also to seek better returns by moving the real estate allocation to Accessible. The only notice of the change in adviser appears in the next annual report in the listing of associated advisers.

Comment: Papis violated Standard V(A). His responsibilities may include the selection of the external advisers, but the decision to change advisers appears to have been arbitrary. If Papis was dissatisfied with the current real estate adviser, he should have conducted a proper solicitation to select the most appropriate adviser.

See also Standard IV(C) Responsibilities of Supervisors, Standard V(B) Communication with Clients and Prospective Clients, and Standard VI(A) Disclosure of Conflicts.

Example 9 (Sufficient Due Diligence):

Andre Shrub owns and operates Conduit, an investment advisory firm. Prior to opening Conduit, Shrub was an account manager with Elite Investment, a hedge fund managed by his good friend Adam Reed. To attract clients to a new Conduit fund, Shrub offers lower-than-normal management fees. He can do so because the fund consists of two top-performing funds managed by Reed. Given his personal friendship with Reed and the prior performance record of these two funds, Shrub believes this new fund is a winning combination for all parties. Clients quickly invest with Conduit to gain access to the Elite funds. No one is turned away because Conduit is seeking to expand its assets under management.

Comment: Shrub violated Standard V(A) by not conducting a thorough analysis of the funds managed by Reed before developing the new Conduit fund. Shrub's reliance on his personal relationship with Reed and his prior knowledge of Elite are insufficient justification for the investments. The funds may be appropriately considered, but a full review of their operating procedures, reporting practices, and transparency are some elements of the necessary due diligence.

See also Standard III(C) Suitability.

Example 10 (Sufficient Due Diligence):

Bob Thompson has been doing research for the portfolio manager of the fixed-income department. His assignment is to do sensitivity analysis on securitized subprime mortgages. He has discussed with the manager possible scenarios to use to calculate expected returns. A key assumption in such calculations is housing price appreciation (HPA) because it drives "prepays" (prepayments of mortgages) and losses. Thompson is concerned with the significant appreciation experienced over the previous five years as a result of the increased availability of funds from subprime mortgages. Thompson insists that the analysis should include a scenario run with −10% for Year 1, −5% for Year 2, and then (to project a worst-case scenario) 0% for Years 3 through 5. The manager replies that these assumptions are too dire because there has never been a time in their available database when HPA was negative.

Thompson conducts his research to better understand the risks inherent in these securities and evaluates these securities in the worst-case scenario, a less likely but possible environment. Based on the results of the enhanced scenarios, Thompson does not recommend the purchase of the securitization. Against the general market trends, the manager follows Thompson's recommendation and does not invest. The following year, the housing market collapses. In avoiding the subprime investments, the manager's portfolio outperforms its peer group that year.

> *Comment*: Thompson's actions in running the scenario test with inputs beyond the historical trends available in the firm's databases adhere to the principles of Standard V(A). His concerns over recent trends provide a sound basis for further analysis. Thompson understands the limitations of his model, when combined with the limited available historical information, to accurately predict the performance of the funds if market conditions change negatively.
>
> See also Standard I(B) Independence and Objectivity.

Example 11 (Use of Quantitatively Oriented Models):

Espacia Liakos works in sales for Hellenica Securities, a firm specializing in developing intricate derivative strategies to profit from particular views on market expectations. One of her clients is Eugenie Carapalis, who has become convinced that commodity prices will become more volatile over the coming months. Carapalis asks Liakos to quickly engineer a strategy that will benefit from this expectation. Liakos turns to Hellenica's modeling group to fulfill this request. Because of the tight deadline, the modeling group outsources parts of the work to several trusted third parties. Liakos implements the disparate components of the strategy as the firms complete them.

Within a month, Carapalis is proven correct: Volatility across a range of commodities increases sharply. But her derivatives position with Hellenica returns huge losses, and the losses increase daily. Liakos investigates and realizes that although each of the various components of the strategy had been validated, they had never been evaluated as an integrated whole. In extreme conditions, portions of the model worked at cross-purposes with other portions, causing the overall strategy to fail dramatically.

> *Comment*: Liakos violated Standard V(A). Members and candidates must understand the statistical significance of the results of the models they recommend and must be able to explain them to clients. Liakos did not take adequate care to ensure a thorough review of the whole model; its components were evaluated only individually. Because Carapalis clearly intended to implement the strategy as a whole rather than as separate parts, Liakos should have tested how the components of the strategy interacted as well as how they performed individually.

Example 12 (Successful Due Diligence/Failed Investment):

Alton Newbury is an investment adviser to high-net-worth clients. A client with an aggressive risk profile in his investment policy statement asks about investing in the Top Shelf hedge fund. This fund, based in Calgary, Alberta, Canada, has reported 20% returns for the first three years. The fund prospectus states that its strategy involves long and short positions in the energy sector and extensive leverage. Based on his analysis of the fund's track record, the principals involved in managing the fund, the fees charged, and the fund's risk profile, Newbury recommends the fund to the client and secures a position in it. The next week, the fund announces that it has suffered a loss of 60% of its value and is suspending operations and redemptions until after a regulatory review. Newbury's client calls him in a panic and asks for an explanation.

> *Comment*: Newbury's actions were consistent with Standard V(A). Analysis of an investment that results in a reasonable basis for recommendation does not guarantee that the investment has no downside risk. Newbury should discuss the analysis process with the client while reminding him or her that past performance does not lead to guaranteed future gains and that losses in an aggressive investment portfolio should be expected.

Example 13 (Quantitative Model Diligence):

Barry Cannon is the lead quantitative analyst at CityCenter Hedge Fund. He is responsible for the development, maintenance, and enhancement of the proprietary models the fund uses to manage its investors' assets. Cannon reads several high-level mathematical publications and blogs to stay informed of current developments. One blog, run by "Expert CFA," presents some intriguing research that may benefit one of CityCenter's current models. Cannon is under pressure from firm executives to improve the model's predictive abilities, and he incorporates the factors discussed in the online research. The updated output recommends several new investments to the fund's portfolio managers.

> *Comment*: Cannon has violated Standard V(A) by failing to have a reasonable basis for the new recommendations made to the portfolio managers. He needed to diligently research the effect of incorporating the new factors before offering the output recommendations. Cannon may use the blog for ideas, but it is his responsibility to determine the effect on the firm's proprietary models.
>
> See Standard VII(B) regarding the violation by "Expert CFA" in the use of the CFA designation.

Example 14 (Selecting a Service Provider):

Ellen Smith is a performance analyst at Artic Global Advisors, a firm that manages global equity mandates for institutional clients. She was asked by her supervisor to review five new performance attribution systems and recommend one that would more appropriately explain the firm's investment strategy to clients. On the list was a system she recalled learning about when visiting an exhibitor booth at a recent conference. The system is highly quantitative and something of a "black box" in how it calculates the attribution values. Smith recommended this option without researching the others because the sheer complexity of the process was sure to impress the clients.

> *Comment*: Smith's actions do not demonstrate a sufficient level of diligence in reviewing this product to make a recommendation for selecting the service. Besides not reviewing or considering the other four potential

systems, she did not determine whether the "black box" attribution process aligns with the investment practices of the firm, including its investments in different countries and currencies. Smith must review and understand the process of any software or system before recommending its use as the firm's attribution system.

Example 15 (Subadviser Selection):

Craig Jackson is working for Adams Partners, Inc., and has been assigned to select a hedge fund subadviser to improve the diversification of the firm's large fund-of-funds product. The allocation must be in place before the start of the next quarter. Jackson uses a consultant database to find a list of suitable firms that claim compliance with the GIPS standards. He calls more than 20 firms on the list to confirm their potential interest and to determine their most recent quarterly and annual total return values. Because of the short turnaround, Jackson recommends the firm with the greatest total return values for selection.

Comment: By considering only performance and GIPS compliance, Jackson has not conducted sufficient review of potential firms to satisfy the requirements of Standard V(A). A thorough investigation of the firms and their operations should be conducted to ensure that their addition would increase the diversity of clients' portfolios and that they are suitable for the fund-of-funds product.

Example 16 (Manager Selection):

Timothy Green works for Peach Asset Management, where he creates proprietary models that analyze data from the firm request for proposal questionnaires to identify managers for possible inclusion in the firm's fund-of-funds investment platform. Various criteria must be met to be accepted to the platform. Because of the number of respondents to the questionnaires, Green uses only the data submitted to make a recommendation for adding a new manager.

Comment: By failing to conduct any additional outside review of the information to verify what was submitted through the request for proposal, Green has likely not satisfied the requirements of Standard V(A). The amount of information requested from outside managers varies among firms. Although the requested information may be comprehensive, Green should ensure sufficient effort is undertaken to verify the submitted information before recommending a firm for inclusion. This requires that he goes beyond the information provided by the manager on the request for proposal questionnaire and may include interviews with interested managers, reviews of regulatory filings, and discussions with the managers' custodian or auditor.

Example 17 (Technical Model Requirements):

Jérôme Dupont works for the credit research group of XYZ Asset Management, where he is in charge of developing and updating credit risk models. In order to perform accurately, his models need to be regularly updated with the latest market data.

Dupont does not interact with or manage money for any of the firm's clients. He is in contact with the firm's US corporate bond fund manager, John Smith, who has only very superficial knowledge of the model and who from time to time asks very basic questions regarding the output recommendations. Smith does not consult Dupont with respect to finalizing his clients' investment strategies.

Dupont's recently assigned objective is to develop a new emerging market corporate credit risk model. The firm is planning to expand into emerging credit, and the development of such a model is a critical step in this process. Because Smith seems to follow the model's recommendations without much concern for its quality as he develops his clients' investment strategies, Dupont decides to focus his time on the development of the new emerging market model and neglects to update the US model.

After several months without regular updates, Dupont's diagnostic statistics start to show alarming signs with respect to the quality of the US credit model. Instead of conducting the long and complicated data update, Dupont introduces new codes into his model with some limited new data as a quick "fix." He thinks this change will address the issue without needing to complete the full data update, so he continues working on the new emerging market model.

Several months following the quick "fix," another set of diagnostic statistics reveals nonsensical results and Dupont realizes that his earlier change contained an error. He quickly corrects the error and alerts Smith. Smith realizes that some of the prior trades he performed were due to erroneous model results. Smith rebalances the portfolio to remove the securities purchased on the basis of the questionable results without reporting the issue to anyone else.

> *Comment*: Smith violated Standard V(A) because exercising "diligence, independence, and thoroughness in analyzing investments, making investment recommendations, and taking investment actions" means that members and candidates must understand the technical aspects of the products they provide to clients. Smith does not understand the model he is relying on to manage money. Members and candidates should also make reasonable enquiries into the source and accuracy of all data used in completing their investment analysis and recommendations.
>
> Dupont violated Standard V(A) even if he does not trade securities or make investment decisions. Dupont's models give investment recommendations, and Dupont is accountable for the quality of those recommendations. Members and candidates should make reasonable efforts to test the output of pre-programmed analytical tools they use. Such validation should occur before incorporating the tools into their decision-making process.
>
> See also Standard V(B) Communication with Clients and Prospective Clients.

48 STANDARD V(B) COMMUNICATION WITH CLIENTS AND PROSPECTIVE CLIENTS

- [ ] demonstrate a thorough knowledge of the CFA Institute Code of Ethics and Standards of Professional Conduct by interpreting the Code and Standards in various situations involving issues of professional integrity
- [ ] recommend practices and procedures designed to prevent violations of the Code and Standards

Members and Candidates must:

1. Disclose to clients and prospective clients the nature of the services provided, along with information about the cost to the client associated with those services.
2. Disclose to clients and prospective clients the basic format and general principles of the investment processes they use to analyze investments, select securities, and construct portfolios and must promptly disclose any changes that might materially affect those processes.
3. Disclose to clients and prospective clients significant limitations and risks associated with the investment process.
4. Use reasonable judgment in identifying which factors are important to their investment analyses, recommendations, or actions and include those factors in communications with clients and prospective clients.
5. Distinguish between fact and opinion in the presentation of investment analyses and recommendations.

Guidance

Highlights:

- *Nature of Services and Information on Cost*
- *Informing Clients of the Investment Process*
- *Different Forms of Communication*
- *Identifying Risk and Limitations*
- *Report Presentation*
- *Distinction between Facts and Opinions in Reports*

Standard V(B) addresses member and candidate conduct with respect to communicating with clients. Developing and maintaining clear, frequent, and thorough communication practices is critical to providing high-quality financial services to clients. When clients understand the information communicated to them, they also can understand exactly how members and candidates are acting on their behalf, which gives clients the opportunity to make well-informed decisions about their investments. Such understanding can be accomplished only through clear communication.

Disclosing Nature of Services and Information about Costs to Clients and Prospective Clients

A fundamental goal of the Code and Standards is to protect client interests and allow clients to make fully informed decisions about their investments and financial well-being. Providing clients with a description of the nature of the services they can expect from investment professionals and information about the costs to the client for those services is critical to achieving this goal. The disclosures required by Standard V(B) will permit clients to make informed decisions as to whether to engage in professional services with members or candidates or their firms.

Full and fair disclosure builds trust with clients, and the disclosure of information about costs benefits clients and protects their interests. Standard V(B) makes clear that required disclosures cover all professional services provided by members and candidates. A clear understanding of the services that members and candidates provide is a foundational element of the client relationship. Clients must understand what services the member or candidate will provide and, critically, what services will not be provided so that members and candidates can set appropriate expectations. It is best practice for members and candidates with client-facing responsibilities to clearly set out in written form at the outset of the engagement a description of the nature and parameters of the professional services as part of the engagement agreement, contract, or other documents memorializing the terms of the client relationship.

In addition to understanding the nature of the services, clients must understand the cost they will be expected to pay for those services so they can make informed decisions about the professional services being provided. This standard requires members and candidates to inform their clients and prospective clients about the services they will receive and the associated costs. Disclosures regarding the cost of the services to clients mandated by Standard V(B) are those expected to be charged to and paid for by the client. Members and candidates should provide a reasonable amount of detail regarding the costs incurred by clients. The standard, however, does not require members and candidates to provide specific dollar amounts. For example, a firm that charges clients a quarterly fee based on the market value of assets under management will be unable to specify a dollar amount in advance. Members and candidates are also not required to disclose a description of the costs to the firm of providing those services. Again, best practice is for members and candidates with client-facing responsibilities to disclose information about the nature of the services and the related costs at the outset of the relationship as part of the client agreement.

The disclosure responsibilities of members and candidates under this standard are ongoing. Initial disclosures at the outset of the relationship alone may not meet the requirements of the standard. If the services or costs change, members and candidates must update the disclosures and provide the updated information to all impacted clients and prospective clients on a timely basis.

In addition, the scope of the disclosures is not limited to only those costs charged by the entity with which the client is in a direct relationship. Members and candidates with client-facing responsibilities must provide disclosures about all of the costs that are associated with the investment services and products that are provided to the client. This includes information on costs arising out of services provided by affiliates, related entities, or third parties for products and services utilized by members, candidates, or their firms in providing their services to clients. Members and candidates may not rely on the sophistication of clients and their supposed understanding of the nature and details of the investment process as a reason for not providing the information required by this standard. However, the information may be tailored to the knowledge and sophistication of each individual client.

The manner in which members and candidates provide the disclosures required by Standard V(B) is at their individual discretion so long as the disclosures are appropriate, accurate, timely, and complete. Best practice dictates that such disclosures be made in written form. Often, in large firms, disclosures about charges to and payments expected by clients are dictated by firm policy and practice. However, this does not relieve members or candidates of their responsibility to provide this information when that is part of their professional responsibilities. While members and candidates rely on and can be directed to use firm-generated disclosures, members and candidates should ensure that these disclosures meet the requirements of the Code and Standards. They have the responsibility to call to their firm's attention when the communication is lacking, flawed, or insufficient to meet the members' and candidates' responsibilities under the Code and Standards. In such a case, members and candidates should, when possible, supplement disclosures from the firm that they consider insufficient to meet the requirements of this standard. Ultimately, if members or candidates cannot rectify or supplement inadequate disclosures mandated by the firm, they should document their objections and take steps to dissociate from the activity.

Generally, this standard affects only client-facing members. While CFA Institute encourages all investment professionals to help ensure that clients receive sufficient disclosures, the standard does not impose a duty on members and candidates who do not interact with clients to ensure that others, not subject to the Code and Standards, comply with Standard V(B). As with other standards that may not be applicable to the professional responsibilities of all members and candidates (e.g., investment performance, suitability), those members and candidates who are part of a team of investment professionals providing services to clients but who do not have client-facing responsibilities need not expand their realm of responsibility to ensure appropriate disclosures to clients are made regarding the nature of services and the associated costs.

Informing Clients of the Investment Process

Members and candidates must adequately describe to clients and prospective clients the manner in which they conduct the investment decision-making process. Such disclosure should address factors that have positive and negative influences on the recommendations, including significant risks and limitations of the investment process used. The member or candidate must keep clients and other interested parties informed on an ongoing basis about changes to the investment process, especially newly identified significant risks and limitations. Only by thoroughly understanding the nature of the investment product or service can a client determine whether changes to that product or service could materially affect his or her investment objectives.

Understanding the basic characteristics of an investment is of great importance in judging the suitability of that investment on a standalone basis, but it is especially important in determining the impact each investment will have on the characteristics of a portfolio. Although the risk and return characteristics of a common stock might seem to be essentially the same for any investor when the stock is viewed in isolation, the effects of those characteristics greatly depend on the other investments held. For instance, if the particular stock will represent 90% of an individual's investments, the stock's importance in the portfolio is vastly different from what it would be to an investor with a highly diversified portfolio for whom the stock will represent only 2% of the holdings.

A firm's investment policy may include the use of outside advisers to manage various portions of clients' assets under management. Members and candidates should inform the clients about the specialization or diversification expertise provided by the external adviser(s). This information allows clients to understand the full mix of products and strategies being applied that may affect their investment objectives.

Different Forms of Communication

For purposes of Standard V(B), communication is not confined to a written report of the type traditionally generated by an analyst researching a security, company, or industry. A presentation of information can be made via any means of communication, including in-person recommendation or description, telephone conversation, media broadcast, or transmission by computer (e.g., on the internet).

Computer and mobile device communications have rapidly evolved over the past few years. Members and candidates using any social media service to communicate business information must be diligent in their efforts to avoid unintended problems because these services may not be available to all clients. When providing information to clients through new technologies, members and candidates should take reasonable steps to ensure that such delivery would treat all clients fairly and, if necessary, be considered publicly disseminated.

The nature of client communications is highly diverse—from one word ("buy" or "sell") to in-depth reports of more than 100 pages. A communication may contain a general recommendation about the market, asset allocations, or classes of investments (e.g., stocks, bonds, real estate) or may relate to a specific security. If recommendations are contained in capsule form (such as a recommended stock list), members and candidates should notify clients that additional information and analyses are available from the producer of the report.

Identifying Risks and Limitations

Members and candidates must outline to clients and prospective clients significant risks and limitations of the analysis contained in their investment products or recommendations. The type and nature of significant risks will depend on the investment process that members and candidates are following and on the personal circumstances of the client. In general, the use of leverage constitutes a significant risk and should be disclosed.

Members and candidates must adequately disclose the general market-related risks and the risks associated with the use of complex financial instruments that are deemed significant. Other types of risks that members and candidates may consider disclosing include, but are not limited to, counterparty risk, country risk, sector or industry risk, security-specific risk, and credit risk.

Investment securities and vehicles may have limiting factors that influence a client's or potential client's investment decision. Members and candidates must report to clients and prospective clients the existence of limitations significant to the decision-making process. Examples of such factors and attributes include, but are not limited to, investment liquidity and capacity. Liquidity is the ability to liquidate an investment on a timely basis at a reasonable cost. Capacity is the investment amount beyond which returns will be negatively affected by new investments.

The appropriateness of risk disclosure should be assessed on the basis of what was known at the time the investment action was taken (often called an *ex ante* basis). Members and candidates must disclose significant risks known to them at the time of the disclosure. Members and candidates cannot be expected to disclose risks they are unaware of at the time recommendations or investment actions are made. In assessing compliance with Standard V(B), it is important to establish knowledge of a purported significant risk or limitation. A one-time investment loss that occurs after the disclosure does not constitute a pertinent factor in assessing whether significant risks and limitations were properly disclosed. Having no knowledge of a risk or limitation that subsequently triggers a loss may reveal a deficiency in the diligence and reasonable basis of the research of the member or candidate but may not reveal a breach of Standard V(B).

Report Presentation

Once the analytical process has been completed, the member or candidate who prepares the report must include those elements that are important to the analysis and conclusions of the report so that the reader can follow and challenge the report's reasoning. A report writer who has done adequate investigation may emphasize certain areas, touch briefly on others, and omit certain aspects deemed unimportant. For instance, a report may dwell on a quarterly earnings release or new-product introduction and omit other matters as long as the analyst clearly stipulates the limits to the scope of the report.

Investment advice based on quantitative research and analysis must be supported by readily available reference material and should be applied in a manner consistent with previously applied methodology. If changes in methodology are made, they should be highlighted.

Distinction between Facts and Opinions in Reports

Standard V(B) requires that opinion be separated from fact. Violations often occur when reports fail to separate the past from the future by not indicating that earnings estimates, changes in the outlook for dividends, or future market price information are *opinions* subject to future circumstances.

In the case of complex quantitative analyses, members and candidates must clearly separate fact from statistical conjecture and should identify the known limitations of an analysis. Members and candidates may violate Standard V(B) by failing to identify the limits of statistically developed projections because such omission leaves readers unaware of the limits of the published projections.

Members and candidates should explicitly discuss with clients and prospective clients the assumptions used in the investment models and processes to generate the analysis. Caution should be used in promoting the perceived accuracy of any model or process to clients because the ultimate output is merely an estimate of future results and not a certainty.

49 STANDARD V(B): RECOMMENDED PROCEDURES

Because the selection of relevant factors is an analytical skill, determination of whether a member or candidate has used reasonable judgment in excluding and including information in research reports depends heavily on case-by-case review rather than a specific checklist.

Members and candidates should encourage their firms to have a rigorous methodology for reviewing research that is created for publication and dissemination to clients.

To assist in the after-the-fact review of a report, the member or candidate must maintain records indicating the nature of the research and should, if asked, be able to supply additional information to the client (or any user of the report) covering factors not included in the report.

STANDARD V(B): APPLICATION OF THE STANDARD

50

Example 1 (Costs of Services to Clients):

The nature of ABC Capital Private Equity Fund III's investments requires ABC Capital to routinely provide structuring advice to the companies in which the fund invests, for which ABC Capital charges a fee to those companies. It is the policy of ABC Capital to remit the fees it earns for restructuring advice to the fund if the investment in the underlying company decreases in value, but it retains the fees if the investment in the underlying company increases in value. The private placement memorandum does not disclose this arrangement because the firm's CEO, Alex Alphonso, views this as a common industry practice and that it provides a "win-win" for investors. ABC Capital's services contribute significantly to the returns enjoyed by investors in the ABC Capital Private Equity Fund III, and ABC Capital earns a substantial fee.

> *Comment*: Alphonso is in violation of Standard V(B) because the compensation received by ABC Capital has not been disclosed to clients who are investors in the fund. Alphonso may not rely on the sophistication of clients and their assumed understanding of the nature and details of the fee arrangements with underlying companies in which ABC Capital invests in as a reason for not providing the information required by this standard. This is true even though investors in ABC Private Equity Fund III benefit from the arrangement.

Example 2 (Costs of Services to Clients):

January James is an investment adviser tasked with completing a manager search for a client's portfolio. The search mandate is to identify a shortlist of investment managers who offer core fixed-income strategies managed to the benchmark identified in the client's investment policy statement. James begins her search with a set of criteria defined by her firm's manager research process policy. She identifies three candidates who fulfill these criteria but notices that her top-ranked manager has significantly higher fees than the other candidates on her list. Her firm's search criteria list fees as less important relative to the other criteria for ranking investment managers. To present investment performance for uniform comparison, James creates a fee comparison chart that lists each manager's performance on a gross-of-fee basis. She presents gross-of-fee performance over the same time periods and relative to the same benchmark. She also calculates the total amount of fees that would have been paid during each of the performance time periods presented. Finally, she lists each manager's fee schedule and any additional fees that may be charged outside the published fees. She explains to her client that prior to final selection, the investment managers will be required to present their final fee proposal.

> *Comment*: James's presentation of manager fees is appropriate because she provided a uniform comparison of manager services. Her presentation adheres to Standard V(B) Communication with Clients and Prospective Clients, which requires disclosure about the nature of services provided, along with information about the cost associated with those services.

Example 3 (Disclosure of Changed Fee Calculation Methodology):

Marc Maalouf works in a branch office for a large wealth management firm. The firm's fees are based on a percentage of the value of the assets managed in each client account. The firm has a standard method for valuing assets and calculating fees for all of its clients, which is disclosed to each client at the outset of the relationship. Maalouf becomes aware that, over time, the firm has transitioned to (1) using the market value of client assets at the end of the billing cycle instead of the average daily balance of the account and (2) including cash and cash equivalents in the fee calculation, which were previously excluded.

> *Comment*: Advisory fees are critical information that a client needs to know. Developing and maintaining clear, frequent, and thorough communication with clients about costs for the investment adviser's services allows them to make well-informed decisions about their investments, including about whether to engage or retain an investment adviser. Maalouf and his firm may change the advisory fee calculation methodology and policies over time for existing accounts, but Maalouf must make clients aware of any such changes. It is improper to change fee calculation methodology without disclosure, even if it results in lower fees.

Example 4 (Sufficient Disclosure of Investment System):

Sarah Williamson, director of marketing for Country Technicians, Inc., is convinced that she has found the perfect formula for increasing Country Technicians' income and diversifying its product base. Williamson plans to build on Country Technicians' reputation as a leading money manager by marketing an exclusive and expensive investment advice letter to high-net-worth individuals. One hitch in the plan is the complexity of Country Technicians' investment system—a combination of technical trading rules (based on historical price and volume fluctuations) and portfolio construction rules designed to minimize risk. To simplify the newsletter, she decides to include only each week's top five "buy" and "sell" recommendations and to leave out details of the valuation models and the portfolio structuring scheme.

> *Comment*: Williamson's plans for the newsletter violate Standard V(B). Williamson need not describe the investment system in detail in order to implement the advice effectively, but she must inform clients of Country Technicians' basic process and logic. Without understanding the basis for a recommendation, clients cannot possibly understand its limitations or its inherent risks.

Example 5 (Providing Opinions as Facts):

Richard Dox is a mining analyst for East Bank Securities. He has just finished his report on Boisy Bay Minerals. Included in his report is his own assessment of the geological extent of mineral reserves likely to be found on the company's land. Dox completed this calculation on the basis of the core samples from the company's latest drilling. According to Dox's calculations, the company has more than 500,000 ounces of gold on the property. Dox concludes his research report as follows: "Based on the fact that the company has 500,000 ounces of gold to be mined, I recommend a strong *buy*."

Comment: If Dox issues the report as written, he will violate Standard V(B). His calculation of the total gold reserves for the property based on the company's recent sample drilling is a quantitative opinion, not a fact. Opinion must be distinguished from fact in research reports.

Example 6 (Proper Description of a Security):

Olivia Thomas, an analyst at Government Brokers, Inc., which is a brokerage firm specializing in government bond trading, has produced a report that describes an investment strategy designed to benefit from an expected decline in U.S. interest rates. The firm's derivative products group has designed a structured product that will allow the firm's clients to benefit from this strategy. Thomas's report describing the strategy indicates that high returns are possible if various scenarios for declining interest rates are assumed. Citing the proprietary nature of the structured product underlying the strategy, the report does not describe in detail how the firm is able to offer such returns or the related risks in the scenarios, nor does the report address the likely returns of the strategy if, contrary to expectations, interest rates rise.

Comment: Thomas has violated Standard V(B) because her report fails to describe properly the basic characteristics of the actual and implied risks of the investment strategy, including how the structure was created and the degree to which leverage was embedded in the structure. The report should include a balanced discussion of how the strategy would perform in the case of rising as well as falling interest rates, preferably illustrating how the strategies might be expected to perform in the event of a reasonable variety of interest rate- and credit risk-spread scenarios. If liquidity issues are relevant with regard to the valuation of either the derivatives or the underlying securities, provisions the firm has made to address those risks should also be disclosed.

Example 7 (Notification of Fund Mandate Change):

May & Associates is an aggressive growth manager that has represented itself since its inception as a specialist at investing in small-cap U.S. stocks. One of May's selection criteria is a maximum capitalization of US$250 million for any given company. After a string of successful years of superior performance relative to its peers, May has expanded its client base significantly, to the point at which assets under management now exceed US$3 billion. For liquidity purposes, May's chief investment officer (CIO) decides to lift the maximum permissible market-cap ceiling to US$500 million and change the firm's sales and marketing literature accordingly to inform prospective clients and third-party consultants.

Comment: Although May's CIO is correct about informing potentially interested parties as to the change in investment process, he must also notify May's existing clients. Among the latter group might be a number of clients who not only retained May as a small-cap manager but also retained mid-cap and large-cap specialists in a multiple-manager approach. Such clients could regard May's change of criteria as a style change that distorts their overall asset allocations.

Example 8 (Notification of Fund Mandate Change):

Rather than lifting the ceiling for its universe from US$250 million to US$500 million, May & Associates extends its small-cap universe to include a number of non-US companies.

> *Comment*: Standard V(B) requires that May's CIO advise May's clients of this change because the firm may have been retained by some clients specifically for its prowess at investing in U.S. small-cap stocks. Other changes that require client notification are introducing derivatives to emulate a certain market sector or relaxing various other constraints, such as portfolio beta. In all such cases, members and candidates must disclose changes to all interested parties.

Example 9 (Notification of Changes to the Investment Process):

RJZ Capital Management is an active value style equity manager that selects stocks by using a combination of four multifactor models. The firm has found favorable results when back testing the most recent 10 years of available market data in a new dividend discount model (DDM) designed by the firm. This model is based on projected inflation rates, earnings growth rates, and interest rates. The president of RJZ decides to replace its simple model that uses price to trailing 12-month earnings with the new DDM.

> *Comment*: Because the introduction of a new and different valuation model represents a material change in the investment process, RJZ's president must communicate the change to the firm's clients. RJZ is moving away from a model based on hard data toward a new model that is at least partly dependent on the firm's forecasting skills. Clients would likely view such a model as a significant change rather than a mere refinement of RJZ's process.

Example 10 (Notification of Changes to the Investment Process):

RJZ Capital Management loses the chief architect of its multifactor valuation system. Without informing its clients, the president of RJZ decides to redirect the firm's talents and resources toward developing a product for passive equity management—a product that will emulate the performance of a major market index.

> *Comment:* By failing to disclose to clients a substantial change to its investment process, the president of RJZ has violated Standard V(B).

Example 11 (Notification of Changes to the Investment Process):

At Fundamental Asset Management, Inc., the responsibility for selecting stocks for addition to the firm's "approved" list has just shifted from individual security analysts to a committee consisting of the research director and three senior portfolio managers. Eleanor Morales, a portfolio manager with Fundamental Asset Management, thinks this change is not important enough to communicate to her clients.

Comment: Morales must disclose the process change to all her clients. Some of Fundamental's clients might be concerned about the morale and motivation among the firm's best research analysts after such a change. Moreover, clients might challenge the stock-picking track record of the portfolio managers and might even want to monitor the situation closely.

Example 12 (Sufficient Disclosure of Investment System):

Amanda Chinn is the investment director for Diversified Asset Management, which manages the endowment of a charitable organization. Because of recent staff departures, Diversified has decided to limit its direct investment focus to large-cap securities and supplement the needs for small-cap and mid-cap management by hiring outside fund managers. In describing the planned strategy change to the charity, Chinn's update letter states, "As investment director, I will directly oversee the investment team managing the endowment's large-capitalization allocation. I will coordinate the selection and ongoing review of external managers responsible for allocations to classes." The letter also describes the reasons for the change and the characteristics external managers must have to be considered.

Comment: Standard V(B) requires the disclosure of the investment process used to construct the portfolio of the fund. Changing the investment process from managing all classes of investments within the firm to the use of external managers is one example of information that needs to be communicated to clients. Chinn and her firm have embraced the principles of Standard V(B) by providing their client with relevant information. The charity can now make a reasonable decision about whether Diversified Asset Management remains the appropriate manager for its fund.

Example 13 (Notification of Changes to the Investment Process):

Michael Papis is the chief investment officer of his state's retirement fund. The fund has always used outside advisers for the real estate allocation, and this information is clearly presented in all fund communications. Thomas Nagle, a recognized sell-side research analyst and Papis's business school classmate, recently left the investment bank he worked for to start his own asset management firm, Accessible Real Estate. Nagle is trying to build his assets under management and contacts Papis about gaining some of the retirement fund's allocation. In the previous few years, the performance of the retirement fund's real estate investments was in line with the fund's benchmark but was not extraordinary. Papis decides to help out his old friend and also to seek better returns by moving the real estate allocation to Accessible. The only notice of the change in adviser appears in the next annual report in the listing of associated advisers.

Comment: Papis has violated Standard V(B). He attempted to hide the nature of his decision to change external managers by making only a limited disclosure. The plan recipients and the fund's trustees need to be aware when changes are made to ensure that operational procedures are being followed.

See also Standard IV(C) Responsibilities of Supervisors, Standard V(A) Diligence and Reasonable Basis, and Standard VI(A) Disclosure of Conflicts.

Example 14 (Notification of Errors):

Jérôme Dupont works for the credit research group of XYZ Asset Management, where he is in charge of developing and updating credit risk models. In order to perform accurately, his models need to be regularly updated with the latest market data.

Dupont does not interact with or manage money for any of the firm's clients. He is in contact with the firm's US corporate bond fund manager, John Smith, who has only very superficial knowledge of the model and who from time to time asks very basic questions regarding the output recommendations. Smith does not consult Dupont with respect to finalizing his clients' investment strategies.

Dupont's recently assigned objective is to develop a new emerging market corporate credit risk model. The firm is planning to expand into emerging credit, and the development of such a model is a critical step in this process. Because Smith seems to follow the model's recommendations without much concern for its quality as he develops his clients' investment strategies, Dupont decides to focus his time on the development of the new emerging market model and neglects to update the US model.

After several months without regular updates, Dupont's diagnostic statistics start to show alarming signs with respect to the quality of the US credit model. Instead of conducting the long and complicated data update, Dupont introduces new codes into his model with some limited new data as a quick "fix." He thinks this change will address the issue without needing to complete the full data update, so he continues working on the new emerging market model.

Several months following the quick "fix," another set of diagnostic statistics reveals nonsensical results and Dupont realizes that his earlier change contained an error. He quickly corrects the error and alerts Smith. Smith realizes that some of the prior trades he performed were due to erroneous model results. Smith rebalances the portfolio to remove the securities purchased based on the questionable results without reporting the issue to anyone else.

> *Comment*: Smith violated V(B) by not disclosing a material error in the investment process. Clients should have been informed about the error and the corrective actions the firm was undertaking on their behalf.
>
> See also Standard V(A) Diligence and Reasonable Basis

Example 15 (Notification of Risks and Limitations):

Quantitative analyst Yuri Yakovlev, has developed an investment strategy that selects small-cap stocks on the basis of quantitative signals. Yakovlev's strategy typically identifies only a small number of stocks (10–20) that tend to be illiquid, but according to his backtests, the strategy generates significant risk-adjusted returns. The partners at Yakovlev's firm, QSC Capital, are impressed by these results. After a thorough examination of the strategy's risks, stress testing, historical backtesting, and scenario analysis, QSC decides to seed the strategy with US$10 million of internal capital in order for Yakovlev to create a track record for the strategy.

After two years, the strategy has generated performance returns greater than the appropriate benchmark and the Sharpe ratio of the fund is close to 1.0. On the basis of these results, QSC decides to actively market the fund to large institutional investors. While creating the offering materials, Yakovlev informs the marketing team that the capacity of the strategy is limited. The extent of the limitation is difficult to ascertain with precision; it depends on market liquidity and other factors in his model that can evolve over time. Yakovlev indicates that given the current market conditions, investments in the fund beyond US$100 million of capital could become more difficult and negatively affect expected fund returns.

Alan Wellard, the manager of the marketing team, is a partner with 30 years of marketing experience and explains to Yakovlev that these are complex technical issues that will muddy the marketing message. According to Wellard the offering material should focus solely on the great track record of the fund. Yakovlev does not object because the fund, with US$12 million of capital, is very far from the US$100 million threshold.

> *Comment*: Yakovlev and Wellard have not appropriately disclosed a significant limitation associated with the investment product. Yakovlev believes this limitation, once reached, will materially affect the returns of the fund. While the fund is currently far from the US$100 million mark, current and prospective investors must be made aware of this capacity issue. If significant limitations are complicated to grasp and clients do not have the technical background required to understand them, Yakovlev and Wellard should either educate the clients or ascertain whether the fund is suitable for each client.

Example 16 (Notification of Risks and Limitations):

Brickell Advisers offers investment advisory services mainly to South American clients. Julietta Ramon, a risk analyst at Brickell, describes to clients how the firm uses value at risk (VaR) analysis to track the risk of its strategies. Ramon assures clients that calculating a VaR at a 99% confidence level, using a 20-day holding period, and applying a methodology based on an ex-ante Monte Carlo simulation is extremely effective. The firm has never had losses greater than those predicted by this VaR analysis.

> *Comment*: Ramon has not sufficiently communicated the risks associated with the investment process to satisfy the requirements of Standard V(B). The losses predicted by a VaR analysis depend greatly on the inputs used in the model. The size and probability of losses can differ significantly from what an individual model predicts. Ramon must disclose how the inputs were selected and the potential limitations and risks associated with the investment strategy.

Example 17 (Notification of Risks and Limitations):

Lily Smith attended an industry conference and noticed that John Baker, an investment manager with Baker Associates, attracted a great deal of attention from the conference participants. On the basis of her knowledge of Baker's reputation and the interest he received at the conference, Smith recommends adding Baker Associates to the approved manager platform. Her recommendation to the approval committee included the statement "John Baker is well respected in the industry, and his insights are consistently sought after by investors. Our clients are sure to benefit from investing with Baker Associates."

> *Comment*: Smith is not appropriately separating facts from opinions in her recommendation to include the manager within the platform. Her actions conflict with the requirements of Standard V(B). Smith is relying on her opinions about Baker's reputation and the fact that many attendees were talking with him at the conference. Smith should also review the requirements of Standard V(A) regarding reasonable basis to determine the level of review necessary to recommend Baker Associates.

51 STANDARD V(C) RECORD RETENTION

- ☐ demonstrate a thorough knowledge of the CFA Institute Code of Ethics and Standards of Professional Conduct by interpreting the Code and Standards in various situations involving issues of professional integrity
- ☐ recommend practices and procedures designed to prevent violations of the Code and Standards

Members and Candidates must develop and maintain appropriate records to support their investment analyses, recommendations, actions, and other investment-related communications with clients and prospective clients.

Guidance

Highlights:

- *New Media Records*
- *Records Are Property of the Firm*
- *Local Requirements*

Members and candidates must retain records that substantiate the scope of their research and reasons for their actions or conclusions. The retention requirement applies to decisions to buy or sell a security as well as reviews undertaken that do not lead to a change in position. Which records are required to support recommendations or investment actions depends on the role of the member or candidate in the investment decision-making process. Records may be maintained either in hard copy or electronic form.

Some examples of supporting documentation that assists the member or candidate in meeting the requirements for retention are as follows:

- personal notes from meetings with the covered company,
- press releases or presentations issued by the covered company,
- computer-based model outputs and analyses,
- computer-based model input parameters,
- risk analyses of securities' impacts on a portfolio,
- selection criteria for external advisers,
- notes from clients from meetings to review investment policy statements, and
- outside research reports.

New Media Records

The increased use of new and evolving technological formats (e.g., social media) for gathering and sharing information creates new challenges in maintaining the appropriate records and files. The nature or format of the information does not remove a member's or candidate's responsibility to maintain a record of information used in his or her analysis or communicated to clients.

Members and candidates should understand that although employers and local regulators are developing digital media retention policies, these policies may lag behind the advent of new communication channels. Such lag places greater responsibility on the individual for ensuring that all relevant information is retained. Examples of non-print media formats that should be retained include, but are not limited to,

- e-mails,
- text messages,
- blog posts, and
- social media posts.

Records Are Property of the Firm

As a general matter, records created as part of a member's or candidate's professional activity on behalf of his or her employer are the property of the firm. When a member or candidate leaves a firm to seek other employment, the member or candidate cannot take the property of the firm, including original forms or copies of supporting records of the member's or candidate's work, to the new employer without the express consent of the previous employer. The member or candidate cannot use historical recommendations or research reports created at the previous firm because the supporting documentation is unavailable. For future use, the member or candidate must re-create the supporting records at the new firm with information gathered through public sources or directly from the covered company and not from memory or sources obtained at the previous employer.

Local Requirements

Local regulators often impose requirements on members, candidates, and their firms related to record retention that must be followed. Firms may also implement policies detailing the applicable time frame for retaining research and client communication records. Fulfilling such regulatory and firm requirements satisfies the requirements of Standard V(C). In the absence of regulatory guidance or firm policies, CFA Institute recommends maintaining records for at least seven years.

STANDARD V(C): RECOMMENDED PROCEDURES

52

The responsibility to maintain records that support investment action generally falls with the firm rather than individuals. Members and candidates must, however, archive research notes and other documents, either electronically or in hard copy, that support their current investment-related communications. Doing so will assist their firms in complying with requirements for preservation of internal or external records.

53 STANDARD V(C): APPLICATION OF THE STANDARD

Example 1 (Record Retention and IPS Objectives and Recommendations):

One of Nikolas Lindstrom's clients is upset by the negative investment returns of his equity portfolio. The investment policy statement for the client requires that the portfolio manager follow a benchmark-oriented approach. The benchmark for the client includes a 35% investment allocation in the technology sector. The client acknowledges that this allocation was appropriate, but over the past three years, technology stocks have suffered severe losses. The client complains to the investment manager for allocating so much money to this sector.

> *Comment*: For Lindstrom, having appropriate records is important to show that over the past three years, the portion of technology stocks in the benchmark index was 35%, as called for in the IPS. Lindstrom should also have the client's IPS stating that the benchmark was appropriate for the client's investment objectives. He should also have records indicating that the investment has been explained appropriately to the client and that the IPS was updated on a regular basis. Taking these actions, Lindstrom would be in compliance with Standard V(C).

Example 2 (Record Retention and Research Process):

Malcolm Young is a research analyst who writes numerous reports rating companies in the luxury retail industry. His reports are based on a variety of sources, including interviews with company managers, manufacturers, and economists; on-site company visits; customer surveys; and secondary research from analysts covering related industries.

> *Comment*: Young must carefully document and keep copies of all the information that goes into his reports, including the secondary or third-party research of other analysts. Failure to maintain such files would violate Standard V(C).

Example 3 (Records as Firm, Not Employee, Property):

Martin Blank develops an analytical model while he is employed by Green Partners Investment Management, LLP (GPIM). While at the firm, he systematically documents the assumptions that make up the model as well as his reasoning behind the assumptions. As a result of the success of his model, Blank is hired to be the head of the research department of one of GPIM's competitors. Blank takes copies of the records supporting his model to his new firm.

> *Comment*: The records created by Blank supporting the research model he developed at GPIM are the records of GPIM. Taking the documents with him to his new employer without GPIM's permission violates Standard V(C). To use the model in the future, Blank must re-create the records supporting his model at the new firm.

STANDARD VI: CONFLICTS OF INTEREST

54

- [ ] demonstrate a thorough knowledge of the CFA Institute Code of Ethics and Standards of Professional Conduct by interpreting the Code and Standards in various situations involving issues of professional integrity
- [ ] recommend practices and procedures designed to prevent violations of the Code and Standards

Standard VI(A) Avoid or Disclose Conflicts

Members and Candidates must avoid or make full and fair disclosure of all matters that could reasonably be expected to impair their independence and objectivity or interfere with respective duties to their clients, prospective clients, and employer. Members and Candidates must ensure that such disclosures are prominent, are delivered in plain language, and communicate the relevant information effectively.

Guidance

Highlights:

- *Disclosure of Conflicts to Employers*
- *Disclosure of Conflicts to Clients*
- *Cross-Departmental Conflicts*
- *Conflicts with Stock Ownership*
- *Conflicts as a Board Member or Director*

A conflict of interest is any matter that could reasonably be expected to impair independence and objectivity or raise a question about whether actions, judgment, or decision making is free from bias. Conflicts of interest occur when there is a personal or professional interest that may impair a member's or candidate's ability to perform his or her professional responsibilities in an independent and objective manner. Conflicts of interest often arise in the investment profession. Conflicts can occur between the interests of clients, the interests of employers, and the member's or candidate's own personal interests. Common sources for conflict are compensation structures, especially incentive and bonus structures that provide immediate returns for members and candidates with little or no consideration of long-term value creation. Identifying and managing conflicts of interest is critically important to engaging in ethical conduct.

Best practice is to avoid actual conflicts or the appearance of conflicts of interest. When it is not reasonable for members and candidates to avoid a conflict, clear and complete disclosure to mitigate the conflict is necessary.

Standard VI(A) protects investors and employers by requiring members and candidates to avoid or fully disclose to clients, potential clients, and employers all actual and potential conflicts of interest. When a member or candidate has made full disclosure of an unavoidable conflict, the member's or candidate's employer, clients, and prospective clients will have the information needed to evaluate the objectivity of the investment advice or action taken on their behalf.

To be effective, disclosures must be prominent and must be made in plain language and in a manner designed to effectively communicate the information. Members and candidates are responsible for determining how often, in what manner, and in what particular circumstances the disclosure of conflicts must be made. Best practice dictates updating disclosures when the nature of a conflict of interest changes materially—for example, if the nature of a conflict of interest worsens through the introduction of bonuses based on each quarter's profits as opposed to annual profits. In making and updating disclosures of conflicts of interest, members and candidates should err on the side of caution to ensure that conflicts are effectively communicated.

Disclosure of Conflicts to Employers

Disclosure of conflicts to employers may be appropriate in many instances. When reporting conflicts of interest to employers, members and candidates must give their employers enough information to assess the impact of the conflict. By complying with employer guidelines, members and candidates allow their employers to avoid potentially embarrassing and costly ethical or regulatory violations.

Reportable situations include conflicts that would interfere with rendering unbiased investment advice and conflicts that would cause a member or candidate to act not in the employer's best interest. The same circumstances that generate conflicts to be reported to clients and prospective clients also dictate reporting to employers. Ownership of stocks analyzed or recommended, participation on outside boards, and financial or other pressures that could influence a decision are to be promptly reported to the employer so that their impact can be assessed and a decision on how to resolve the conflict can be made.

The mere appearance of a conflict of interest may create problems for members, candidates, and their employers. Therefore, many of the conflicts previously mentioned may be explicitly prohibited by an employer in order to avoid those conflicts altogether. For example, many employers restrict personal trading, outside board membership, and related activities to prevent situations that might not normally be considered problematic from a conflict-of-interest point of view but that could give the appearance of a conflict of interest. Members and candidates must comply with these employer restrictions. Members and candidates should take reasonable steps to avoid conflicts. However, if the conflicts are not resolved, they must report conflicts promptly.

Standard VI(A) also deals with a member's or candidate's conflicts of interest that might be detrimental to the employer's business. Any potential conflict situation that could prevent clear judgment about or full commitment to the execution of a member's or candidate's duties to the employer should be avoided. If the member or candidate does not avoid the conflict, it must be reported to the member's or candidate's employer.

Disclosure of Conflicts to Clients

Members and candidates must maintain their objectivity when rendering investment advice or taking investment action. Investment advice or actions may be perceived to be tainted in numerous situations. For instance, a member or candidate may not be objective if he or she owns stock in the company that is the subject of an investment recommendation or if the member or candidate has a close personal relationship with the company managers. Requiring members and candidates to disclose all matters that reasonably could be expected to impair the member's or candidate's objectivity when a conflict exists mitigates the conflict and allows clients and prospective clients to judge motives and possible biases for themselves.

While avoiding conflicts altogether is preferred, often in the investment industry, a conflict or the perception of a conflict is not reasonably avoidable. The most obvious conflicts of interest, which must always be avoided or disclosed, are relationships between an issuer and the member, the candidate, or his or her firm (such as a directorship or consultancy by a member; investment banking, underwriting, and financial relationships; broker/dealer market-making activities; and material beneficial ownership of stock). For the purposes of Standard VI(A), members and candidates beneficially own securities or other investments if they have a direct or indirect pecuniary interest in the securities, have the power to vote or direct the voting of the shares of the securities or investments, or have the power to dispose or direct the disposition of the security or investment.

A member or candidate must take reasonable steps to determine whether a conflict of interest exists and disclose to clients any known conflicts of the member's or candidate's firm. As an example, disclosure of broker/dealer market-making activities alerts clients that a purchase or sale might be made from or to the firm's proprietary account and that the firm has a special interest in the price of the stock.

Additionally, disclosures must be made to clients regarding conflicts that may arise in fee arrangements, subadvisory agreements, or other situations involving nonstandard fee structures. Equally important is the disclosure of arrangements in which the firm benefits directly from investment recommendations. An obvious conflict of interest is the rebate of a portion of the service fee some classes of mutual funds charge to investors. Members and candidates must disclose such relationships so clients can fully understand such conflicts.

Cross-Departmental Conflicts

Other circumstances may give rise to actual or potential conflicts of interest. For instance, a sell-side analyst working for a broker/dealer may be encouraged, not only by members of her or his own firm but also by corporate issuers themselves, to write research reports about particular companies. The buy-side analyst is likely to be faced with similar conflicts as banks exercise their underwriting and security-dealing powers. The marketing division may ask an analyst to recommend the stock of a certain company in order to obtain business from that company.

The potential for conflicts of interest also exists with broker-sponsored limited partnerships formed to invest venture capital. Members and candidates may be expected not only to follow issues from these partnerships once they are offered to the public but also to promote the issues in the secondary market after public offerings. Members and candidates must resolve situations presenting potential conflicts of interest or disclose them in accordance with the principles set forth in Standard VI(A).

Conflicts with Stock Ownership

The most prevalent conflict requiring disclosure under Standard VI(A) is a member's or candidate's ownership of stock in companies that he or she recommends to clients or that clients hold. The simplest method for preventing a conflict is to avoid the conflict by prohibiting members and candidates from owning any such securities, but this approach may be overly burdensome and too restrictive. Members and candidates must disclose any beneficial ownership interest in a security or other investment that the member or candidate is recommending. Conflicts arising from personal investing are discussed more fully in the guidance for Standard VI(B).

Conflicts as a Board Member or Director

Service as a board member or director poses three basic conflicts of interest. First, a conflict may exist between the duties owed to clients and the duties owed to shareholders of the company. Second, investment personnel who serve as directors may receive securities or options to purchase securities of the company as compensation for serving on the board, which could raise questions about trading actions that might increase the value of those securities. Third, board service creates the opportunity to receive material nonpublic information involving the company. Even though the information is confidential, the perception could be that information not available to the public is being communicated to a director's firm—whether a broker, investment adviser, or other type of organization. When members or candidates providing investment services also serve as directors, they should be isolated from those making investment decisions by the use of firewalls or similar restrictions.

55 STANDARD VI(A): APPLICATION OF THE STANDARD

Example 1 (Conflict of Interest and Business Relationships):

Henry Weiss is a research analyst with Williamsburg Company, a broker and investment banking firm. Williamsburg's merger and acquisition department has represented Jimco, a conglomerate, in all of Jimco's acquisitions for 20 years. From time to time, Williamsburg officers sit on the boards of directors of various Jimco subsidiaries. Weiss is writing a research report on Jimco.

> *Comment*: Weiss must disclose in his research report Williamsburg's special relationship with Jimco. Broker/dealer management of and participation in public offerings must be disclosed in research reports. Because the position of underwriter to a company entails a special past and potential future relationship with a company that is the subject of investment advice, it threatens the independence and objectivity of the report writer and must be disclosed.

Example 2 (Conflict of Interest and Business Stock Ownership):

The investment management firm of Dover & Roe sells a 25% interest in its partnership to a multinational bank holding company, First of New York. Immediately after the sale, Roy Hobbs, president of Dover & Roe, changes her recommendation for First of New York's common stock from "sell" to "buy" and adds First of New York's commercial paper to Dover & Roe's approved list for purchase.

> *Comment*: Best practice would be for Hobbs to discontinue research coverage of First of New York because the new ownership interest in this company creates a conflict of interest. At minimum, Hobbs must disclose the new relationship with First of New York to all Dover & Roe clients. Hobbs must also require the ownership interest to be disclosed to clients by the firm's portfolio managers when they make specific investment recommendations or take investment actions with respect to First of New York's securities.

Example 3 (Conflict of Interest and Personal Stock Ownership):

Karl Fargmon, a research analyst who follows firms producing office equipment, has been recommending purchase of Kincaid Printing because of its innovative new line of copiers. After his initial report on the company, Fargmon's wife inherits from a distant relative US$3 million of Kincaid stock. One year after his initial report on the company, Fargmon is asked to write a follow-up report on Kincaid.

> *Comment*: At minimum, Fargmon must disclose his wife's ownership of the Kincaid stock to his employer and in his follow-up report. Best practice is to avoid the conflict by asking his employer to assign another analyst to draft the follow-up report.

Example 4 (Conflict of Interest and Personal Stock Ownership):

Julie Roberts is speculating in penny stocks for her own account and purchases 100,000 shares of Drew Mining, Inc., for US$0.30 a share. She intends to sell these shares at the sign of any substantial upward price movement of the stock. A week later, her employer asks her to write a report on penny stocks in the mining industry to be published in two weeks. Even without owning the Drew stock, Roberts would recommend it in her report as a "buy." A surge in the price of the stock to the US$2 range is likely to result once the report is issued.

> *Comment*: Roberts must disclose the conflict to her employer and should consider declining the research assignment on Drew Mining. If Roberts's employer has her write the report despite the conflict, Roberts must disclose the conflict in her report.

Example 5 (Conflict of Interest and Compensation Arrangements):

Sarah Snead, a portfolio manager for Thomas Investment Counsel, LLC, specializes in managing public retirement funds and defined benefit pension plan accounts, all of which have long-term investment objectives. A year ago, Snead's employer, in an attempt to motivate and retain key investment professionals, introduced a bonus compensation system that rewards portfolio managers on the basis of quarterly performance relative to their peers and to certain benchmark indexes. In an attempt to improve the short-term performance of her accounts, Snead changes her investment strategy and purchases several high-beta stocks for client portfolios. These purchases are seemingly contrary to the clients' investment policy statements (IPSs). No change in objective or strategy has been recommended by Snead during the year.

> *Comment*: Snead has violated Standard VI(A) by failing to inform her clients of the changes in her compensation arrangement with her employer, which created a conflict of interest between her compensation and her clients' IPSs. Firms may pay employees on the basis of performance, but pressure by Thomas Investment Counsel to achieve short-term performance goals conflicts with the requirement to take only investment actions that are consistent with the objectives of Snead's accounts.

Example 6 (Conflict of Interest and Compensation Arrangements):

Kevin Carter is a representative with Bengal International, a registered broker/dealer. Carter is approached by a stock promoter for Badger Company, who offers to pay Carter additional compensation for sales of Badger Company's stock to Carter's clients. Carter accepts the stock promoter's offer but does not disclose the arrangement to his clients or to his employer. Carter sells shares of the stock to his clients.

> *Comment*: Carter has violated Standard VI(A) by failing to disclose to clients that he is receiving additional compensation for recommending and selling Badger stock. At minimum, Carter must disclose the arrangement with Badger to his clients so they may evaluate whether Carter's recommendations to buy Badger were affected by this arrangement. Best practice is for Carter to avoid this conflict of interest altogether by declining the offer of additional compensation from Badger Company.

Example 7 (Conflict of Interest and Requested Favors):

Henri Papis is the chief investment officer of his state's retirement fund. The fund has always used external managers for the real estate allocation, and this information is clearly presented in all fund communications. Eric Nagle, a recognized sell-side research analyst and Papis's business school classmate, recently left the investment bank he worked for to start his own asset management firm, Accessible Real Estate. Nagle is trying to build his assets under management, and he contacts Papis about gaining some of the retirement fund's real estate allocation. In the previous few years, the performance of the retirement fund's real estate investments was in line with the fund's benchmark but was not extraordinary. Papis decides to help out his old friend and also to seek better returns by moving the real estate allocation to Accessible. The only notice of the change in managers appears in the next annual report in the listing of external managers.

> *Comment*: Papis has violated Standard VI(A) by not disclosing to his employer his personal relationship with Nagle. Disclosure of his past history with Nagle would allow his firm to determine whether the conflict may have impaired Papis's independence in deciding to change external managers.

56 STANDARD VI(B) PRIORITY OF TRANSACTIONS

- [ ] demonstrate a thorough knowledge of the CFA Institute Code of Ethics and Standards of Professional Conduct by interpreting the Code and Standards in various situations involving issues of professional integrity
- [ ] recommend practices and procedures designed to prevent violations of the Code and Standards

> Investment transactions for clients and employers must have priority over investment transactions in which a Member or Candidate is the beneficial owner.

Guidance

Highlights:

- *Avoiding Potential Conflicts*
- *Personal Trading Secondary to Trading for Clients*
- *Standards for Nonpublic Information*
- *Impact on All Accounts with Beneficial Ownership*

Standard VI(B) reinforces the responsibility of members and candidates to give the interests of their clients and employers priority over their personal financial interests. This standard is designed to prevent any potential conflict of interest or the appearance of a conflict of interest with respect to personal transactions. Client interests have priority. Client transactions must take precedence over transactions made on behalf of the member's or candidate's firm or personal transactions.

Avoiding Potential Conflicts

Conflicts between the client's interest and an investment professional's personal interest may occur. Although conflicts of interest exist, nothing is inherently unethical about individual managers, advisers, or mutual fund employees making money from personal investments as long as (1) the client is not disadvantaged by the trade, (2) the investment professional does not benefit personally from trades undertaken for clients, and (3) the investment professional complies with applicable regulatory requirements.

Some situations occur where a member or candidate may need to enter a personal transaction that runs counter to current recommendations or what the portfolio manager is doing for client portfolios. For example, a member or candidate may be required at some point to sell an asset to make a college tuition payment or a down payment on a home, to meet a margin call, or so on. The sale may be contrary to the long-term advice the member or candidate is currently providing to clients. In these situations, the same three criteria given in the preceding paragraph should be applied in the transaction so as to not violate Standard VI(B).

Personal Trading Secondary to Trading for Clients

Standard VI(B) states that transactions for clients and employers must have priority over transactions in securities or other investments for which a member or candidate is the beneficial owner. The objective of the standard is to prevent personal transactions from adversely affecting the interests of clients or employers. A member or candidate having the same investment positions or being co-invested with clients does not always create a conflict. Some clients in certain investment situations require members or candidates to have aligned interests. Personal investment positions or transactions of members or candidates or their firm should never, however, adversely affect client investments.

Standards for Nonpublic Information

Standard VI(B) covers the activities of members and candidates who have knowledge of pending transactions that may be made on behalf of their clients or employers, who have access to nonpublic information during the normal preparation of research recommendations, or who take investment actions. Members and candidates are prohibited from conveying nonpublic information to any person whose relationship to the member or candidate makes the member or candidate a beneficial owner of the person's securities. Members and candidates must not convey this information to any other person if the nonpublic information can be deemed material.

Impact on All Accounts with Beneficial Ownership

Members or candidates may undertake transactions in accounts for which they are a beneficial owner only after their clients and employers have had adequate opportunity to act on a recommendation. Personal transactions include those made for the member's or candidate's own account, for family (including spouse, children, and other immediate family members) accounts, and for accounts in which the member or candidate has a direct or indirect pecuniary interest, such as a trust or retirement account. Family accounts that are client accounts should be treated like any other firm account and should neither be given special treatment nor be disadvantaged because of the family relationship. If a member or candidate has a beneficial ownership in the account, however, the member or candidate may be subject to preclearance or reporting requirements of the employer or applicable law.

57 STANDARD VI(B): RECOMMENDED PROCEDURES

Policies and procedures designed to prevent potential conflicts of interest, and even the appearance of a conflict of interest, with respect to personal transactions are critical to establishing investor confidence in the securities industry. Therefore, members and candidates should urge their firms to establish such policies and procedures. Because investment firms vary greatly in assets under management, types of clients, number of employees, and so on, each firm should have policies regarding personal investing that are best suited to the firm. Members and candidates should then prominently disclose these policies to clients and prospective clients.

The specific provisions of each firm's standards will vary, but all firms should adopt certain basic procedures to address the conflict areas created by personal investing. These procedures include the following:

- *Limited participation in equity IPOs*: Some eagerly awaited IPOs rise significantly in value shortly after the issue is brought to market. Because the new issue may be highly attractive and sought after, the opportunity to participate in the IPO may be limited. Therefore, purchases of IPOs by investment personnel create conflicts of interest in two principal ways. First, participation in an IPO may have the appearance of taking away an attractive investment opportunity from clients for personal gain—a clear breach of the duty of loyalty to clients. Second, personal purchases in IPOs may have the appearance that the investment opportunity is being bestowed as an incentive to make future investment decisions for the benefit of the party providing the opportunity. Members and candidates can avoid these conflicts or appearances of conflicts of interest by not participating in IPOs.

Reliable and systematic review procedures should be established to ensure that conflicts relating to IPOs are identified and appropriately dealt with by supervisors. Members and candidates should preclear their participation in IPOs, even in situations without any conflict of interest between a member's or candidate's participation in an IPO and the client's interests. Members and candidates should not benefit from the position that their clients occupy in the marketplace—through preferred trading, the allocation of limited offerings, or oversubscription.

- *Restrictions on private placements*: Strict limits should be placed on investment personnel acquiring securities in private placements, and appropriate supervisory and review procedures should be established to prevent noncompliance.

Firms do not routinely use private placements for clients (e.g., venture capital deals) because of the high risk associated with them. Conflicts related to private placements are more significant to members and candidates who manage large pools of assets or act as plan sponsors because these managers may be offered special opportunities, such as private placements, as a reward or an enticement for continuing to do business with a particular broker.

Participation in private placements raises conflict-of-interest issues that are similar to issues surrounding IPOs. Investment personnel should not be involved in transactions, including (but not limited to) private placements, that could be perceived as favors or gifts that seem designed to influence future judgment or to reward past business deals.

Whether the venture eventually proves to be good or bad, managers have an immediate conflict concerning private placement opportunities. If and when the investments go public, participants in private placements have an incentive to recommend the investments to clients regardless of the suitability of the investments for their clients. Doing so increases the value of the participants' personal portfolios.

- *Establish blackout/restricted periods*: Investment personnel involved in the investment decision-making process should establish blackout periods prior to trades for clients so that managers cannot take advantage of their knowledge of client activity by "front-running" client trades (trading for one's personal account before trading for client accounts).

Individual firms must decide who within the firm should be required to comply with the trading restrictions. At a minimum, all individuals who are involved in the investment decision-making process should be subject to the same restricted period. Each firm must determine specific requirements related to blackout and restricted periods that are most relevant to the firm while ensuring that the procedures are governed by the guiding principles set forth in the Code and Standards. Size of firm and type of securities purchased are relevant factors. For example, in a large firm, a blackout requirement is, in effect, a total trading ban because the firm is continually trading in most securities. In a small firm, the blackout period is more likely to prevent the investment manager from front-running.

- *Reporting requirements*: Supervisors should establish reporting procedures for investment personnel, including disclosure of personal holdings/beneficial ownerships, confirmations of trades to the firm and the employee, and preclearance procedures. Once trading restrictions are in place, they must be enforced. The best method for monitoring and enforcing procedures to eliminate conflicts of interest in personal trading is through reporting requirements, including the following:

  - *Disclosure of holdings in which the employee has a beneficial interest*: Disclosure by investment personnel to the firm should be made upon commencement of the employment relationship and at least annually thereafter. To address privacy considerations, disclosure of personal holdings should be handled in a confidential manner by the firm.
  - *Providing duplicate confirmations of transactions*: Investment personnel should be required to direct their brokers to supply to firms duplicate copies or confirmations of all their personal securities transactions and copies of periodic statements for all securities accounts. The duplicate confirmation requirement has two purposes: (1) The requirement sends a message that there is independent verification, which reduces the likelihood of unethical behavior, and (2) it enables verification of the accounting of the flow of personal investments that cannot be determined from merely looking at holdings.
  - *Preclearance procedures*: Investment personnel should examine all planned personal trades to identify possible conflicts prior to the execution of the trades. Preclearance procedures are designed to identify possible conflicts before a problem arises.

- *Disclosure of policies*: Members and candidates should fully disclose to investors their firm's policies regarding personal investing. The information about employees' personal investment activities and policies will foster an atmosphere of full and complete disclosure and calm the public's legitimate concerns about the conflicts of interest posed by investment personnel's personal trading. The disclosure must provide helpful information to investors; it should not be simply boilerplate language, such as "investment personnel are subject to policies and procedures regarding their personal trading."

58 STANDARD VI(B): APPLICATION OF THE STANDARD

Example 1 (Personal Trading):

Research analyst Marlon Long does not recommend purchase of a common stock for his employer's account because he wants to purchase the stock personally and does not want to wait until the recommendation is approved and the stock is purchased by his employer.

> *Comment*: Long has violated Standard VI(B) by taking advantage of his knowledge of the stock's value before allowing his employer to benefit from that information.

Example 2 (Trading for Family Member Account):

Carol Baker, the portfolio manager of an aggressive growth mutual fund, maintains an account in her husband's name at several brokerage firms with which the fund and a number of Baker's other individual clients do a substantial amount of business. Whenever a hot issue becomes available, she instructs the brokers to buy it for her husband's account. Because such issues normally are scarce, Baker often acquires shares in hot issues but her clients are not able to participate in them.

> *Comment*: To avoid violating Standard VI(B), Baker must acquire shares for her mutual fund first and acquire them for her husband's account only after doing so, even though she might miss out on participating in new issues via her husband's account. She also must disclose the trading for her husband's account to her employer because this activity creates a conflict between her personal interests and her employer's interests.

Example 3 (Family Accounts as Equals):

Erin Toffler, a portfolio manager at Esposito Investments, manages the retirement account established with the firm by her parents. Whenever IPOs become available, she first allocates shares to all her other clients for whom the investment is appropriate; only then does she place any remaining portion in her parents' account, if the issue is appropriate for them. She has adopted this procedure so that no one can accuse her of favoring her parents.

> *Comment*: Toffler has violated Standard VI(B) by breaching her duty to her parents by treating them differently from her other accounts simply because of the family relationship. As fee-paying clients of Esposito Investments, Toffler's parents are entitled to the same treatment as any other client of the firm. If Toffler has beneficial ownership in the account, however, and Esposito Investments has preclearance and reporting requirements for personal transactions, she may have to preclear the trades and report the transactions to Esposito.

Example 4 (Personal Trading and Disclosure):

Gary Michaels is an entry-level employee who holds a low-paying job serving both the research department and the investment management department of an active investment management firm. He purchases a sports car and begins to wear expensive clothes after only a year of employment with the firm. The director of the investment management department, who has responsibility for monitoring the personal stock transactions of all employees, investigates and discovers that Michaels has made substantial investment gains by purchasing stocks just before they were put on the firm's recommended "buy" list. Michaels was regularly given the firm's quarterly personal transaction form but declined to complete it.

> *Comment*: Michaels violated Standard VI(B) by placing personal transactions ahead of client transactions. In addition, his supervisor violated Standard IV(C) Responsibilities of Supervisors by permitting Michaels to continue to perform his assigned tasks without having signed the quarterly personal transaction form. Note also that if Michaels had communicated information about the firm's recommendations to a person who traded the security, that action would be a misappropriation of the information and a violation of Standard II(A) Material Nonpublic Information.

Example 5 (Trading Prior to Report Dissemination):

A brokerage's insurance analyst, Denise Wilson, makes a closed-circuit TV report to her firm's branches around the country. During the broadcast, she includes negative comments about a major company in the insurance industry. The following day, Wilson's report is printed and distributed to the sales force and public customers. The report recommends that both short-term traders and intermediate investors take profits by selling that insurance company's stock. Seven minutes after the broadcast, however, Ellen Riley, head of the firm's trading department, had closed out a long "call" position in the stock. Shortly thereafter, Riley established a sizable "put" position in the stock. When asked about her activities, Riley claimed she took the actions to facilitate anticipated sales by institutional clients.

> *Comment*: Riley did not give customers an opportunity to buy or sell in the options market before the firm itself did. By taking action before the report was disseminated, Riley's firm may have depressed the price of the calls and increased the price of the puts. The firm could have avoided a conflict of interest if it had waited to trade for its own account until its clients had an opportunity to receive and assimilate Wilson's recommendations. As it is, Riley's actions violated Standard VI(B).

STANDARD VI(C) REFERRAL FEES 59

- ☐ demonstrate a thorough knowledge of the CFA Institute Code of Ethics and Standards of Professional Conduct by interpreting the Code and Standards in various situations involving issues of professional integrity
- ☐ recommend practices and procedures designed to prevent violations of the Code and Standards

> Members and Candidates must disclose to their employer, clients, and prospective clients, as appropriate, any compensation, consideration, or benefit received from or paid to others for the recommendation of products or services.

Guidance

Standard VI(C) states the responsibility of members and candidates to inform their employer, clients, and prospective clients of any benefit received for referrals of customers and clients. Such disclosures allow clients or employers to evaluate (1) any partiality shown in any recommendation of services and (2) the full cost of the services. Members and candidates must disclose when they pay a fee or provide compensation to others who have referred prospective clients to the member or candidate.

Appropriate disclosure means that members and candidates must advise the client or prospective client, before entry into any formal agreement for services, of any benefit given or received for the recommendation of any services provided by the member or candidate. In addition, the member or candidate must disclose the nature of the consideration or benefit—for example, flat fee or percentage basis, one-time or continuing benefit, based on performance, benefit in the form of provision of research, or other noncash benefit—together with the estimated dollar value. Consideration includes all fees, whether paid in cash, in soft dollars, or in kind.

60 STANDARD VI(C): RECOMMENDED PROCEDURES

Members and candidates should encourage their employers to develop procedures related to referral fees. The firm may completely restrict such fees. If the firm does not adopt a strict prohibition of such fees, the procedures should indicate the appropriate steps for requesting approval.

Employers should have investment professionals provide to the clients notification of approved referral fee programs and provide the employer regular (at least quarterly) updates on the amount and nature of compensation received.

61 STANDARD VI(C): APPLICATION OF THE STANDARD

Example 1 (Disclosure of Referral Arrangements and Outside Parties):

Brady Securities, Inc., a broker/dealer, has established a referral arrangement with Lewis Brothers, Ltd., an investment counseling firm. In this arrangement, Brady Securities refers all prospective tax-exempt accounts, including pension, profit-sharing, and endowment accounts, to Lewis Brothers. In return, Lewis Brothers makes available to Brady Securities on a regular basis the security recommendations and reports of its research staff, which registered representatives of Brady Securities use in serving customers. In addition, Lewis Brothers conducts monthly economic and market reviews for Brady Securities personnel and directs all stock commission business generated by referral accounts to Brady Securities.

Willard White, a partner in Lewis Brothers, calculates that the incremental costs involved in functioning as the research department of Brady Securities are US$20,000 annually.

Referrals from Brady Securities last year resulted in fee income of US$200,000 for Lewis Brothers, and directing all stock trades through Brady Securities resulted in additional costs to Lewis Brothers' clients of US$10,000.

Diane Branch, the chief financial officer of Maxwell Inc., contacts White and says that she is seeking an investment manager for Maxwell's profit-sharing plan. She adds, "My friend Harold Hill at Brady Securities recommended your firm without qualification, and that's good enough for me. Do we have a deal?" White accepts the new account but does not disclose his firm's referral arrangement with Brady Securities.

> *Comment*: White has violated Standard VI(C) by failing to inform the prospective customer of the referral fee payable in services and commissions for an indefinite period to Brady Securities. Such disclosure could have caused Branch to reassess Hill's recommendation and make a more critical evaluation of Lewis Brothers' services.

Example 2 (Disclosure of Interdepartmental Referral Arrangements):

James Handley works for the trust department of Central Trust Bank. He receives compensation for each referral he makes to Central Trust's brokerage department and personal financial management department that results in a sale. He refers several of his clients to the personal financial management department but does not disclose the arrangement within Central Trust to his clients.

> *Comment*: Handley has violated Standard VI(C) by not disclosing the referral arrangement at Central Trust Bank to his clients. Standard VI(C) does not distinguish between referral payments paid by a third party for referring clients to the third party and internal payments paid within the firm to attract new business to a subsidiary. Members and candidates must disclose all such referral fees. Therefore, Handley is required to disclose, at the time of referral, any referral fee agreement in place among Central Trust Bank's departments. The disclosure should include the nature and the value of the benefit and should be made in writing.

Example 3 (Disclosure of Referral Arrangements and Informing Firm):

Katherine Roberts is a portfolio manager at Katama Investments, an advisory firm specializing in managing assets for high-net-worth individuals. Katama's trading desk uses a variety of brokerage houses to execute trades on behalf of its clients. Roberts asks the trading desk to direct a large portion of its commissions to Naushon, Inc., a small broker/dealer run by one of Roberts' business school classmates. Katama's traders have found that Naushon is not very competitive on pricing, and although Naushon generates some research for its trading clients, Katama's other analysts have found most of Naushon's research to be not especially useful. Nevertheless, the traders do as Roberts asks, and in return for receiving a large portion of Katama's business, Naushon recommends the investment services of Roberts and Katama to its wealthiest clients. This arrangement is not disclosed to either Katama or the clients referred by Naushon.

> *Comment*: Roberts is violating Standard VI(C) by failing to inform her employer of the referral arrangement.

Example 4 (Disclosure of Referral Arrangements and Outside Organizations):

Alex Burl is a portfolio manager at Helpful Investments, a local investment advisory firm. Burl is on the advisory board of his child's school, which is looking for ways to raise money to purchase new playground equipment for the school. Burl discusses a plan with his supervisor in which he will donate to the school a portion of his service fee from new clients referred by the parents of students at the school. Upon getting the approval from Helpful, Burl presents the idea to the school's advisory board and directors. The school agrees to announce the program at the next parent event and asks Burl to provide the appropriate written materials to be distributed. A week following the distribution of the flyers, Burl receives the first school-related referral. In establishing the client's investment policy statement, Burl clearly discusses the school's referral and outlines the plans for distributing the donation back to the school.

> *Comment*: Burl has not violated Standard VI(C) because he secured the permission of his employer, Helpful Investments, and the school prior to beginning the program and because he discussed the arrangement with the client at the time the investment policy statement was designed.

Example 5 (Disclosure of Referral Arrangements and Outside Parties):

The sponsor of a state employee pension is seeking to hire a firm to manage the pension plan's emerging market allocation. To assist in the review process, the sponsor has hired Thomas Arrow as a consultant to solicit proposals from various advisers. Arrow is contracted by the sponsor to represent its best interest in selecting the most appropriate new manager. The process runs smoothly, and Overseas Investments is selected as the new manager.

The following year, news breaks that Arrow is under investigation by the local regulator for accepting kickbacks from investment managers after they are awarded new pension allocations. Overseas Investments is included in the list of firms allegedly making these payments. Although the sponsor is happy with the performance of Overseas since it has been managing the pension plan's emerging market funds, the sponsor still decides to have an independent review of the proposals and the selection process to ensure that Overseas was the appropriate firm for its needs. This review confirms that, even though Arrow was being paid by both parties, the recommendation of Overseas appeared to be objective and appropriate.

> *Comment*: Arrow has violated Standard VI(C) because he did not disclose the fee being paid by Overseas. Withholding this information raises the question of a potential lack of objectivity in the recommendation of Overseas by Arrow; this aspect is in addition to questions about the legality of having firms pay to be considered for an allocation.
>
> Regulators and governmental agencies may adopt requirements concerning allowable consultant activities. Local regulations sometimes include having a consultant register with the regulatory agency's ethics board. Regulator policies may include a prohibition on acceptance of payments from investment managers receiving allocations and require regular reporting of contributions made to political organizations and candidates. Arrow would have to adhere to these requirements as well as the Code and Standards.

STANDARD VII: RESPONSIBILITIES AS A CFA INSTITUTE MEMBER OR CFA CANDIDATE

62

- [ ] demonstrate a thorough knowledge of the CFA Institute Code of Ethics and Standards of Professional Conduct by interpreting the Code and Standards in various situations involving issues of professional integrity
- [ ] recommend practices and procedures designed to prevent violations of the Code and Standards

Standard VII(A) Conduct as Participants in CFA Institute Programs

Members and Candidates must not engage in any conduct that compromises the reputation or integrity of CFA Institute or the CFA designation or the integrity, validity, or security of CFA Institute programs.

Guidance

Highlights:

- *Confidential Program Information*
- *Additional CFA Program Restrictions*
- *Expressing an Opinion*

Standard VII(A) covers the conduct of CFA Institute members and candidates involved with the CFA Program and prohibits any conduct that undermines the public's confidence that the CFA charter represents a level of achievement based on merit and ethical conduct. There is an array of CFA Institute programs beyond the CFA Program that provide additional educational and credentialing opportunities, including the Certificate in Investment Performance Measurement (CIPM®) Program and the CFA Institute Investment Foundations® Program. The standard's function is to hold members and candidates to a high ethical criterion while they are participating in or involved with any CFA Institute program. Conduct covered includes but is not limited to

- giving or receiving assistance (cheating) on any CFA Institute examinations;
- violating the rules, regulations, and testing policies of CFA Institute programs;
- providing confidential program or exam information to candidates or the public;
- disregarding or attempting to circumvent security measures established for any CFA Institute examinations;
- improperly using an association with CFA Institute to further personal or professional goals; and
- misrepresenting information on the Professional Conduct Statement or in the CFA Institute Continuing Education Program.

Confidential Program Information

CFA Institute is vigilant about protecting the integrity of CFA Institute programs' content and examination processes. CFA Institute program rules, regulations, and policies prohibit candidates from disclosing confidential material gained during the exam process.

Examples of information that cannot be disclosed by candidates sitting for an exam include but are not limited to

- specific details of questions appearing on the exam and
- broad topical areas and formulas tested or not tested on the exam.

All aspects of the exam, including questions, broad topical areas, and formulas, tested or not tested, are considered confidential until such time as CFA Institute elects to release them publicly. This confidentiality requirement allows CFA Institute to maintain the integrity and rigor of exams for future candidates. Standard VII(A) does not prohibit candidates from discussing nonconfidential information or curriculum material with others or in study groups in preparation for the exam.

Candidates increasingly use online forums and new technology as part of their exam preparations. CFA Institute actively polices blogs, forums, and related social networking groups for information considered confidential. The organization works with both individual candidates and the sponsors of online or offline services to promptly remove any and all violations. As noted in the discussion of Standard I(A)–Knowledge of the Law, candidates, members, and the public are encouraged to report suspected violations to CFA Institute.

Additional CFA Program Restrictions

The CFA Program rules, regulations, and policies define additional allowed and disallowed actions concerning the exams. Violating any of the testing policies, such as the calculator policy, personal belongings policy, or the Candidate Pledge, constitutes a violation of Standard VII(A). Candidates will find all of these policies on the CFA Program portion of the CFA Institute website (www.cfainstitute.org). Exhibit 2 provides the Candidate Pledge, which highlights the respect candidates must have for the integrity, validity, and security of the CFA exam.

Members may participate as volunteers in various aspects of the CFA Program. Standard VII(A) prohibits members from disclosing and/or soliciting confidential material gained prior to or during the exam and grading processes with those outside the CFA exam development process.

Examples of information that cannot be shared by members involved in developing, administering, or grading the exams include but are not limited to

- questions appearing on the exam or under consideration,
- deliberation related to the exam process, and
- information related to the scoring of questions.

Members may also be asked to offer assistance with other CFA Institute programs, including but not limited to the CIPM and Investment Foundations programs. Members participating in any CFA Institute program should do so with the same level of integrity and confidentiality as is required of participation in the CFA Program.

Expressing an Opinion

Standard VII(A) does *not* cover expressing opinions regarding CFA Institute, the CFA Program, or other CFA Institute programs. Members and candidates are free to disagree and express their disagreement with CFA Institute on its policies, its procedures, or any advocacy positions taken by the organization. When expressing a personal opinion, a candidate is prohibited from disclosing content-specific information, including any actual exam question and the information as to subject matter covered or not covered in the exam.

Exhibit 2: Sample of CFA Program Testing Policies

Candidate Pledge	As a candidate in the CFA Program, I am obligated to follow Standard VII(A) of the CFA Institute Standards of Professional Conduct, which states that members and candidates must not engage in any conduct that compromises the reputation or integrity of CFA Institute or the CFA designation or the integrity, validity, or security of the CFA exam. ▪ Prior to this exam, I have not given or received information regarding the content of this exam. During this exam, I will not give or receive any information regarding the content of this exam. ▪ After this exam, I will not disclose **ANY** portion of this exam and I will not remove **ANY** exam materials from the testing room in original or copied form. I understand that all exam materials, including my answers, are the property of CFA Institute and will not be returned to me in any form. ▪ I will follow **ALL** rules of the CFA Program as stated on the CFA Institute website and the back cover of the exam book. My violation of any rules of the CFA Program will result in CFA Institute voiding my exam results and may lead to suspension or termination of my candidacy in the CFA Program.

STANDARD VII(A): APPLICATION OF THE STANDARD

63

Example 1 (Sharing Exam Questions):

Travis Nero serves as a proctor for the administration of the CFA examination in his city. In the course of his service, he reviews a copy of the Level II CFA exam on the evening prior to the exam's administration and provides information concerning the exam questions to two candidates who use it to prepare for the exam.

> *Comment*: Nero and the two candidates have violated Standard VII(A). By giving information about the exam questions to two candidates, Nero provided an unfair advantage to the two candidates and undermined the integrity and validity of the Level II CFA exam as an accurate measure of the knowledge, skills, and abilities necessary to earn the right to use the CFA designation. By accepting the information, the candidates also compromised the integrity and validity of the Level II CFA exam and undermined the ethical framework that is a key part of the designation.

Example 2 (Bringing Written Material into Exam Room):

Loren Sullivan is enrolled to take the Level II CFA exam. He has been having difficulty remembering a particular formula, so prior to entering the exam room, he writes the formula on the palm of his hand. During the afternoon section of the exam, a proctor notices Sullivan looking at the palm of his hand. She asks to see his hand and finds the formula.

> *Comment*: Because Sullivan wrote down information from the Candidate Body of Knowledge (CBOK) and took that written information into the exam room, his conduct compromised the validity of his exam performance and violated Standard VII(A). Sullivan's conduct was also in direct contradiction with the rules and regulations of the CFA Program, the Candidate Pledge, and the CFA Institute Code and Standards.

Example 3 (Writing after Exam Period End):

At the conclusion of the morning section of the Level I CFA exam, the proctors announce, "Stop writing now." John Davis has not completed the exam, so he continues to randomly fill in ovals on his answer sheet. A proctor approaches Davis's desk and reminds him that he should stop writing immediately. Davis, however, continues to complete the answer sheet. After the proctor asks him to stop writing two additional times, Davis finally puts down his pencil.

> *Comment*: By continuing to complete his exam after time was called, Davis has violated Standard VII(A). By continuing to write, Davis took an unfair advantage over other candidates, and his conduct compromised the validity of his exam performance. Additionally, by not heeding the proctor's repeated instructions, Davis violated the rules and regulations of the CFA Program.

Example 4 (Sharing Exam Content):

After completing the Level II CFA exam, Annabelle Rossi posts on her blog about her experience. She posts the following: "Level II is complete! I think I did fairly well on the exam. It was really difficult, but fair. I think I did especially well on the derivatives questions. And there were tons of them! I think I counted 18! The ethics questions were really hard. I'm glad I spent so much time on the Code and Standards. I was surprised to see there were no questions at all about IPO allocations. I expected there to be a couple. Well, off to celebrate getting through it. See you tonight?"

> *Comment*: Rossi did not violate Standard VII(A) when she wrote about how difficult she found the exam or how well she thinks she may have done. By revealing portions of the CBOK covered on the exam and areas not covered, however, she did violate Standard VII(A) and the Candidate Pledge. Depending on the time frame in which the comments were posted, Rossi not only may have assisted future candidates but also may have provided an unfair advantage to candidates yet to sit for the same exam, thereby undermining the integrity and validity of the Level II CFA exam.

Example 5 (Sharing Exam Content):

Level I candidate Etienne Gagne has been a frequent visitor to an internet forum designed specifically for CFA Program candidates. The week after completing the Level I CFA exam, Gagne and several others begin a discussion thread on the forum about the most challenging questions and attempt to determine the correct answers.

> *Comment*: Gagne has violated Standard VII(A) by providing and soliciting confidential exam information, which compromises the integrity of the exam process and violates the Candidate Pledge. In trying to determine correct answers to specific questions, the group's discussion included question-specific details considered to be confidential to the CFA Program.

Example 6 (Sharing Exam Content):

CFA4Sure is a company that produces test-preparation materials for CFA Program candidates. Many candidates register for and use the company's products. The day after the CFA exam, CFA4Sure sends an e-mail to all its customers asking them to share with the company the hardest questions from the exam so that CFA4Sure can better prepare its customers for the next exam administration. Marisol Pena e-mails a summary of the questions she found most difficult on the exam.

> *Comment*: Pena has violated Standard VII(A) by disclosing a portion of the exam questions. The information provided is considered confidential until publicly released by CFA Institute. CFA4Sure is likely to use such feedback to refine its review materials for future candidates. Pena's sharing of the specific questions undermines the integrity of the exam while potentially making the exam easier for future candidates.
>
> If the CFA4Sure employees who participated in the solicitation of confidential CFA Program information are CFA Institute members or candidates, they also have violated Standard VII(A).

Example 7 (Discussion of Exam Grading Guidelines and Results):

Prior to participating in grading CFA exams, Wesley Whitcomb is required to sign a CFA Institute Grader Agreement. As part of the Grader Agreement, Whitcomb agrees not to reveal or discuss the exam materials with anyone except CFA Institute staff or other graders. Several weeks after the conclusion of the CFA exam grading, Whitcomb tells several colleagues who are candidates in the CFA Program which question he graded. He also discusses the guideline answer and adds that few candidates scored well on the question.

> *Comment*: Whitcomb violated Standard VII(A) by breaking the Grader Agreement and disclosing information related to a specific question on the exam, which compromised the integrity of the exam process.

Example 8 (Compromising CFA Institute Integrity as a Volunteer):

Jose Ramirez is an investor-relations consultant for several small companies that are seeking greater exposure to investors. He is also the program chair for the CFA Institute society in the city where he works. Ramirez schedules only companies that are his clients to make presentations to the society and excludes other companies.

> *Comment*: Ramirez, by using his volunteer position at CFA Institute to benefit himself and his clients, compromises the reputation and integrity of CFA Institute and thus violates Standard VII(A).

Example 9 (Compromising CFA Institute Integrity as a Volunteer):

Marguerite Warrenski is a member of the CFA Institute GIPS Executive Committee, which oversees the creation, implementation, and revision of the GIPS standards. As a member of the Executive Committee, she has advance knowledge of confidential information regarding the GIPS standards, including any new or revised standards the committee is considering. She tells her clients that her Executive Committee membership will allow her to better assist her clients in keeping up with changes to the Standards and facilitating their compliance with the changes.

> *Comment*: Warrenski is using her association with the GIPS Executive Committee to promote her firm's services to clients and potential clients. In defining her volunteer position at CFA Institute as a strategic business advantage over competing firms and implying to clients that she would use confidential information to further their interests, Warrenski is compromising the reputation and integrity of CFA Institute and thus violating Standard VII(A). She may factually state her involvement with the Executive Committee but cannot infer any special advantage to her clients from such participation.

64 STANDARD VII(B) REFERENCE TO CFA INSTITUTE, THE CFA DESIGNATION, AND THE CFA PROGRAM

- ☐ demonstrate a thorough knowledge of the CFA Institute Code of Ethics and Standards of Professional Conduct by interpreting the Code and Standards in various situations involving issues of professional integrity
- ☐ recommend practices and procedures designed to prevent violations of the Code and Standards

When referring to CFA Institute, CFA Institute membership, the CFA designation, or candidacy in the CFA Program, Members and Candidates must not misrepresent or exaggerate the meaning or implications of membership in CFA Institute, holding the CFA designation, or candidacy in the CFA Program.

Guidance

Highlights:

- *CFA Institute Membership*
- *Using the CFA Designation*
- *Referring to Candidacy in the CFA Program*

Standard VII(B) is intended to prevent promotional efforts that make promises or guarantees that are tied to the CFA designation. Individuals must not exaggerate the meaning or implications of membership in CFA Institute, holding the CFA designation, or candidacy in the CFA Program.

Standard VII(B) is not intended to prohibit factual statements related to the positive benefit of earning the CFA designation. However, statements referring to CFA Institute, the CFA designation, or the CFA Program that overstate the competency of an individual or imply, either directly or indirectly, that superior performance can be expected from someone with the CFA designation are not allowed under the standard.

Statements that highlight or emphasize the commitment of CFA Institute members, CFA charterholders, and CFA candidates to ethical and professional conduct or mention the thoroughness and rigor of the CFA Program are appropriate. Members and candidates may make claims about the relative merits of CFA Institute, the CFA Program, or the Code and Standards as long as those statements are implicitly or explicitly stated as the opinion of the speaker. Statements that do not express opinions have to be supported by facts.

Standard VII(B) applies to any form of communication, including but not limited to communications made in electronic or written form (such as on firm letterhead, business cards, professional biographies, directory listings, printed advertising, firm brochures, or personal resumes) and oral statements made to the public, clients, or prospects.

CFA Institute Membership

The term "CFA Institute member" refers to "regular" and "affiliate" members of CFA Institute who have met the membership requirements as defined in the CFA Institute Bylaws. Once accepted as a CFA Institute member, the member must satisfy the following requirements to maintain his or her status:

- remit annually to CFA Institute a completed Professional Conduct Statement, which renews the commitment to abide by the requirements of the Code and Standards and the CFA Institute Professional Conduct Program, and
- pay applicable CFA Institute membership dues on an annual basis.

If a CFA Institute member fails to meet any of these requirements, the individual is no longer considered an active member. Until membership is reactivated, individuals must not present themselves to others as active members. They may state, however, that they were CFA Institute members in the past or refer to the years when their membership was active.

Using the CFA Designation

Those who have earned the right to use the Chartered Financial Analyst® designation are encouraged to do so but only in a manner that does not misrepresent or exaggerate the meaning or implications of the designation. The use of the designation may be accompanied by an accurate explanation of the requirements that have been met to earn the right to use the designation.

"CFA charterholders" are those individuals who have earned the right to use the CFA designation granted by CFA Institute. These people have satisfied certain requirements, including completion of the CFA Program and required years of acceptable work experience. Once granted the right to use the designation, individuals must also satisfy the CFA Institute membership requirements (see above) to maintain their right to use the designation.

If a CFA charterholder fails to meet any of the membership requirements, he or she forfeits the right to use the CFA designation. Until membership is reactivated, individuals must not present themselves to others as CFA charterholders. They may state, however, that they were charterholders in the past.

Given the growing popularity of social media, where individuals may anonymously express their opinions, pseudonyms or online profile names created to hide a member's identity should not be tagged with the CFA designation.

Use of the CFA designation by a CFA charterholder is governed by the terms and conditions of the annual Professional Conduct Statement Agreement, entered into between CFA Institute and its membership prior to commencement of use of the CFA designation and reaffirmed annually.

Referring to Candidacy in the CFA Program

Candidates in the CFA Program may refer to their participation in the CFA Program, but such references must clearly state that an individual is a *candidate* in the CFA Program and must not imply that the candidate has achieved any type of partial designation. A person is a candidate in the CFA Program if

- the person's application for registration in the CFA Program has been accepted by CFA Institute, as evidenced by issuance of a notice of acceptance, and the person is enrolled to sit for a specified examination or
- the registered person has sat for a specified examination but exam results have not yet been received.

If an individual is registered for the CFA Program but declines to sit for an exam or otherwise does not meet the definition of a candidate as described in the CFA Institute Bylaws, then that individual is no longer considered an active candidate. Once the person is enrolled to sit for a future examination, his or her CFA Program candidacy resumes.

CFA Program candidates must never state or imply that they have a partial designation as a result of passing one or more levels or cite an expected completion date of any level of the CFA Program. Final award of the charter is subject to meeting the CFA Program requirements and approval by the CFA Institute Board of Governors.

If a candidate passes each level of the exam in consecutive years and wants to state that he or she did so, that is not a violation of Standard VII(B) because it is a statement of fact. If the candidate then goes on to claim or imply superior ability by obtaining the designation in only three years, however, he or she is in violation of Standard VII(B).

Exhibit 3 provides examples of proper and improper references to the CFA designation.

Exhibit 3: Proper and Improper References to the CFA Designation

Proper References	Improper References
"Completion of the CFA Program has enhanced my portfolio management skills."	"CFA charterholders achieve better performance results."
"John Smith passed all three CFA Program exams in three consecutive years."	"John Smith is among the elite, having passed all three CFA exams in three consecutive attempts."
"The CFA designation is globally recognized and attests to a charterholder's success in a rigorous and comprehensive study program in the field of investment management and research analysis."	"As a CFA charterholder, I am the most qualified to manage client investments."
"The credibility that the CFA designation affords and the skills the CFA Program cultivates are key assets for my future career development."	"As a CFA charterholder, Jane White provides the best value in trade execution."
"I enrolled in the CFA Program to obtain the highest set of credentials in the global investment management industry."	"Enrolling as a candidate in the CFA Program ensures one of becoming better at valuing debt securities."
"I passed Level I of the CFA Program."	"CFA, Level II"
"I am a 2010 Level III candidate in the CFA Program."	"CFA, Expected 2011"
"I passed all three levels of the CFA Program and may be eligible for the CFA charter upon completion of the required work experience."	"CFA, Expected 2011" "John Smith, Charter Pending"

STANDARD VII(B): RECOMMENDED PROCEDURES 65

Misuse of a member's CFA designation or CFA candidacy or improper reference to it is common by those in a member's or candidate's firm who do not possess knowledge of the requirements of Standard VII(B). As an appropriate step to reduce this risk, members and candidates should disseminate written information about Standard VII(B) and the accompanying guidance to their firm's legal, compliance, public relations, and marketing departments (see www.cfainstitute.org).

For materials that refer to employees' affiliation with CFA Institute, members and candidates should encourage their firms to create templates that are approved by a central authority (such as the compliance department) as being consistent with Standard VII(B). This practice promotes consistency and accuracy in the firm of references to CFA Institute membership, the CFA designation, and CFA candidacy.

66 STANDARD VII(B): APPLICATION OF THE STANDARD

Example 1 (Passing Exams in Consecutive Years):

An advertisement for AZ Investment Advisors states that all the firm's principals are CFA charterholders and all passed the three exams on their first attempt. The advertisement prominently links this fact to the notion that AZ's mutual funds have achieved superior performance.

> *Comment*: AZ may state that all principals passed the three exams on the first try as long as this statement is true, but it must not be linked to performance or imply superior ability. Implying that (1) CFA charterholders achieve better investment results and (2) those who pass the exams on the first try may be more successful than those who do not violates Standard VII(B).

Example 2 (Right to Use CFA Designation):

Five years after receiving his CFA charter, Louis Vasseur resigns his position as an investment analyst and spends the next two years traveling abroad. Because he is not actively engaged in the investment profession, he does not file a completed Professional Conduct Statement with CFA Institute and does not pay his CFA Institute membership dues. At the conclusion of his travels, Vasseur becomes a self-employed analyst accepting assignments as an independent contractor. Without reinstating his CFA Institute membership by filing his Professional Conduct Statement and paying his dues, he prints business cards that display "CFA" after his name.

> *Comment*: Vasseur has violated Standard VII(B) because his right to use the CFA designation was suspended when he failed to file his Professional Conduct Statement and stopped paying dues. Therefore, he no longer is able to state or imply that he is an active CFA charterholder. When Vasseur files his Professional Conduct Statement, resumes paying CFA Institute dues to activate his membership, and completes the CFA Institute reinstatement procedures, he will be eligible to use the CFA designation.

Example 3 ("Retired" CFA Institute Membership Status):

After a 25-year career, James Simpson retires from his firm. Because he is not actively engaged in the investment profession, he does not file a completed Professional Conduct Statement with CFA Institute and does not pay his CFA Institute membership dues. Simpson designs a plain business card (without a corporate logo) to hand out to friends with his new contact details, and he continues to put "CFA" after his name.

> *Comment*: Simpson has violated Standard VII(B). Because he failed to file his Professional Conduct Statement and ceased paying dues, his membership has been suspended and he has given up the right to use the CFA designation. CFA Institute has procedures, however, for reclassifying a member and charterholder as "retired" and reducing the annual dues. If he wants to obtain retired status, he needs to file the appropriate paperwork with CFA Institute. When Simpson receives his notification from CFA Institute

that his membership has been reclassified as retired and he resumes paying reduced dues, his membership will be reactivated and his right to use the CFA designation will be reinstated.

Example 4 (Stating Facts about CFA Designation and Program):

Rhonda Reese has been a CFA charterholder since 2000. In a conversation with a friend who is considering enrolling in the CFA Program, she states that she has learned a great deal from the CFA Program and that many firms require their employees to be CFA charterholders. She would recommend the CFA Program to anyone pursuing a career in investment management.

Comment: Reese's comments comply with Standard VII(B). Her statements refer to facts: The CFA Program enhanced her knowledge, and many firms require the CFA designation for their investment professionals.

Example 5 (Order of Professional and Academic Designations):

Tatiana Prittima has earned both her CFA designation and a PhD in finance. She would like to cite both her accomplishments on her business card but is unsure of the proper method for doing so.

Comment: The order of designations cited on such items as resumes and business cards is a matter of personal preference. Prittima is free to cite the CFA designation either before or after citing her PhD. Multiple designations must be separated by a comma.

Example 6 (Use of Fictitious Name):

Barry Glass is the lead quantitative analyst at CityCenter Hedge Fund. Glass is responsible for the development, maintenance, and enhancement of the proprietary models the fund uses to manage its investors' assets. Glass reads several high-level mathematical publications and blogs to stay informed on current developments. One blog, run by "Expert CFA," presents some intriguing research that may benefit one of CityCenter's current models. Glass is under pressure from firm executives to improve the model's predictive abilities, and he incorporates the factors discussed in the online research. The updated output recommends several new investments to the fund's portfolio managers.

Comment: "Expert CFA" has violated Standard VII(B) by using the CFA designation inappropriately. As with any research report, authorship of online comments must include the charterholder's full name along with any reference to the CFA designation.

See also Standard V(A), which Glass has violated for guidance on diligence and reasonable basis.

PRACTICE PROBLEMS

1. Which of the following is a correct statement of a member's or candidate's duty under the Code and Standards?

   A. In the absence of specific applicable law or other regulatory requirements, the Code and Standards govern the member's or candidate's actions.

   B. A member or candidate is required to comply only with applicable local laws, rules, regulations, or customs, even though the Code and Standards may impose a higher degree of responsibility or a higher duty on the member or candidate.

   C. A member or candidate who trades securities in a securities market where no applicable local laws or stock exchange rules regulate the use of material nonpublic information may take investment action based on material nonpublic information.

2. Ward is scheduled to visit the corporate headquarters of Evans Industries. Ward expects to use the information he obtains there to complete his research report on Evans stock. Ward learns that Evans plans to pay all of Ward's expenses for the trip, including costs of meals, hotel room, and air transportation. Which of the following actions would be the *best* course for Ward to take under the Code and Standards?

   A. Accept the expense-paid trip and write an objective report.

   B. Pay for all travel expenses, including costs of meals and incidental items.

   C. Accept the expense-paid trip but disclose the value of the services accepted in the report.

3. An investment management firm has been hired by ETV Corporation to work on an additional public offering for the company. The firm's brokerage unit now has a "sell" recommendation on ETV, but the head of the investment banking department has asked the head of the brokerage unit to change the recommendation from "sell" to "buy." According to the Standards, the head of the brokerage unit would be permitted to:

   A. increase the recommendation by no more than one increment (in this case, to a "hold" recommendation).

   B. place the company on a restricted list and give only factual information about the company.

   C. assign a new analyst to decide whether the stock deserves a higher rating.

4. Long has been asked to be the keynote speaker at an upcoming investment conference. The event is being hosted by one of the third-party investment managers currently used by his pension fund. The manager offers to cover all conference and travel costs for Long and make the conference registrations free for three additional members of his investment management team. To ensure that the conference obtains the best speakers, the host firm has arranged for an exclusive golf outing for the day following the conference on a local championship-caliber

course. Which of the following is *least likely* to violate Standard I(B)?

A. Long may accept only the offer to have his conference-related expenses paid by the host firm. B.

B. Long may accept the offer to have his conference-related expenses paid and may attend the exclusive golf outing at the expense of the hosting firm.

C. Long may accept the entire package of incentives offered to speak at this conference.

5. Grey recommends the purchase of a mutual fund that invests solely in long-term US Treasury bonds. He makes the following statements to his clients:
I. "The payment of the bonds is guaranteed by the US government; therefore, the default risk of the bonds is virtually zero."
II. "If you invest in the mutual fund, you will earn a 10% rate of return each year for the next several years based on historical performance of the market."
Did Grey's statements violate the CFA Institute Code and Standards?

A. Neither statement violated the Code and Standards.

B. Only Statement I violated the Code and Standards.

C. Only Statement II violated the Code and Standards.

6. Michelieu tells a prospective client, "I may not have a long-term track record yet, but I'm sure that you'll be very pleased with my recommendations and service. In the three years that I've been in the business, my equity-oriented clients have averaged a total return of more than 26% a year." The statement is true, but Michelieu only has a few clients, and one of his clients took a large position in a penny stock (against Michelieu's advice) and realized a huge gain. This large return caused the average of all of Michelieu's clients to exceed 26% a year. Without this one investment, the average gain would have been 8% a year. Has Michelieu violated the Standards?

A. No, because Michelieu is not promising that he can earn a 26% return in the future

B. No, because the statement is a true and accurate description of Michelieu's track record

C. Yes, because the statement misrepresents Michelieu's track record

7. Anderb, a portfolio manager for XYZ Investment Management Company—a registered investment organization that advises investment firms and private accounts—was promoted to that position three years ago. Bates, her supervisor, is responsible for reviewing Anderb's portfolio account transactions and her required monthly reports of personal stock transactions. Anderb has been using Jonelli, a broker, almost exclusively for brokerage transactions for the portfolio account. For securities in which Jonelli's firm makes a market, Jonelli has been giving Anderb lower prices for personal purchases and higher prices for personal sales than Jonelli gives to Anderb's portfolio accounts and other investors. Anderb has been filing monthly reports with Bates only for those months in which she has no personal transactions, which is about every fourth month. Which of the following is *most likely* to be a violation of the Code and Standards?

A. Anderb failed to disclose to her employer her personal transactions.

B. Anderb owned the same securities as those of her clients.

C. Bates allowed Anderb to use Jonelli as her broker for personal trades.

8. The mosaic theory holds that an analyst:

   A. violates the Code and Standards if the analyst fails to have knowledge of and comply with applicable laws.

   B. can use material public information and nonmaterial nonpublic information in the analyst's analysis.

   C. should use all available and relevant information in support of an investment recommendation.

9. An investment banking department of a brokerage firm often receives material nonpublic information that could have considerable value if used in advising the firm's brokerage clients. In order to conform to the Code and Standards, which one of the following is the best policy for the brokerage firm?

   A. Permanently prohibit both "buy" and "sell" recommendations of the stocks of clients of the investment banking department.

   B. Establish physical and informational barriers within the firm to prevent the exchange of information between the investment banking and brokerage operations.

   C. Monitor the exchange of information between the investment banking department and the brokerage operation.

10. Andrews, a private wealth manager, is conducting interviews for a new research analyst for his firm. One of the candidates is Wright, an analyst with a local investment bank. During the interview, while Wright is describing his analytical skills, he mentions a current merger in which his firm is acting as the adviser. Andrews has heard rumors of a possible merger between the two companies, but no releases have been made by the companies concerned. Which of the following actions by Andrews is *least likely* a violation of the Code and Standards?

    A. Waiting until the next day before trading on the information to allow time for it to become public

    B. Notifying all investment managers in his firm of the new information so none of their clients are disadvantaged

    C. Placing the securities mentioned as part of the merger on the firm's restricted trading list

11. During a round of golf, Rodriguez, chief financial officer of Mega Retail, mentions to Hart, a local investment adviser and long-time personal friend, that Mega is having an exceptional sales quarter. Rodriguez expects the results to be almost 10% above the current estimates. The next day, Hart initiates the purchase of a large stake in the local exchange-traded retail fund for her personal account.

    A. Hart violated the Code and Standards by investing in the exchange-traded fund that included Mega Retail.

    B. Hart did not violate the Code and Standards because she did not invest directly in securities of Mega Retail.

C. Rodriguez did not violate the Code and Standards because the comments made to Hart were not intended to solicit an investment in Mega Retail.

12. Pietro, president of Local Bank, has hired the bank's market maker, Vogt, to seek a merger partner. Local is currently listed on a stock exchange and has not reported that it is seeking strategic alternatives. Vogt has discussed the possibility of a merger with several firms, but they have all decided to wait until after the next period's financial data are available. The potential buyers believe the results will be worse than the results of prior periods and will allow them to pay less for Local Bank. Pietro wants to increase the likelihood of structuring a merger deal quickly. Which of the following actions would *most likely* be a violation of the Code and Standards?

    A. Pietro could instruct Local Bank to issue a press release announcing that it has retained Vogt to find a merger partner.

    B. Pietro could place a buy order for 2,000 shares (or four times the average weekly volume) through Vogt for his personal account.

    C. After confirming with Local's chief financial officer, Pietro could instruct Local to issue a press release reaffirming the firm's prior announced earnings guidance for the full fiscal year.

13. Stewart has been hired by Goodner Industries, Inc., to manage its pension fund. Stewart's duty of loyalty, prudence, and care is owed to:

    A. the management of Goodner.

    B. the participants and beneficiaries of Goodner's pension plan.

    C. the shareholders of Goodner.

14. One of the discretionary accounts managed by Farnsworth is the Jones Corporation employee profit-sharing plan. Jones, the company president, recently asked Farnsworth to vote the shares in the profit-sharing plan in favor of the slate of directors nominated by Jones Corporation and against the directors sponsored by a dissident stockholder group. Farnsworth does not want to lose this account, because he directs all the account's trades to a brokerage firm that provides Farnsworth with useful information about tax-free investments. Although this information is not of value in managing the Jones Corporation account, it does help in managing several other accounts. The brokerage firm providing this information also offers the lowest commissions for trades and provides best execution. Farnsworth investigates the director issue, concludes that the management-nominated slate is better for the long-run performance of the company than the dissident group's slate, and votes accordingly. Farnsworth:

    A. violated the Standards in voting the shares in the manner requested by Jones but not in directing trades to the brokerage firm.

    B. did not violate the Standards in voting the shares in the manner requested by Jones or in directing trades to the brokerage firm.

    C. violated the Standards in directing trades to the brokerage firm but not in voting the shares as requested by Jones.

15. Carter works for Invest Today, a local asset management firm. A broker that provides Carter with proprietary research through client brokerage arrangements is offering a new trading service. The broker is offering low-fee, execution-only

trades to complement its traditional full-service, execution-and-research trades. To entice Carter and other asset managers to send additional business its way, the broker will apply the commissions paid on the new service toward satisfying the brokerage commitment of the prior full-service arrangements. Carter has always been satisfied with the execution provided on the full-service trades, and the new, low-fee trades are comparable to the fees of other brokers currently used for the accounts that prohibit soft dollar arrangements.

A. Carter can trade for his accounts that prohibit soft dollar arrangements under the new, low-fee trading scheme.

B. Carter cannot use the new trading scheme because the commissions are prohibited by the soft dollar restrictions of the accounts.

C. Carter should trade only through the new, low-fee scheme and should increase his trading volume to meet his required commission commitment.

16. Which statement about a manager's use of client brokerage commissions violates the Code and Standards?

A. A client may direct a manager to use that client's brokerage commissions to purchase goods and services for that client.

B. Client brokerage commissions should be used to benefit the client and should be commensurate with the value of the brokerage and research services received.

C. Client brokerage commissions may be directed to pay for the investment manager's operating expenses.

17. Stafford is a portfolio manager for a specialized real estate mutual fund. Her firm clearly describes in the fund's prospectus its soft dollar policies. Stafford decides that entering the CFA Program will enhance her investment decision-making skill and decides to use the fund's soft dollar account to pay the registration and exam fees for the CFA Program. Which of the following statements is *most likely* correct?

A. Stafford did not violate the Code and Standards, because the prospectus informed investors of the fund's soft dollar policies.

B. Stafford violated the Code and Standards because improving her investment skills is not a reasonable use of the soft dollar account.

C. Stafford violated the Code and Standards because the CFA Program does not meet the definition of research allowed to be purchased with brokerage commissions.

18. Which one of the following actions will help ensure the fair treatment of brokerage firm clients when a new investment recommendation is made?

A. Informing all people in the firm in advance that a recommendation is to be disseminated.

B. Distributing recommendations to institutional clients prior to individual accounts.

C. Minimizing the time between the decision and the dissemination of a recommendation.

19. Smith, a research analyst with a brokerage firm, decides to change his recommendation for the common stock of Green Company, Inc., from a "buy" to a "sell." He mails this change in investment advice to all the firm's clients on Wednesday. The day after the mailing, a client calls with a buy order for 500 shares of Green Company. In this circumstance, Smith should:

    A. accept the order.

    B. advise the customer of the change in recommendation before accepting the order.

    C. not accept the order, because it is contrary to the firm's recommendation.

20. Brown works for an investment counseling firm. Green, a new client of the firm, is meeting with Brown for the first time. Green used another counseling firm for financial advice for years, but she has switched her account to Brown's firm. After spending a few minutes getting acquainted, Brown explains to Green that she has discovered a highly undervalued stock that offers large potential gains. She recommends that Green purchase the stock. Brown has committed a violation of the Standards. What should she have done differently?

    A. Brown should have determined Green's needs, objectives, and tolerance for risk before making a recommendation of any type of security.

    B. Brown should have thoroughly explained the characteristics of the company to Green, including the characteristics of the industry in which the company operates.

    C. Brown should have explained her qualifications, including her education, training, and experience and the meaning of the CFA designation.

21. ABC Investment Management acquires a new, very large account with two concentrated positions. The firm's current policy is to add new accounts for the purpose of performance calculation after the first full month of management. Cupp is responsible for calculating the firm's performance returns. Before the end of the initial month, Cupp notices that one of the significant holdings of the new accounts is acquired by another company, causing the value of the investment to double. Because of this holding, Cupp decides to account for the new portfolio as of the date of transfer, thereby allowing ABC Investment to reap the positive impact of that month's portfolio return.

    A. Cupp did not violate the Code and Standards, because the GIPS standards allow composites to be updated on the date of large external cash flows.

    B. Cupp did not violate the Code and Standards, because companies are allowed to determine when to incorporate new accounts into their composite calculation.

    C. Cupp violated the Code and Standards because the inclusion of the new account produces an inaccurate calculation of the monthly results according to the firm's stated policies.

22. Paper was recently terminated as one of a team of five managers of an equity fund. The fund had two value-focused managers and terminated one of them to reduce costs. In a letter sent to prospective employers, Paper presents, with written permission of the firm, the performance history of the fund to demonstrate

his past success.

A. Paper did not violate the Code and Standards.

B. Paper violated the Code and Standards by claiming the performance of the entire fund as his own.

C. Paper violated the Code and Standards by including the historical results of his prior employer.

23. Bronson provides investment advice to the board of trustees of a private university endowment fund. The trustees have provided Bronson with the fund's financial information, including planned expenditures. Bronson receives a phone call on Friday afternoon from Murdock, a prominent alumnus, requesting that Bronson fax him comprehensive financial information about the fund. According to Murdock, he has a potential contributor but needs the information that day to close the deal and cannot contact any of the trustees. According to the Standards, Bronson should:

A. send Murdock the information because disclosure would benefit the client.

B. not send Murdock the information to preserve confidentiality.

C. send Murdock the information, provided Bronson promptly notifies the trustees.

24. Townsend was recently appointed to the board of directors of a youth golf program that is the local chapter of a national not-for-profit organization. The program is beginning a new fundraising campaign to expand the number of annual scholarships it provides. Townsend believes many of her clients make annual donations to charity. The next week in her regular newsletter to all clients, she includes a small section discussing the fundraising campaign and her position on the organization's board.

A. Townsend did not violate the Code and Standards.

B. Townsend violated the Code and Standards by soliciting donations from her clients through the newsletter.

C. Townsend violated the Code and Standards by not getting approval of the organization before soliciting her clients.

25. Which of the following statements is *correct* under the Code and Standards?

A. CFA Institute members and candidates are prohibited from undertaking independent practice in competition with their employer.

B. Written consent from the employer is necessary to permit independent practice that could result in compensation or other benefits in competition with a member's or candidate's employer.

C. Members and candidates are prohibited from making arrangements or preparations to go into a competitive business before terminating their relationship with their employer.

26. A former hedge fund manager, Jackman, has decided to launch a new private wealth management firm. From his prior experiences, he believes the new firm needs to achieve US$1 million in assets under management in the first year. Jackman offers a US$10,000 incentive to any adviser who joins his firm with a

minimum of US$200,000 in committed investments. Jackman places notice of the opening on several industry web portals and career search sites. Which of the following is *correct* according to the Code and Standards?

A. A member or candidate is eligible for the new position and incentive if he or she can arrange for enough current clients to switch to the new firm and if the member or candidate discloses the incentive fee.

B. A member or candidate may not accept employment with the new firm because Jackman's incentive offer violates the Code and Standards.

C. A member or candidate is not eligible for the new position unless he or she is currently unemployed because soliciting the clients of the member's or candidate's current employer is prohibited.

27. Jurgen is a portfolio manager. One of her firm's clients told Jurgen that he will compensate her beyond the compensation provided by her firm on the basis of the capital appreciation of his portfolio each year. Jurgen should:

A. turn down the additional compensation because it will result in conflicts with the interests of other clients' accounts.

B. turn down the additional compensation because it will create undue pressure on her to achieve strong short-term performance.

C. obtain permission from her employer prior to accepting the compensation arrangement.

28. Willier is the research analyst responsible for following Company X. All the information he has accumulated and documented suggests that the outlook for the company's new products is poor, so the stock should be rated a weak "hold." During lunch, however, Willier overhears a financial analyst from another firm whom he respects offer opinions that conflict with Willier's forecasts and expectations. Upon returning to his office, Willier releases a strong "buy" recommendation to the public. Willier:

A. violated the Standards by failing to distinguish between facts and opinions in his recommendation.

B. violated the Standards because he did not have a reasonable and adequate basis for his recommendation.

C. was in full compliance with the Standards.

29. Scott works for a regional brokerage firm. He estimates that Walkton Industries will increase its dividend by US$1.50 a share during the next year. He realizes that this increase is contingent on pending legislation that would, if enacted, give Walkton a substantial tax break. The US representative for Walkton's home district has told Scott that although she is lobbying hard for the bill and prospects for its passage are favorable, concern of the US Congress over the federal deficit could cause the tax bill to be voted down. Walkton Industries has not made any statements about a change in dividend policy. Scott writes in his research report, "We expect Walkton's stock price to rise by at least US$8.00 a share by the end of the year because the dividend will increase by US$1.50 a share. Investors buying the stock at the current time should expect to realize a total return of at least 15% on the stock." Which of the following statements is true?

A. Scott violated the Standards because he used material inside information.

B. Scott violated the Standards because he failed to separate opinion from fact.

C. Scott violated the Standards by basing his research on uncertain predictions of future government action.

30. Cannan has been working from home on weekends and occasionally saves correspondence with clients and completed work on her home computer. Because of worsening market conditions, Cannan is one of several employees released by her firm. While Cannan is looking for a new job, she uses the files she saved at home to request letters of recommendation from former clients. She also provides to prospective clients some of the reports as examples of her abilities.

    A. Cannan violated the Code and Standards because she did not receive permission from her former employer to keep or use the files after her employment ended.

    B. Cannan did not violate the Code and Standards because the files were created and saved on her own time and computer.

    C. Cannan violated the Code and Standards because she is prohibited from saving files on her home computer.

31. Smith is a financial analyst with XYZ Brokerage Firm. She is preparing a purchase recommendation on JNI Corporation. Which of the following situations is *most likely* to represent a conflict of interest for Smith that would have to be avoided or disclosed?

    A. Smith frequently purchases items produced by JNI.

    B. XYZ holds for its own account a substantial common stock position in JNI.

    C. Smith's brother-in-law is a supplier to JNI.

32. Jamison is a junior research analyst at Howard & Howard, a brokerage and investment banking firm. Howard & Howard's mergers and acquisitions department has represented the Britland Company in all its acquisitions for the past 20 years. Two of Howard & Howard's senior officers are directors of various Britland subsidiaries. Jamison has been asked to write a research report on Britland. What is the best course of action for her to follow?

    A. Jamison may write the report but must refrain from expressing any opinions because of the special relationships between the two companies.

    B. Jamison should not write the report, because the two Howard & Howard officers serve as directors for subsidiaries of Britland.

    C. Jamison may write the report if she discloses the director relationship between the two companies.

33. Which of the following statements clearly *conflicts* with the recommended procedures for compliance presented in the CFA Institute *Standards of Practice Handbook*?

    A. Firms should disclose to clients the personal investing policies and procedures established for their employees.

    B. Prior approval must be obtained for the personal investment transactions of all employees.

C. For confidentiality reasons, personal transactions and holdings should not be reported to employers unless mandated by regulatory organizations.

34. Rose, a portfolio manager for a local investment advisory firm, is planning to sell a portion of his personal investment portfolio to cover the costs of his child's tuition. Rose wants to sell a portion of his holdings in Household Products, but his firm recently upgraded the stock to "strong buy." Which of the following describes Rose's options under the Code and Standards?

    A. Based on his firm's "buy" recommendation, Rose cannot sell the shares, because he would be improperly prospering from the inflated recommendation.

    B. Rose is free to sell his personal holdings once his firm is properly informed of his intentions.

    C. Rose can sell his personal holdings but only when a client of the firm places an order to buy shares of Household.

35. Which of the following statements is a stated purpose of disclosure in Standard VI(C) Referral Fees?

    A. Disclosure will allow the client to request discounted service fees.

    B. Disclosure will help the client evaluate any possible partiality shown in the recommendation of services.

    C. Disclosure means advising a prospective client about the referral arrangement once a formal client relationship has been established.

36. Park is very frustrated after taking the Level II CFA exam. While she was studying for the exam, to supplement the curriculum provided, she ordered and used study material from a third-party provider. Park believes the additional material focused her attention on specific topic areas that were not tested while ignoring other areas. She posts the following statement on the provider's discussion board: "I am very dissatisfied with your firm's CFA Program Level II material. I found the exam extremely difficult and myself unprepared for specific questions after using your product. How could your service provide such limited instructional resources on the analysis of inventories and taxes when the exam had multiple questions about them? I will not recommend your products to other candidates." Which of the following statements is true?

    A. Park violated the Code and Standards by purchasing third-party review material.

    B. Park violated the Code and Standards by providing her opinion on the difficulty of the exam.

    C. Park violated the Code and Standards by providing specific information on topics tested on the exam.

37. Albert and Tye, who recently started their own investment advisory business, have registered to take the Level III CFA examination. Albert's business card reads, "Judy Albert, CFA Level II." Tye has not put anything about the CFA designation on his business card, but promotional material that he designed for the business describes the CFA requirements and indicates that Tye participates in the CFA Program and has completed Levels I and II. Which of the following

statements is true?

A. Albert violated the Standards, but Tye did not.

B. Tye violated the Standards, but Albert did not.

C. Both Albert and Tye violated the Standards.

38. Rule has worked as a portfolio manager for a large investment management firm for the past 10 years. Rule earned his CFA charter last year and has decided to open his own investment management firm. After leaving his current employer, Rule creates some marketing material for his new firm. He states in the material, "In earning the CFA charter, a highly regarded credential in the investment management industry, I further enhanced the portfolio management skills learned during my professional career. While completing the examination process in three consecutive years, I consistently received the highest possible scores on the topics of ethics, alternative investments, and portfolio management." Did Rule violate Standard VII(B) Reference to CFA Institute, the CFA Designation, and the CFA Program in his marketing material?

    A. Rule violated Standard VII(B) in stating that he completed the exams in three consecutive years.

    B. Rule violated Standard VII(B) in stating that he received the highest scores in the topics of ethics, alternative investments, and portfolio management.

    C. Rule did not violate Standard VII(B).

39. Quinn sat for the Level III CFA exam this past weekend. He updates his resume with the following statement: "In finishing the CFA Program, I improved my skills related to researching investments and managing portfolios. I will be eligible for the CFA charter upon completion of the required work experience."

    A. Quinn violated the Code and Standards by claiming he improved his skills through the CFA Program.

    B. Quinn violated the Code and Standards by incorrectly stating that he is eligible for the CFA charter.

    C. Quinn did not violate the Code and Standards with his resume update.

SOLUTIONS

1. The correct answer is A because this question relates to Standard I(A) Knowledge of the Law—specifically, global application of the Code and Standards. Members and candidates who practice in multiple jurisdictions may be subject to various securities laws and regulations. If applicable law is more strict than the requirements of the Code and Standards, members and candidates must adhere to applicable law; otherwise, members and candidates must adhere to the Code and Standards. Therefore, answer A is correct. Answer B is incorrect because members and candidates must adhere to the higher standard set by the Code and Standards if local applicable law is less strict. Answer C is incorrect because when no applicable law exists, members and candidates are required to adhere to the Code and Standards, and the Code and Standards prohibit the use of material nonpublic information.

2. The correct answer is B. The best course of action under Standard I(B) Independence and Objectivity is to avoid a conflict of interest whenever possible. Therefore, for Ward to pay for all his expenses is the correct answer. Answer C details a course of action in which the conflict would be disclosed, but this solution is not as appropriate as avoiding the conflict of interest. Answer A would not be the best course because it would not remove the appearance of a conflict of interest; even though the report would not be affected by the reimbursement of expenses, it could appear to be.

3. The correct answer is B. This question relates to Standard I(B) Independence and Objectivity. When asked to change a recommendation on a company stock to gain business for the firm, the head of the brokerage unit must refuse in order to maintain his independence and objectivity in making recommendations. He must not yield to pressure by the firm's investment banking department. To avoid the appearance of a conflict of interest, the firm should discontinue issuing recommendations about the company. Answer A is incorrect; changing the recommendation in any manner that is contrary to the analyst's opinion violates the duty to maintain independence and objectivity. Answer C is incorrect because merely assigning a new analyst to decide whether the stock deserves a higher rating will not address the conflict of interest.

4. Answer A is correct. Standard I(B) Independence and Objectivity emphasizes the need for members and candidates to maintain their independence and objectivity. Best practices dictate that firms adopt a strict policy not to accept compensation for travel arrangements. At times, however, accepting paid travel would not compromise one's independence and objectivity. Answers B and C are incorrect because the added benefits—free conference admission for additional staff members and an exclusive golf retreat for the speaker—could be viewed as inducements related to the firm's working arrangements and not solely related to the speaking engagement. Should Long wish to bring other team members or participate in the golf outing, he or his firm should be responsible for the associated fees.

5. The correct answer is C. This question involves Standard I(C) Misrepresentation. Statement I is a factual statement that discloses to clients and prospects accurate information about the terms of the investment instrument. Statement II, which guarantees a specific rate of return for a mutual fund, is an opinion stated as a fact and, therefore, violates Standard I(C). If Statement II were rephrased to include a qualifying statement, such as "in my opinion, investors may earn . . . ," it would not be in violation of the Standards.

6. The correct answer is C. This question relates to Standard I(C) Misrepresentation. Although Michelieu's statement about the total return of his clients' accounts on average may be technically true, it is misleading because the majority of the gain resulted from one client's large position taken against Michelieu's advice. Therefore, this statement misrepresents the investment performance the member is responsible for. He has not taken steps to present a fair, accurate, and complete presentation of performance. Answer B is thus incorrect. Answer A is incorrect because although Michelieu is not guaranteeing future results, his words are still a misrepresentation of his performance history.

7. The correct answer is A. This question involves three of the Standards. Anderb, the portfolio manager, has been obtaining more favorable prices for her personal securities transactions than she gets for her clients, which is a breach of Standard III(A) Loyalty, Prudence, and Care. In addition, she violated Standard I(D) Misconduct by failing to adhere to company policy and by hiding her personal transactions from her firm. Anderb's supervisor, Bates, violated Standard IV(C) Responsibilities of Supervisors; although the company had requirements for reporting personal trading, Bates failed to adequately enforce those requirements. Answer B does not represent a violation because Standard VI(B) Priority of Transactions requires that personal trading in a security be conducted after the trading in that security of clients and the employer. The Code and Standards do not prohibit owning such investments, although firms may establish policies that limit the investment opportunities of members and candidates. Answer C does not represent a violation because the Code and Standards do not contain a prohibition against employees using the same broker for their personal accounts that they use for their client accounts. This arrangement should be disclosed to the employer so that the employer may determine whether a conflict of interest exists.

8. The correct answer is B. This question deals with Standard II(A) Material Nonpublic Information. The mosaic theory states that an analyst may use material public information and nonmaterial nonpublic information in creating a larger picture than shown by any individual piece of information and the conclusions the analyst reaches become material only after the pieces are assembled. Answers A and C are accurate statements relating to the Code and Standards but do not describe the mosaic theory.

9. The correct answer is B. The best policy to prevent violation of Standard II(A) Material Nonpublic Information is the establishment of firewalls in a firm to prevent exchange of insider information. The physical and informational barrier of a firewall between the investment banking department and the brokerage operation prevents the investment banking department from providing information to analysts on the brokerage side who may be writing recommendations on a company stock. Prohibiting recommendations of the stock of companies that are clients of the investment banking department is an alternative, but answer A states that this prohibition would be permanent, which is not the best answer. Once an offering is complete and the material nonpublic information obtained by the investment banking department becomes public, resuming publishing recommendations on the stock is not a violation of the Code and Standards, because the information of the investment banking department no longer gives the brokerage operation an advantage in writing the report. Answer C is incorrect because no exchange of information should be occurring between the investment banking department and the brokerage operation, so monitoring of such exchanges is not an effective compliance procedure for preventing the use of material nonpublic information.

10. Answer C is correct. The guidance for Standard II(A) Material Nonpublic Information recommends adding securities to the firm's restricted list when the firm has or may have material nonpublic information. By adding these securities to this list, Andrews would uphold this standard. Because waiting until the next day will not ensure that news of the merger is made public, answer A is incorrect. Negotiations between the two companies may take much longer, and the merger may never happen. Andrews must wait until the information is disseminated to the market before he trades on that information. Answer B is incorrect because Andrews should not disclose the information to other managers; no trading is allowed on material nonpublic information.

11. Answer A is correct. Hart's decision to invest in the retail fund appears directly correlated with Rodriguez's statement about the successful quarter of Mega Retail and thus violates Standard II(A) Material Nonpublic Information. Rodriguez's information would be considered material because it would influence the share price of Mega Retail and probably influence the price of the entire exchange-traded retail fund. Thus, answer B is incorrect. Answer C is also incorrect because Rodriguez shared information that was both material and nonpublic. Company officers regularly have such knowledge about their firms, which is not a violation. The sharing of such information, however, even in a conversation between friends, does violate Standard II(A).

12. Answer B is correct. Through placing a personal purchase order that is significantly greater than the average volume, Pietro is violating Standard II(B) Market Manipulation. He is attempting to manipulate an increase in the share price and thus bring a buyer to the negotiating table. The news of a possible merger and confirmation of the firm's earnings guidance may also have positive effects on the price of Local Bank, but Pietro's actions in instructing the release of the information does not represent a violation through market manipulation. Announcements of this nature are common and practical to keep investors informed. Thus, answers A and C are incorrect.

13. The correct answer is B. Under Standard III(A) Loyalty, Prudence, and Care, members and candidates who manage a company's pension fund owe these duties to the participants and beneficiaries of the pension plan, not the management of the company or the company's shareholders.

14. The correct answer is B. This question relates to Standard III(A) Loyalty, Prudence, and Care—specifically, a member's or candidate's responsibility for voting proxies and the use of client brokerage. According to the facts stated in the question, Farnsworth did not violate Standard III(A). Although the company president asked Farnsworth to vote the shares of the Jones Corporation profit-sharing plan a certain way, Farnsworth investigated the issue and concluded, independently, the best way to vote. Therefore, even though his decision coincided with the wishes of the company president, Farnsworth is not in violation of his responsibility to be loyal and to provide care to his clients. In this case, the participants and the beneficiaries of the profit-sharing plan are the clients, not the company's management. Had Farnsworth not investigated the issue or had he yielded to the president's wishes and voted for a slate of directors that he had determined was not in the best interest of the company, Farnsworth would have violated his responsibilities to the beneficiaries of the plan. In addition, because the brokerage firm provides the lowest commissions and best execution for securities transactions, Farnsworth has met his obligations to the client in using this brokerage firm. It does not matter that the brokerage firm also provides research information that is not useful for the account generating the commission, because Farnsworth is not paying extra client money for that information.

15. Answer A is correct. The question relates to Standard III(A) Loyalty, Prudence, and Care. Carter believes the broker offers effective execution at a fee that is comparable with those of other brokers, so he is free to use the broker for all accounts. Answer B is incorrect because the accounts that prohibit soft dollar arrangements do not want to fund the purchase of research by Carter. The new trading scheme does not incur additional commissions from clients, so it would not go against the prohibitions. Answer C is incorrect because Carter should not incur unnecessary or excessive "churning" of the portfolios (excessive trading) for the purpose of meeting the brokerage commitments of soft dollar arrangements.

16. The correct answer is C. This question involves Standard III(A) Loyalty, Prudence, and Care and the specific topic of soft dollars or soft commissions. Answer C is the correct choice because client brokerage commissions may not be directed to pay for the investment manager's operating expenses. Answer B describes how members and candidates should determine how to use brokerage commissions—that is, if the use is in the best interests of clients and is commensurate with the value of the services provided. Answer A describes a practice that is commonly referred to as "directed brokerage." Because brokerage is an asset of the client and is used to benefit the client, not the manager, such practice does not violate a duty of loyalty to the client. Members and candidates are obligated in all situations to disclose to clients their practices in the use of client brokerage commissions.

17. Answer C is correct. According to Standard III(A) Loyalty, Prudence, and Care, the CFA Program would be considered a personal or firm expense and should not be paid for with the fund's brokerage commissions. Soft dollar accounts should be used only to purchase research services that directly assist the investment manager in the investment decision-making process, not to assist the management of the firm or to further education. Thus, answer A is incorrect. Answer B is incorrect because the reasonableness of how the money is used is not an issue; the issue is that educational expense is not research.

18. The correct answer is C. This question, which relates to Standard III(B) Fair Dealing, tests the knowledge of the procedures that will assist members and candidates in treating clients fairly when making investment recommendations. The step listed in answer C will help ensure the fair treatment of clients. Answer A may have negative effects on the fair treatment of clients. The more people who know about a pending change, the greater the chance that someone will inform some clients before the information's release. The firm should establish policies that limit the number of people who are aware in advance that a recommendation is to be disseminated. Answer B, distributing recommendations to institutional clients before distributing them to individual accounts, discriminates among clients on the basis of size and class of assets and is a violation of Standard III(B).

19. The correct answer is B. This question involves Standard III(B) Fair Dealing. Smith disseminated a change in the stock recommendation to his clients but then received a request contrary to that recommendation from a client who probably had not yet received the recommendation. Prior to executing the order, Smith should take additional steps to ensure that the customer received the change of recommendation. Answer A is incorrect because the client placed the order prior to receiving the recommendation and, therefore, does not have the benefit of Smith's most recent recommendation. Answer C is also incorrect; simply because the client request is contrary to the firm's recommendation does not mean a member can override a direct request by a client. After Smith contacts the client to ensure that the client received the changed recommendation, if the client still

wants to place a buy order for the shares, Smith is obligated to comply with the client's directive.

20. The correct answer is A. In this question, Brown is providing investment recommendations before making inquiries about the client's financial situation, investment experience, or investment objectives. Brown is thus violating Standard III(C) Suitability. Answers B and C provide examples of information members and candidates should discuss with their clients at the outset of the relationship, but these answers do not constitute a complete list of those factors. Answer A is the best answer.

21. Answer C is correct. Cupp violated Standard III(D) Performance Presentations when he deviated from the firm's stated policies solely to capture the gain from the holding being acquired. Answer A is incorrect because the firm does not claim GIPS compliance and the GIPS standards require external cash flows to be treated in a consistent manner with the firm's documented policies. Answer B is incorrect because the firm does not state that it is updating its composite policies. If such a change were to occur, all cash flows for the month would have to be reviewed to ensure their consistent treatment under the new policy.

22. Answer B is correct. Paper violated Standard III(D) Performance Presentation by not disclosing that he was part of a team of managers that achieved the results shown. If he had also included the return of the portion he directly managed, he would not have violated the standard. Thus, answer A is incorrect. Answer C is incorrect because Paper received written permission from his prior employer to include the results.

23. The correct answer is B. This question relates to Standard III(A) Loyalty, Prudence, and Care and Standard III(E) Preservation of Confidentiality. In this case, the member manages funds of a private endowment. Clients, who are, in this case, the trustees of the fund, must place trust in members and candidates. Bronson cannot disclose confidential financial information to anyone without the permission of the fund, regardless of whether the disclosure may benefit the fund. Therefore, answer A is incorrect. Answer C is incorrect because Bronson must notify the fund and obtain the fund's permission before publicizing the information.

24. Answer A is correct. Townsend has not provided any information about her clients to the leaders or managers of the golf program; thus, she has not violated Standard III(E) Preservation of Confidentiality. Providing contact information about her clients for a direct-mail solicitation would have been a violation. Answer B is incorrect because the notice in the newsletter does not violate Standard III(E). Answer C is incorrect because the golf program's fundraising campaign had already begun, so discussing the opportunity to donate was appropriate.

25. The correct answer is B. Under Standard IV(A) Loyalty, members and candidates may undertake independent practice that may result in compensation or other benefit in competition with their employer as long as they obtain consent from their employer. Answer C is not consistent with the Standards, because the Standards allow members and candidates to make arrangements or preparations to go into competitive business as long as those arrangements do not interfere with their duty to their current employer. Answer A is not consistent with the Standards, because the Standards do not include a complete prohibition against undertaking independent practice.

26. Answer C is correct. Standard IV(A) Loyalty discusses activities permissible to members and candidates when they are leaving their current employer; soliciting

clients is strictly prohibited. Thus, answer A is inconsistent with the Code and Standards, even with the required disclosure. Answer B is incorrect because the offer does not directly violate the Code and Standards. There may be out-of-work members and candidates who can arrange the necessary commitments without violating the Code and Standards.

27. The correct answer is C. This question involves Standard IV(B) Additional Compensation Arrangements. The arrangement described in the question—whereby Jurgen would be compensated beyond the compensation provided by her firm, on the basis of an account's performance—is not a violation of the Standards as long as Jurgen discloses the arrangement in writing to her employer and obtains permission from her employer prior to entering into the arrangement. Answers A and B are incorrect; although the private compensation arrangement could conflict with the interests of other clients and lead to short-term performance pressures, members and candidates may enter into such agreements as long as they have disclosed the arrangements to their employer and obtained permission for the arrangement from their employer.

28. The correct answer is B. This question relates to Standard V(A) Diligence and Reasonable Basis. The opinion of another financial analyst is not an adequate basis for Willier's action in changing the recommendation. Answer C is thus incorrect. So is answer A because, although it is true that members and candidates must distinguish between facts and opinions in recommendations, the question does not illustrate a violation of that nature. If the opinion overheard by Willier had sparked him to conduct additional research and investigation that justified a change of opinion, then a changed recommendation would be appropriate.

29. The correct answer is B. This question relates to Standard V(B) Communication with Clients and Prospective Clients. Scott issued a research report stating that he expects the price of Walkton Industries stock to rise by US$8 a share "because the dividend will increase" by US$1.50 per share. He made this statement knowing that the dividend will increase only if Congress enacts certain legislation, an uncertain prospect. By stating that the dividend will increase, Scott failed to separate fact from opinion. The information regarding passage of legislation is not material nonpublic information, because it is conjecture, and the question does not state whether the US representative gave Scott her opinion on the passage of the legislation in confidence. She could have been offering this opinion to anyone who asked. Therefore, statement A is incorrect. It may be acceptable to base a recommendation, in part, on an expectation of future events, even though they may be uncertain. Therefore, answer C is incorrect.

30. Answer A is correct. According to Standard V(C) Record Retention, Cannan needed the permission of her employer to maintain the files at home after her employment ended. Without that permission, she should have deleted the files. All files created as part of a member's or candidate's professional activity are the property of the firm, even those created outside normal work hours. Thus, answer B is incorrect. Answer C is incorrect because the Code and Standards do not prohibit using one's personal computer to complete work for one's employer.

31. The correct answer is B. This question involves Standard VI(A) Avoid or Disclose Conflicts—specifically, the holdings of an analyst's employer in company stock. XYZ ownership of the stock of the company that is the subject of the research report creates a conflict of interest that must be disclosed in the research report. XYZ could avoid the conflict by not having Smith prepare a recommendation for JNI or any other company in which XYZ has an ownership interest. Answers A and C do not describe conflicts of interest that Smith would have to avoid or disclose. Answer A describes the use of a firm's products, which would not be a re-

quired disclosure, because it will likely not create a conflict of interest. In answer C, the relationship between the analyst and the company through a relative is so tangential that it does not create a conflict of interest necessitating disclosure.

32. The correct answer is B. This question involves Standard VI(A) Avoid or Disclose Conflicts. The question establishes a conflict of interest in which an analyst, Jamison, is asked to write a research report on a company that is a client of her employer. In addition, two directors of the company are senior officers of Jamison's employer. Best practice would be to avoid the conflicts of interest by not providing a research report on companies that are clients of or have a director relationship with Howard & Howard. If the conflicts are not avoided, both the client relationship and director relationship must be disclosed by Jamison in her research report. Answer C is incorrect because Jamison would be disclosing only one of the conflicts. Answer A is incorrect because whether Jamison expresses any opinions in the report is irrelevant to her duty to disclose all conflicts of interest. Not expressing opinions does not relieve the analyst of the responsibility to disclose the special relationships between the two companies.

33. The correct answer is C. This question asks about compliance procedures relating to personal investments of members and candidates. The statement in answer C clearly conflicts with the recommended procedures in the *Standards of Practice Handbook*. Employers should compare personal transactions of employees with those of clients on a regular basis regardless of the existence of a requirement by any regulatory organization. Such comparisons ensure that employees' personal trades do not conflict with their duty to their clients, and the comparisons can be conducted in a confidential manner. The statement in answer A does not conflict with the procedures in the *Handbook*. Disclosure of such policies will give full information to clients regarding potential conflicts of interest on the part of those entrusted to manage their money. Answer B is incorrect because firms are encouraged to establish policies whereby employees clear their personal holdings and transactions with their employers.

34. The correct answer is B. Standard VI(B) Priority of Transactions does not limit transactions of company employees that differ from current recommendations as long as the sale does not disadvantage current clients. Thus, answer A is incorrect. Answer C is incorrect because the Standard does not require the matching of personal and client trades.

35. The correct answer is B. Answer B gives one of the two primary reasons listed in the *Handbook* for disclosing referral fees to clients under Standard VI(C) Referral Fees. (The other is to allow clients and employers to evaluate the full cost of the services.) Answer A is incorrect because Standard VI(C) does not require members or candidates to discount their fees when they receive referral fees. Answer C is inconsistent with Standard VI(C) because disclosure of referral fees, to be effective, should be made to prospective clients before entering into a formal client relationship with them.

36. Answer C is correct. Standard VII(A) Conduct as Members and Candidates in the CFA Program prohibits providing information to candidates or the public that is considered confidential to the CFA Program. In revealing that questions related to the analysis of inventories and analysis of taxes were on the exam, Park violated this standard. Answer B is incorrect because the guidance for the standard explicitly acknowledges that members and candidates are allowed to offer their opinions about the CFA Program. Answer A is incorrect because candidates are not prohibited from using outside resources.

37. The correct answer is A. Standard VII(B) Reference to CFA Institute, the CFA

Designation, and the CFA Program is the subject of this question. The reference on Albert's business card implies that there is a "CFA Level II" designation; Tye merely indicates in promotional material that he is participating in the CFA Program and has completed Levels I and II. Candidates may not imply that there is some sort of partial designation earned after passing a level of the CFA exam. Therefore, Albert violated Standard VII(B). Candidates may communicate that they are participating in the CFA Program, however, and may state the levels that they have completed. Therefore, Tye has not violated Standard VII(B).

38. Answer B is correct, according to Standard VII(B) Reference to CFA Institute, the CFA Designation, and the CFA Program. CFA Program candidates do not receive their actual scores on the exam. Topic and subtopic results are grouped into three broad categories, and the exam is graded only as "pass" or "fail." Although candidates may achieve a topical score of "above 70%," they cannot factually state that they received the highest possible score, because that information is not reported. Thus, answer C is incorrect. Answer A is incorrect as long as the member or candidate actually completed the exams consecutively. Standard VII(B) does not prohibit the communication of factual information about completing the CFA Program in three consecutive years.

39. Answer B is correct. According to Standard VII(B) Reference to CFA Institute, the CFA Designation, and the CFA Program, Quinn cannot claim to have finished the CFA Program or be eligible for the CFA charter until he officially learns that he passed the Level III CFA exam. Until the results for the most recent exam are released, those who sat for the exam should continue to refer to themselves as "candidates." Thus, answer C is incorrect. Answer A is incorrect because members and candidates may discuss areas of practice in which they believe the CFA Program improved their personal skills.

LEARNING MODULE

3

Application of the Code and Standards: Level III

LEARNING OUTCOMES

Mastery	The candidate should be able to:
☐	evaluate practices, policies, and conduct relative to the CFA Institute Code of Ethics and Standards of Professional Conduct
☐	explain how the practices, policies, or conduct does or does not violate the CFA Institute Code of Ethics and Standards of Professional Conduct

INTRODUCTION

1

The purpose of this learning module is to provide examples of how the CFA Institute Code of Ethics and Standards of Professional Conduct (Code and Standards) can be applied in situations requiring professional and ethical judgment. Exhibit 1 presents a useful framework to help navigate the ethical decision-making process and apply the Code and Standards. The framework's components do not need to be addressed in the sequence shown, but a review of the outcome should conclude the process. This review provides insights for improved decision making in the future.

Exhibit 1: A Framework for Ethical Decision Making

- Identify: Relevant facts, stakeholders and duties owed, ethical principles, conflicts of interest
- Consider: Situational influences, additional guidance, alternative actions
- Decide and act
- Reflect: Was the outcome as anticipated? Why or why not?

These cases involve individuals in private wealth and institutional asset management settings and discussion as to whether actions, taken or not taken, are in violation of the Code and Standards. As you work through these cases, think about how applying the ethical decision-making framework might have changed the decisions and actions

Note: The quoted material that follows is from the most recent edition of the Standards of Practice Handbook, 11th edition (2014), which includes the Standards themselves, as well as the guidance for them.

of those in the scenarios. Referencing the Code and Standards will help in identifying applicable ethical principles upon which sound decisions and appropriate behavior can be based. The learning module concludes with practice problems in item-set format.

2 SOVEREIGN INVESTMENT CORPORATION

- ☐ evaluate practices, policies, and conduct relative to the CFA Institute Code of Ethics and Standards of Professional Conduct
- ☐ explain how the practices, policies, or conduct does or does not violate the CFA Institute Code of Ethics and Standards of Professional Conduct

Anthony Corrales and Victoria Adebayo worked together at a UK hedge fund (HFI) that specializes in making alternative investments in developing markets.[1] Recently, Adebayo decided to return to her home country and accept a position as chief financial officer and chief investment officer at her country's Sovereign Investment Corporation (SIC). SIC's mandate is to benefit the country's developing economy by financing local projects that generate positive investment returns and attract global partners to co-invest with SIC. A secondary goal for SIC is to develop the country's capital markets by promoting more activity and growth in the local stock market. To achieve these objectives, SIC has an investment company called National Investments (NI). In exchange for investment proceeds, investors are issued shares in NI that are listed on the country's sole national exchange. By bringing in outside investors, the capital invested by NI has a leverage effect on the local economy and society. Adebayo is excited about the opportunity to work for SIC and lead NI's investing activities. She makes appropriate arrangements for the move home.

Soon after Adebayo starts in her new role, one of the country's regional governors, who also leads the country's opposing political party, strenuously advocates for SIC to make a sizable investment in a complex mining project in an underpopulated, remote area of the nation. The project is expected to bring economic benefits to the governor's region but requires a major capital commitment. The country's minister of finance, who hired Adebayo, has different priorities. He wants SIC to fund a moderately sized urban infrastructure project. Although less capital intensive than the mining project, this project is expected to create hundreds of jobs for supporters of the political party currently in power.

Adebayo knows that although both projects are potentially important to the country, investing in both simultaneously would strain the team's resources. She quickly decides that NI should invest in the urban infrastructure project before investing in the mining project. Adebayo thinks this sequencing of investment by NI offers the benefit of supporting the current political party in power while postponing investment in the mining project until a time when the opposition party gains control of the government in a future election. She also believes the urban infrastructure project may be more profitable in the short term, thus helping to attract new investment partners. With more capital from outside investors and the extra time, Adebayo believes NI would then have sufficient funding and expertise to invest in the second, more capital intensive and complex project.

1 This case is by Jon Stokes, JD, and is based on cases from *Ethics in Practice: Ethics in Investment Management Casebook*. Consistent with the 11th edition of the *Standards of Practice Handbook*.

KNOWLEDGE CHECK

1. Did Adebayo's decision to invest in the urban infrastructure project rather than the mining project most likely violate the CFA Institute Code and Standards?

   A. No

   B. Yes, with regard to diligence and reasonable basis

   C. Yes, with regard to suitability

   Solution:

   B is correct. Standard V(A) Diligence and Reasonable Basis requires members to exercise diligence, independence, and thoroughness, as well as to have a reasonable and adequate basis to support investment action. Adebayo's decision to invest "quickly" without apparent analysis is made based on political, not investment or financial, considerations. Adebayo is facing political pressures from senior governmental supporters of each project. She must thoroughly and independently investigate each potential investment and be resolute in maintaining her independence and objectivity to act in the best interests of NI and its investors. In addition, Adebayo must not be swayed or influenced by conflicts of interest resulting from outside situational influences or pressures.

   A is incorrect because Adebayo's decision to invest "quickly" without apparent analysis is made based on political, not investment, considerations and violates her responsibilities to exercise diligence, independence, and thoroughness in analyzing investments and taking investment action. She does not have a reasonable and adequate basis, supported by appropriate research and investigation, for any investment analysis, recommendation, or action.

   C is incorrect. Both investments are suitable in meeting the goals of NI and may be justified on their merit in having a positive socioeconomic impact for the country. The mining project is likely to increase the country's wealth through increased economic activity and at the same time deliver a potentially attractive ROI. The infrastructure project will similarly enhance the local economy by providing long-term employment for hundreds of workers.

2. Which of the following would most likely mitigate any political bias influencing Adebayo's decisions regarding how to invest NI assets?

   A. Requiring all investments be approved by a higher governmental authority

   B. Developing a rigorous governance framework for investment decisions

   C. Requiring Adebayo to disclose conflicts of interest

   Solution:

   B is correct. NI should have a robust and rigorous governance framework for making investment decisions that supports an appropriate level of due diligence undertaken and facilitates Adebayo's duty to make independent and objective investment decisions free of bias, as required by Standard I(B) Independence and Objectivity. NI's development orientation does not justify taking a less-than-rigorous investment approach. If NI is to originate deals locally and bring in co-investors, it must demonstrate that it is acting in investors' best interests and is not subject to political pressures or other situational influences.

A is incorrect because deferring the decision to a higher governmental authority would not mitigate and may in fact enhance political influence on the investment decision rather than ensure each project is objectively considered for its individual investment merit.

C is incorrect because disclosing outside negative situational influences or conflicts of interest does not replace the need to act with independent and objective judgement when analyzing and selecting investment opportunities.

Anthony Corrales, CFA, Partner, Hedge Fund Investors

Anthony Corrales, CFA, Adebayo's former colleague and partner at the hedge fund HFI, contacts Adebayo and expresses interest in making a significant investment in NI. Corrales asks Adebayo for detailed information regarding NI's current financial condition, future projections, and projects. She gives him the standard investor disclosure package. After closely examining the material, Corrales decides it is an excellent investment for the hedge fund. He is confident Adebayo will deliver a strong ROI for NI, which in turn will generate strong performance for HFI.

To demonstrate his conviction and convince his hedge fund partners of the opportunity, Corrales immediately invests 25% of his personal portfolio in NI in return for shares. After several days of deliberation, the hedge fund partners decide to invest HFI assets in NI but seek assurances that NI will maintain its aggressive investment strategy and commitment to high returns. Adebayo assures Corrales and the other hedge fund partners that NI is committed to providing its investors with high rates of return. Corrales asks Adebayo to provide him directly with regular updates on NI's investment performance, financial health, future funding plans, and project status. After the hedge fund's investment with SIC is made public, shares in NI trade higher on the exchange.

Corrales is also interested in making private market investments directly for HFI. To help in this endeavor, the hedge fund uses local subadvisers to identify promising investment opportunities and navigate local laws and regulations. For their role, the subadvisers are paid from assets of the hedge fund, and although they have minimal or no experience as financial consultants or advisers, all subadvisers have close connections with local high-ranking government officials. Payments are made by the subadvisers on behalf of the hedge fund to cover substantial "deal fees" and other expenses to facilitate governmental support for each investment. Corrales does not require the local business partners to provide details of their activities or to identify what specific expenses the fees cover. Corrales views these expenditures as necessary to the fund's investment success and reports them as operating expenses to the fund's investors.

KNOWLEDGE CHECK

1. Which of Adebayo's interactions with Corrales most likely violates the CFA Institute Code and Standards?

   A. Sharing information about NI's current investments and financial condition

   B. Promising to provide updates directly to Corrales and the hedge fund partners

C. Committing that she will maximize return on investment for NI's investors

Solution:

C is correct. Standard III(C) Suitability requires CFA Institute members responsible for managing assets to a specific mandate, strategy, or style to take only investment actions that are consistent with that mandate. In the case of NI, Adebayo has a dual mandate to invest in projects that have both a beneficial socioeconomic impact and a positive expected investment return. This dual mandate is in contrast to traditional investment mandates that focus only on ROI regardless of outside or other impact. NI's investors are informed up front that investment return is not the single determining factor for NI's investment decisions. Any assurances by Adebayo to the hedge fund or other investors that promise a set rate of return or prioritize return maximization would be contrary to NI's mandate.

A is incorrect. Transparency is a fundamental principle in the Code and Standards. It would be appropriate and reasonable for Adebayo to provide detailed information about NI to potential investors, such as her former hedge fund partners, so they can conduct appropriate due diligence on NI. Although Adebayo must be careful to avoid improperly disclosing confidential information or material nonpublic information to potential investors, the facts make clear that Adebayo shares the information she is regularly disclosing to other potential investors. Adebayo can develop trust with the investment community, for NI's benefit, by providing ongoing transparency and accountability regarding her investment actions.

B is incorrect. Although Adebayo must be careful that she treats NI investors fairly, it may be acceptable in some circumstances to regularly communicate directly with a particular investor. This holds true as long as all investors of NI are treated fairly and receive the same disclosures about the financial prospects and other information about NI, with no preference for those investors with whom Adebayo has a close relationship. There is no indication from the facts that Adebayo is not also providing this same "hands on" service to other NI investors.

2. Did Corrales's investment for his own portfolio most likely violate the CFA Institute Code and Standards?

A. No

B. Yes, with regard to conflicts of interest

C. Yes, with regard to priority of transactions

Solution:

C is correct. In this instance, Corrales engaged in the unethical and often illegal practice of front-running, or trading in advance for one's personal account prior to trading for client accounts for economic advantage. Standard VI(B) Priority of Transactions states that investment transactions for clients must have priority over investment transactions for personal benefit. After the hedge fund invests in NI, the value of NI shares increases, benefiting Corrales through an increase in the value of his personal investment. This practice is unethical and violates Standard VI(B) even if his personal investment does not disadvantage the hedge fund in any way. Corrales should have waited to invest in NI until after the hedge fund had completed its investment in NI.

A is incorrect because Corrales is violating Standard VI(B) Priority of Transactions.

B is incorrect. Purchasing the same investments as your employer or investing in the same assets as your clients does not necessarily create a conflict of interest, although best practice recommends that such "co-investing" be disclosed.

3. By hiring subadvisers in a developing country to source investment opportunities, Corrales is most likely violating the Standard of Professional Conduct relating to:

   A. misrepresentation.

   B. diligence and reasonable basis.

   C. independence and objectivity.

   Solution:

   A is correct. By reporting subadvisory payments as legitimate hedge fund "operating expenses," Corrales is misrepresenting the nature of the payments to hide illegal activity and is in violation of Standard I(C) Misrepresentation. Although it is acceptable to hire subadvisers to assist in sourcing investment opportunities, Corrales is not hiring a subadviser to assist in the investment decision-making process but is essentially engaged in bribery and facilitating local corruption.

   Such conduct would violate multiple standards. To ensure inside access to investment opportunities for the hedge fund, Corrales pays locally connected individuals with minimal or no financial experience to influence government officials and secure access to investment deals. The "deal fees" are corrupt transactions and are not supported by any documentation that details legitimate investment expenses. Corrales very likely violates Standard I(A) Knowledge of the Law because his conduct would most likely violate applicable anti-bribery laws.

   B is incorrect. To better serve clients, investment professionals may choose to delegate to third parties work that requires specialization, knowledge, or expertise. For example, an investment adviser may hire subadvisers to handle a particular strategy or investment style outside the scope of the adviser's ability or experience. An adviser can hire a subadviser to manage an asset allocation invested in a particular market, and the payments to the subadviser would be legitimate investment expenses that could properly be passed on to investors in the hedge fund. Under Standard V(A) Diligence and Reasonable Basis, investment advisers who hire subadvisers must ensure they have the necessary knowledge or expertise to meet the need for diligence and thoroughness in using subadvisers in the investment decision-making process.

   C is incorrect. Investment professionals may rely on the recommendations of subadvisers who have a particular specialization or specific knowledge or expertise when selecting investment opportunities without having separate or objective reasons for choosing those investments independent from the subadviser's recommendation.

Ani Mehrotra, CFA, Junior Analyst, National Investments

Back at NI, Adebayo hires Ani Mehrotra, a young analyst and recent CFA® charterholder who serves on the board of the CFA Institute local society. Mehrotra's responsibilities include globally promoting NI to potential investors. He is excited about his new role and is looking forward to working with Adebayo. Mehrotra asks Adebayo why she has not been participating in events held by the local society, given how active she was with CFA Society of the UK. Adebayo tells him that since taking her new role, she has not paid her CFA Institute membership dues or had the time to engage actively with the society. Mehrotra notices that Adebayo continues to use the CFA designation on her business card and on all marketing materials. When Mehrotra asks Adebayo about her use of the designation, she tells him that because she passed the exams and earned the charter, the credential is like a university degree that cannot be taken away.

During a sales presentation by Mehrotra and Adebayo, the potential client notes that his firm considers only investment opportunities that have CFA charterholders in senior investment positions. He asks Adebayo if all of NI's senior investment professionals are CFA charterholders. Adebayo responds, "Yes, that is correct." Mehrotra defers to Adebayo, his supervisor, and says nothing.

In serving as a board member in the CFA Institute local society, Mehrotra seeks to "give back" to the CFA Program by mentoring local candidates. He volunteers to lead the exam preparation course given by his local society for candidates in the CFA Program. After the exam, the society hosts a celebration for the students. During the celebration, a number of Mehrotra's students describe their experiences sitting for the exam. Most give their opinion on the relative difficulty of the exam, and some describe their surprise about areas of the curriculum that were not tested. Mehrotra asks the students their opinion on the most difficult exam questions. He hopes to use this information to help ensure his future students are better prepared.

KNOWLEDGE CHECK

1. With regard to communicating information to a potential investor about the qualifications of NI's investment team, who violated the CFA Institute Code and Standards?

   A. Only Adebayo

   B. Both Adebayo and Mehrotra

   C. Neither Adebayo or Mehrotra

   Solution:

   B is correct. Standard VII(B) Reference to CFA Institute, the CFA Designation, and the CFA Program states that when referring to the CFA designation, CFA Institute members and candidates "must not misrepresent . . . holding the designation." The CFA designation is not like a degree from a university in that once granted the right to use the designation, individuals must also satisfy CFA Institute membership requirements (including paying dues and submitting a Professional Conduct Statement annually) to maintain the right to refer to themselves as CFA charterholders. Although Adebayo earned her charter, her membership is considered lapsed because she has not been paying her CFA Institute dues. Until her membership is reactivated, she must not use the CFA designation or present herself as a charterholder to potential investors, although she may state she was previously a CFA Institute member.

   Mehrotra hears Adebayo refer to herself as a charterholder, but he knows that because Adebayo has not paid her dues, her CFA Institute membership has lapsed. Standard I(A) Knowledge of the Law prohibits members from knowingly participating or assisting in the violations of others and requires members to dissociate from any unethical or illegal conduct. Mehrotra's acquiescence and silence during Adebayo's misrepresentation to the client, at minimum, assists Adebayo's violation of the standard. By keeping silent about false information given to a potential investor, when doing so is potentially harmful to that investor, Mehrotra's behavior constitutes assisting in the violations of those who provide that false information even if there is no active conduct by Mehrotra. Best practice, although difficult, would be for Mehrotra to address Adebayo directly about her conduct and ask her to reinstate her membership or correct the statement made to the potential investor. If Adebayo refuses to take corrective action, Mehrotra could bring this conduct to the attention of the SIC's compliance department for them to address. Mehrotra should dissociate from the activity by not participating in any future sales meetings with Adebayo.

A is incorrect because Mehrotra violated Standard I(A) Knowledge of the Law, as outlined earlier.

C is incorrect because Adebayo violated Standard VII(B) Reference to CFA Institute, the CFA Designation, and the CFA Program and Mehrotra violated Standard I(A) Knowledge of the Law, as outlined earlier.

2. Which of Mehrotra's actions with respect to the local society's preparatory course least likely violates the CFA Institute Code and Standards?

   A. Soliciting information about the exam questions from students in an effort to improve the course for future preparatory classes

   B. Relating information about the exam to candidates in future preparatory classes to help prepare them for the exam

   C. Sharing his students' opinions about the difficulty of the exam to candidates in future preparatory classes to emphasize the need to thoroughly prepare

Solution:

C is correct. CFA Institute Standard VII(A) Conduct as Participants in CFA Institute Programs states that candidates must not engage in any conduct that compromises the integrity, validity, or security of CFA Institute programs. This standard is designed to protect the integrity and security of future exams. The standard includes giving or receiving assistance on any CFA exams and providing confidential program or exam information to candidates or the public. Candidates may generally disclose whether they believed the CFA exam was difficult relative to their expectations. It is acceptable for Mehrotra to advise future preparatory classes that his previous students found the CFA exam to be more difficult than expected and thus students should study the curriculum and prepare as much as possible.

A is incorrect. Candidates cannot provide specific information about the exam regarding the questions or the subjects tested within a topic area. Mehrotra violated Standard VII(A) by soliciting information about specific exam questions.

B is incorrect. Candidates can discuss their exam experience in general terms. However, they cannot provide specific information about the exam questions or curriculum subjects that are or are not tested on the exam. Mehrotra cannot pass such information to future candidates without violating Standard VII(A). For example, although CFA Institute makes known to candidates that ethics is one of 10 topic areas tested on the exam, there may not be an exam question on the subject of material nonpublic information. A candidate saying the ethics topic in the exam was difficult is not in violation of Standard VII(A), but a candidate saying there were no exam questions on insider information would violate Standard VII(A).

Marcia Lopez

June 2017 was a life-changing month for Marcia Lopez.[2] She earned a master's degree in finance from a top national university, sat for the Level I CFA exam, and accepted a job offer in her hometown as an associate in the wealth management division of BankGlobal, a multinational financial services firm.

In August, Lopez finds out that she passed Level I and begins working for BankGlobal. On her first day at BankGlobal, Lopez meets with her supervisor, David Hockett, CFA. Hockett has worked in the wealth management industry for almost 25 years and has been with BankGlobal for the past 10 years. He is eager to share his expertise with Lopez, which will enable her to assume greater client management responsibilities under his supervision. During their meeting, Hockett reviews BankGlobal's code of ethics, the specific policies and procedures needed to ensure compliance with their code, the CFA Institute Code and Standards, and all applicable securities laws and regulations. At the end of the meeting, Lopez asks him to approve her Business Card Request form, on which she describes herself as a "CFA, Level I." Hockett tells her that she should also put on her business card the year she expects to receive her CFA designation so clients can track her success in the program.

KNOWLEDGE CHECK

1. Did Lopez violate the Code and Standards in her description of herself on the Business Card Request form?

   A. Yes

   B. No, because she found out in August that she passed Level I

   C. No, because she knows the year that she expects to receive her CFA designation

   Solution:

   A is correct. Putting on her business card "CFA, Level I" and the year in which she expects to receive the CFA designation is a violation of Standard VII(B) Reference to CFA Institute, the CFA Designation, and the CFA Program. "Candidates in the CFA Program may refer to their participation in the CFA Program, but such references must clearly state that an individual is a *candidate* in the CFA Program and must not imply that the candidate has achieved any type of partial designation." Moreover, CFA candidates must never "cite an expected completion date of any level of the CFA Program."

   B is incorrect. The fact that she found out she passed Level I is irrelevant to the standard. By putting "CFA, Level I" and the year she expects to receive her designation, Lopez violated Standard VII(B) Reference to CFA Institute, the CFA Designation, and the CFA Program.

   C is incorrect. Lopez cannot know the year she expects to receive the designation because she needs to pass Levels II and III and gain sufficient relevant work experience—all of which involve future uncertainty. Even if knowing the date were possible, putting the year she expects to receive her designation violates Standard VII(B) Reference to CFA Institute, the CFA Designation, and the CFA Program.

2 This case is by Charles H. Kard, CFA, CFP, and Michael G. McMillan, PhD, CFA, in *Ethics Cases*. Consistent with the 11th edition of the *Standards of Practice Handbook*.

David Hockett and Team

Later that day, Hockett introduces Lopez to the four other members of his wealth management team. The team manages $900 million in assets for 150 high-net-worth clients. Almost 80% of the team's assets are managed in discretionary accounts, with the balance managed in non-discretionary accounts. For the past two years, the portfolios managed by Hockett's team have outperformed their benchmarks and most other wealth management teams at BankGlobal. This is partly due to the close relationships that the team has developed with the securities analysts in BankGlobal's research department. Because of bottlenecks in BankGlobal's information technology (IT) department, it generally takes about 45 minutes for changes in the analysts' recommendations to be published on the firm's website and emailed to clients. As a result, the analysts often call Hockett's team about changes in their recommendations before IT has published the information on BankGlobal's website. After receiving these calls, the team immediately acts on any analyst changes for their discretionary accounts to prevent their clients' portfolios from being adversely impacted when the recommendations are posted or to take advantage of better-than-expected reports.

KNOWLEDGE CHECK

1. By acting on the analysts' recommendations for their discretionary accounts, are members of Hockett's team violating the Code and Standards?

   A. No

   B. Yes, because they are not dealing fairly with all clients

   C. Yes, because they are acting on material nonpublic information

   Solution:

   B is correct. By acting on the analysts' recommendation changes for their discretionary accounts before the changes are publicly disseminated, the team is violating Standard III(B) Fair Dealing. Standard III(B) requires members and candidates to "deal fairly and objectively with all clients when providing investment analysis, making investment recommendations, taking investment action, or engaging in other professional activities." The guidance to Standard III(B) states, "Members and candidates must make every effort to treat all individual and institutional clients in a fair and impartial manner. A member or candidate may have multiple relationships with an institution; for example, the member or candidate may be a corporate trustee, pension fund manager, manager of funds for individuals employed by the customer, loan originator, or creditor. A member or candidate must exercise care to treat all clients fairly."

   A is incorrect. By acting on the analysts' recommendation changes for only some clients before the investment recommendations are publicly disseminated to all clients, Hockett's team is not treating all BankGlobal clients in a fair and impartial manner. Hockett is giving preferential treatment to his discretionary accounts at the expense of other clients, such as the non-discretionary accounts managed by Hockett's team and clients of other BankGlobal wealth teams.

   C is incorrect. The research team develops their recommendations for management of all BankGlobal's client accounts. These clients pay BankGlobal for its research. If other investors would like to access BankGlobal research, they can do so by becoming clients of the bank. The guidance to Standard II(A) Material Nonpublic Information states, "Information is material if it would significantly alter the total mix of information currently available

> about a security." To be considered material, there would need to be a clear indication that the general investing public relies on the information of BankGlobal. There is no indication in the material that BankGlobal recommendations are distributed to or highly valued by the general investing public.

The Kochanskis

After several months of learning about the wealth management division's operations and products, Hockett believes Lopez is ready to meet with prospective clients. Next week, Hockett is meeting with Marty and Mary Kochanski for the first time. The Kochanskis were referred to Hockett by Gary White, their business banker at BankGlobal. The Kochanskis are both 61 years of age, and they recently retired after Mary sold her medical insurance consulting business for $7.4 million. Hockett invites Lopez to participate in the meeting with the couple and asks her to prepare a presentation on BankGlobal's wealth management capabilities. Hockett also asks her to create a model "balanced portfolio" that he intends to recommend to the Kochanskis at the meeting.

Lopez is excited and immediately begins work on the presentation. To develop the Kochanskis' "balanced portfolio," Lopez prepares a list of fixed-income funds, equity mutual funds, and exchange-traded funds (ETFs). The list includes mutual funds and ETFs from BankGlobal's proprietary offerings, as well as those from other firms. Lopez then selects the top two performing equity and fixed-income funds with the highest five-year returns. To create a balanced portfolio, she gives an equal weight to each fund. Unsure how to present the model portfolio's past performance, Lopez uses an average of the four funds' five-year annualized rates of return and labels it "total portfolio return." For comparison purposes, Lopez shows the annual rates of return realized over a five-year period for a "composite portfolio" consisting of the team's discretionary accounts of similar size to the Kochanskis' that also have a balanced objective. To simplify the presentation, she excludes terminated accounts.

The day before they are to meet with the Kochanskis, Hockett reviews Lopez's presentation. Although he is impressed with the quality of her work, he asks her why she did not use only BankGlobal's proprietary mutual funds to create the Kochanskis' balanced portfolio. Hockett tells Lopez that, whenever possible, she should always use BankGlobal's products since they are "as good as any other firm's" and that the team receives a higher fee by using them. In addition, he states that "as employees and shareholders of BankGlobal, we have a fiduciary duty to maximize our shareholders' wealth." Before leaving to go home that evening, Lopez changes the funds in the Kochanskis' model portfolio to include only BankGlobal's proprietary funds and then updates the presentation.

The next morning, Hockett and Lopez meet with the Kochanskis. At the time White referred them to Hockett, White told Hockett only how much the Kochanskis wanted to invest, their ages, and their employment status. At the face-to-face meeting, the Kochanskis share that while they have a solid understanding of the health care and medical insurance businesses, they don't know enough about financial markets and securities to manage their own investments. Instead, they would prefer to have an investment professional manage their money, allowing them more time to travel and enjoy their grandchildren. During the 30-minute meeting with the Kochanskis, Hockett and Lopez go through Lopez's presentation and explain why a balanced portfolio is best suited for them.

KNOWLEDGE CHECK

1. Did Hockett and Lopez violate the Code and Standards in their recommendation of a balanced portfolio to the Kochanskis?

   A. Yes

   B. No, because they know the Kochanskis' investment objectives and risk tolerance

   C. No, because the balanced portfolio is most suitable for the Kochanskis given their age and wealth

   Solution:

   A is correct. Hockett and Lopez violated the Code and Standards. By developing and recommending a balanced portfolio for the Kochanskis without knowing their clients' investment objectives, risk tolerance, horizon, and so on, Hockett and Lopez violated Standard III(C) Suitability: "When Members and Candidates are in an advisory relationship with a client, they must:

   - Make a reasonable inquiry into a client's or prospective client's investment experience, risk and return objectives, and financial constraints prior to making any investment recommendation or taking investment action and must reassess and update this information regularly.
   - Determine that an investment is suitable to the client's financial situation and consistent with the client's written objectives, mandates, and constraints before making an investment recommendation or taking investment action.
   - Judge the suitability of investments in the context of the client's total portfolio."

   Hockett and Lopez should have developed an investment policy statement for the Kochanskis *before* they recommended any investments.

   B is incorrect. Hockett and Lopez violated Standard III(C) Suitability because they did not know their clients' investment objectives, risk tolerance, horizon, and so on, when they developed and recommended the balanced portfolio. Hockett and Lopez should have developed an investment policy statement for the Kochanskis before they recommended any investments.

   C is incorrect. Without knowing the Kochanskis' investment objectives, risk tolerance, horizon, and so on, it is simply not possible to know that the balanced portfolio as constructed is most suitable for the Kochanskis. Thus, the actions of Hockett and Lopez are in violation of Standard III(C) Suitability.

2. Which one of the following caused Lopez to violate the Code and Standards in her presentation of past performance information?

   A. Exclusion of terminated accounts

   B. Using an average return for the model portfolio's performance

   C. Using discretionary accounts of similar size to the Kochanskis' account

   Solution:

   A is correct. Lopez violated Standard III(D) Performance Presentation in her use and presentation of the composite portfolio's performance because she did not include the performance of terminated accounts. In addition, she included only the team's discretionary accounts of similar size to the Kochanskis.' Lopez should have included terminated and current discretionary accounts that were similar in her composite portfolio's performance. There is no need to include non-discretionary accounts because clients make their own investment decisions for such accounts.

B is incorrect. Using an average of the four funds' performance to present the model portfolio's performance is acceptable since the Kochanskis' knowledge of investments is unknown to Lopez. This easy-to-understand approach is appropriate for sharing information with novice investors. According to the guidance for Standard III(D), "Members and candidates can also meet their obligations under Standard III(D) by considering the knowledge and sophistication of the audience to whom a performance presentation is addressed."

C is incorrect. Lopez presented a composite based on accounts similar in nature to the one being recommended. According to the guidance for Standard III(D), "Members and candidates can also meet their obligations under Standard III(D) by presenting the performance of the weighted composite of similar portfolios rather than using a single representative account."

The Kochanskis are impressed with Lopez's presentation and BankGlobal's broad array of products and services, its commitment to clients, and its long-term view of the markets. As a result, they decide to open an account and invest their $7.4 million in the balanced portfolio.

Following the meeting with the Kochanskis, Hockett calls White to thank him for the referral. White replies, "Glad to do it. The new incentive referral program implemented in the corporate banking division in January of this year has been very rewarding for me. I receive a $250 gift certificate each time I refer one of my banking clients to the wealth management division. Because our referral program is internal and uses gift certificates, I do not have to disclose this to clients."

Hockett replies, "In January of this year, the wealth management division also established a new incentive program in order to motivate and retain key people, like myself and my team. All portfolio managers are now paid a quarterly bonus based on the performance of client accounts relative to certain benchmark indexes. Although 90% of our client accounts are conservative, with long-term investment objectives, we have been able to generate short-term 'alpha' in these accounts by investing 15%–20% of their portfolios in high-beta stocks that appear to have low risk. As a result, we have not had to change client investment objectives or their investment policy statements. Our returns have been great, and clients are pleased with our performance. Until that changes, I don't see a need to mention the incentive program to clients."

After work, Lopez posts the following message to her old high school friends on social media: "Just opened an account for Mr. Kochanski and his wife."

KNOWLEDGE CHECK

1. Is Hockett violating the Code and Standards by generating "alpha" for conservative client accounts?

   A. Yes

   B. No, because the stocks are high-beta, low-risk securities

   C. No, because client investment objectives and investment policy statements are unchanged

   Solution:

   A is correct. Hockett is violating Standard III(C) Suitability by investing in high-beta stocks for client accounts with long-term objectives in order to achieve his short-term quarterly performance bonus. According to Standard III(C), "When Members and Candidates are responsible for managing a portfolio to a specific mandate, strategy, or style, they must make only investment recommendations or take only investment actions that are consistent with the stated objectives and constraints of the portfolio." High-beta stocks by their very nature have risk.

Hockett is also violating Standard III(C) by investing 15%–20% of his clients' portfolios in high-beta stocks that "appear low risk." These high-beta stocks are contrary to the long-term risk profile established in the clients' investment policy statements (IPSs). Hockett changed the investment strategy for his clients in an attempt to gain short-term rewards offered by his firm's new compensation arrangement and not in response to changes in their investment needs and corresponding investment policy statements.

B is incorrect. High-beta stocks are not low risk. Hockett's statement is incorrect, and he is violating Standard III(C) by investing 15%–20% of clients' portfolios in high-beta stocks that are contrary to the long-term risk profile established in the clients' IPSs. Hockett has changed the investment strategy of his clients in an attempt to reap short-term rewards offered by his firm's new compensation arrangement.

C is incorrect. The fact that client investment objectives and investment policy statements are unchanged is irrelevant. Hockett violated Standard III(C) by investing 15%–20% of clients' portfolios in high-beta stocks that are contrary to the long-term risk profile established in the clients' IPSs. Hockett has changed the investment strategy of his clients in an attempt to reap short-term rewards offered by his firm's new compensation arrangement.

2. Did Lopez violate the Code and Standards in her use of social media?

   A. Yes

   B. No, because Lopez did not provide any specific information on the investments or dollar amounts

   C. No, because Lopez posted a message only to her old high school friends, not to people in the industry

Solution:

A is correct. Lopez violated Standard III(E) Preservation of Confidentiality by posting about the Kochanskis' opening of an account. According to Standard III(E), "Members and Candidates must keep information about current, former, and prospective clients confidential unless: 1. The information concerns illegal activities on the part of the client or prospective client, 2. Disclosure is required by law, or 3. The client or prospective client permits disclosure of the information." Standard III(E) requires that even the presence of a client account be kept confidentially within the firm unless the client has been informed and has consented to the disclosure of the information.

B is incorrect. Standard III(E) requires all information about current, former, or prospective clients be kept confidential, not just information about their investments or dollar amounts. Posting the name of the Kochanskis as new clients violated the required confidentiality.

C is incorrect. Standard III(E) requires all information about current, former, or prospective clients be kept confidential. This confidentiality extends beyond the investment industry to the population as a whole. By posting the name of the Kochanskis as new clients in a message to her high school friends, Lopez violated the confidentiality required under Standard III(E).

CASTLE BIOTECHNOLOGY CASE: DAVID PLUME, PHD, CFA

3

- ☐ evaluate practices, policies, and conduct relative to the CFA Institute Code of Ethics and Standards of Professional Conduct
- ☐ explain how the practices, policies, or conduct does or does not violate the CFA Institute Code of Ethics and Standards of Professional Conduct

Castle Biotechnology (CB) is a biopharmaceutical company dedicated to acquiring, developing, and commercializing pharmaceutical and biotechnology products.[3] These products are developed within CB and through the nine biopharmaceutical companies it controls. Fifteen months ago, CB purchased a controlling interest in Global Capital Management (Global), a full-service investment banking and asset management firm that provides a range of services that include underwriting, institutional sales, trading, equity research, and retail brokerage.

Shakira Chung, CFA, is CB's president, and Yusef Anders, CFA, is CB's chief executive. This morning, they are meeting to discuss the latest financial results of CB and its subsidiaries.

Anders says, "Shakira, your idea to purchase Global was brilliant. Global gives CB an in-house underwriter and a private sales force of 700 brokers to raise money to finance the research and development activities of the nine companies in our portfolio. Since acquiring Global, its brokers and research analysts have raised more than $75 million from investors around the world. Currently, Global has deals in progress to raise an additional $45 million."

Chung replies, "Yusef, we have built a unique model that inherently aligns CB's business objectives with the financial interests of Global's clients. We should be proud of the deals we have completed and the large amount of capital we have raised for our subsidiaries since we acquired Global."

Two of the biopharmaceutical companies in CB's portfolio that Global has recently taken public are Street Pharmaceuticals (STRX) and Appaloosa Biotech (APBX). Even though each company issued 75% of its shares to the public, CB stills retains voting control of each company. CB also has the right to receive a significant grant of each company's common stock each year.

David Plume, PhD, CFA

David Plume, PhD, CFA, follows the biopharmaceutical industry for Global. Prior to joining Global, Plume worked as a biochemist at CB for 15 years. During that time, he developed close professional and personal relationships with Chung and Anders. As a result, they encouraged him to become an equity analyst at Global after CB acquired it. Chung and Anders felt Plume's extensive, in-depth knowledge of the biotechnology

3 This case is by Michael G. McMillan, PhD, CFA, in *Ethics Cases*. Consistent with the 11th edition of the *Standards of Practice Handbook*.

and pharmaceutical industries would be a great help to Global. He would not only be able to write "perceptive" research reports on the companies in CB's portfolio, but he also would be able to help Global's corporate finance department identify which of its companies should be taken public. As part of his compensation package at Global, Plume receives an annual bonus equal to 0.10% of the gross proceeds raised for each initial public offering (IPO) he works on.

Prior to STRX and APBX going public with their IPOs, Plume spent a good deal of time with Global's investment bankers explaining the products each company was developing, their market potential, and the regulatory process required before their drugs could be approved for patient use by government regulators. On their first day of trading, the stock prices of STRX and APBX increased by 70% and 65%, respectively. Since then, however, their stock prices have declined 36% and 54%, respectively.

Shortly after STRX and APBX went public with their IPOs, Plume published positive research reports for both companies. In a note published on Global's website, Plume wrote that "STRX and APBX are the biopharmaceutical companies of the future. Although both are small and have no revenues to date, each company is developing a 'life-changing drug' currently undergoing clinical trials. As a result, I rate their stocks a 'buy' and predict their share prices will more than double in 9–12 months."

In his research reports, Plume does not mention that Global is owned by Castle, the same company that controls STRX and APBX, because this information is disclosed in each company's offering prospectus. He does state, however, that "one or more directors, officers, and/or employees of Global Capital and its affiliated companies or independent contractors affiliated with Global may be a director of the issuer of the securities mentioned herein." Plume also does not disclose that he owns Class A preferred shares of CB and options on CB's common stock, which were given/granted to him while he was a CB employee.

Three months after issuing his research report with a "buy" rating on APBX, Plume sells APBX short in his personal portfolio. He does not disclose the sale, because he was never a beneficial owner of APBX's stock.

KNOWLEDGE CHECK

1. Did Plume violate the Code and Standards by not disclosing in his research report that Global is owned by Castle?

   A. Yes

   B. No, because this does not affect his duty to Global or his duty to clients

   C. No, because this information is disclosed in each company's offering prospectus

   Solution:

   A is correct. By not disclosing that Global is owned by Castle in his research report, Plume is in violation of Standard VI(A) Avoid or Disclose Conflicts, which states that "Members and Candidates must avoid or make full and fair disclosure of all matters that could reasonably be expected to impair their independence and objectivity or interfere with respective duties to their clients, prospective clients, and employer. Members and Candidates must ensure that such disclosures are prominent, are delivered in plain language, and communicate the relevant information effectively."

   By not disclosing in his research reports the relationships between Castle, its nine subsidiaries, and Global, Plume is in violation of Standard VI(A). CB's ownership of Global and Plume's close relationships with CB's management raise questions about Plume's ability to remain independent and objective.

B is incorrect. Plume must disclose to his clients that Global is owned by Castle. Thus, the non-disclosure means he failed in his duty of full and fair disclosure of any conflicts of interest that may affect his clients.

C is incorrect. The fact that the relationships between Plume, CB, its subsidiaries, and Global are disclosed in the offering prospectus is necessary but not sufficient to meet Standard VI(A) because they may not communicate the information effectively or in a prominent manner.

2. Did Plume violate the Code and Standards by not disclosing his ownership of CB's Class A preferred shares and common stock options in his research report?

   A. Yes

   B. No, because he does not own shares of STRX and APBX

   C. No, because he does not have a beneficial interest in STRX and APBX

Solution:

A is correct. By not disclosing his ownership of CB's preferred shares and stock options in his research report, Plume is in violation of Standard VI(A) Avoid or Disclose Conflicts. Because of this ownership in CB, Plume has a beneficial ownership interest in the securities of STRX and APBX, both of which he recommended as "buys." The most obvious conflict that must always be disclosed involves relationships between an issuer and the member, the candidate, or his or her firm. For the purposes of Standard VI(A), members and candidates beneficially own securities or other investments if they have a direct or indirect pecuniary interest in the securities, have the power to direct the voting of the shares of the securities or investments, or have the power to dispose of or direct the disposition of the security or investment.

B is incorrect. Plume does not need to own shares in STRX and APBX directly to have a beneficial interest in the two companies. His ownership of CB's preferred shares and its common stock options, along with CB's voting control of each company, gives him a beneficial ownership interest in STRX and APBX. This situation creates a conflict of interest that requires disclosure.

C is incorrect. Plume's ownership of CB's preferred shares and its common stock options give him a beneficial ownership interest in STRX and APBX. This beneficial interest leads to the conflict of interest that requires disclosure of his holding of CB's Class A preferred shares and options on CB common stock.

3. Did Plume violate the Code and Standards by not disclosing in his research report his annual bonus based on his IPO work?

   A. Yes

   B. No, because it does not represent an additional compensation arrangement

   C. No, because it does not affect his duty of loyalty, prudence, and care to clients

Solution:

A is correct. By not disclosing his annual bonus in his research report, Plume is in violation of Standard I(B) Independence and Objectivity, which states, "Members and Candidates must use reasonable care and judgment to achieve and maintain independence and objectivity in their professional activities. Members and Candidates must not offer, solicit, or accept any gift, benefit, compensation, or consideration that reasonably could be expected to compromise their own or another's independence and objectivity."

Plume's annual bonus is equal to 0.10% of the gross proceeds for each IPO he works on with the corporate finance department. Can a member or candidate remain objective if on behalf of the firm, the member or candidate obtains or assists in obtaining fees for service? As a sell-side analyst, Plume may be encouraged by Global or CB to write potentially biased research reports about particular companies (i.e., the ones in CB's portfolio) to the exclusion of covering companies that may be more suitable for Global's clients. The guidance for Standard I(B) states, "Compensation arrangements should not link analyst remuneration directly to investment banking assignments in which the analysts may participate as a team member." The guidance also states, "Having analysts work with investment bankers is appropriate only when the conflicts are adequately and effectively managed and disclosed. Firm managers have a responsibility to provide an environment in which analysts are neither coerced nor enticed into issuing research that does not reflect their true opinions. Firms should require public disclosure of actual conflicts of interest to investors." Global can avoid the conflict by removing this incentive from Plume's compensation package.

B is incorrect. Plume's bonus is based on the gross proceeds of each IPO he works on, and so it does constitute an additional compensation arrangement. The compensation arrangement creates a conflict of interest that must be disclosed.

C is incorrect. Because Plume's bonus is based on the gross proceeds of each IPO he works on, it is reasonable to expect that his independence and objectivity may be compromised. This arrangement links his compensation directly to his participation in his investment banking assignments and thus creates a conflict of interest.

4. Did Plume violate the Code and Standards by selling APBX short in his personal portfolio?

   A. Yes

   B. No, because he was not a beneficial owner of APBX

   C. No, because he sold the shares short after issuing his research report

Solution:

A is correct. By selling ABPX short in his personal portfolio, Plume is in violation of Standard VI(A) Avoid or Disclose Conflicts, which states that "Members and Candidates must avoid or make full and fair disclosure of all matters that could reasonably be expected to impair their independence and objectivity or interfere with respective duties to their clients, prospective clients, and employer. Members and Candidates must ensure that such disclosures are prominent, are delivered in plain language, and communicate the relevant information effectively." Selling APBX short in his personal portfolio while having a "buy" recommendation on the stock is a conflict of interest that Plume needs to disclose. Global could avoid this conflict by prohibiting such transactions by its employees.

B is incorrect. Plume's ownership of CB's preferred shares and its common stock options, along with CB's voting control of each company, gives him a beneficial ownership interest in STRX and APBX. Selling APBX short after he issues a "buy" recommendation creates a conflict of interest that Plume must disclose to clients.

C is incorrect. Selling APBX short after he issues a "buy" recommendation creates a conflict of interest that Plume must disclose to clients.

CASTLE BIOTECHNOLOGY CASE 2: SANDRA BENNING, CFA, AND CLARIS DEACON

4

- ☐ evaluate practices, policies, and conduct relative to the CFA Institute Code of Ethics and Standards of Professional Conduct
- ☐ explain how the practices, policies, or conduct does or does not violate the CFA Institute Code of Ethics and Standards of Professional Conduct

Sandra Benning, CFA, is an investment adviser (broker) at Global and a rising star because of her exceptional skill in brokering stocks and developing relationships. Her clients include corporations, their senior executives, pension plans, and high-net worth individuals. Benning recently joined Global after working as an investment adviser at Kodiak Securities. While at Kodiak, she used her personal social media platforms, such as LinkedIn, X, and Facebook, as well as "old fashioned" email, to communicate with her clients. After she resigned from Kodiak, she immediately used her social media accounts to inform her clients of her departure and solicited them to follow her to Global. Global paid her a signing bonus of $250,000 based on the percentage of her Kodiak clients who moved their accounts to Global. One of the reasons Benning joined Global was to give her clients greater access to Global's initial public offerings. Global pays its investment advisers an annual year-end bonus based on the level of their clients' IPO participation. Benning does not disclose either bonus to clients.

KNOWLEDGE CHECK

1. Did Benning violate the Code and Standards in her use of social media and email to solicit former clients?

   A. No

   B. Yes, because Benning has a duty of loyalty to Kodiak

   C. Yes, because Benning is not preserving her clients' confidentiality

   Solution:

   A is correct. Benning's solicitation of former clients via social media does not violate the Code and Standards. Standard IV(A) Loyalty states, "The Code and Standards also do not prohibit former employees from contacting clients of their previous firm, in the absence of a noncompete agreement." In the absence of a noncompete agreement, as long as Benning maintains her duty of loyalty to Kodiak before joining Global, does not take steps to solicit clients until she has left Kodiak, and does not use material from Kodiak without the firm's permission after she has left the firm, she is not in violation of the Code and Standards.

   B is incorrect. In this case, Benning did not solicit clients until after she resigned from Kodiak. Benning used her personal social media platforms to connect with her clients, and she did not contact them until after she resigned from Kodiak. She did not use material from Kodiak without the firm's permission.

C is incorrect. Benning did not reveal confidential client information in her use of social medial to solicit former clients.

2. Did Benning violate the Code and Standards by not disclosing to clients the signing bonus received from Global to bring clients over from Kodiak?

   A. Yes

   B. No, because the bonus is not a referral fee

   C. No, because the bonus represents additional compensation

Solution:

A is correct. By not disclosing to her Kodiak clients the signing bonus she received from Global, Benning is in violation of Standard VI(A) Avoid or Disclose Conflicts. Benning's decision to solicit her Kodiak clients to move to Global could have been influenced by the fact that her signing bonus from Global was based on the percentage of her Kodiak clients who moved their accounts to Global. This creates an actual or potential conflict of interest that she must disclose to her former Kodiak clients. Global can avoid this conflict by not compensating Benning in this way.

According to Standard VI(A) Avoid or Disclose Conflicts, "Members and Candidates must avoid or make full and fair disclosure of all matters that could reasonably be expected to impair their independence and objectivity or interfere with respective duties to their clients, prospective clients, and employer." Standard VI(A) protects investors and employers by requiring members and candidates to avoid or fully disclose to clients, potential clients, and employers all actual and potential conflicts of interest.

B is incorrect. It is true that the bonus paid by Global represents compensation paid by the employer to the employee for services provided and is not a referral fee. It is also true, however, that the signing bonus could reasonably be expected to impair Benning's independence and objectivity or interfere with her respective duties to her clients, prospective clients, and her employer, which is in violation of Standard I(B). If such a potential conflict of interest exists, Standard VI(A) requires Benning to fully and fairly disclose it. Referral fees are defined in Standard VI(C) Referral Fees as "any compensation, consideration, or benefit received from or paid to others for the recommendation of products or services." Members and candidates must disclose referral fees to their employers, clients, and prospective clients, as appropriate.

C is incorrect. Additional compensation is defined in Standard IV(B) Additional Compensation Arrangements as "gifts, benefits, compensation, or consideration that competes with or might reasonably be expected to create a conflict of interest with their employer's interest unless they obtain written consent from all parties involved." Additional compensation arrangements generally refer to conflicts of interest the member or candidate has with their employer, not clients and prospects. The bonus does not represent additional compensation. It does, however, create an actual/potential conflict of interest.

3. Does Benning's non-disclosure of her year-end bonus that is based on the level of her clients' IPO participation place her in violation of the Code and Standards?

   A. No

   B. Yes, because the bonus represents a conflict of interest

   C. Yes, because the bonus represents additional compensation

   Solution:

   B is correct. Benning's year-end bonus is based on the level of her clients' participation in IPOs. This situation creates a conflict of interest between Benning and her clients. Is she recommending IPOs to clients based on their best interest or hers? Benning is in violation of Standard VI(A) Avoid or Disclose of Conflicts, which states that "Members and Candidates must avoid or make full and fair disclosure of all matters that could reasonably be expected to impair their independence and objectivity or interfere with respective duties to their clients, prospective clients, and employer. Members and Candidates must ensure that such disclosures are prominent, are delivered in plain language, and communicate the relevant information effectively." Global can avoid this conflict by not compensating Benning in this way.

   A is incorrect. Benning's year-end bonus is based on the level of her clients' participation in IPOs, which creates a conflict of interest between Benning and her clients that must be avoided or disclosed under Standard VI(A). Global can avoid this conflict by not compensating Benning in this way.

   C is incorrect. The bonus is not additional compensation, which is defined in Standard IV(B) as "gifts, benefits, compensation, or consideration that competes with or might reasonably be expected to create a conflict of interest with their employer's interest." In this case, the bonus is between the employer and the employee and does not create a conflict of interest between Global and Benning. The year-end bonus does, however, create a conflict of interest between Benning and her clients that must be disclosed under Standard VI(A). Global can avoid this conflict by not compensating Benning in this way.

Currently, Global is planning a highly anticipated initial public offering for Frontier Therapeutics (FTSX), a company in CB's portfolio. To determine interest in this IPO, Benning contacts her clients via social media and email and invites them to submit an application to participate in the FTSX public offering. In the invitation, she cautions her clients that "confirming your indication of interest does not guarantee an allocation of shares in the offering." She also warns that "depending on client demand, clients requesting IPO shares might receive all, some, or none of the shares they requested." On highly anticipated (oversubscribed) IPOs, Global's policy is to allocate the IPO shares to institutional clients who plan on purchasing additional shares on the first day of trading. Following Global's policy, Benning calls her institutional clients who expressed an interest in FTSX to ask if they plan on purchasing additional shares of FTSX on its first day of trading. For clients who indicate they plan on buying additional shares, Benning will allocate shares of FTSX to them in the IPO.

Once all client indications of interest have been submitted, Global then uses this information to determine an offering price for FTSX and the "basis of allotment" (i.e., the number of shares to be allocated) to each adviser/broker for their clients.

Global uses the following criteria to make its IPO allocation decisions:

- The level of business a client has conducted with the firm
- The long- or short-term interest of a client in the issuer

- The size of a client's anticipated long-term investment
- The client's track record of investment in similar issues
- The client's apparent interest in the issuer, as evidenced by attendance at road shows
- The size of the client's account
- The existing or potential business relationships between the client and Global

The day before FTSX's first day of trading (public listing), Benning emails her high-net-worth individual clients who were allocated shares of FTSX and warns them not to flip (sell) their shares when FTSX begins trading or else they will be excluded from future IPO allocations. She then phones her corporate clients (those with an existing investment banking relationship with Global) and tells them they are free to sell their shares of FTSX at the end of its first trading day. The following day, at the end of trading, FTSX's stock price closes down, at 65% of its initial offering price.

KNOWLEDGE CHECK

1. Does Benning violate the Code and Standards by allocating FTSX shares to institutional clients who plan on purchasing additional shares when it begins trading?

   A. Yes

   B. No, because Benning is following her employer's policy

   C. No, because Benning is treating all her clients fairly

   Solution:

   A is correct. This is an example of a tie-in agreement, where the underwriter requires the investor to buy more shares of a new issue in the secondary market as a condition of buying shares in the IPO. It is intended to artificially increase demand and support a higher share price. Tie-in agreements are a violation of Standard II(B) Market Manipulation: "Members and Candidates must not engage in practices that distort prices or artificially inflate trading volume with the intent to mislead market participants." By allocating shares of FTSX to institutional clients who agree to purchase additional shares on the first day of trading, Global and Benning may be distorting security prices or trading volume on the first day of trading by deceiving investors that rely on information in the market. The guidance for Standard II(B) states, "Transaction-based manipulation involves instances where a member or candidate knew or should have known that his or her actions could affect the pricing of a security." It appears that Benning and Global are artificially creating demand for FTSX shares (and increasing its price on the first day of trading) by allocating IPO shares only to clients who plan to purchase additional shares on the first day of trading.

   This practice also violates Standard III(B) Fair Dealing: "Members and Candidates must deal fairly and objectively with all clients when providing investment analysis, making investment recommendations, taking investment action, or engaging in other professional activities." In this case, Benning is not treating all her institutional clients fairly, because she is allocating IPO shares only to those clients who agree to purchase additional shares after FTSX begins trading on the first day. The overall criteria and policy used by Global to determine client allocations also are in violation of Standard III(B).

B is incorrect. Irrespective of whether she followed her employer's policy, Benning's actions are in violation of Standard II(B) Market Manipulation and Standard III(B) Fair Dealing.

C is incorrect. In this case, Benning is not treating all her institutional clients fairly because she is only allocating IPO shares to those clients who agree to purchase additional shares after FTSX begins trading on the first day. Benning's allocation to institutional investors violates Standard III(B) Fair Dealing: "Members and Candidates must deal fairly and objectively with all clients when providing investment analysis, making investment recommendations, taking investment action, or engaging in other professional activities."

Claris Deacon

Benning's newest client is Claris Deacon, a long-time family friend. To date, Deacon has made three visits to Benning's office to set up her investment account and portfolio. During her first visit, she completed and signed a New Account Agreement and a Limited Trade Authorization form, giving Benning discretion to transact securities in Deacon's account. During Deacon's second visit, she opened a cash management account that linked her brokerage account to an in-house checking (transaction) account. In her third visit, Deacon completed and signed an Option Account Application and Agreement, authorizing Benning to transact equity options in her account. After the third visit, Benning changed some of the language in the Option Account Application and Agreement pertaining to Deacon's suitability for the options she would be recommending. To save Deacon from having to make yet another trip to her office to initial the changes on the form, Benning initials the form on Deacon's behalf.

While traveling with her husband a week later, Deacon calls Benning because she is unable to transfer money from her brokerage account to her checking account. Upon further investigation, Benning discovers that the link between the accounts had not been activated. Proud of the superior customer service she provides to her clients, Benning immediately calls her client and obtains Deacon's authorization to sign the Account Linking form on Deacon's behalf. Within 24 hours, Deacon has access to her account.

A month later, Benning receives a phone call from Deacon's husband, Steve, who informs her that his wife is having serious health issues. He asks Benning to redeem \$15,000 worth of mutual fund shares and send the proceeds as soon as possible. Over the next few weeks, Benning completes several redemptions and withdrawals from Deacon's account at Steve's request. Benning makes a note on the trade form each time a redemption is processed, indicating she has spoken with Steve, who is acting on Deacon's behalf.

KNOWLEDGE CHECK

1. In opening and servicing Deacon's account, does Benning violate the Code and Standards?

   A. Yes

   B. No, because Benning was acting in Deacon's best interest

C. No, because Benning was exercising prudent judgment, loyalty, and reasonable care

Solution:

A is correct. By changing the language on the Option Account Application and Agreement and initialing the form on behalf of Deacon, Benning is in violation of Standard I(D) Misconduct. Signing the Account Linking form on behalf of Deacon is also a violation of Standard I(D). According to Standard I(D) Misconduct, "Members and Candidates must not engage in any professional conduct involving dishonesty, fraud, or deceit or commit any act that reflects adversely on their professional reputation, integrity, or competence." The approval Benning received over the telephone to sign the Account Linking form is insufficient. Benning needs Deacon to personally sign the authorization.

By redeeming shares and transacting (withdrawals) in Deacon's account at her husband's request, Benning is in violation of Standard III(A) Loyalty, Prudence, and Care. Benning has no authority or authorization from Deacon, the account holder, allowing Deacon's husband, Steve, to redeem shares and approve withdrawals from her account. To transact in the account, Steve would need to be a cosigner on all the account documents or have a "power of attorney" written authorization signed by Deacon granting him the right to act on Deacon's behalf. According to Standard III(A), "Members and Candidates have a duty of loyalty to their clients and must act with reasonable care and exercise prudent judgment." Members and candidates must also be aware of whether they have "custody" or effective control of client assets. If so, a heightened level of responsibility arises.

B is incorrect. Even if Benning was acting in Deacon's best interests by making and initialing the changes on the Option Account Application and Agreement form and signing the Account Linking form, these changes cannot be implemented without Deacon's own written approval and thus are in violation of the Standards. In addition, she should not have transacted in Deacon's account at her husband's request without Deacon's authorization.

C is incorrect. Benning is *not* showing loyalty, prudence, or care by taking actions that violate Standard III(A). These actions include making and initialing the changes on the Option Account Application and Agreement form and signing the Account Linking form. These changes cannot be effected without Deacon's own written approval and are in violation of the Standards. In addition, Benning should not have transacted in Deacon's account at her husband's request without Deacon's authorization.

5 LIONSGATE LIMITED & BANK OF AUSTRALIA CASE 1

☐ evaluate practices, policies, and conduct relative to the CFA Institute Code of Ethics and Standards of Professional Conduct

☐ explain how the practices, policies, or conduct does or does not violate the CFA Institute Code of Ethics and Standards of Professional Conduct

Lionsgate Limited (LL) is a publicly listed Australian fund manager.[4] The firm has benefited greatly from the Superannuation Guarantee program that was created in 1992. This program requires all the country's employees aged 18–70 to contribute a percentage of their earnings to a tax-advantaged retirement account or superannuation fund. In addition, legislation enacted in 2005 gives all employees the right to select a superannuation fund administered by a retail financial services company, such as LL. LL offers a range of mutual funds.

Tony Hill and Team

LL's flagship fund is the Lionsgate Victory Capital Fund (VCF), an equity mutual fund that is managed by Tony Hill and his team of 16 analysts. In LL's marketing material, Hill states, "For the period ending 31 December 2018, the Victory Capital Fund is the best-performing fund in Australian equities over the 10-year period. The VCF has delivered returns of 28.7%, gross of fees over the 1-year period, and 13.2% annually since inception in 2005. During this time, assets under management (AUM) in Australian dollars increased from \$18 million to \$14 billion."

Hill has become the main media engagement person for the VCF and LL. He has a half-hour show on Sky News Business Channel, writes a weekly financial column for the *Australian Financial Review*, and regularly appears on daytime and evening talk shows, where he talks about the VCF and its holdings. Like the other guests on these shows, Hill does not receive financial compensation for his appearances. Instead, the shows' sponsors provide him with "thank you gift bags," containing wine, retail gift cards, restaurant gift certificates, and travel discounts on hotels and airfare. Hill does not disclose the receipt of these gift bags to LL.

In 2006, Nicole Martin, CFA, was hired as an intern at LL to cover the paper, chemical, and publishing industries. After graduating at the top of her class from a prestigious university, Nicole accepted a full-time position on Hill's team, covering the metals, mining, and energy industries. As Hill's outside activities increased, Martin assumed more responsibility for security selection and investment decision making for the VCF. For the past three years, the performance of the VCF has been directly attributable to her and the other analysts, although both she and Hill still state publicly that he is in charge of all investment decision making for the VCF.

As the VCF's "star stock picker," Hill is often invited to provide a fund update at LL's quarterly board meetings. Hill uses the most recent board meeting to announce his resignation and to notify the board he is starting his own fund management firm. Recognizing Hill's departure could have a negative impact on LL's stock price as well as cash flows into the VCF, the board asks Hill to keep his plans to resign confidential until the end of LL's fiscal year (in two weeks) to give it time to find his replacement. Hill agrees. After the board meeting, Hill has a "closed door" meeting with his team and announces his plan to resign and start his own firm. He then asks the team if they want to join him. Ten of the analysts agree to resign with him and work in his new firm. Martin and the five remaining analysts tell him they will remain at LL, and they leave the meeting. Hill tells the analysts who will join him, "Team, we have a lot of work to do over the next two weeks. We'll need to use time after work and on weekends to lease office space and to individually register with the government authorities in the name of our new firm. Since we have not signed a noncompete agreement with LL, we can begin soliciting former clients the day we open our new firm."

4 This case is by Susan Morey and Michael G. McMillan, PhD, CFA, in *Ethics Cases*. Consistent with the 11th Edition of the *Standards of Practice Handbook*.

KNOWLEDGE CHECK

1. Do Hill's statements in the Lionsgate Limited marketing materials violate the Code and Standards?

   A. No

   B. Yes, because he stated the Victory Capital Fund's returns gross of fees

   C. Yes, because he is not distinguishing between fact and opinion in discussing the fund's performance

   Solution:

   A is correct. There is no evidence to suggest Hill's statements are false or opinion based. In speaking about the fund's performance, Hill is stating facts. In addition, Hill states the performance is gross of fees or "pre-fees." According to Standard III(D) Performance Presentation, "When communicating investment performance information, Members and Candidates must make reasonable efforts to ensure that it is fair, accurate, and complete." The guidance for Standard III(D) states, "Members and candidates can also meet their obligations under Standard III(D) by including disclosures that fully explain the performance results being reported (for example, stating, when appropriate, that results are simulated when model results are used, clearly indicating when the performance record is that of a prior entity, or disclosing whether the performance is gross of fees, net of fees, or after tax)."

   B is incorrect. Hill states the performance is gross of fees or "pre-fees." The guidance for Standard III(D) states, "Members . . . can also meet their obligations under Standard III(D) by including disclosures that fully explain the performance results being reported (for example, . . . disclosing whether the performance is gross of fees, net of fees, or after tax)."

   C is incorrect. It is clear in this case that in speaking about the fund's performance, Hill is stating facts, not opinions.

2. Does Hill violate the Code and Standards by accepting "thank you gift bags" from the talk show sponsors?

   A. No

   B. Yes, because he does not disclose this to his employer

   C. Yes, because his independence and objectivity are being compromised

   Solution:

   A is correct. According to Standard IV(B) Additional Compensation Arrangements, "Members and Candidates must not accept gifts, benefits, compensation, or consideration that competes with or might reasonably be expected to create a conflict of interest with their employer's interest unless they obtain written consent from all parties involved." Hill's appearance on these shows does not create a conflict of interest with the interests of LL or the VCF.

   B is incorrect. No conflict of interest is created in this situation. By not disclosing his receipt of the "thank you gift bags," Hill is not in violation of the Code and Standards.

   C is incorrect. Hill's acceptance of the "thank you gift bags" does not create a conflict of interest between Hill and his employer or between Hill and his clients. Therefore, Hill's independence and objectivity are not compromised. Hill is not in violation of Standard I(B) Independence and Objectivity.

3. Has Martin or Hill violated the Code and Standards by publicly stating that Hill is in charge of investment decision making for the VCF?

   A. Yes

   B. No, because Hill still works for the VCF

   C. No, because Martin and Hill both publicly state that Hill is in charge of investment decision making

   Solution:

   A is correct. Martin and Hill have failed to disclose to clients and prospective clients that Martin has assumed more responsibility for security selection and investment decision making at the fund and that she and the other analysts—not Hill—are primarily responsible for the fund's performance. Martin and Hill both violated Standard V(B) Communication with Clients and Prospective Clients: "Members and Candidates must: 1. Disclose to clients and prospective clients the basic format and general principles of the investment processes they use to analyze investments, select securities, and construct portfolios and must promptly disclose any changes that might materially affect those processes."

   B is incorrect. Although Hill still works for the VCF, Martin has assumed more responsibility for security selection and investment decision making at the VCF, such that she and the other analysts are primarily responsible for the fund's performance.

   C is incorrect. While Martin and Hill both publicly state Hill is in charge, it is not true. Martin—not Hill—is now primarily responsible for security selection and investment decision making at the VCF.

4. Did Hill violate the Code and Standards with respect to announcing his resignation in the "closed door" meeting with his team?

   A. No

   B. Yes, he should not have announced his plan to resign to his team.

   C. Yes, he should have publicly announced his resignation immediately after the board meeting.

   Solution:

   B is correct. Hill violated the Code and Standards by telling his team about his planned resignation after the board's request that he keep this information strictly confidential until fiscal year end (in two weeks). Despite the board's request, Hill informed his team the same day. Hill's conduct violates Standard IV(A): Duties to Employers, Loyalty. While the board's request may be considered as an outward-facing directive, it can also be considered an internally-facing directive. By telling his team about his resignation after the board's request that he keep this information confidential until fiscal year end, Hill is not honoring the board's request and is being disloyal to his employer. Hill would have been free to discuss his resignation with his team prior to his informing the board of his plans and prior to the board's request for confidentiality.

   A is incorrect. Hill did violate Standard IV(A): Loyalty. By telling his team about his resignation after the board's request that he keep this information confidential until fiscal year end, Hill is not honoring the board's request and is being disloyal to his employer.

C is incorrect. There is no duty under the Code and Standards for Hill to announce his resignation immediately after the board meeting.

5. Did Hill violate the Code and Standards by asking his team to join him at his new firm?

   A. No

   B. Yes, because Hill was the supervisor of the team

   C. Yes, because Hill owed a duty of loyalty to his current employer

   Solution:

   A is correct. It is not a violation for Hill to ask his team to join him at his new firm. The Guidance to Standard IV(A): Duties to Employers, Loyalty states, "A departing employee is generally free to make arrangements or preparations to go into a competitive business before terminating the relationship with his or her employer as long as such preparations do not breach the employee's duty of loyalty." Asking his team to join him at his new firm does not breach the duty of loyalty. However, any planning and activity on behalf of the new firm (such as the leasing of office space and individual registration) must be done by Hill and the individuals joining him on their own time.

   B is incorrect. The fact that Hill was the supervisor of the team does not change his responsibility to his employer under Standard IV(A). Thus, he was not in violation of this Standard for the reasons given in the answer to A.

   C is incorrect. Hill does owe a duty to his employer under Standard IV(A); however, asking his team to join him at his new firm does not breach the duty of loyalty under the criteria of this standard. Thus, Hill is not in violation of the Code and Standards.

6. Did Hill and his team violate the Code and Standards by leasing office space for the new firm and registering with the government authorities before resigning from Lionsgate?

   A. No

   B. Yes, because Hill and his team owe a duty of loyalty to Lionsgate

   C. Yes, because Hill and his team owe a duty of loyalty to Lionsgate's clients

   Solution:

   A is correct. It is not a violation for Hill and the team to lease office space and register with the government authorities before resigning from Lionsgate. According to Standard IV(A): Duties to Employers, Loyalty, "In matters related to their employment, Members and Candidates must act for the benefit of their employer and not ... cause harm to their employer." Moreover, Guidance to Standard IV(A) states, "A departing employee is generally free to make arrangements or preparations to go into a competitive business before terminating the relationship with his or her employer as long as such preparations do not breach the employee's duty of loyalty." Hill and the team are making preparations outside of work and on weekends; their actions to start a new business do not occur during hours when their employer would expect them to be at work. Thus, they are not in violation of the standard. Hill and the team are also not violating Standard III(A): Duties to Clients, Loyalty, Prudence, and Care because their actions are taking place during non-work hours, not when they should be working for the benefit of their clients.

B is incorrect. Hill and the individuals joining him at the new firm are using their time outside of work and on weekends to lease office space and to individually register with government authorities. Because they are not using work time, they are not breaching their duty of loyalty to Lionsgate, as defined in Standard IV(A): Duties to Employers, Loyalty.

C is incorrect. In using their time outside of work and on weekends to plan for the new firm, Hill and his team are not placing their own interests ahead of their clients' interests. They are not in violation of Standard III(A): Duties to Clients, Loyalty, Prudence, and Care.

7. Did Hill violate the Code and Standards by telling his team to begin soliciting former clients the day they open the new firm?

   A. No

   B. Yes, because Hill owes a duty of loyalty to Lionsgate

   C. Yes, because Hill has a responsibility as their supervisor

Solution:

A is correct. Hill is not in violation of the Code and Standards. The Guidance to Standard IV(A): Duties to Employers, Loyalty states, "When members and candidates are planning to leave their current employer, they must continue to act in the employer's best interest. They must not engage in any activities that would conflict with this duty until their resignation becomes effective." The Guidance also states, "A member or candidate who is contemplating seeking other employment must not contact existing clients or potential clients prior to leaving his or her employer for purposes of soliciting their business for the new employer." By telling his team to begin solicitation on the new firm's opening day—not prior to its opening—there is no conflict of interest or violation of loyalty.

B is incorrect. The Guidance to Standard IV(A): Duties to Employers, Loyalty states, "When members and candidates are planning to leave their current employer, they must continue to act in the employer's best interest. They must not engage in any activities that would conflict with this duty until their resignation becomes effective." The Guidance also states, "A member or candidate who is contemplating seeking other employment must not contact existing clients or potential clients prior to leaving his or her employer for purposes of soliciting their business for the new employer." Hill tells his team to begin client solicitation on the new firm's opening day, not prior to its opening. At that time, Hill and his team will no longer work for Lionsgate.

C is incorrect. Hill is not violating Standard IV(C): Duties to Employers, Responsibilities of Supervisors. According to this standard, "Members and Candidates must make reasonable efforts to ensure that anyone subject to their supervision or authority complies with applicable laws, rules, regulations, and the Code and Standards." Hill did not ask anyone under his supervision to violate any of the Standards.

6 LIONSGATE LIMITED & BANK OF AUSTRALIA CASE 2

☐ evaluate practices, policies, and conduct relative to the CFA Institute Code of Ethics and Standards of Professional Conduct

☐ explain how the practices, policies, or conduct does or does not violate the CFA Institute Code of Ethics and Standards of Professional Conduct

Rob Portman, CFA, is a salesperson at LL who oversees the sales of the VCF to institutions and high-net-worth individuals. For each of the past five years, Portman has achieved his annual sales goal and has received a sizable bonus as a result. Portman is hoping this year will be no different. With two weeks remaining in LL's fiscal year, Portman is planning a big event next week for prospective clients that he hopes will enable him to achieve his sales goal.

Portman knows how much "prestige" institutional clients and high-net-worth individuals place on having Hill manage their money. To make the fund more attractive to prospective and current clients, Portman always discusses Hill's stock-picking acumen and Hill's success as the key investment decision maker for the VCF. In addition, he always invites Hill to meetings with important clients. However, when clients have investment-related questions about the fund's purchases and sales, he always refers them to Martin, who he refers to as Hill's "assistant."

Tonight is Portman's big event. Since LL's board meeting, Portman has heard rumors about Hill and members of his team leaving the firm. To clarify Hill's situation, Portman meets with LL's chief investment officer (CIO), who attended the recent board meeting. The CIO tells Portman to ignore the rumors about Hill and proceed with his planned event. Later that day, Portman learns from Sky News Business Channel that the CIO and two board members have sold shares in LL and the VCF. As a result, Portman sells his shares in LL and the VCF.

KNOWLEDGE CHECK

1. Did Portman violate the Code and Standards by inviting Hill to important client meetings and discussing Hill's stock-picking acumen?

   A. No

   B. Yes, because Portman is misrepresenting Hill's role in the investment process to clients

   C. Yes, because Portman is misrepresenting the VCF investment strategy and its limitations and risks

   Solution:

   B is correct. By inviting Hill to client meetings and referring to Martin as Hill's "assistant," Portman is giving clients the impression that Hill is responsible for stock selection and investment decision making at the fund. Portman is in violation of Standard I(C) Misrepresentation: "Members and Candidates must not knowingly make any misrepresentations relating to investment analysis, recommendations, actions, or other professional activities."

   A is incorrect. Portman is in violation of Standard I(C) Misrepresentation. By inviting Hill to client meetings and referring to Martin as Hill's "assistant," Portman is giving clients the impression that Hill is responsible for stock selection and investment decision making at the fund.

C is incorrect. Although Portman is misrepresenting Hill's role in executing the VCF's investment strategy, he is not misrepresenting the investment strategy itself.

2. Did Lionsgate's CIO and the two board members violate the Code and Standards by selling their shares in LL and the VCF?

   A. No

   B. Yes, because they owe a duty of loyalty to Lionsgate

   C. Yes, because they acted on material nonpublic information

Solution:

C is correct. By selling their shares before Hill's resignation was announced, they acted on material nonpublic information. According to Standard II(A) Material Nonpublic Information, "Members and Candidates who possess material nonpublic information that could affect the value of an investment must not act or cause others to act on the information." Information is "material" if its disclosure would probably have an impact on the price of a security or if reasonable investors would want to know the information before making an investment decision.

A is incorrect. They are clearly in violation of Standard II(A) Material Nonpublic Information.

B is incorrect. Although the CIO and two board members do owe a duty of loyalty to Lionsgate, they are not in violation of Standard IV(A) Loyalty by selling their shares in LL and the VCF. Instead, they are in violation of Standard II(A) Material Nonpublic Information.

3. Did Portman violate the Code and Standards by selling his shares in LL and the VCF?

   A. No

   B. Yes, because he owes a duty of loyalty to Lionsgate

   C. Yes, because he is acting on material nonpublic information

Solution:

A is correct. In this case, Portman does not know definitively whether Hill is resigning. In addition to the rumors he heard, Portman's sell decision is based on learning from Sky News Business Channel that the CIO and two board members sold their shares. Portman's decision to sell is not based on material nonpublic information, because this information was publicly reported. He is not in violation of Standard II(A) Material Nonpublic Information.

B is incorrect. Although Portman does owe a duty to his employer, Lionsgate, he is not in violation of Standard IV(A) Loyalty by selling his shares in LL and the VCF.

C is incorrect. In selling his shares in LL and the VCF, Portman is not acting on material nonpublic information and therefore is not in violation of Standard II(A) Material Nonpublic Information.

Kirk Graeme, CFA

Lionsgate Limited is partially owned by the Bank of Australia Financial Group (BOA). BOA consists of a retail bank, a capital market division (investment and corporate banking), and a wealth management division. Kirk Graeme, CFA, is a financial adviser in BOA's wealth management division. He is regarded as a subject matter expert at the firm because of the well-supported research he does on new issues and his experience in buying and selling them.

Although all accounts that Graeme manages are fee based, he does receive additional commissions (paid by the issuer) for new issue purchases.

BOA (through its capital market group) is a member of the syndicate for new issues purchased by Graeme. As a syndicate member, BOA also shares in fees and commissions paid by the issuer. BOA's policy does not require commission disclosure on new issues since clients receive prospectuses for new issue purchases that disclose commissions paid to the syndicate member. Graeme, however, does disclose his new issue commissions to clients who ask for this information.

In 2016 and 2017, Graeme earned a total of $477,000 in commissions from new issues, while BOA earned fees and commissions of $1,908,900 on the same transactions. From 2016 to 2017, Graeme's assets under management remained relatively unchanged; however, Graeme more than doubled the dollar value of new issue purchases relative to his AUM. Unfortunately, many of these new issues performed poorly. By the end of 2017, Graeme had sold—often significantly below purchase price—many of the issues he purchased in 2016. Despite the underperformance, Graeme continues to research and recommend new issues following the same process he has always used.

KNOWLEDGE CHECK

1. Did Graeme violate the Code and Standards with respect to his disclosure of new issue commissions earned on sales only to those clients who ask for the information?

   A. No, he does not need to disclose the commissions, because BOA's policy does not require it.

   B. No, he does not need to disclose the commissions, because clients receive this disclosure in the prospectuses for the new issues.

   C. Yes, he does need to disclose the commissions.

   Solution:

   C is correct. Graeme is in violation of Standard VI(A) Avoid or Disclose Conflicts, which states that "Members and Candidates must avoid or make full and fair disclosure of all matters that could reasonably be expected to impair their independence and objectivity or interfere with respective duties to clients, prospective clients, and employer. Members and Candidates must ensure that such disclosures are prominent, are delivered in plain language, and communicate the relevant information effectively." Graeme can avoid the conflict by not accepting commissions from new issues. If he does not avoid the conflict, Graeme must inform all clients, not just those who ask, of the commissions he receives on new issues so that his clients have the information necessary to evaluate the objectivity of the investment advice or action taken by him on their behalf.

   A is incorrect. There is a violation because the commissions could reasonably be expected to impair Graeme's objectivity. Standard VI(A) requires Graeme to disclose the conflict of interest that these commissions create to all his clients regardless of BOA's policy in this regard.

> B is incorrect. There is a violation because the commissions could reasonably be expected to impair Graeme's objectivity. Graeme can avoid the conflict by not accepting the commissions. If he accepts the commissions, Standard VI(A) requires Graeme to disclose the conflict created by these commissions to all his clients regardless of what appears in the prospectuses of the new issues.

The Delaneys

In January 2017, Graeme opened a $250,000 joint account for Melissa and Rodney Delaney. During their initial conversation, the Delaneys stated that the account represented the majority of their investable assets, that their investment time horizon was 15–20 years, and that they had a low tolerance for risk. After this conversation, approximately half of Graeme's recommended purchases to the Delaneys were new issues; new issues represented approximately three-quarters of the dollar value of all purchases in their account. Between January and October 2017, the longest period of time that a new issue was held in their account was five months. Since opening the Delaneys' account, the majority of purchases were new issues. During this period, Graeme also made new issue purchases for the majority of his other client accounts.

At the end of 2017, Graeme met with his supervisor, Jane Balmer. During the meeting, Balmer raised concerns about the turnover in Graeme's accounts and his use of new issues. Balmer also escalated her concerns by reporting them to BOA's director of compliance. After his meeting with Balmer, Graeme significantly reduced his new issue purchases and turnover in his "book of business."

> **KNOWLEDGE CHECK**
>
> 1. Did Graeme violate the Code and Standards in managing the Delaneys' account?
>
>   **A.** No
>
>   **B.** Yes, because their risk tolerance is low
>
>   **C.** Yes, because their time horizon is 15–20 years
>
>   **Solution:**
>
>   B is correct. The Delaneys stated that their risk tolerance is low, which means they were unwilling to accept high levels of volatility in their portfolio. By purchasing new issues in their account and holding them for less than five months, Graeme's actions are unsuitable for the Delaneys' risk tolerance. As stated, the majority of the purchases Graeme made for the Delaneys were new issue purchases. Graeme violated Standard III(C) Suitability: "When Members and Candidates are in an advisory relationship with a client, they must: . . . b. determine that an investment is suitable to the client's financial situation and consistent with the client's written objectives, mandates, and constraints before making an investment recommendation or taking investment action." In addition, members and candidates must "judge the suitability of investments in the context of the client's total portfolio."
>
>   A is incorrect. Graeme violated Standard III(C) by purchasing new issues for the Delaneys' account that were unsuitable for the Delaneys' risk tolerance.
>
>   C is incorrect. It is the Delaneys' low risk tolerance—not their long time horizon—that makes the purchase of new issues unsuitable. Graeme violated Standard III(C).

2. Did Balmer follow the Code and Standards in addressing her concerns about Graeme's use of new issues?

   A. No

   B. Yes, because she escalated her concerns to the director of compliance

   C. Yes, because she raised her concerns with Graeme, who responded accordingly

   Solution:

   A is correct. Balmer violated Standard IV(C) Responsibilities of Supervisors, which states that "Members and Candidates must make reasonable efforts to ensure that anyone subject to their supervision or authority complies with applicable laws, rules, regulations, and the Code and Standards." Moreover, the guidance for this standard states, "Once a supervisor learns that an employee has violated or may have violated the law or the Code and Standards, the supervisor must promptly initiate an assessment to determine the extent of the wrongdoing. Relying on an employee's statements about the extent of the violation or assurances that the wrongdoing will not reoccur is not enough." Balmer should have initiated an investigation to ascertain the extent of Graeme's wrongdoing.

   B is incorrect. Rather than just escalating her concerns to the director of compliance, Balmer should have initiated an investigation to ascertain the extent of Graeme's wrongdoing.

   C is incorrect. Rather than just raising her concerns with Graeme, Balmer should have initiated an investigation to ascertain the extent of Graeme's wrongdoing.

David Milgram

Five years ago, Graeme opened an account for David Milgram, a 67-year-old retired chemical engineer. At that time, Graeme worked with Milgram to set Milgram's investment policy statement, which has remained in place ever since. Last month, Milgram sent a written complaint to Graeme's supervisor, Jane Balmer, titled "Request for an Urgent Review of My Account." In the complaint letter, Milgram stated, "I am concerned about the dismal performance of my account. The decrease in value is causing me considerable alarm. As a result, I would like to meet with you and Graeme. I am wondering about setting a new direction and getting a second opinion on the suitability of my holdings. At this point, however, I want to hear Graeme's side of the story and make a plan to stop the decline in my account value and get out of this mess."

After receiving the letter, Balmer calls Graham into her office to discuss the complaint and Milgram's account. However, she does not report Graeme or the complaint to BOA's director of compliance. The next day, Graeme meets with Balmer and Milgram at BOA's office. During the meeting, Graeme reviews Milgram's portfolio and updates the investment policy statement that he created when Milgram opened his account. Graeme also discusses the quality of the securities in Milgram's portfolio and advises him that he should not focus on the portfolio value alone. Satisfied with Graeme's explanation, Milgram leaves BOA's office.

KNOWLEDGE CHECK

1. Did Graeme violate the Code and Standards in the handling of Milgram's account?

   A. Yes

   B. No, because he updates Milgram's investment policy statement

   C. No, because he reviews Milgram's portfolio and the quality of security holdings with him

   Solution:

   A is correct. Graeme did not update Milgram's IPS for five years after it was first put in place. Graeme violated Standard III(C) Suitability. The guidance for Standard III(C) states that "updating the IPS should be repeated at least annually and also prior to material changes to any specific investment recommendations or decisions on behalf of the client."

   B is incorrect. Graeme has not updated Milgram's IPS since it was first put in place five years ago, which places him in violation of Standard III(C).

   C is incorrect. Graeme has not updated Milgram's IPS since it was first put in place, which places him in violation of Standard III(C).

2. Did Balmer violate the Code and Standards in the handling of Milgram's complaint?

   A. No

   B. Yes, because she did not report the complaint to BOA's department of compliance

   C. Yes, because she did not initiate an investigation of the complaint

   Solution:

   A is correct. Balmer did not violate the Code and Standards. As soon as she was made aware of the complaint, she initiated an investigation by calling Graeme into her office. She sat in on the meeting, where Graeme reviewed Milgram's account and IPS. According to Standard IV(C) Responsibilities of Supervisors, "Members and Candidates must make reasonable efforts to ensure that anyone subject to their supervision or authority complies with applicable laws, rules, regulations, and the Code and Standards." According to the guidance for this standard, "Once a supervisor learns that an employee has violated or may have violated the law or the Code and Standards, the supervisor must promptly initiate an assessment to determine the extent of the wrongdoing. Relying on an employee's statements about the extent of the violation or assurances that the wrongdoing will not reoccur is not enough."

   B is incorrect. Reporting the misconduct up the chain of command and warning the employee to cease the activity are not enough to meet Standard IV(C). Instead, as soon as Balmer received the complaint, she initiated an investigation by calling Graeme into her office to discuss and review Milgram's account. This is the requirement of Standard IV(C).

   C is incorrect. Balmer did initiate an investigation by summoning Graeme into her office to discuss the complaint. Balmer continued her investigation by attending the meeting with Milgram when Graeme reviewed Milgram's account and IPS.

7 GABBY SIM

- [ ] evaluate practices, policies, and conduct relative to the CFA Institute Code of Ethics and Standards of Professional Conduct
- [ ] explain how the practices, policies, or conduct does or does not violate the CFA Institute Code of Ethics and Standards of Professional Conduct

Global Harvest Bank (GHB) is an independent private bank that offers clients a range of services, including advisory lending and banking solutions, investment management, succession planning, tax reporting, and custody services.[5] GHB is headquartered in Singapore and has offices in Hong Kong SAR, Luxembourg, Zurich, and the Cayman Islands.

Gabby Sim was hired by GHB after graduating with first-class honors in finance from an international two-year MBA program. On her first day at the bank, Sim meets with her supervisor and the chief investment officer of GHB, Ahmad Yousoff, CFA, who oversees her onboarding experience.

After meeting with Sim, Yousoff meets with the president of GHB, Irene Wong, and two board members, David Tan and Audrey Chuong, CFA, to discuss the memorandum of understanding (MOU) that was recently signed by MGM2, a new institutional client. MGM2 is a strategic investment and development company that is wholly owned by the government of Saspara through its Ministry of Finance. The mission of MGM2 is to promote Sasparian economic development through global partnerships and foreign direct investment. Tan and Chuong have worked tirelessly over the past year to build a relationship with MGM2 on behalf of GHB. As a reward for their hard work, Yousoff and Wong decided to pay Tan and Chuong a portion of the annual investment advisory fees generated by MGM2. Yousoff did not disclose this fee-sharing arrangement in the MOU he provided to MGM2. During the meeting, Chuong asks Yousoff to meet with Bo Hie, a Sasparian businessman who helped found MGM2 and also played an instrumental role in developing relations between GHB and MGM2. Chuong, however, does not tell Yousoff that Hie recently hired her son in an executive role in his company.

KNOWLEDGE CHECK

1. Did Yousoff violate the Code and Standards by not disclosing the fee-sharing arrangement in the MOU?

   A. Yes

   B. No, because it is a fee-sharing arrangement and not a referral fee

5 This case is by Laurel Teo, CFA, and Michael G. McMillan, PhD, CFA, in *Ethics Cases*. Consistent with the 11th edition of the *Standards of Practice Handbook*.

C. No, because the referral fee arrangement was decided after the relationship with MGM2 had been established

Solution:

B is correct. Yousoff is not in violation of the Code and Standards. The fee-sharing arrangement is a reward paid to Tan and Chuong for their efforts to bring MGM2 on as a client. The fee arrangement is not a referral fee. Tan and Chuong did not refer MGM2 to GHB. A referral fee is compensation, consideration, or benefit received from or paid to others for the recommendation of products or services.

For referral fees, Standard VI(C) Referral Fees applies: "Members and Candidates must disclose to their employer, clients, and prospective clients, as appropriate, any compensation, consideration, or benefit received from or paid to others for the recommendation of products or services." The guidance for this standard explains, "Appropriate disclosure means that members and candidates must advise the client or prospective client, before entry into any formal agreement for services, of any benefit given or received for the recommendation of any services provided by the member or candidate."

A is incorrect. The fee-sharing arrangement is a reward paid to Tan and Chuong for their efforts to bring MGM2 on as a client. It is not a referral fee, so they are not in violation of Standard VI(C) Referral Fees.

C is incorrect. The fee-sharing arrangement is not a referral fee, so Yousoff does not have to disclose this arrangement in the MOU. Yousoff would need to disclose the arrangement if payment represented a conflict of interest. However, the case facts provide no evidence that a conflict of interest is present.

2. Did Chuong violate the Code and Standards by not disclosing information about her son to Yousoff?

   A. No

   B. Yes, because this situation represents a conflict of interest

   C. Yes, because Chuong is misrepresenting her relationship with Hie

Solution:

B is correct. Hie's hiring of Chuong's son in an executive position at Hie's firm could reasonably be expected to impair Chuong's independence and objectivity with respect to interactions between MGM2 and GHB. Standard VI(A) Avoid or Disclose Conflicts requires Chuong to disclose this conflict.

A is incorrect. A conflict of interest exists, and Chuong violated the Code and Standards by not disclosing the hiring of her son by Hie.

C is incorrect. This situation is not a violation of Standard I(C) Misrepresentation. By not disclosing information about her son, Chuong did not knowingly make any misrepresentation relating to investment analysis, recommendations, actions, or other professional activities.

Busy setting up the MGM2 account, Yousoff asks Sim to meet with Hie. During their meeting, Hie tells Sim that he wants to open an account in the name of his firm, Bad Moon Rising, Ltd. Sim has Hie complete and sign the Application for Opening an Account/Custody Account for Legal Entities and the Establishment of the Beneficial Owner's Identity form, which identifies him as the sole beneficial owner of the Bad Moon Rising account. Hie also completes and signs the Resolutions form, which lists Hie as the sole authorized signatory on the account. Included in the account opening documents is a copy of a page from Hie's Sasparian passport, which includes his photograph. Hie then presents Sim with a check for $15 million that is drawn on one of his personal bank accounts located in the Cayman Islands. When Sim begins to ask the firm's required questions for new clients on investment experience, objectives, and risk tolerance, Hie interrupts her and states, "I am a very busy man and do not have time to answer all these questions. Initially, I only plan to invest in short-term US government (risk-free) securities in this account, so your questions are irrelevant. Later, I plan to invest in securities in other asset classes. In addition, because of the confidential nature of my business relationships, please destroy all notes you have made during this meeting and use the following fact sheet to document our conversation":

Occupation:	Consultant
Employer:	Self-employed
Net Worth:	$110 million
Investment Objective:	Long term
Return Goal:	5%–10% per year
Risk Profile:	Conservative

Before leaving the meeting, Hie tells Sim, "You can expect a number of large deposits into my account from MGM2 over the next few months. Some of these deposits will then be wired to other accounts that I have set up around the world. If you process these transactions in a timely manner, I will pay you a bonus at the end of the year. In addition, since you are fluent in English, Mandarin Chinese, and a number of Chinese dialects, such as Hokkien and Cantonese, I will be referring a number of my elderly Chinese relatives to you. Many of them live in Singapore and either do not understand English or have little knowledge of the language. To this end, please meet with my mother-in-law, Madam Tan Swee Neo."

Hie continues, "Lastly, because of the sensitive nature of my work with MGM2 and the large sums of money involved, do not talk to anyone about this account or its transactions. Please do not email or correspond in writing to me concerning the Bad Moon Rising account. Instead, call me on my cell phone or instant message me to notify me whenever a deposit is received and a withdrawal has been executed." Sim agrees, and Hie concludes the meeting by telling Sim, "If you need any more information, please talk with GHB board members Tan and Chuong, who I am sure can answer any additional questions that you may have." Later that day, Sim uses the fact sheet that Hie provided to prepare his investment policy statement and destroys the other notes she took during their meeting. When she meets with Yousoff to tell him about her meeting with Hie, she does not mention the bonus that Hie has promised to pay her at the end of the year. Sim opens the account for Hie.

KNOWLEDGE CHECK

1. Did Sim violate the Code and Standards by fulfilling Hie's request to destroy documentation of their conversation?

   A. Yes

   B. No, because Sim is preserving Hie's confidentiality

   C. No, because Sim is exercising her duty of loyalty, prudence, and care

   Solution:

   A is correct. Sim violated Standard V(C) Record Retention: "Members and Candidates must develop and maintain appropriate records to support their investment analyses, recommendations, actions, and other investment-related communications with clients and prospective clients." The guidance for Standard V(C) states, "Members and candidates must retain records that substantiate the scope of their research and reasons for their actions or conclusions." Some examples of supporting documentation include "notes from clients from meetings to review investment policy statements." By destroying all notes from their meeting, Sim is not maintaining appropriate records to support her investment actions.

B is incorrect. Sim has a duty to her firm to retain records supporting her recommendations to and actions for clients of the firm. Keeping these records in no way compromises her duty of confidentiality to Hie under Standard III(E) Preservation of Confidentiality.

C is incorrect. The destruction of the documentation is not directly related to the actions considered necessary under Standard III(A) Loyalty, Prudence, and Care.

2. Did Sim violate the Code and Standards by not disclosing her bonus arrangement with Hie to Yousoff?

   A. Yes

   B. No, because the bonus will not create a conflict of interest

   C. No, because the bonus does not represent additional compensation

Solution:

A is correct. By not disclosing her bonus arrangement with Hie, Sim violated the Code and Standards. According to Standard IV(B) Additional Compensation Arrangements, "Members and Candidates must not accept gifts, benefits, compensation, or consideration that competes with or might reasonably be expected to create a conflict of interest with their employer's interest unless they obtain written consent from all parties involved." Hie's promise of a bonus if Sim processes his transactions in a timely manner could conflict with Sim's responsibilities to her other clients or other clients of GHB.

Sim also violated Standard I(B) Independence and Objectivity. Per the guidance for the standard, "Members and candidates may accept bonuses or gifts from clients as long as they disclose them to their employer. . . . Disclosure is required, however, so that supervisors can monitor such situations to guard against employees favoring a gift-giving client to the detriment of other fee-paying clients."

B is incorrect. Hie's bonus has the potential to create a conflict of interest for Sim, thus jeopardizing her independence and objectivity. At a minimum, Sim must disclose the bonus arrangement to Yousoff, her employer.

C is incorrect. Hie's bonus is additional compensation to Sim. At a minimum, Sim must disclose the bonus arrangement to Yousoff, her employer.

3. In opening Hie's account, did Sim violate the Code and Standards?

   A. Yes

   B. No, because Hie plans to invest in risk-free securities

   C. No, because Hie signed the required forms and provided Sim with a fact sheet with all the necessary information

Solution:

A is correct. Sim did not complete the required section on Hie's investment experience, objectives, and risk tolerance of new clients; the information Hie provided was not sufficient for Sim to develop an appropriate IPS. Sim violated Standard III(C) Suitability. The guidance for the standard states, "When an advisory relationship exists, members and candidates must gather client information at the inception of the relationship. Such information includes the client's financial circumstances, personal data (such as age and occupation) that are relevant to investment decisions, attitudes toward risk, and objectives in investing. This information should be incorporated into a written investment policy statement (IPS) that addresses the client's risk tolerance, return requirements, and all investment constraints (including time horizon, liquidity needs, tax concerns, legal and regulatory factors, and unique circumstances)."

B is incorrect. A client's statement regarding his or her desired investment strategy, especially without a fully formed IPS, does not meet the requirements of Standard III(C) Suitability.

C is incorrect. The fact sheet does not provide enough information for Sim to develop an investment policy statement for Hie; therefore, Sim's actions violate the requirements of Standard III(C) Suitability.

Two days after the Bad Moon Rising account is opened, $70 million is wired into it from an MGM2 account in Saspara. When Sim calls Hie to notify him about this deposit and ask what he wants to do with it, Hie tells her that a portion of the money will be used "to purchase real estate for MGM2 in the United States." He then faxes her a copy of an investment agreement between MGM2, as the client, and Bad Moon Rising, as the investment manager. According to this agreement, MGM2 was a "founding investor in Bad Moon Rising that wishes to support and assist Bad Moon Rising in realizing its purpose by providing an initial capital contribution of $70 million."

Sim, however, has concerns about the deposit size and justification for the $70 million deposit since it is from a state-owned entity, so she discusses it with Yousoff. Sim's plan is to set up another meeting with Hie and an official from MGM2, who can confirm the deposit and further explain the source and use of the deposit. Yousoff, however, tells her not to do this since Hie already provided documentation from MGM2 in the form of the investment agreement. Instead, Yousoff suggests to Sim that she speak with Tan and Chuong. That afternoon, Sim calls the two GHB board members to tell them about the $70 million deposit in Hie's account and faxes them a copy of the investment agreement Hie provided. After reviewing this information, Tan and Chuong confirm its validity and Hie's role with MGM2.

KNOWLEDGE CHECK

1. Did Yousoff violate the Code and Standards by instructing Sim to speak with Tan and Chuong?

   A. Yes

   B. No, because Tan and Chuong know and have worked with Hie

   C. No, because Hie already submitted documentation confirming the source and purpose of the $70 million deposit

Solution:

A is correct. Suggesting that Sim speak with Tan and Chuong does not absolve Yousoff of his responsibilities as a supervisor. Yousoff violated Standard IV(C) Responsibilities of Supervisors: "Members and Candidates must make reasonable efforts to ensure that anyone subject to their supervision or authority complies with applicable laws, rules, regulations, and the Code and Standards." In this case, Yousoff should have encouraged Sim to arrange a meeting with Hie and an official of MGM2 to confirm the source and purpose of the funds.

B is incorrect. A reasonable effort would have involved Sim arranging a meeting with Hie and an official of MGM2 (and ideally Yousoff also) to confirm the source and purpose of the funds. Neither Tan nor Chuong have firsthand knowledge of the actual transaction under scrutiny.

C is incorrect. Sim has expressed concern about the documentation of the transaction (its size and justification). Under Standard IV(C), Yousoff is required to make a reasonable effort to detect violations of the laws, rules, and the Code and Standards. Accepting the existing documentation violates this duty.

2. Did Sim violate client confidentiality by talking to Tan and Chuong about Hie's account?

   A. Yes

   B. No, because Hie instructed Sim to speak with Tan and Chuong

   C. No, because Tan, Chuong, and Hie worked together to develop the relationship between GHB and MGM2

Solution:

B is correct. Hie has given specific permission to Sim to seek information from Tan and Chuong when he tells her as they conclude their meeting together, "If you need any more information, please talk with GHB board members, Tan and Chuong, who I am sure can answer any additional questions that you may have." As a result, Sim did not violate the Code and Standards in her disclosure of confidential information regarding her client, Hie.

According to the guidance for Standard III(E) Preservation of Confidentiality, the standard "requires that members and candidates preserve the confidentiality of information communicated to them by their clients, prospective clients, and former clients. This standard is applicable when (1) the member or candidate receives information because of his or her special ability to conduct a portion of the client's business or personal affairs and (2) the member or candidate receives information that arises from or is relevant to that portion of the client's business that is the subject of the special or confidential relationship."

According to the standard, then, a member or candidate can break confidence when permission is granted by the client. In this case, Hie has given his permission to Sim by telling her to seek information as needed from board members Tan and Chuong, so Sim is not in violation of the Code and Standards.

A is incorrect. Hie gave her permission to speak with Tan and Chuong, so Sim did not violate Standard III(E) Preservation of Confidentiality by disclosing confidential information about Hie.

C is incorrect. The fact that Tan, Chuong, and Hie worked together to develop the relationship between GHB and MGM2 does not allow Sim to discuss Hie's information with Tan and Chuong. Sim did not violate Standard III(E), however, because Hie gave her permission to speak with Tan and Chuong.

Over the next few months, MGM2 wires a total of $100 million into the Bad Moon Rising account in four separate transactions. Each transfer is a foreign exchange transaction completed through financial institutions in Saspara and processed through different US correspondent bank accounts. To justify these substantial fund transfers from MGM2, Hie tells Sim that MGM2 has entered into a number of real estate purchase agreements that he will be handling for them. He also provides her with copies of several agreements that are signed by Yousoff, GHB's CIO. Hie later transfers most of the $100 million to his bank accounts in Switzerland, Luxembourg, and the Cayman Islands.

Sim, however, remains suspicious about the size and frequency of the activity in Hie's account, so she meets with Yousoff to discuss her concerns. During the meeting, Sim tells Yousoff, "Hie recently transferred $50 million into and out of his account in less than a week. I can't find any reason or motivation for why this transaction had to pass through his GHB account and not come directly from the MGM2 account to its real estate partners. I believe that Hie may be using this account to launder money." In response, Yousoff tells her, "As Hie's investment adviser, your job should be to focus on processing these transactions in a timely manner. Remember, the president and the board of directors are watching you. Given that two of our board members established this relationship with MGM2, we have to assume that these board members represented the will of the bank's owners as far as these relationships and transactions are concerned. Therefore, we have to be very careful about how we handle their transactions and ensure they are handled smoothly, efficiently, and quickly. I have reviewed the large number of deposits and withdrawals in Hie's account, and my only concern is the speed with which they are processed."

KNOWLEDGE CHECK

1. Based on Yousoff's response to Sim about the transactions in Hie's account, what is the first course of action for Sim to take?

   A. Contact GHB's compliance department.

   B. Contact the regulator in her jurisdiction.

   C. Take no action since she has informed Yousoff of her concerns.

   Solution:

   A is correct. The guidance for Standard I(A) Knowledge of the Law states, "When in doubt about the appropriate action to undertake, it is recommended that a member or candidate seek the advice of compliance personnel or legal counsel concerning legal requirements. If a potential violation is being committed by a fellow employee, it may also be prudent for the member or candidate to seek the advice of the firm's compliance department or legal counsel."

   B is incorrect. Informing Yousoff produced no action toward resolving the concerns Sim has, and so according to Standard I(A), the next step for Sim is to seek the advice of compliance personnel or legal counsel regarding her concerns. The guidance for Standard I(A) states, "Although the Code and Standards do not compel members and candidates to report violations to their governmental or regulatory organizations unless such disclosure is mandatory under applicable law, . . . such disclosure may be prudent under certain circumstances."

   C is incorrect. Informing Yousoff produced no action toward resolving the concerns Sim has regarding these transactions. According to Standard I(A), Sim's responsibility is to take the next step and seek the advice of compliance personnel or legal counsel regarding her concerns.

Per Hie's request, Sim meets with Madam Tan Swee Neo for the first time. Madam Tan is a 70-year-old retired seamstress who has made her fortune buying and selling real estate. Since retiring from her job, Madam Tan has put most of her life savings in fixed deposits (certificates of deposit). Periodically, she invests the balance in the equities of lower-risk energy utility companies when she receives tips from her friends and relatives. Recently, however, her goals changed. She now wants to invest even more of her portfolio in conservative equities so that she can pay for her grandchildren's private school and college expenses.

Madam Tan tells Sim that she heard from her friends about an oil-linked structured note sold by GHB. "My friends tell me that these notes pay 10% a year, which is much higher than what I can get from fixed deposits. My energy stocks have been doing so badly; I need something new," Madam Tan adds. Sim offers Madam Tan a brochure on the structured note; however, the brochure is in English, which Madam Tan does not read. Sim provides a verbal summary of the product overview in Mandarin, explaining to Madam Tan that the product's return is linked to the performance of a basket of oil futures indexes. Although Sim does not translate the note's full terms and conditions in fine print, she does caution Madam Tan that the 10% annual coupon payment is not guaranteed and that while there is full principal protection if held to maturity, there will be a penalty for early redemption of the note, which matures in seven years. She also tells Madam Tan that since the product was launched three years ago, the conditions for coupon payment have been met every year. Madam Tan is not sure what oil futures are or how they work. Nevertheless, she decides to put $50,000 into the notes. Sim executes the transaction at Madam Tan's request.

KNOWLEDGE CHECK

1. Did Sim violate the Code and Standards by purchasing oil-linked structured notes for Madam Tan?

   A. Yes

   B. No, because Madam Tan asked her to purchase the notes

   C. No, because she warned Madam Tan that the 10% annual coupon payment is not guaranteed

   Solution:

   A is correct. Sim violated Standard III(C) Suitability. The structured notes are unsuitable for Madam Tan. Although Madam Tan has previously invested in real estate, since retiring, she has invested in fixed deposits and lower-risk energy utility stocks. She now wishes to invest more of her portfolio in conservative equites. In addition, Madam Tan shares that she is unsure what oil futures are or how they work.

   The guidance for Standard III(C) states that it "requires that members and candidates who are in an investment advisory relationship with clients consider carefully the needs, circumstances, and objectives of the clients when determining the appropriateness and suitability of a given investment or course of investment action. . . . Members and candidates may receive requests from a client for trades that do not properly align with the risk and return objectives outlined in the client's investment policy statement. These transaction requests may be based on the client's individual biases or professional experience. Members and candidates will need to make reasonable efforts to balance their clients' trading requests with their responsibilities to follow the agreed-on investment policy statement."

   B is incorrect. In this case, Sim violated Standard III(C) Suitability because the structured notes are not suitable for Madam Tan given her investment needs and objectives. The guidance for the standard states, "Members and candidates will need to make reasonable efforts to balance their clients' trading requests with their responsibilities to follow the agreed-on investment policy statement." When the transaction may have a material impact on the portfolio, the client's IPS should be updated to ensure the client understands the potential effect of the requested trade on his or her risk/return targets.

C is incorrect. Simply warning Madam Tan that the annual coupon is not guaranteed is insufficient to show Madam Tan that structured notes are not suitable for her investment needs and objectives. Handing Madam Tan a brochure written in English on the structured note has little value if she doesn't understand English and therefore is insufficient to meet Standard III(C).

A year later, Madam Tan is upset when she does not receive any payments from the structured notes. While visiting with her relatives in a neighboring country, she hears from her nephew who works at the state oil company that oil prices are likely to continue to slide over the next several years. Alarmed that this will worsen her investment, Madam Tan phones Sim. She tells Sim to immediately redeem the structured notes and switch the funds into a three-month fixed deposit. Sim suggests that Madam Tan consider the full costs and risks involved in redeeming before proceeding further, but Madam Tan says she cannot spend too much time on expensive international calls and instructs Sim to just "act on it right away." Because Madam Tan called Sim on her mobile phone rather than her office phone, Sim is not able to record the conversation. Sim completes the transactions because of the urgency of the request.

When Madam Tan returns home from her travel, she is shocked to find that her original $50,000 investment has shrunk to $30,000 upon redemption. She calls Sim and demands an explanation. Sim reminds her that she warned Madam Tan about the early redemption penalty a year ago when Madam Tan was considering the product. Madam Tan exclaims, "Yes, but I didn't realize the penalty would be so high! And I thought the product would be low risk since you told me there have been payments in each of the last three years." Outraged at the 40% loss in what had been half of her life savings, Madam Tan files a complaint against Sim.

KNOWLEDGE CHECK

1. In redeeming Madam Tan's structured notes and switching her funds to a fixed deposit, did Sim violate the Code and Standards?

   A. Yes

   B. No, because Sim followed Madam Tan's request to redeem the structured notes immediately

   C. No, because Sim has acted with reasonable care and prudent judgment

   Solution:

   A is correct. Sim violated Standard III(A) Loyalty, Prudence, and Care by redeeming the structured notes. Sim did not act with reasonable care or prudent judgment in executing the redemption immediately without fully explaining the associated costs to Madam Tan and investigating how the economic environment might impact the risk of the structured notes. It can also be argued that she violated Standard III(C) Suitability. According to the guidance for this standard, it "requires that members and candidates who are in an investment advisory relationship with clients consider carefully the needs, circumstances, and objectives of the clients when determining the appropriateness and suitability of a given investment or course of investment action. . . . Members and candidates may receive requests from a client for trades that do not properly align with the risk and return objectives outlined in the client's investment policy statement. These transaction requests may be based on the client's individual biases or professional experience. Members and candidates will need to make reasonable efforts to balance their clients' trading requests with their responsibilities to follow the agreed-on investment policy statement."

B is incorrect. Madam Tan's request to immediately redeem the structured notes was not in alignment with her IPS and reflected her lack of experience. In this circumstance, Standard III(C) requires Sim to make a reasonable effort to balance Madam Tan's request with her stated IPS objectives of investing in conservative equities so that she can pay for her grandchildren's private school and college expenses.

C is incorrect. Sim did not act with reasonable care or prudent judgment by immediately executing the redemption of the structured notes without first ensuring she fully explained the associated costs to Madam Tan. Sim also should have investigated whether Madam Tan's fears regarding the economic environment and its impact on the risk of the structured notes had any justification before she executed the redemption. Sim violated Standard III(A) Loyalty, Prudence, and Care.

PRACTICE PROBLEMS

The following information relates to questions 1-6

Jason Locke, CFA, has recently been hired as the chief investment officer of the Escarpment Regional Government Employees' Pension Fund (the Fund). Currently, he is conducting evaluations of all external managers employed by the Fund to ensure that they are providing the highest possible returns for their mandates while complying with all applicable laws and regulations.

Locke is evaluating the activity of Niagara Growth Managers (NGM), a local money manager with an allocation of 10% of the Fund's assets. He realizes that any reduction in the allocation to this local manager will be met with considerable political pressure. The investment policy statement for NGM's portion of the Fund's assets states that NGM is to actively manage an equity portfolio of local small-cap, high-tech companies.

Upon his review of NGM's activity, Locke is concerned about two items that he would like to have explained. At a meeting with NGM's portfolio manager, Emma Black, CFA, Locke asks her to comment on each item:

Commodity Positions

> **Locke:** "Over the last year, several large positions in commodities have been taken by the Fund's portfolio. This is inconsistent with the IPS."
>
> **Black:** "Commodities have significantly outperformed high-tech equities recently. I added commodities to larger clients' portfolios on a temporary basis. Clients were not informed, because the positions will be sold once market sentiment shifts. I have not managed commodities before, but I am getting good returns."
>
> **Locke:** "I am uncomfortable with these investments in this portfolio."

IPO Share Allocation

> **Locke:** "The Fund's portfolio received 50,000 shares of an initial public offering on 1 April. On 15 May, 30,000 shares were removed at the current market price."
>
> **Black:** "There was a problem with NGM's IPO allocation algorithm. Initially, you were overallocated. When we discovered the error, your account was adjusted."
>
> **Locke:** "Short-term interest should have been credited to the Fund for use of its cash to cover the trade. In any case, this was an IPO of a large international high-tech company. It was not an appropriate investment for the portfolio."

After the meeting, Locke is not satisfied with Black's comments and decides that further action is required. He also decides that he will allow NGM to continue to manage Fund assets until he finishes his evaluation. This decision is based on the superior returns of the NGM-managed assets, the significant diversification this portfolio adds to the Fund, and the political implications of firing the local money manager.

The next week, Locke calls Black and outlines several conditions that must be fulfilled for NGM to continue as a manager for the Fund. One of the conditions outlined relates to trade allocation.

Trade Allocation

> **Locke:** "Provide written trade allocation procedures consistent with the CFA Institute Standards of Professional Conduct."
>
> **Black:** "I will mail you a copy of our new procedures stating that trade allocations must be reviewed at the end of each month against the client's IPS. They also say that interest will be credited to accounts that have been incorrectly allocated shares and debited from those accounts that should have received shares."

With his evaluation complete, Locke must now consider whether to retain NGM as one of the Fund's asset managers.

1. According to the CFA Institute Standards of Professional Conduct, Locke owes his primary duty of loyalty in managing the Fund to:

   A. the plan trustees.

   B. all the pension plan beneficiaries.

   C. the Escarpment regional government.

2. With respect to the commodity positions, which of the following actions *best* describes Black's violation of the CFA Institute Standards of Professional Conduct? Black violated the Standards by:

   A. buying an asset class in which she has no prior management experience.

   B. buying assets that are inconsistent with the portfolio's investment policy statement.

   C. failing to notify the client that she would temporarily deviate from the client's investment policy statement.

3. With regard to the IPO share allocation, are NGM's method of trade correction on 15 May and Locke's demand for a short-term interest credit consistent with the CFA Institute Standards of Professional Conduct?

   A. Yes

   B. No, only the method of trade correction is consistent.

   C. No, only the demand for a short-term interest credit is consistent.

4. After his initial meeting with Black, does Locke's decision to allow NGM to continue managing the portfolio violate the CFA Institute Standards of Professional Conduct?

   A. No

   B. Yes, because he allowed political factors to influence his decision

   C. Yes, because he is obligated to immediately suspend NGM until he finishes his evaluation

5. With regard to Locke's condition regarding trade allocation, does Black's response violate the Standards of Professional Conduct with respect to allocation

reviews *and* interest adjustments?

A. Yes

B. No, it violates the Standards only with respect to allocation reviews.

C. No, it violates the Standards only with respect to interest adjustments.

6. Based on his complete evaluation, what is Locke's *best* course of action with respect to NGM's management of the Fund's assets?

   A. Reduce NGM's allocation of the Fund's assets until NGM has demonstrated its compliance with Locke's conditions.

   B. Eliminate NGM as a manager since Locke cannot be sure that NGM will act fairly and in accordance with the Fund's IPS.

   C. Maintain NGM's allocation of the Fund's assets, and concentrate on evaluating managers with larger proportions of the Fund's assets or with substandard performance.

The following information relates to questions 7-12

Elias Nano, a recent MBA graduate and a Level II candidate in the CFA Program, is an unpaid summer intern with Patriarch Investment Counsel and expects to be offered a full-time paid position in the fall. Through his efforts, he is able to convince some family members and friends to become clients of the firm, and he now assists with the management of their accounts. His supervisor congratulates him and states, "These clients are the foundation from which you will be able to build your career as an investment adviser." After working hard all summer, Nano is told that Patriarch will not be able to offer him a paid position.

Nano interviews with a number of firms and tells each one about the accounts that he is managing and expects to be able to bring with him. Because he was merely an intern at Patriarch, he does not believe he owes any particular loyalty to Patriarch. He also believes that he can keep the clients because his former supervisor implied that these were Nano's clients.

Nano subsequently joins Markoe Advisers as an assistant director with supervisory responsibilities. Markoe Advisers is an investment management firm that advertises that it provides customized portfolio solutions for individual and institutional clients. As a matter of policy, Markoe Advisers does not reject as a client any individual meeting the account minimum size. Markoe Advisers has two strategies—aggressive growth equity and growth equity—and is always fully invested. Nano asks his family and friends to transfer their accounts from Patriarch to Markoe Advisers.

As the first CFA candidate to be employed by Markoe Advisers, Nano has been asked to head a team that is reviewing the firm's compliance policies and procedures, which Nano considers inadequate and incomplete. He states his concerns to the firm's president, Mr. Markoe: "Although Markoe Advisers, as a firm, cannot adopt the CFA Institute Code of Ethics and Standards of Professional Conduct, the firm can adopt the CFA Institute Asset Manager Code." Mr. Markoe tells Nano that the firm is considering acquiring another advisory firm that has similar compliance policies and procedures. Mr. Markoe says, "We are not going to consider any compliance changes at this time."

Nano decides to draft a model compliance document to guide discussions about future compliance issues at the firm. Nano's initial draft includes the following components of a compliance policy statement:

- **Performance Presentation**

  Performance data must be documented for each of Markoe Advisers' active accounts, be disclosed upon request, and be compared with the firm's composite, which is composed of active accounts only. Performance data must be presented on a before-tax basis to all clients, with the disclosure that all performance data are presented gross of fees.

- **Suitability of Investments**

  Markoe Advisers, to maintain consistency of performance, will assign each client to one of the firm's two portfolios. Both of these portfolios will be sufficiently broadly diversified to meet the investment objectives of all our clients.

- **Disclosures of Conflicts**

  Markoe Advisers encourages its staff to be involved in the business and civic community. Only business or civic interests that relate to current portfolio holdings need to be reported to the firm.

- **Violations**

  Any violation of the Markoe Advisers compliance policy statement will be reported to the president, and employees will receive an official warning.

- **Compensation**

  All staff members of Markoe Advisers will discuss with their supervisor all outside compensation that they are receiving or may receive.

7. Does Nano comply with the CFA Institute Standards of Professional Conduct when he asks his clients to transfer their accounts to Markoe Advisers?

   A. No

   B. Yes, because he contacted the clients after leaving Patriarch

   C. Yes, because he was an intern and not a paid employee of Patriarch

8. Is Nano's statement with respect to adoption of the CFA Institute Code of Ethics and Standards of Professional Conduct and the CFA Institute Asset Manager Code, respectively, correct?

	CFA Institute Code and Standards	CFA Institute Asset Manager Code
A	No	No
B	No	Yes
C	Yes	No

9. According to the CFA Institute Code and Standards, what action should Nano take after discussing the firm's compliance policy with Mr. Markoe? Nano should:

   A. resign from the firm.

   B. notify the board of directors.

C. decline to accept supervisory responsibilities.

10. Does Nano's draft compliance policy statement conform to the Code and Standards with respect to performance presentation?

  A. No, because terminated accounts are excluded

  B. No, because performance is reported to all clients gross of fees

  C. No, because performance data are presented on a before-tax basis

11. Does Nano's draft compliance policy statement conform to the CFA Institute Code and Standards with respect to suitability of investments and disclosures of conflicts?

	Suitability of investments	Disclosures of conflicts
A	No	No
B	No	Yes
C	Yes	No

12. Does Nano's draft compliance policy statement conform to the CFA Institute Code and Standards with respect to violations and compensation?

	Violations	Compensation
A	No	No
B	No	Yes
C	Yes	No

The following information relates to questions 13-18

Patricia Jollie, CFA, is the fixed-income analyst and portfolio manager at Mahsud Financial Corporation, a small investment firm.

On 5 April, a friend who works for a bond-rating agency mentions to Jollie that a bond the agency is analyzing will experience a rating change. That bond also happens to be in Mahsud Financial's portfolios. Not wanting to trade ahead of the rating change announcement, Jollie decides to wait for distribution of the information through her friend's scheduled interview on a business television program on the afternoon of 8 April. On the morning of 8 April, the information is released on a worldwide financial news service. Jollie immediately changes her mind about waiting for the interview and trades the bonds in Mahsud Financial's portfolios.

On 8 April, Jollie also trades a second bond to rebalance one of Mahsud Financial's portfolios. Jollie knows before executing her transaction that the bond is thinly traded. Although Jollie's trade will materially affect the bond's market price, it is not her intention to create price movement. A colleague witnesses the trade and large bond price change and says, "What a market overreaction; the bond price appears to be distorted now!" The colleague also points out to Jollie that Mahsud Financial's policy on market manipulation states, "Mahsud Financial employees must refrain from making transactions that distort security prices or volume with the intent to mislead market participants."

In conducting fixed-income research, Jollie believes that insight into prospective corporate bond returns can be derived from information that is also relevant to a company's stock. She spends several hours a week in equity investment chat rooms on the internet, and she pays particular attention to the research reports posted by Jill Dean, CFA, a self-employed analyst, on www.Jill_Dean_the_Independent_Analyst.com. Prior to writing each report, Dean is paid a flat fee by the companies whose stocks she researches, but she does not reveal this fact to readers of her reports. She produces reports only for those companies whose stocks she can legitimately give "buy" recommendations after conducting a thorough analysis. Otherwise, she returns the flat fee. Investors have come to recognize all her "buy" ratings as having a sound and reasonable basis.

Jollie considers Dean's summaries and forecasts to be very well crafted. Dean has given Jollie written permission to use her summaries and forecasts, word for word and without attribution, in her own bond analysis reports. On occasion, Jollie has done so. In Dean's other internet postings, she reports the results of relevant academic finance studies. Once Jollie learns of a study by reading Dean's postings, she often reads the original study and mentions the results in her own reports. Jollie always cites the original study only and does not reveal that she learned of the study through Dean.

Mahsud Financial occasionally sponsors seminars on ethics. In the most recent seminar, the main speaker made statements about the relationship between ethics and the law and also about potential conflict of interest sources for research analysts. The seminar speaker's statements were as follows:

Statement 1	An illegal action is unethical, and actions that are legal are ethically sound.
Statement 2	For analysts, a major source of conflict of interest is potential profit resulting from a weak barrier between the employer's research department and investment banking department.
Statement 3	For situations in which conflicts of interest cannot be avoided, Mahsud Financial's written compliance policy should include the following component: "For unavoidable conflicts of interest that the employee judges to be material, employees must disclose the conflicts of interest to clients prominently and in plain language."
Statement 4	On the matter of gifts that might impair employees' objectivity, Mahsud Financial's written compliance policy should also include the following component: "Employees must disclose to Mahsud Financial all client gifts regardless of value."

13. Did Jollie violate the CFA Institute Standards of Professional Conduct by trading on the news of the bond-rating change?

    A. No

    B. Yes, only because she possessed material nonpublic information

    C. Yes, only because she should have waited to trade until after her friend's television interview took place

14. Are Jollie's 8 April trade of the second bond and Mahsud Financial's policy on market manipulation consistent with the Standards with respect to market

manipulation?

A. Both Jollie's 8 April trade of the second bond and Mahsud Financial's policy on market manipulation are consistent with the Standards.

B. Jollie's 8 April trade of the second bond is inconsistent and Mahsud Financial's policy on market manipulation is consistent with the Standards.

C. Jollie's 8 April trade of the second bond is consistent and Mahsud Financial's policy on market manipulation is inconsistent with the Standards.

15. Did Dean violate the Standards in preparing and disseminating her equity reports?

A. No

B. Yes, only by misrepresenting her recommendations as independent

C. Yes, only by accepting payment from the companies on which she produces reports

16. In preparing investment reports, did Jollie violate the Standards with respect to her use of Dean's summaries and forecasts and citation of studies found in Dean's internet postings?

	Use of Dean's summaries and forecasts?	Citation of studies found in Dean's internet postings?
A	No	Yes
B	Yes	No
C	Yes	Yes

17. Are the seminar speaker's Statements 1 and 2 correct?

	Statement 1	Statement 2
A	No	No
B	No	Yes
C	Yes	No

18. Are the seminar speaker's Statements 3 and 4 sufficient to meet the requirements of the related Standards?

	Statement 3	Statement 4
A	No	No
B	No	Yes
C	Yes	No

The following information relates to questions 19-23

Stacia Finnegan, CFA, manages a regional office of Harvest Financial's brokerage business. Her responsibilities include training all personnel in compliance with the firm's standards, policies, procedures, and applicable laws and regulations.

Finnegan is currently providing training on the firm's new PlusAccount, a comprehensive, fee-based brokerage account. "PlusAccounts," she tells the brokers, "are an excellent way to ensure that the financial adviser does not recommend trades for the purpose of generating commissions. Adviser and client interests are aligned." She continues, "You will find that many clients will benefit from converting a traditional brokerage account to a PlusAccount. Be aware, however, that PlusAccounts are not appropriate for all categories of investors, including buy-and-hold clients and certain clients with assets less than $50,000."

Finnegan distributes written compliance procedures for establishing and maintaining PlusAccounts. She carefully explains that regulatory rules "require that we have reasonable grounds for believing that the PlusAccount is appropriate for a particular customer. Additionally, we must review each account on an annual basis to determine whether PlusAccount status remains appropriate. The policies outlined in these documents are designed to ensure compliance with industry standards and regulatory requirements. You must follow these compliance procedures exactly."

Finnegan then distributes and explains the sales and disclosure materials for clients. The materials include the following fee structure:

PlusAccount Annual Fee (as a percentage of assets)*

Account Asset Level	Equity (%)	Mutual Fund/Fixed Income (%)
$0–$250,000	2.00	1.00
Next $250,000	1.50	1.00
Next $250,000	1.25	1.00
Next $250,000	1.00	1.00
More than $1 million	0.75	0.75

**Minimum annual fee of $1,000, billed quarterly.*

Finnegan spends the rest of the afternoon training the staff on detailed procedures and answering their questions.

Chris Klein is a registered broker and financial adviser with Harvest. He is also a Level II candidate in the CFA Program. Klein is excited about the new PlusAccounts and believes they will be attractive for many clients.

One of Klein's clients is Elaine Vanderon, who contributes weekly to her brokerage account. Under Vanderon's directions, Klein invests the weekly contributions in actively managed mutual funds (unit trusts). The funds have below-average management fees and average returns. Commissions for Vanderon average $35 per transaction.

When Vanderon's account reaches $50,000 in assets, Klein recommends conversion to a PlusAccount. He carefully explains that in a PlusAccount, both the cost of investment advice and many implementation costs are wrapped into the management fee billed on a quarterly basis. Stock and bond commissions, he tells Vanderon, are discounted by 70%. Klein informs Vanderon that in a PlusAccount, she can buy or sell thousands of mutual funds or unit trusts (including those in which she invests) for no commissions or transaction charges. He explains that PlusAccounts are ideal for clients who trade often—or as part of a periodic investment program, such as hers. Vanderon reads through the disclosure material provided by Klein and accepts his recommendation.

Klein routinely informs clients about the benefits of PlusAccount status and presents them with all the disclosure materials. Another client Klein encourages to open a PlusAccount is Lee Brown. Brown has accumulated stock holdings of $300,000 and trades equities almost daily. His annual commissions for the previous 12 months equal $9,100. His portfolio is well diversified. He has a high risk tolerance and prefers growth stocks. After explaining the fee structure, Klein tells Brown, "The PlusAccount is ideal for an active trader like you."

One year later, Finnegan is promoted. She delegates supervisory responsibility for Klein and 15 other brokers to her assistant branch manager.

The same month, Klein meets with Vanderon and Brown to review their portfolios and financial situations. Both clients are happy with their PlusAccounts. Vanderon's commission costs have declined to zero. Her account continues to grow in line with her plans and expectations. Brown is also happy with his account. His annual commission costs have declined 70%, to $2,700.

Two months later, Vanderon receives a $1 million inheritance and places it in her PlusAccount. Although he conducted a full review two months earlier, Klein meets with Vanderon to review her financial situation and discuss potential changes to her investment policy. During their meeting, Klein mentions that he has completed the Level III CFA exam. He informs Vanderon, "Completion of the CFA Program has enhanced my portfolio management skills." He tells Vanderon, "As a CFA charterholder, I am the best qualified to manage your investments." Vanderon congratulates Klein on his accomplishment and agrees to consider any changes he recommends to her PlusAccount.

The following month, Klein telephones Vanderon to recommend a highly rated mutual fund. Klein states, "The fund has an excellent performance history and is ranked in the top decile of comparable funds. For the past three- and five-year periods, its average annual return has exceeded the benchmark by 90 bps. Of course, past performance is no guarantee of future returns, but several of my clients hold this fund and are very happy with it. One of them invested $50,000 five years ago. That investment is worth more than $100,000 today." When Vanderon asks about fees, Klein explains that the fund's management fees are 25 bps higher than those of her existing investments. He adds, "Because of your PlusAccount status, you won't incur a brokerage commission for this transaction even though I will receive a referral fee if you invest in the fund."

Six months later, Brown suffers serious medical and financial problems and stops trading. Klein telephones him to review his financial situation. Brown insists that he will make a full recovery and that he will be trading again shortly. During the next 12 months, Brown is too ill to trade. His growing expenses force him to withdraw large amounts from his PlusAccount. Within another 18 months, his PlusAccount value is less than $50,000.

19. When recommending that Vanderon convert to a PlusAccount, did Klein violate any of the Standards?

    A. No

    B. Yes, because he did not have a reasonable basis

    C. Yes, because the account is unsuitable for Vanderon

20. When recommending that Brown convert to a PlusAccount, did Klein violate any

of the Standards?

A. No

B. Yes, relating to suitability

C. Yes, relating to reasonable basis

21. When meeting with Vanderon, did Klein violate any of the Standards?

A. No

B. Yes, because he improperly referenced the CFA designation

C. Yes, because he claimed enhanced portfolio management skills

22. When recommending the mutual fund to Vanderon, did Klein violate any of the Standards?

A. No

B. Yes, relating to suitability

C. Yes, relating to referral fees

23. In her supervisory duties, did Finnegan violate any of the Standards?

A. No

B. Yes, because she failed to ensure that compliance procedures are enforced

C. Yes, because she delegated supervisory authority to her assistant branch manager

The following information relates to questions 24-29

A. J. Vinken, CFA, manages the Stonebridge Fund at Silk Road Capital Management. He develops a growth-stock selection model that produces highly favorable simulated performance results. He would like to use the model in managing the Stonebridge Fund, a large-capitalization equity fund. He drafts a letter for distribution to all shareholders. In it, he discusses in detail his approach to equity selection using the model. He includes both the actual and simulated performance results of the Stonebridge Fund for the past three years, as shown in Exhibit 1.

Exhibit 1: Stonebridge Fund Annual Returns

Year	Stonebridge Fund (Simulated)	Stonebridge Fund (Actual)
1	10.71%	9.22%
2	2.83%	–4.13%

Year	Stonebridge Fund (Simulated)	Stonebridge Fund (Actual)
3	22.23%	22.23%
Average annual return	11.92%	9.11%

Vinken writes, "Using the proprietary selection model for the past three years, the Stonebridge Fund would have earned an average annual return of almost 300 bps in excess of the fund's actual return. Based on these simulated results, I am confident that using the model will yield better performance results in the future; however, Silk Road Capital Management can make no statement of assurance or guarantee regarding future investment returns."

D. S. Khadri, CFA, is also a portfolio manager at Silk Road. She recently assumed management of the small-cap Westlake Fund from Vinken.

Khadri implements an electronic record-retention policy when she becomes the Westlake manager. In accordance with her policy, all records for the fund—including investment analyses, transactions, and investment-related communications with clients and prospective clients—are scanned and electronically stored. Vinken maintained the same records in hard copy format for the five years that he managed the Westlake Fund. Khadri has begun the process of scanning all the past records of the Westlake Fund; however, Vinken complains that Khadri is wasting company resources by scanning old records. Vinken insists that he will continue to maintain only hard copy records for the Stonebridge Fund for the five years required by regulators.

Khadri writes a performance review of the Westlake Fund for its quarterly newsletter. She reports that Silk Road Capital Management is moving toward compliance with the Global Investment Performance Standards (GIPS®). She states, "The Westlake Fund is already partially GIPS compliant. We expect to be fully compliant with the GIPS standards within the next 12 months."

In the quarterly newsletter, Khadri makes the following statements:

Statement 1	China's pegging of the yuan to the US dollar will end within the next 12 months, which will lead to the yuan increasing in value by more than 40%, supporting our overweighting of Chinese-related stocks in the Westlake Fund.
Statement 2	Increased geopolitical uncertainty around the globe should keep oil prices above three-year levels, which supports our recommendation for an overweighting of equities in the small-cap energy sector.

Khadri also reports the following:

"The quarterly return of the Westlake Fund was 4.07%. The quarterly return exceeded the performance of its benchmark, the Russell 2000 Index, by 0.16%. Investors should not expect this type of performance to continue into the foreseeable future.*

*Additional detailed information available upon request."

After the quarterly newsletter is distributed, a client contacts Khadri claiming that the Westlake Fund actually underperformed the benchmark during the quarter. After researching the issue, Khadri confirms that the client is correct and sends him a letter in which she provides the corrected results. In her letter to the client, she blames the discrepancy—which was the result of a human typographical error—on a computer programming error.

24. In his letter regarding the stock selection model, did Vinken violate any of the

Standards?

A. No

B. Yes, because he used simulated performance results

C. Yes, because he claimed that the new model will yield better performance results

25. Are the record-retention policies of both Khadri and Vinken consistent with the Standards?

A. Yes

B. No, Khadri's policy is not consistent.

C. No, Vinken's policy is not consistent.

26. Are Khadri's statements regarding compliance with the GIPS standards consistent with the Standards of Professional Conduct?

A. Yes

B. No, because Khadri may not claim partial compliance

C. No, because Khadri failed to disclose the areas of noncompliance

27. Are Khadri's statements in the quarterly newsletter consistent with the Standards of Professional Conduct?

A. Yes

B. No, because Statement 1 is opinion, not fact

C. No, because Statement 2 is opinion, not fact

28. Are Khadri's newsletter comments regarding returns consistent with the Standards?

A. Yes

B. No, because Khadri used an inappropriate benchmark

C. No, because Khadri did not disclose whether the performance results are before or after fees

29. When responding to the client complaint regarding Westlake's performance, Khadri *least likely* violated the standard relating to:

A. misconduct.

B. misrepresentation.

C. performance presentation.

The following information relates to questions 30-35

Omega Financial, a large financial services firm, makes a market in more than 500 stocks. As a market maker, the firm executes institutional orders, as well as retail orders placed by its private wealth unit, its broker/dealer affiliate, and other third-party broker/dealers.

A page in Omega's compliance manual, which adheres to all legal and regulatory requirements, includes the following information:

OTC Stocks in Which Omega Is a Market Maker

Definitions:	
Riskless principal transaction: an order in which a firm, after receiving a customer's order, executes the order on a principal basis from another market center	
Net trade/trade on a net basis: a principal transaction in which a market maker, after having received an order, executes the order at one price with another broker/dealer or another customer and then sells to (buys from) the customer at a different price	
Compliance Policies:	
Institutional Orders	*Retail Orders*
Riskless principal transactions may be traded on a net basis.	Riskless principal transactions may not be traded on a net basis. They receive the same execution price without markup, markdown, commissions, or fees.

Consistent with regulatory requirements, Omega discloses the information about riskless principal transactions to all clients and third-party broker/dealers. In addition, Omega informs third-party broker/dealers that it will seek best execution on retail orders.

Omega is developing an automated order-handling system to improve efficiencies in order flow. Anticipated benefits of the new system include much faster execution speeds. Additionally, the system design includes a trading mechanism that will execute portions of certain large orders to reduce market impact. The trading mechanism delays some orders to allow the firm to obtain a better overall price.

Xavier Brown, CFA, is responsible for overseeing the project to ensure its timely completion. Brown enlists the compliance department to review the programming during the initial development phase and identify any potential problems. The compliance department compares the order-handling function of the new system to the third-party software currently in use. They identify several potential problems, including delays in execution of certain large market orders and embedded markups and markdowns on stocks in which the firm makes a market. According to the compliance department, changes are necessary to comply with regulatory requirements.

Brown directs the programmers to correct the problems and run tests and simulations. The programmers spend the next few months making changes to the system and adding comments throughout the code that clearly explain the purpose of particular functions. After several months, the programmers report that they have corrected all the identified problems and run the necessary tests and simulations. The following month, the firm switches to the automated order-handling system as planned.

Joy Chen, CFA, trades Xydeo stock for Omega. One month following the switch to the new order-handling system, Chen is able to execute a number of principal riskless transactions for both institutional and retail clients at $25.00 per share. When processing the customer buy orders totaling 500,000 shares, the new system automatically uses the best-publicized price, \$25.01, and then the firm issues client confirmations showing a purchase price of \$25.01.

Stephen Smith, CFA, works across from Chen at the trading desk at Omega. His seat is close to a speaker for the company's squawk box, which is used to broadcast information about current analyst recommendations, news about market events, and information about pending block trades.

Smith's young brother-in-law, Adolfo Garcia, recently accepted a position as a broker at a third-party broker/dealer that trades with Omega. Garcia has a modest income and little savings. He is enthusiastic about investments and has enrolled as a CFA candidate. Smith calls Garcia early each morning to talk about the previous day's events. At the end of their conversation, Smith places the call on speakerphone and resumes his work.

In his office, Garcia can hear Omega's squawk box over the speakerphone. Garcia enjoys listening as Omega analysts discuss changes in ratings, economic forecasts, and capital market developments. He is careful not to trade in stocks mentioned explicitly on the squawk box. Rather, he sometimes researches competitors and other firms operating in the same industry. In one case, he immediately shorts the stock of Tefla Corporation after an Omega analyst downgrades a firm in the same industry.

Garcia frequently places large block orders for low-priced, small-capitalization stocks at the market price. Once the new system is operational, Smith processes the orders through the new trading system mechanism, which delays execution of portions of the orders and allows the firm to obtain a better price for Garcia.

30. For a CFA charterholder, would adhering to Omega's policies regarding riskless principal transactions result in a violation of the CFA Institute Standards of Professional Conduct?

    A. No

    B. Yes, because Omega disadvantages institutional clients

    C. Yes, because disclosure of the policy does not relieve Omega of its obligation to treat clients equally

31. When overseeing the development of the automated trading system, did Brown violate any of the Standards?

    A. No

    B. Yes, because he accepted an assignment for which he was inadequately trained and skilled

    C. Yes, because he did not ensure that the final system complied with regulatory requirements

32. With regard to Chen's trades in Xydeo, do both the institutional and retail trades comply with the Standards?

    A. Only the retail trades comply.

    B. Only the institutional trades comply.

    C. Neither the retail nor the institutional trades comply.

33. When placing the morning phone call on speakerphone, did Smith violate any of

the Standards?

A. No

B. Yes, his duty to Omega

C. Yes, his duty to clients and to Omega

34. When listening to the Omega squawk box, did Garcia violate any of the Standards?

A. No

B. Yes, the standard regarding professionalism

C. Yes, the standard regarding material nonpublic information

35. When shorting Tefla stock, did Garcia violate any of the Standards?

A. No

B. Yes, because he did not have a reasonable basis for the trade

C. Yes, because he was in possession of material nonpublic information

---

The following information relates to questions 36-41

Sebastian Riser, CFA, works as a portfolio manager for Swibank, a small private bank in Switzerland. Riser manages the accounts of his clients according to best practices, keeping clients' interests before those of the bank and his own. He allocates investments in a fair manner when he deems them consistent with the stated objectives and constraints of clients.

Swibank has a Luxembourg subsidiary, which distributes fund-of-funds products. Riser recently received a request to serve on the board of directors for the subsidiary. In this role, Riser would advise management on business strategies, market opportunities, potential clients, and current and prospective fund managers. For his role on the board, Riser would receive an annual payment directly from the subsidiary equivalent to 5% of his total portfolio manager salary in Switzerland.

The following month, Riser accepts the position on the board. The subsidiary registers each new fund-of-funds product with regulatory authorities in Luxembourg and discloses Riser's role as a board member in the required filings, which are public and readily available.

Riser serves as the contact person for the subsidiary's institutional clients in Switzerland and participates in the subsidiary's road shows in Switzerland. His role during these road shows varies. On some occasions, he simply attends the presentations while the operating management sells the products; on other occasions, he gives the actual presentation promoting the products. Riser's name does not appear in the promotional material distributed at the road shows.

Alexander Komm, a long-time colleague of Riser, is the founder of Komm Private Management, which provides asset management, advisory, and trust services to high-net-worth individuals. The firm has several well-managed proprietary funds. Komm offers Riser a position with the firm as managing partner. Riser is flattered but declines the offer, explaining that he is very happy working at

Swibank.

That same week, the subsidiary informs Riser that it needs an experienced fund manager to manage a new publicly traded Japanese equity product. Riser is convinced that Komm Private Management would be qualified and recommends the firm for the new product. After a thorough search process, the subsidiary hires Komm Private Management for the new product.

Six months later, after numerous discussions, Komm finally convinces Riser to join Komm Private Management as a managing partner. The following week, Riser submits his resignation to Swibank. His position on the board of the subsidiary is not dependent on his employment at the bank, and he agrees to serve the remaining three years of his term.

After signing and submitting his employment contract to Komm, Riser takes three weeks of vacation before starting his new position. During this time, he purchases 2,000 shares of the new Japanese equity product for his private account. When he begins working at Komm Private Management, he purchases a large block of shares in the Japanese equity product, which he allocates according to internal procedures to all accounts for which it is suitable.

36. According to the CFA Institute Standards of Professional Conduct, before accepting the position on the board of the subsidiary, Riser should:

    A. receive verbal consent from Swibank.

    B. receive verbal consent from his clients.

    C. disclose to his employer the financial compensation proposed by the subsidiary.

37. When participating in the road shows in Switzerland, Riser *least likely* violated the standard relating to:

    A. avoiding or disclosing conflicts.

    B. independence and objectivity.

    C. additional compensation arrangements.

38. When recommending Komm Private Management, did Riser violate any of the Standards?

    A. No

    B. Yes, relating to duties to employers

    C. Yes, relating to avoiding or disclosing conflicts

39. When resigning from Swibank, did Riser violate any of the Standards?

    A. No

    B. Yes, because he breached his duty of loyalty to his employer

    C. Yes, because he did not resign his position with the Luxembourg subsidiary

40. In his original purchase of 2,000 shares of the Japanese equity product, Riser *least likely* violated the standard relating to:

    A. suitability.

B. priority of transactions.

C. integrity of capital markets.

41. According to the Standards, Riser is not required to disclose to clients his:

   A. holdings of the Japanese equity product.

   B. relationship with the Swibank subsidiary.

   C. compensation from the Swibank subsidiary.

The following information relates to questions 42-47

Prudent Investment Associates (PIA) is a small-cap equity investment management company that uses fundamental equity analysis in its investment decision-making process. All portfolio managers at PIA manage both discretionary and non-discretionary accounts. Kevin Danko, CFA, is PIA's owner and chief investment officer and supervises May Chau, a recently hired portfolio manager. PIA has adopted the CFA Institute Code of Ethics and Standards of Professional Conduct.

Chau is enrolled to sit for the Level III CFA exam. In its marketing brochure, PIA states, "May Chau is a Level III candidate in the CFA Program." A colleague tells Chau this statement may be incorrect according to the CFA Institute Code and Standards and suggests the following change: "May Chau has passed the Level II CFA exam."

PIA has established a relationship with Fair Trading Incorporated (FTI), a regional investment bank and broker/dealer. FTI provides clients with access to research and analysts' recommendations via a user-registered website. This access is available on the condition that clients not forward any of the research and recommendations to any other parties. In exchange for this access and after concluding that FTI provides best execution, Danko directs to FTI most of his trade orders.

FTI also provides to a select group of brokerage clients, including PIA, information regarding several of its investment banking customers. This information includes the customers' own earnings projections. FTI instructs this select group of brokerage clients not to disseminate these earnings projections to the public until released by the investment banking customers.

On a regular basis, Danko reviews the list of "strong buys" on FTI's website to see if there have been any new "buy" recommendations. Danko quickly places orders for discretionary client accounts to purchase shares of any company for which the investment recommendation has been changed to a "strong buy." He takes this action so discretionary account clients do not miss any price appreciation. After each purchase, he instructs Chau to perform the appropriate fundamental analysis on these companies within five business days so the research file is adequately documented.

From time to time, PIA receives initial public offering allocations from FTI. Danko allocates these IPOs to those discretionary accounts that normally participate in IPOs. If the IPO is oversubscribed, he excludes his wife's discretionary non-fee-paying account so that he is not accused of bias when allocating the oversubscribed IPOs.

During a recent presentation, Danko and Chau are asked what procedures PIA uses to ensure employees do not benefit from information prior to executing trades in client accounts. Danko responds that PIA has the following trading procedures:

Procedure 1	Investment personnel are not permitted to trade securities for five business days prior to trades executed in discretionary client accounts.
Procedure 2	Each quarter, a randomly selected group of investment personnel must provide duplicate trade confirmations to the PIA compliance officer.
Procedure 3	Investment personnel must receive prior approval for personal trades only for trades greater than $5,000.

42. Does the reference to Chau's participation in the CFA Program as presented in the marketing brochure or in the suggested change violate the Standards?

   A. No, it does not.

   B. The marketing brochure is a violation, but the suggested change is not a violation.

   C. The suggested change is a violation, but the marketing brochure is not a violation.

43. Did Danko violate the Standards when he directed trades to FTI?

   A. No

   B. Yes, because by trading with FTI, Danko put PIA's interests ahead of his clients

   C. Yes, because Danko has a duty to provide FTI's research to PIA's clients before executing trades

44. According to the Standards, which of the following actions is the *most* appropriate for Danko to take with respect to the use of the earnings projections? Danko should:

   A. disclose the information to the public.

   B. terminate PIA's relationship with FTI.

   C. keep the information confidential and not use it in his analysis.

45. Did Danko's decision to purchase shares that are recommended as a "strong buy" violate the Standards?

   A. No

   B. Yes, because Danko must have a reasonable and adequate basis prior to purchasing the shares

   C. Yes, because Danko must give non-discretionary accounts the opportunity to purchase equities at the same time he purchases equities in the discretionary accounts

46. Did Danko violate the Standards when he allocated oversubscribed IPO issues?

    A. No

    B. Yes, because he should have allocated the oversubscribed IPOs across all discretionary accounts

    C. Yes, because he should have treated his wife's account the same as other discretionary accounts and included it in the oversubscribed IPO allocations

47. Which of PIA's trading procedures is *most* consistent with the Standards?

    A. Procedure 1

    B. Procedure 2

    C. Procedure 3

SOLUTIONS

1. B is correct. Locke's primary duty is to his clients. In the case of a pension plan, the clients are all the ultimate beneficiaries.

2. B is correct. Under no circumstances should a manager take investment action that is inconsistent with the client's IPS.

3. C is correct. Locke's interest claim is legitimate since the Fund's cash was used to purchase equities that were later removed from the account. Therefore, the Fund is owed interest for the period in question.

4. A is correct. Until Locke's investigation is complete, he has no obligation to suspend the manager or take any other action. He believes the manager can and does add value through superior returns and diversification, and thus it may be reasonable to retain NGM if Locke can be satisfied that the manager can act within the constraints of the IPS and the Standards of Professional Conduct. Until the analysis is complete, suspending the manager and leaving the assets unmanaged or temporarily moving them to another manager for safekeeping would not be practical and Locke would be violating his duty to act in his clients' best interests.

5. A is correct. Client suitability for an investment must be reviewed prior to allocation, not afterward. With respect to interest adjustments, clients who were incorrectly allocated shares must be paid for the use of their cash; however, in no instance should clients suffer a loss because of an allocation error by the manager (that is, have interest removed from their portfolio even though shares are put in their account on a backdated basis).

6. B is correct. Locke has a duty to the pension plan beneficiaries to act in their best interests. He would be violating that duty if he continues to employ a manager who does not manage its mandate or demonstrate that it is aware of and complies with its own duties to clients. He must demonstrate his own professional competence by firing the manager.

7. B is correct. Standard IV(A) prohibits employees from soliciting the clients of employers prior to—but not subsequent to—their departure.

8. B is correct. The Code and Standards apply to individual members and candidates of CFA Institute, but firms are encouraged to adopt the Code and Standards as part of their firm code of ethics. The CFA Institute Asset Manager Code has been drafted specifically for firms.

9. C is correct. Standard IV(C) states that members and candidates should decline in writing to accept supervisory responsibilities until a firm adopts reasonable procedures to allow them to adequately exercise such responsibility.

10. A is correct. Standard III(D) states that both terminated and active accounts must be included as part of the performance history.

11. A is correct. By placing all clients in one of the two specialized portfolios it operates, Markoe Advisers is not giving adequate consideration to the individual needs, circumstances, and objectives of each client as required by the Standards. In addition, the Standards require that members and candidates avoid or disclose all actual and potential conflicts of interest, not just those that relate to current portfolio holdings.

12. A is correct. The Standards require that the supervisor promptly initiate an investigation to ascertain the extent of the violation and should take steps to ensure that violations will not be repeated by limiting or monitoring the employees' activities. The Standards also require that members and candidates obtain written permission from their employer before accepting any compensation or benefits from third parties that may create a conflict of interest.

13. A is correct. Jollie did not act on the material nonpublic information she possessed but waited until it became public. According to the *Standards of Practice Handbook*, "It is not necessary . . . to wait for the slowest method of delivery."

14. A is correct. Jollie's transaction is a legitimate market order in a thinly traded security, and Mahsud Financial's policy statement is consistent with the Standards with respect to the integrity of capital markets.

15. B is correct. It is not a violation to accept compensation from an issuer in exchange for research, but such arrangements must be disclosed prominently and in plain language.

16. B is correct. Receiving Dean's written permission does not absolve Jollie of her responsibility to provide attribution. Because Jollie uses the results of the research studies and does not use Dean's interpretation of the studies, it is appropriate to cite the original authors only.

17. B is correct. The first statement is incorrect, and the second statement is correct. What is legal is not necessarily ethical. A weak barrier between the employer's research department and investment banking department is a potential source of conflict.

18. B is correct. Statement 3 is incorrect. Conflicts must be avoided or disclosed. If not avoided, a conflict must be disclosed—prominently and in plain language—regardless of whether the member views the conflict as material. Statement 4 is in compliance with the Standards. The Mahsud Financial disclosure requirement complies with the Standards. Gifts from clients must be disclosed so the employer can determine whether the gift could affect the employee's independence and objectivity.

19. A is correct. Klein did not violate the Standards when recommending a PlusAccount to Vanderon. His actions comply with Standard III(A) Loyalty, Prudence, and Care; Standard III(C) Suitability; and Standard V(A) Diligence and Reasonable Basis. As required, Klein disclosed the fee structure associated with the PlusAccount. Based on the fee structure and Vanderon's trading activity, the PlusAccount appears to be a suitable investment vehicle. By converting to PlusAccount status, Vanderon will incur an annual fee of $1,000 and eliminate approximately $1,800 in annual brokerage commissions. The potential savings of approximately $800 provides a reasonable basis for recommending PlusAccount status.

20. A is correct. Klein did not violate the Standards when recommending a PlusAccount to Brown. His actions comply with Standard III(A) Loyalty, Prudence, and Care; Standard III(C) Suitability; and Standard V(A) Diligence and Reasonable Basis. As required, he disclosed the fee structure. Based on the fee structure and Brown's annual commissions, the PlusAccount appears to be a suitable investment vehicle. By converting to PlusAccount status, Brown will incur an annual fee of $5,750 and save approximately $6,370 in annual brokerage commissions. The potential savings of approximately $620 provides a reasonable basis for recommending PlusAccount status.

21. B is correct. Klein improperly referenced the CFA designation when he stated, "As a CFA charterholder, I am the best qualified to manage your investments." He is in violation of Standard VII(B) Reference to CFA Institute, the CFA Designation, and the CFA Program.

22. C is correct. Klein violated Standard VI(C) Referral Fees because he failed to provide appropriate disclosure. Standard VI(C) states that members must disclose the nature of the consideration or benefit—for example, whether on a flat fee or percentage basis, a one-time or continuing benefit, or based on performance—together with the estimated monetary value. Although Klein acknowledged receipt of referral fees from the fund, he did not disclose an estimated dollar value or the nature of the consideration.

23. B is correct. Finnegan violated Standard IV(C) Responsibilities of Supervisors by failing to ensure that compliance procedures are enforced. As she informed her staff, Harvest "must review each account on an annual basis to determine whether PlusAccount status remains appropriate." Had Vanderon's and Brown's accounts been reviewed annually in accordance with compliance procedures, it would have been clear that the PlusAccount was no longer suitable for either. Delegating supervisory authority to another individual does not violate the Standards.

24. A is correct. Vinken did not violate any of the Standards in his letter. In accordance with Standard III(D) Performance Presentation, he presented fair, accurate, and complete information when he identified actual and simulated performance results. Also in accordance with the standard, he did not guarantee superior future investment returns. In accordance with Standard V(B) Communication with Clients and Prospective Clients, Vinken described to his clients and prospective clients the process and logic of the new investment model. By providing the basic details of the model, Vinken provided his clients the basis for understanding the limitations or inherent risks of the investment strategy.

25. A is correct. The policies of both Khadri and Vinken are consistent with Standard V(C) Record Retention, which states that "Members and Candidates must develop and maintain appropriate records to support their investment analyses, recommendations, actions, and other investment-related communications with clients and prospective clients." The records required to support recommendations and/or investment actions depend on the role of the member or candidate in the investment decision-making process. Records can be maintained in either hard copy or electronic form. Even though they use different methods, Khadri and Vinken each maintain the appropriate records and have adequate systems of record control.

26. B is correct. Khadri is in violation of Standard III(D) Performance Presentation. When claiming compliance with the GIPS standards, firms must meet all the requirements. The GIPS standards, while voluntary, apply only on a firmwide basis. Neither a firm nor a fund can claim partial compliance with the GIPS standards.

27. B is correct. Standard V(B) Communication with Clients and Prospective Clients requires the member or candidate to separate and distinguish "facts from opinions" in the presentation of analyses and investment recommendations. Statement 1 in the newsletter says, "China's pegging of the yuan to the US dollar *will* end within the next 12 months which *will* lead to the yuan increasing in value by more than 40%, supporting our overweighting of Chinese-related stocks in the Westlake Fund." Khadri did not clearly differentiate between opinion and fact. The statement about the future of oil pricing is not as questionable, because Khadri used the term "should," which helps clients understand that this is an

opinion and not a certainty. Members may communicate opinions, estimates, and assumptions about future values and possible events, but they must take care to differentiate fact from opinion.

28. C is correct. Khadri violated Standard III(D) Performance Presentation because he did not disclose whether the performance results are before or after fees. Standard III(D) requires that members and candidates make reasonable efforts to ensure that investment performance information is "fair, accurate, and complete." According to the guidance provided in the *Standards of Practice Handbook*, members should include disclosures that fully explain the performance results (for example, whether the performance is gross of fees, net of fees, or after tax).

29. C is correct. Because Khadri provided the corrected information in her letter to the client, she is least likely to have violated Standard III(D) Performance Presentation. She is more likely to have violated the Standards relating to misconduct and misrepresentation because she knowingly misrepresented the cause of the error. Standard I(D) Misconduct requires that members "not engage in any professional conduct involving dishonesty." Standard I(C) Misrepresentation prohibits members from knowingly making any misrepresentations relating to investment actions and professional activities.

30. A is correct. Markups and markdowns in net trades are considered fees paid by clients. Standard III(B) Fair Dealing requires that members treat all clients fairly in light of their investment objectives and circumstances. Treating institutional and retail investors differently is not a violation. According to the Standards, members can differentiate their services to clients, but different levels of service must be disclosed and should not negatively affect clients. Omega has made the appropriate disclosures to its clients in compliance with legal and regulatory requirements and the Standards.

31. C is correct. Brown is in violation of Standard IV(C) Responsibilities of Supervisors because he did not ensure that the final system complied with regulatory requirements. According to Standard IV(C), Brown has a responsibility to make reasonable efforts to detect and prevent violations of applicable laws, rules, and regulations. Alerted to potential problems by the compliance department, he had a responsibility to ensure that the modifications corrected the potential problems without introducing new problems.

32. B is correct. Only the institutional trades comply with the Standards. All the trades were processed on a net basis. Because the firm disclosed that institutional orders may be executed on a net basis, the institutional trades did not result in a violation. The firm disclosed to clients that in riskless principal trades, retail clients will receive the same execution price without markup. Executing the retail orders on a net basis with a $0.01 markup resulted in a violation of Standard I(C) Misrepresentation and Standard III(B) Fair Dealing.

33. C is correct. Smith violated his duties to both clients and Omega by not protecting confidential information. By providing Garcia access to confidential information, such as changes in recommendations and information regarding block trades, Smith provided Garcia the opportunity to front-run, which could cause harm to both Omega and its clients. Thus, Smith's actions violated his duty of loyalty, prudence, and care to his clients and his duty of loyalty to his employer, Standards III(A) and IV(A), respectively.

34. B is correct. Garcia violated Standard I: Professionalism by engaging in eavesdropping on confidential information, including changes in analyst recommendations and pending block trades. According to Standard I(D) Misconduct,

members must not engage in professional conduct involving dishonesty, deceit, or fraud or commit any act that reflects adversely on their professional reputation, integrity, or competence. Garcia engaged in deceitful conduct in obtaining information from the squawk box. His actions reflect adversely on his professional reputation and integrity and thus violated Standard I(D). Although he listened to the material nonpublic information on pending block trades, Garcia is not in violation of Standard II(A) Material Nonpublic Information because he did not act on it. Possession of such material nonpublic information is not a violation of the standard, but acting on the information is.

35. C is correct. Garcia was in possession of material nonpublic information and acted on it, in violation of Standard II(A). After the analyst's recommendation has been issued and/or distributed publicly, Garcia would be free to make the trade. Because this is a personal purchase, the standard relating to diligence and reasonable basis is not applicable.

36. C is correct. According to Standard IV(B) Additional Compensation Arrangements, members must not accept compensation that competes with their employer's interest unless they obtain written consent from all parties involved. Thus, Riser must receive written, not verbal, consent from his employer before accepting the position on the subsidiary's board. According to the recommended procedures for compliance, Riser should make an immediate written report to his employer specifying the terms of the agreement, the nature of the compensation, the approximate amount of the compensation, and the duration of the agreement. The Standards do not require that members receive permission from clients before accepting board positions.

37. C is correct. Riser least likely violated Standard IV(B) Additional Compensation Arrangements when participating in the road shows. Standard IV(B) provides guidance regarding the acceptance and disclosure of compensation that might conflict with an employer's interests. Participating in the road shows and receiving compensation from the subsidiary do not appear to conflict with his employer's interests.

    When participating in the road shows, Riser may have violated Standard I(B) Independence and Objectivity and Standard VI(A) Avoid or Disclose Conflicts. Standard I(B) requires that members use reasonable care and judgment to achieve and maintain independence and objectivity in their professional activities. Riser's role as board member could jeopardize his objectivity and create a conflict of interest. Standard VI(A) requires that members avoid or make full and fair disclosure of all matters that could reasonably be expected to impair their independence and objectivity or interfere with respective duties to their clients, prospective clients, and employer. Full disclosure allows clients to judge motives and possible biases for themselves. Since Riser did not avoid the conflict, Standard VI(A) requires disclosure and Riser does not appear to have made adequate disclosure.

38. C is correct. Standard VI(A) requires all conflicts to be avoided or disclosed. Although Riser's recommendation may be based solely on his knowledge of the firm's track record, his prior relationship with Komm, including the job offer, is a conflict and must be disclosed so the subsidiary will have all the information needed to evaluate the objectivity of his recommendation.

39. A is correct. No violation occurred. Riser is not required to resign his position with the subsidiary. Riser did not engage in any activities that would conflict with his employer's interest before his resignation became effective.

40. A is correct. Riser least likely violated Standard III(C) Suitability when purchas-

ing shares for his own account. Riser may, however, have violated Standard II(A) Material Nonpublic Information and Standard VI(B) Priority of Transactions when making the purchase. If, when trading for his own account, Riser knew that he will place a large block trade for Komm Private Management clients, he may have been in possession of material nonpublic information. Standard VI(B) covers the activities of all members who have knowledge of pending transactions that may be made on behalf of their clients or employers. Riser has accepted the position of managing partner, has recommended the manager for the product, and knew or should have known that he will purchase the product for at least some Komm Private Management clients once he begins work at Komm. His purchase ahead of Komm Private Management's clients might be front-running. Best practice would be to delay his private account purchase until after he purchases shares for clients.

41. C is correct. Standard VI(A) Avoid or Disclose Conflicts states that "Members and Candidates must avoid or make full and fair disclosure of all matters that could reasonably be expected to impair their independence and objectivity or interfere with respective duties to their clients, prospective clients, and employer." Riser's holdings of the Japanese equity product and his position on the board of the subsidiary could impair his objectivity. Each conflict must be avoided or disclosed to clients. He need not disclose his compensation from the subsidiary, because it is not a referral fee.

42. A is correct. Both the first and second presentations are consistent with the CFA Institute Code and Standards. According to the Standards, candidates may reference their participation in the CFA Program as long as they are active, but they cannot imply a partial designation. A statement about the level of the exam successfully passed or a level of the exam upcoming is appropriate, whereas indicating or implying a partial designation or citing a future date of expected completion of a level in the CFA Program is prohibited.

43. A is correct. Danko directed his trading with FTI only after taking into account FTI's ability to provide best execution. There is no indication that FTI requires a certain amount of trading for access to the website, only that access is provided in exchange for orders. This arrangement for trading in return for research services is discussed in the guidance for Standard III(A) Loyalty, Prudence, and Care.

44. C is correct. The information that Danko received is material nonpublic information. Disclosing the information to the public is not his role. Further, earning gains for his clients does not excuse the violation and is not a justifiable reason for taking action on the material nonpublic information. The only entities that should release the information are the corporations or another entity with their permission, perhaps FTI.

45. B is correct. Investment decision making based on speed or on third-party research alone is insufficient for meeting Standard V(A) Diligence and Reasonable Basis.

46. A is correct. When an issue is oversubscribed, allocations cannot be made to accounts where members and candidates have beneficial interest; client orders must be filled first.

47. A is correct. A blackout period is appropriate for investment decision-making personnel so that managers do not take advantage of their knowledge of trading activity and "front-run" the trade. The actual detail of the blackout period is not specified in the Standards, only that one should exist.

LEARNING MODULE

4

Asset Manager Code of Professional Conduct

by Kurt N. Schacht, JD, CFA, Jonathan J. Stokes, JD, and Glenn Doggett, CFA.

Kurt N. Schacht, JD, CFA, is at CFA Institute (USA). Jonathan J. Stokes, JD, is at CFA Institute (USA). Glenn Doggett, CFA, is at CFA Institute (USA).

LEARNING OUTCOMES

Mastery	*The candidate should be able to:*
☐	explain the purpose of the Asset Manager Code and the benefits that may accrue to a firm that adopts the Code
☐	explain the ethical and professional responsibilities required by the six General Principles of Conduct of the Asset Manager Code
☐	determine whether an asset manager's practices and procedures are consistent with the Asset Manager Code
☐	recommend practices and procedures designed to prevent violations of the Asset Manager Code

INTRODUCTION, ADOPTING THE CODE AND CLAIMING COMPLIANCE 1

☐	explain the purpose of the Asset Manager Code and the benefits that may accrue to a firm that adopts the Code

Asset managers hold a unique place of trust in the lives of millions of investors. Investment professionals and firms that undertake and perform their responsibilities with honesty and integrity are critical to maintaining investors' trust and confidence and to upholding the client covenant of trust, loyalty, prudence, and care. CFA Institute and its members are committed to reinforcing those principles. The CFA Institute mission is to lead the investment profession globally by setting the highest standards of ethics, education, and professional excellence. To foster this culture of ethics and professionalism, CFA Institute offers this voluntary code of conduct. It is designed to be broadly adopted within the industry as a template and guidepost for investors seeking managers who adhere to sound ethical practice.

The Asset Manager Code of Professional Conduct outlines the ethical and professional responsibilities of firms that manage assets on behalf of clients. Whereas the CFA Institute Code of Ethics and Standards of Professional Conduct address individual conduct, this Code is meant to apply, on a global basis, to firms that manage client assets as separate accounts or pooled funds (including collective investment schemes, mutual funds, and fund of funds organizations); we refer to such firms as "Managers." In part, this document responds to requests from Managers to extend the scope of the Code and Standards to the firm level. Although many institutional asset managers, particularly those in well-regulated jurisdictions, already have such a code in place, they should use this Code to evaluate their own code and ensure that all of this Code's principles have been included. This Code also has been developed for use by asset managers, including hedge fund managers, who may not already have such a code in place. This second edition of the Code includes provisions relating to risk management as well as guidance for Managers seeking to claim compliance.

Ethical leadership begins at the highest level of an organization; therefore, the Code should be adopted by the Manager's senior management, board of directors, and similar oversight bodies. Such adoption sends a strong message regarding the importance of ethical behavior at the firm. Rather than creating rules that apply only to certain people or groups, this Code is intended to cover all employees of the firm. Although not every employee is actively involved in conduct covered in the Code, a code that is broadly applied reinforces the need for all employees to understand the ethical issues involved in the asset management business. By adopting and enforcing a code of conduct for their organizations, Managers demonstrate their commitment to ethical behavior and the protection of investors' interests. In doing so, the Managers also protect and enhance the reputation of their organizations.

The Code sets forth minimum ethical standards for providing asset management services for clients. It is meant to be general in nature and allows flexibility for asset managers of various sizes and structures to develop the particular policies and procedures necessary to implement the Code. The goal of this Code is to set forth a useful framework for all asset managers to provide services in a fair and professional manner and to fully disclose key elements of those services to clients, regardless of whether individual Managers are required to register or comply with applicable securities laws or regulations. Unregistered hedge fund managers, in particular, are encouraged to adopt the Code and implement its provisions to ensure fair dealing and integrity and to promote self-regulation in this dynamic sector.

We recognize that in the highly regulated and complex business of investment management, the adoption of a code of ethics by itself is not sufficient to ensure ethical conduct. To be implemented effectively, the principles and standards embodied in the Code must be supported by appropriate compliance procedures. The specific procedures that translate principle into practice will depend on a variety of factors, including the business of the Manager, the type of clients, the size of the Manager (based on assets under management and on number of employees), the regulatory régime with which the Manager must comply, and other factors.

Managers must adhere to all applicable laws and regulations governing their activities. Thus, the provisions of this Code may need to be supplemented with additional provisions to meet the requirements of applicable security regulation in markets around the world. Inevitably, in some markets, the Code will closely reflect or be aligned with existing regulation or accepted best practice and in other markets, the Code will expand on the existing work of regulatory authorities or may even break new ground. Furthermore, Managers operate in different types of market structures, which may affect the manner in which the Code can be applied. Despite these differences, the Code provides a universal set of principles and standards relevant to all asset managers.

Clients have a responsibility to be aware of, understand, and monitor how their assets are invested. Yet, to fulfill this responsibility, clients must be able to count on full and fair disclosure from their Managers. Providing clients with a code of ethics that sets a framework for how the Manager conducts business is an important step toward developing the trust and confidence necessary for a successful investment management relationship.

Adopting the Code and Claiming Compliance

Adoption of or compliance with the Asset Manager Code of Professional Conduct requires firms to adhere to all the principles of conduct and provisions set forth in the Code. Many asset management firms already have codes of ethics and other policies and procedures that address or go beyond the principles and provisions of the Code. Adoption of or compliance with the Code does not require a firm to amend its existing code of ethics or other policies and procedures as long as they are at least consistent with the principles and provisions set forth in the Code. Managers are strongly encouraged to review and consider the material in the Appendix when developing and reviewing their codes and other policies and procedures, although because of the many variables in size and complexity among asset management firms, compliance with the Code does not require strict adherence to this guidance.

If the Manager has not complied with each of the principles of conduct and provisions of the Code, the Manager cannot represent that it is in compliance with the Code. Statements referring to partial or incomplete compliance (e.g., "the firm complies with the Asset Manager Code *except for* . . ." or "the firm complies with parts A, B, and C of the Asset Manager Code") are prohibited.

Once a Manager has met each of the required elements of the Code, the firm must make the following statement whenever the firm claims compliance with the Code:

> "[Insert name of Firm] claims compliance with the CFA Institute Asset Manager Code of Professional Conduct. This claim has not been verified by CFA Institute."

Acknowledgement of Claim of Compliance to CFA Institute

Managers also must notify CFA Institute of their claim of compliance with the Asset Manager Code of Professional Conduct through the CFA Institute online notification process at www.cfainstitute.org/assetcode. This acknowledgement form is for communication and information-gathering purposes only and does not represent that CFA Institute engages in enforcement or quality control of an organization's claim of compliance. CFA Institute does not verify either the Manager's claim of compliance or actual compliance with the Code.

GENERAL PRINCIPLES OF CONDUCT AND ASSET MANAGER CODE OF PROFESSIONAL CONDUCT 2

☐ explain the ethical and professional responsibilities required by the six General Principles of Conduct of the Asset Manager Code

Managers have the following responsibilities to their clients. Managers must:

1. Act in a professional and ethical manner at all times.
2. Act for the benefit of clients.
3. Act with independence and objectivity.
4. Act with skill, competence, and diligence.
5. Communicate with clients in a timely and accurate manner.
6. Uphold the applicable rules governing capital markets.

Asset Manager Code of Professional Conduct

A. Loyalty to Clients

Managers must:

1. Place client interests before their own.
2. Preserve the confidentiality of information communicated by clients within the scope of the Manager–client relationship.
3. Refuse to participate in any business relationship or accept any gift that could reasonably be expected to affect their independence, objectivity, or loyalty to clients.

B. Investment Process and Actions

Managers must:

1. Use reasonable care and prudent judgment when managing client assets.
2. Not engage in practices designed to distort prices or artificially inflate trading volume with the intent to mislead market participants.
3. Deal fairly and objectively with all clients when providing investment information, making investment recommendations, or taking investment action.
4. Have a reasonable and adequate basis for investment decisions.
5. When managing a portfolio or pooled fund according to a specific mandate, strategy, or style:

   a. Take only investment actions that are consistent with the stated objectives and constraints of that portfolio or fund.

   b. Provide adequate disclosures and information so investors can consider whether any proposed changes in the investment style or strategy meet their investment needs.

6. When managing separate accounts and before providing investment advice or taking investment action on behalf of the client:

   a. Evaluate and understand the client's investment objectives, tolerance for risk, time horizon, liquidity needs, financial constraints, any unique circumstances (including tax considerations, legal or regulatory constraints, etc.) and any other relevant information that would affect investment policy.

   b. Determine that an investment is suitable to a client's financial situation.

C. Trading

Managers must:

1. Not act or cause others to act on material nonpublic information that could affect the value of a publicly traded investment.
2. Give priority to investments made on behalf of the client over those that benefit the Managers' own interests.
3. Use commissions generated from client trades to pay for only investment-related products or services that directly assist the Manager in its investment decision making process, and not in the management of the firm.
4. Maximize client portfolio value by seeking best execution for all client transactions.
5. Establish policies to ensure fair and equitable trade allocation among client accounts.

D. Risk Management, Compliance, and Support

Managers must:

1. Develop and maintain policies and procedures to ensure that their activities comply with the provisions of this Code and all applicable legal and regulatory requirements.
2. Appoint a compliance officer responsible for administering the policies and procedures and for investigating complaints regarding the conduct of the Manager or its personnel.
3. Ensure that portfolio information provided to clients by the Manager is accurate and complete and arrange for independent third-party confirmation or review of such information.
4. Maintain records for an appropriate period of time in an easily accessible format.
5. Employ qualified staff and sufficient human and technological resources to thoroughly investigate, analyze, implement, and monitor investment decisions and actions.
6. Establish a business-continuity plan to address disaster recovery or periodic disruptions of the financial markets.
7. Establish a firmwide risk management process that identifies, measures, and manages the risk position of the Manager and its investments, including the sources, nature, and degree of risk exposure.

E. Performance and Valuation

Managers must:

1. Present performance information that is fair, accurate, relevant, timely, and complete. Managers must not misrepresent the performance of individual portfolios or of their firm.
2. Use fair-market prices to value client holdings and apply, in good faith, methods to determine the fair value of any securities for which no independent, third-party market quotation is readily available.

F. Disclosures

Managers must:

1. Communicate with clients on an ongoing and timely basis.
2. Ensure that disclosures are truthful, accurate, complete, and understandable and are presented in a format that communicates the information effectively.
3. Include any material facts when making disclosures or providing information to clients regarding themselves, their personnel, investments, or the investment process.
4. Disclose the following:
   a. Conflicts of interests generated by any relationships with brokers or other entities, other client accounts, fee structures, or other matters.
   b. Regulatory or disciplinary action taken against the Manager or its personnel related to professional conduct.
   c. The investment process, including information regarding lock-up periods, strategies, risk factors, and use of derivatives and leverage.
   d. Management fees and other investment costs charged to investors, including what costs are included in the fees and the methodologies for determining fees and costs.
   e. The amount of any soft or bundled commissions, the goods and/or services received in return, and how those goods and/or services benefit the client.
   f. The performance of clients' investments on a regular and timely basis.
   g. Valuation methods used to make investment decisions and value client holdings.
   h. Shareholder voting policies.
   i. Trade allocation policies.
   j. Results of the review or audit of the fund or account.
   k. Significant personnel or organizational changes that have occurred at the Manager.
   l. Risk management processes.

3 APPENDIX 6: A. LOYALTY TO CLIENTS

- ☐ determine whether an asset manager's practices and procedures are consistent with the Asset Manager Code
- ☐ recommend practices and procedures designed to prevent violations of the Asset Manager Code

Appendix 6—Recommendations and Guidance

Adoption of the Code is insufficient by itself for a Manager to meet its ethical and regulatory responsibilities. Managers must adopt detailed policies and procedures to effectively implement the Code. This section provides guidance explaining the Code and includes recommendations and illustrative examples to assist Managers that are seeking to implement the Code. These examples are not meant to be exhaustive, and the policies and procedures needed to support the Code will depend on the particular circumstances of each organization and the legal and regulatory environment in which the Manager operates.

The following guidance highlights particular issues that Managers should consider when developing their internal policies and procedures that accompany the Code. The guidance is not intended to cover all issues or aspects of a Manager's operations that would have to be included in such policies and procedures to fully implement and support the Code.

A. Loyalty to Clients

Managers must:

1. **Place client interests before their own.**

   Client interests are paramount. Managers should institute policies and procedures to ensure that client interests supersede Manager interests in all aspects of the Manager–client relationship, including (but not limited to) investment selection, transactions, monitoring, and custody. Managers should take reasonable steps to avoid situations in which the Manager's interests and client interests conflict and should institute operational safeguards to protect client interests. Managers should implement compensation arrangements that align the financial interests of clients and Managers and avoid incentives that could result in Managers taking action in conflict with client interests.

2. **Preserve the confidentiality of information communicated by clients within the scope of the Manager–client relationship.**

   As part of their ethical duties, Managers must hold information communicated to them by clients or other sources within the context of the Manager–client relationship strictly confidential and must take all reasonable measures to preserve that confidentiality. This duty applies when Managers obtain information on the basis of their confidential relationship with the client or their special ability to conduct a portion of the client's business or personal affairs. Managers should create a privacy policy that addresses how confidential client information will be collected, stored, protected, and used.

   The duty to maintain confidentiality does not supersede a duty (and in some cases the legal requirement) to report suspected illegal activities involving client accounts to the appropriate authorities. Where appropriate, Managers should consider creating and implementing a written anti-money-laundering policy to prevent their organizations from being used for money laundering or the financing of any illegal activities.

3. **Refuse to participate in any business relationship or accept any gift that could reasonably be expected to affect their independence, objectivity, or loyalty to clients.**

As part of holding clients' interests paramount, Managers must establish policies for accepting gifts or entertainment in a variety of contexts. To avoid the appearance of a conflict, Managers must refuse to accept gifts or entertainment from service providers, potential investment targets, or other business partners of more than a minimal value. Managers should define what the minimum value is and should confer with local regulations which may also establish limits.

Managers should establish a written policy limiting the acceptance of gifts and entertainment to items of minimal value. Managers should consider creating specific limits for accepting gifts (e.g., amount per time period per vendor) and prohibit the acceptance of any cash gifts. Employees should be required to document and disclose to the Manager, through their supervisor, the firm's compliance office, or senior management, the acceptance of any gift or entertainment.

This provision is not meant to preclude Managers from maintaining multiple business relationships with a client as long as potential conflicts of interest are managed and disclosed.

4 APPENDIX 6: B. INVESTMENT PROCESS AND ACTIONS

- ☐ determine whether an asset manager's practices and procedures are consistent with the Asset Manager Code
- ☐ recommend practices and procedures designed to prevent violations of the Asset Manager Code

Managers must:

1. **Use reasonable care and prudent judgment when managing client assets.**

   Managers must exhibit the care and prudence necessary to meet their obligations to clients. Prudence requires caution and discretion. The exercise of prudence requires acting with the care, skill, and diligence that a person acting in a like capacity and familiar with such matters would use under the same circumstances. In the context of managing a client's portfolio, prudence requires following the investment parameters set forth by the client and balancing risk and return. Acting with care requires Managers to act in a prudent and judicious manner in avoiding harm to clients.

2. **Not engage in practices designed to distort prices or artificially inflate trading volume with the intent to mislead market participants.**

   Market manipulation is illegal in most jurisdictions and damages the interests of all investors by disrupting the efficient functioning of financial markets and causing deterioration in investor confidence.

   Market manipulation includes practices that distort security prices or values or artificially inflate trading volumes with the intent to deceive persons or entities that rely on information in the market. Such practices may involve, for example, transactions that deceive market participants by distorting the price-setting mechanism of financial instruments and the dissemination of false or misleading information. Transaction-based manipulation includes, but is not limited to, transactions that artificially distort prices or volume to give the impression of activity or price movement in a financial instrument (e.g., trading in illiquid stocks at the end of a measurement period to drive up the price and improve Manager performance) and securing a large position with the intent to exploit and manipulate the price of an asset and/or a related derivative. Information-based manipulation includes, but is not limited to, spreading knowingly false rumors to induce trading by others and pressuring sell-side analysts to rate or recommend a security in such a way that benefits the Manager or the Manager's clients.

3. **Deal fairly and objectively with all clients when providing investment information, making investment recommendations, or taking investment action.**

   To maintain the trust that clients place in them, Managers must deal with all clients in a fair and objective manner. Managers must not give preferential treatment to favored clients to the detriment of other clients. In some cases, clients may pay for a higher level of service or certain services and certain products may only be made available to certain qualifying clients (e.g., certain funds may be open only to clients with assets above a certain level). These practices are permitted as long as they are disclosed and made available to all clients.

   This provision is not intended to prevent Managers from engaging in secondary investment opportunities—referred to in some jurisdictions as "side-letter," "sidecar," or "tag-along" arrangements—with certain clients as long as such opportunities are fairly allocated among similarly situated clients for whom the opportunity is suitable.

4. **Have a reasonable and adequate basis for investment decisions.**

   Managers must act with prudence and make sure their decisions have a reasonable and adequate basis. Prior to taking action on behalf of their clients, Managers must analyze the investment opportunities in question and should act only after undertaking due diligence to ensure there is sufficient knowledge about specific investments or strategies. Such analysis will depend on the style and strategy being used. For example, a Manager implementing a passive strategy will have a very different basis for investment actions from that of a Manager that uses an active strategy.

   Managers can rely on external third-party research as long as Managers have made reasonable and diligent efforts to determine that such research has a reasonable basis. When evaluating investment research, Managers should consider the assumptions used, the thoroughness of the analysis performed, the timeliness of the information, and the objectivity and independence of the source.

   Managers should have a thorough understanding of the securities in which they invest and the strategies they use on behalf of clients. Managers should understand the structure and function of the securities, how they are traded, their liquidity, and any other risks (including counterparty risk).

   Managers who implement complex and sophisticated investment strategies should understand the structure and potential vulnerabilities of such strategies and communicate these in an understandable manner to their clients. For example, when implementing complex derivative strategies, Managers should understand the various risks and conduct statistical analysis (i.e., stress testing) to determine how the strategy will perform under different conditions. By undertaking adequate due diligence, Managers can better judge the suitability of investments for their clients.

5. **When managing a portfolio or pooled fund according to a specific mandate, strategy, or style:**

    a. **Take only investment actions that are consistent with the stated objectives and constraints of that portfolio or fund.**

    When Managers are given a specific mandate by clients or offer a product, such as a pooled fund for which the Managers do not know the specific financial situation of each client, the Managers must manage the funds or portfolios within the stated mandates or strategies. Clients need to be able to evaluate the suitability of the investment funds or strategies for themselves. Subsequently, they must be able to trust that Managers will not diverge from the stated or agreed-on mandates or strategies. When market events or opportunities change to such a degree that Managers wish to have flexibility to take advantage of those occurrences, such flexibility is not improper but should be expressly understood and agreed to by Managers and clients. Best practice is for Managers to disclose such events to clients when they occur or, at the very least, in the course of normal client reporting.

    b. **Provide adequate disclosures and information so investors can consider whether any proposed changes in the investment style or strategy meet their investment needs.**

    To give clients an opportunity to evaluate the suitability of investments, Managers need to provide adequate information to them about any proposed material changes to their investment strategies or styles. They must provide this information well in advance of such changes. Clients should be given enough time to consider the proposed changes and take any actions that may be necessary. If the Manager decides to make a material change in the investment strategy or style, clients should be permitted to redeem their investment, if desired, without incurring any undue penalties.

6. **When managing separate accounts and before providing investment advice or taking investment action on behalf of the client:**

    a. **Evaluate and understand the client's investment objectives, tolerance for risk, time horizon, liquidity needs, financial constraints, any unique circumstances (including tax considerations, legal or regulatory constraints, etc.) and any other relevant information that would affect investment policy.**

    Prior to taking any investment actions for clients, Managers must take the necessary steps to understand and evaluate the client's financial situation, constraints, and other relevant factors. Without understanding the client's situation, the Manager cannot select and implement an appropriate investment strategy. Ideally, each client will have an investment policy statement (IPS) that includes a discussion of risk tolerances (both the ability and willingness of the client to bear risk), return objectives, time horizon, liquidity requirements, liabilities, tax considerations, and any legal, regulatory, or other unique circumstances.

The purpose of the IPS is to provide Managers with written strategic plans to direct investment decisions for each client. The Manager should take an opportunity to review the IPS for each client, offer any suggestions on clarifying the IPS, and discuss with the client the various techniques and strategies to be used to meet the client's investment goals. Managers should review each client's IPS with the client at least annually and whenever circumstances suggest changes may be needed.

The information contained in an IPS allows Managers to assess whether a particular strategy or security is suitable for a client (in the context of the rest of the client's portfolio), and the IPS serves as the basis for establishing the client's strategic asset allocation. (Note: In some cases, the client will determine the strategic asset allocation; in other cases, that duty will be delegated to the Manager). The IPS should also specify the Manager's role and responsibilities in managing the client's assets and establish schedules for review and evaluation. The Manager should reach agreement with the client as to an appropriate benchmark or benchmarks by which the Manager's performance will be measured and any other details of the performance evaluation process (e.g., when performance measurement should begin).

b. **Determine that an investment is suitable to a client's financial situation.**

Managers must evaluate investment actions and strategies in light of each client's circumstances. Not all investments are suitable for every client, and Managers have a responsibility to ensure that only appropriate investments and investment strategies are included in a client's portfolio. Ideally, individual investments should be evaluated in the context of clients' total assets and liabilities, which may include assets held outside of the Manager's account, to the extent that such information is made available to the Manager and is explicitly included in the context of the client's IPS.

APPENDIX 6: C. TRADING

5

- ☐ determine whether an asset manager's practices and procedures are consistent with the Asset Manager Code
- ☐ recommend practices and procedures designed to prevent violations of the Asset Manager Code

Managers must:

1. **Not act or cause others to act on material nonpublic information that could affect the value of a publicly traded investment.**

Trading on material nonpublic information, which is illegal in most jurisdictions, erodes confidence in capital markets, institutions, and investment professionals and promotes the perception that those with inside and special access can take unfair advantage of the general investing public. Although trading on such information may lead to short-term profitability, over time, individuals and the profession as a whole suffer if investors avoid capital markets because they perceive them to be unfair by favoring the knowledgeable insider.

Different jurisdictions and regulatory regimes may define materiality differently, but in general, information is "material" if it is likely that a reasonable investor would consider it important and if it would be viewed as significantly altering the total mix of information available. Information is "nonpublic" until it has been widely disseminated to the marketplace (as opposed to a select group of investors).

Managers must adopt compliance procedures, such as establishing information barriers (e.g., fire walls), to prevent the disclosure and misuse of material nonpublic information. In many cases, pending trades or client or fund holdings may be considered material nonpublic information, and Managers must be sure to keep such information confidential. In addition, merger and acquisition information, prior to its public disclosure, is generally considered material nonpublic information. Managers should evaluate company-specific information that they may receive and determine whether it meets the definition of material nonpublic information.

This provision is not meant to prevent Managers from using the mosaic theory to draw conclusions—that is, combine pieces of material public information with pieces of nonmaterial nonpublic information to draw conclusions that are actionable.

2. **Give priority to investments made on behalf of the client over those that benefit the Managers' own interests.**

   Managers must not execute their own trades in a security prior to client transactions in the same security. Investment activities that benefit the Manager must not adversely affect client interests. Managers must not engage in trading activities that work to the disadvantage of clients (e.g., front-running client trades).

   In some investment arrangements, such as limited partnerships or pooled funds, Managers put their own capital at risk alongside that of their clients to align their interests with the interests of their clients. These arrangements are permissible only if clients are not disadvantaged.

   Managers should develop policies and procedures to monitor and, where appropriate, limit the personal trading of their employees. In particular, Managers should require employees to receive approval prior to any personal investments in initial public offerings or private placements. Managers should develop policies and processes designed to ensure that client transactions take precedence over employee or firm transactions. One method is to create a restricted list and/or watch list of securities that are owned in client accounts or may be bought or sold on behalf of clients in the near future; prior to trading securities on such a list, employees would be required to seek approval. In addition, Managers could require employees to provide the compliance officer with copies of trade confirmations each quarter and annual statements of personal holdings.

3. **Use commissions generated from client trades to pay for only investment-related products or services that directly assist the Manager in its investment decision-making process, and not in the management of the firm.**

Managers must recognize that commissions paid (and any benefits received in return for commissions paid) are the property of the client. Consequently, any benefits offered in return for commissions must benefit the Manager's clients.

To determine whether a benefit generated from client commissions is appropriate, Managers must determine whether it will directly assist in the Manager's investment decision-making process. The investment decision-making process can be considered the qualitative and quantitative process and the related tools used by the Manager in rendering investment advice to clients. The process includes financial analysis, trading and risk analysis, securities selection, broker selection, asset allocation, and suitability analysis.

Some Managers have chosen to eliminate the use of soft commissions (also known as soft dollars) to avoid any conflicts of interest that may exist. Managers should disclose their policy on how benefits are evaluated and used for the client's benefit. If Managers choose to use a soft commission or bundled brokerage arrangement, they should disclose this use to their clients. Managers should consider complying with industry best practices regarding the use and reporting of such an arrangement, which can be found in the CFA Institute Soft Dollar Standards.

4. **Maximize client portfolio value by seeking best execution for all client transactions.**

   When placing client trades, Managers have a duty to seek terms that secure best execution for and maximize the value of each client's portfolio (i.e., ensure the best possible result overall). Managers must seek the most favorable terms for client trades within each trades' particular circumstances (such as transaction size, market characteristics, liquidity of security, and security type). Managers also must decide which brokers or venues provide best execution while considering, among other things, commission rates, timeliness of trade executions, and the ability to maintain anonymity, minimize incomplete trades, and minimize market impact.

   When a client directs the Manager to place trades through a specific broker or through a particular type of broker, Managers should alert the client that by limiting the Manager's ability to select the broker, the client may not be receiving best execution. The Manager should seek written acknowledgment from the client of receiving this information.

5. **Establish policies to ensure fair and equitable trade allocation among client accounts.**

   When placing trades for client accounts, Managers must allocate trades fairly so that some client accounts are not routinely traded first or receive preferential treatment. Where possible, Managers should use block trades and allocate shares on a pro-rata basis by using an average price or some other method that ensures fair and equitable allocations. When allocating shares of an initial or secondary offering, Managers should strive to ensure that all clients for whom the security is suitable are given opportunities to participate. When Managers do not receive a large enough allocation to allow all eligible clients to participate fully in a particular offering, they must ensure that certain clients are not given preferential treatment and should establish a system to ensure that new issues are allocated fairly (e.g., pro rata). Manager's trade allocation policies should specifically address how initial public offerings and private placements are to be handled.

6 APPENDIX 6: D. RISK MANAGEMENT, COMPLIANCE AND SUPPORT

- ☐ determine whether an asset manager's practices and procedures are consistent with the Asset Manager Code
- ☐ recommend practices and procedures designed to prevent violations of the Asset Manager Code

Managers must:

1. **Develop and maintain policies and procedures to ensure that their activities comply with the provisions of this Code and all applicable legal and regulatory requirements.**

   Detailed and firmwide compliance policies and procedures are critical tools to ensure that Managers meet their legal requirements when managing client assets. In addition, the fundamental, principle-based, ethical concepts embodied in the Code should be put into operation by the implementation of specific policies and procedures.

   Documented compliance procedures assist Managers in fulfilling the responsibilities enumerated in the Code and ensure that the standards expressed in the Code are adhered to in the day-to-day operation of the firms. The appropriate compliance programs, internal controls, and self-assessment tools for each Manager will depend on such factors as the size of the firm and the nature of its investment management business.

2. **Appoint a compliance officer responsible for administering the policies and procedures and for investigating complaints regarding the conduct of the Manager or its personnel.**

   Effective compliance programs require Managers to appoint a compliance officer who is competent, knowledgeable, and credible and is empowered to carry out his or her duties. Depending on the size and complexity of the Manager's operations, Managers may designate an existing employee to also serve as the compliance officer, may hire a separate individual for that role, or may establish an entire compliance department. Where possible, the compliance officer should be independent from the investment and operations personnel and should report directly to the CEO or board of directors.

   The compliance officer and senior management should regularly make clear to all employees that adherence to compliance policies and procedures is crucial and that anyone who violates them will be held liable. Managers should consider requiring all employees to acknowledge that they have received a copy of the Code (as well as any subsequent material amendments), that they understand and agree to comply with it, and that they will report any suspected violations of the Code to the designated compliance officer. Compliance officers should take steps to implement appropriate employee training and conduct continuing self-evaluation of the Manager's compliance practices to assess the effectiveness of the practices.

Among other things, the compliance officer should be charged with reviewing firm and employee transactions to ensure the priority of client interests. Because personnel, regulations, business practices, and products constantly change, the role of the compliance officer (particularly the role of keeping the firm up to date on such matters) is particularly important.

The compliance officer should document and act expeditiously to address any compliance breaches and work with management to take appropriate disciplinary action.

3. **Ensure that portfolio information provided to clients by the Manager is accurate and complete and arrange for independent third-party confirmation or review of such information.**

   Managers have a responsibility to ensure that the information they provide to clients is accurate and complete. By receiving an independent third-party confirmation or review of that information, clients have an additional level of confidence that the information is correct, which may enhance the Manager's credibility. Such verification is also good business practice because it may serve as a risk management tool to help the Manager identify potential problems. The confirmation of portfolio information may take the form of an audit or review, as is the case with most pooled vehicles, or may take the form of copies of account statements and trade confirmations from the custodian bank where the client assets are held.

4. **Maintain records for an appropriate period of time in an easily accessible format.**

   Managers must retain records that substantiate their investment activities, the scope of their research, the basis for their conclusions, and the reasons for actions taken on behalf of their clients. Managers should also retain copies of other compliance-related records that support and substantiate the implementation of the Code and related policies and procedures, as well as records of any violations and resulting actions taken. Records can be maintained either in hard copy or electronic form.

   Regulators often impose requirements related to record retention. In the absence of such regulation, Managers must determine the appropriate minimum time frame for keeping the organization's records. Unless otherwise required by local law or regulation Managers should keep records for at least seven years.

5. **Employ qualified staff and sufficient human and technological resources to thoroughly investigate, analyze, implement, and monitor investment decisions and actions.**

   To safeguard the Manager–client relationship, Managers need to allocate all the resources necessary to ensure that client interests are not compromised. Clients pay significant sums to Managers for professional asset management services, and client assets should be handled with the greatest possible care.

   Managers of all sizes and investment styles struggle with issues of cost and efficiency and tend to be cautious about adding staff in important operational areas. Nevertheless, adequate protection of client assets requires appropriate administrative, back-office, and compliance support. Managers should ensure that adequate internal controls are in place to prevent fraudulent behavior.

   A critical consideration is employing only *qualified* staff. Managers must ensure that client assets are invested, administered, and protected by qualified and experienced staff. Employing qualified staff reflects a client-first attitude and helps ensure that Managers are applying the care and prudence necessary to meet their obligations to clients. This provision is not meant to prohibit the outsourcing of certain functions, but the Manager retains the liability and responsibility for any outsourced work.

Managers have a responsibility to clients to deliver the actual services they claim to offer. Managers must use adequate resources to carry out the necessary research and analysis to implement their investment strategies with due diligence and care. Also, Managers must have adequate resources to monitor the portfolio holdings and investment strategies. As investment strategies and instruments become increasingly sophisticated, the need for sufficient resources to analyze and monitor them becomes ever more important.

6. **Establish a business-continuity plan to address disaster recovery or periodic disruptions of the financial markets.**

   Part of safeguarding client interests is establishing procedures for handling client accounts and inquiries in situations of national, regional, or local emergency or market disruption. Commonly referred to as business-continuity or disaster-recovery planning, such preparation is increasingly important in an industry and world highly susceptible to a wide variety of disasters and disruptions.

   The level and complexity of business-continuity planning depends on the size, nature, and complexity of the organization. At a minimum, Managers should consider having the following:

   - adequate backup, preferably off-site, for all account information;
   - alternative plans for monitoring, analyzing, and trading investments if primary systems become unavailable;
   - plans for communicating with critical vendors and suppliers;
   - plans for employee communication and coverage of critical business functions in the event of a facility or communication disruption; and
   - plans for contacting and communicating with clients during a period of extended disruption.

   Numerous other factors may need to be considered when creating the plan. According to the needs of the organization, these factors may include establishing backup office and operational space in the event of an extended disruption and dealing with key employee deaths or departures.

   As with any important business planning, Managers should ensure that employees and staff are knowledgeable about the plan and are specifically trained in areas of responsibility. Plans should be tested on a firmwide basis at intervals to promote employee understanding and identify any needed adjustments.

7. **Establish a firmwide risk management process that identifies, measures, and manages the risk position of the Manager and its investments, including the sources, nature, and degree of risk exposure.**

   Many investors, including those investing in hedge funds and alternative investments or leveraged strategies, invest specifically to increase their risk-adjusted returns. Assuming some risk is a necessary part of that process. The key to sound risk management by Managers is seeking to ensure that the risk profile desired by clients matches the risk profile of their investments. Risk management should complement rather than compete with the investment management process. Investment managers must implement risk management techniques that are consistent with their investment style and philosophy.

The types of risks faced by Managers include, but are not limited to, market risk, credit risk, liquidity risk, counterparty risk, concentration risk, and various types of operational risk. Such types of risks should be analyzed by Managers as part of a comprehensive risk management process for portfolios, investment strategies, and the firm. These examples are illustrative only and may not be applicable to all investment organizations.

Although portfolio managers consider risk issues as part of formulating an investment strategy, the firm's risk management process must be objective, independent, and insulated from influence of portfolio managers. Managers may wish to describe to clients how the risk management framework complements the portfolio management process while remaining separate from that process. Managers should consider outsourcing risk management activities if a separate risk management function is not appropriate or feasible because of the size of the organization.

An effective risk management process will identify risk factors for individual portfolios as well as for the Manager's activities as whole. It will often be appropriate for managers to perform stress tests, scenario tests, and backtests as part of developing risk models that comprehensively capture the full range of their actual and contingent risk exposures. The goal of such models is to determine how various changes in market and investment conditions could affect investments. The risk models should be continuously evaluated and challenged, and Managers should be prepared to describe the models to clients. Despite the importance of risk models, however, effective risk management ultimately depends on the experience, judgment, and ability of the Managers in analyzing their risk metrics.

APPENDIX 6: E. PERFORMANCE AND EVALUATION 7

- ☐ determine whether an asset manager's practices and procedures are consistent with the Asset Manager Code
- ☐ recommend practices and procedures designed to prevent violations of the Asset Manager Code

Managers must:

1. **Present performance information that is fair, accurate, relevant, timely, and complete. Managers must not misrepresent the performance of individual portfolios or of their firm.**

   Although past performance is not necessarily indicative of future performance, historical performance records are often used by prospective clients as part of the evaluation process when hiring asset managers. Managers have a duty to present performance information that is a fair representation of their record and includes all relevant factors. In particular, Managers should be certain not to misrepresent their track records by taking credit for performance that is not their own (i.e., when they were not managing a particular portfolio or product) or by selectively presenting certain time periods or investments (i.e., cherry picking). Any hypothetical or backtested performance must be clearly identified as such. Managers should provide as much additional portfolio transparency as feasibly possible. Any forward-looking information provided to clients must also be fair, accurate, and complete.

A model for fair, accurate, and complete performance reporting is embodied in the Global Investment Performance Standards (GIPS®), which are based on the principles of fair representation and full disclosure and are designed to meet the needs of a broad range of global markets. By adhering to these standards for reporting investment performance, Managers help assure investors that the performance information being provided is both complete and fairly presented. When Managers comply with the GIPS standards, both prospective and existing clients benefit because they can have a high degree of confidence in the reliability of the performance numbers the Managers are presenting. This confidence may, in turn, enhance clients' sense of trust in their Managers.

2. **Use fair-market prices to value client holdings and apply, in good faith, methods to determine the fair value of any securities for which no independent, third-party market quotation is readily available.**

   In general, fund Managers' fees are calculated as a percentage of assets under management. In some cases, an additional fee is calculated as a percentage of the annual returns earned on the assets. Consequently, a conflict of interest may arise where the portfolio Manager has the additional responsibility of determining end-of-period valuations and returns on the assets.

   These conflicts may be overcome by transferring responsibility for the valuation of assets (including foreign currencies) to an independent third party. For pooled funds that have boards of directors comprising independent members, the independent members should have the responsibility of approving the asset valuation policies and procedures and reviewing the valuations. For pooled funds without independent directors, we recommend that this function be undertaken by independent third parties who are expert in providing such valuations.

   Managers should use widely accepted valuation methods and techniques to appraise portfolio holdings of securities and other investments and should apply these methods on a consistent basis.

8 APPENDIX 6: F. DISCLOSURES

- ☐ determine whether an asset manager's practices and procedures are consistent with the Asset Manager Code
- ☐ recommend practices and procedures designed to prevent violations of the Asset Manager Code

Managers must:

1. **Communicate with clients on an ongoing and timely basis.**

   Developing and maintaining clear, frequent, and thorough communication practices is critical to providing high-quality financial services to clients. Understanding the information communicated to them allows clients to know how Managers are acting on their behalf and gives clients the opportunity to make well-informed decisions regarding their investments. Managers must determine how best to establish lines of communication that fit their circumstances and that enable clients to evaluate their financial status.

2. **Ensure that disclosures are truthful, accurate, complete, and understandable and are presented in a format that communicates the information effectively.**

   Managers must not misrepresent any aspect of their services or activities, including (but not limited to) their qualifications or credentials, the services they provide, their performance records, and characteristics of the investments or strategies they use. A misrepresentation is any untrue statement or omission of fact or any statement that is otherwise false or misleading. Managers must ensure that misrepresentation does not occur in oral representations, marketing (whether through mass media or printed brochures), electronic communications, or written materials (whether publicly disseminated or not).

   To be effective, disclosures must be made in plain language and in a manner designed to effectively communicate the information to clients and prospective clients. Managers must determine how often, in what manner, and under what particular circumstances disclosures must be made.

3. **Include any material facts when making disclosures or providing information to clients regarding themselves, their personnel, investments, or the investment process.**

   Clients must have full and complete information to judge the abilities of Managers and their actions in investing client assets. "Material" information is information that reasonable investors would want to know relative to whether or not they would choose to use or continue to use the Manager.

4. **Disclose the following:**

   a. **Conflicts of interests generated by any relationships with brokers or other entities, other client accounts, fee structures, or other matters.**

      Conflicts of interests often arise in the investment management profession and can take many forms. Best practice is to avoid such conflicts if possible. When Managers cannot reasonably avoid conflicts, they must carefully manage them and disclose them to clients. Disclosure of conflicts of interests protects investors by providing them with the information they need to evaluate the objectivity of their Managers' investment advice and actions taken on behalf of clients and by giving them the information to judge the circumstances, motives, and possible Manager bias for themselves. Examples of some of the types of activities that can constitute actual or potential conflicts of interest are the use of soft dollars or bundled commissions, referral and placement fees, trailing commissions, sales incentives, directed brokerage arrangements, allocation of investment opportunities among similar portfolios, Manager or employee holdings in the same securities as clients, whether the Manager co-invests alongside clients, and use of affiliated brokers.

b. **Regulatory or disciplinary action taken against the Manager or its personnel related to professional conduct.**

Past professional conduct records are an important factor in an investor's selection of a Manager. Such records include actions taken against a Manager by any regulator or other organization. Managers must fully disclose any significant instances in which the Manager or an employee was found to have violated standards of conduct or other standards in such a way that reflects badly on the integrity, ethics, or competence of the organization or the individual.

c. **The investment process, including information regarding lock-up periods, strategies, risk factors, and use of derivatives and leverage.**

Managers must disclose to clients and prospects the manner in which investment decisions are made and implemented. Such disclosures should address the overall investment strategy and should include a discussion of the specific risk factors inherent in such a strategy.

Understanding the basic characteristics of an investment is an important factor in judging the suitability of each investment on a stand-alone basis, but it is especially important in determining the effect each investment will have on the characteristics of the client's portfolio. Only by thoroughly understanding the nature of the investment product or service can a client determine whether changes to that product or service could materially affect his or her investment objectives.

d. **Management fees and other investment costs charged to investors, including what costs are included in the fees and the methodologies for determining fees and costs.**

Investors are entitled to full and fair disclosures of costs associated with the investment management services provided. Material that should be disclosed includes information relating to any fees to be paid to the Managers on an ongoing basis and periodic costs that are known to the Managers and that will affect investors' overall investment expenses. At a minimum, Managers should provide clients with gross- and net-of-fees returns and disclose any unusual expenses.

A general statement that certain fees and other costs will be assessed to investors may not adequately communicate the total amount of expenses that investors may incur as a result of investing. Therefore, Managers must not only use plain language in presenting this information but must clearly explain the methods for determining all fixed and contingent fees and costs that will be borne by investors and also must explain the transactions that will trigger the imposition of these expenses.

Managers should also retrospectively disclose to each client the actual fees and other costs charged to the clients, together with itemizations of such charges when requested by clients. This disclosure should include the specific management fee, any incentive fee, and the amount of commissions Managers paid on behalf of clients during the period. In addition, Managers must disclose to prospective clients the average or expected expenses or fees clients are likely to incur.

e. **The amount of any soft or bundled commissions, the goods and/or services received in return, and how those goods and/or services benefit the client.**

Commissions belong to the client and should be used in their best interests. Any soft or bundled commissions should be used only to benefit the client. Clients deserve to know how their commissions are spent, what is received in return for them, and how those goods and/or services benefit them.

f. **The performance of clients' investments on a regular and timely basis.**

Clients may reasonably expect to receive regular performance reporting about their accounts. Without such performance information, even for investment vehicles with lock-up periods, clients cannot evaluate their overall asset allocations (i.e., including assets not held or managed by the Managers) and determine whether rebalancing is necessary. Accordingly, unless otherwise specified by the client, Managers must provide regular, ongoing performance reporting. Managers should report to clients at least quarterly, and when possible, such reporting should be provided within 30 days after the end of the quarter.

g. **Valuation methods used to make investment decisions and value client holdings.**

Clients deserve to know whether the assets in their portfolios are valued on the basis of closing market values, third-party valuations, internal valuation models, or other methods. This type of disclosure allows clients to compare performance results and determine whether different valuation sources and methods may explain differences in performance results. This disclosure should be made by asset class and must be meaningful (i.e., not general or boilerplate) so that clients can understand how the securities are valued.

h. **Shareholder voting policies.**

As part of their fiduciary duties, Managers that exercise voting authority over client shares must vote them in an informed and responsible manner. This obligation includes the paramount duty to vote shares in the best interests of clients.

To fulfill their duties, Managers must adopt policies and procedures for the voting of shares and disclose those policies and procedures to clients. These disclosures should specify, among other things, guidelines for instituting regular reviews for new or controversial issues, mechanisms for reviewing unusual proposals, guidance in deciding whether additional actions are warranted when votes are against corporate management, and systems to monitor any delegation of share-voting responsibilities to others. Managers also must disclose to clients how to obtain information on the manner in which their shares were voted.

i. **Trade allocation policies.**

By disclosing their trade allocation policies, Managers give clients a clear understanding of how trades are allocated and provide realistic expectations of what priority they will receive in the investment allocation process. Managers must disclose to clients any changes in the trade allocation policies. By establishing and disclosing trade allocation policies that treat clients fairly, Managers foster an atmosphere of openness and trust with their clients.

j. **Results of the review or audit of the fund or account.**

If a Manager submits its funds or accounts (generally pooled or mutual funds) for an annual review or audit, it must disclose the results to clients. Such disclosure enables clients to hold Managers accountable and alerts them to any potential problems.

k. **Significant personnel or organizational changes that have occurred at the Manager.**

Clients should be made aware of significant changes at the Manager in a timely manner. "Significant" changes would include personnel turnover, merger and acquisition activities of the Manager, and similar actions.

l. **Risk management processes.**

Managers must disclose their risk management processes to clients. Material changes to the risk management process also must be disclosed. Managers should further consider regularly disclosing specific risk information and specific information regarding investment strategies related to each client. Managers must provide clients information detailing what relevant risk metrics they can expect to receive at the individual product/portfolio level.

PRACTICE PROBLEMS

The following information relates to questions 1-6

Henry Schmidt, David Zane, and Andrew Ronoldo founded SZR LLC (SZR), an investment advisory firm managing portfolios for individuals. Although none of the founders holds the CFA charter, SZR has adopted the CFA Institute Asset Manager Code of Professional Conduct.

SZR's client portfolios average $50,000 and are entirely invested in SZR's commingled fund, managed by Ronoldo. Ronoldo implements a quantitative enhanced index process in SZR's fund and has consistently added moderate performance (alpha) over the fund's mid-cap benchmark index. After five years of strong performance, Ronoldo worries that the mid-cap fund will lag broad market indexes, so he decides to broaden the fund's strategy. After doing research, he adds micro-cap, foreign, and convertible preferred stocks to the fund and doubles some holdings so that their weights are much larger than they are in the benchmark index. Since the fund achieves even stronger performance, both against the benchmark mid-cap index and major market indexes, Ronoldo plans to describe the new strategy in the company's next annual newsletter, due to be sent to clients in three months.

As a prominent member of the community, Schmidt has just joined the board of a local company, Trezeguet Baking Company, which recently went public. Trezeguet's shares are in most micro-capitalization (cap) indexes. As a board member, Schmidt receives a small annual stipend of $2,000; however, he is granted several thousand stock options, which he can exercise after 24 months' board service. Since his stipend is insignificant and he will not exercise his options for at least 24 months, Schmidt does not disclose his Trezeguet board service to SZR clients.

One of SZR's clients is president of Sastre International. Because of SZR's success, this client hires SZR to manage $800 million of Sastre International's corporate cash in a separate account, but asks that its hiring of SZR not be made public. Sastre's board asks Ronoldo to direct all of the Sastre account trades through a local financial advisor, to thank the advisor for selecting SZR. Ronoldo is concerned that this direction may limit SZR's ability to achieve best execution, but after Sastre acknowledges in writing that this is their preference, Ronoldo agrees to follow Sastre's direction.

As head of operations, Zane wishes to simplify trading and implements a new trade policy: first place trades for the Sastre account through the local financial advisor and then submit the commingled fund's trades through national brokerage houses and electronic networks. The local financial advisor is pleased with this arrangement, as he is able to buy securities before other clients; he informs Zane that he'll recommend SZR to additional clients.

Schmidt, SZR's sales director, sends the commingled fund's stellar performance track record to several investment consultants, who serve as "gatekeepers" for large institutional clients, but he is told that SZR is too small to be considered by their clients. After Schmidt reveals that Sastre has recently hired SZR, and offers to negotiate the same special fee discount that has been given to Sastre, one consultant agrees to consider SZR for its clients. The consultant indicates that if SZR agrees to sponsor the consulting firm's annual conference, Schmidt will meet many potential clients. Schmidt considers this conference sponsorship, but decides that it is too costly for SZR's budget, so he declines the offer.

As SZR grows, Zane hires his brother-in-law, John Karna (top salesman for a local auto parts company) as Compliance Officer. Karna is tasked with writing SZR's Code of Ethics and its Investment Policies and Procedures Manual. Karna is also put in charge of the firm's Business Continuity Plan. The plan consists of his taking home, each evening, the computer records of SZR's daily trades.

1. Does Ronoldo violate the CFA Institute Asset Manager Code of Professional Conduct with respect to his broader investment strategy?

   A. No.

   B. Yes, with respect to client disclosure only.

   C. Yes, with respect to reasonable and adequate basis only.

2. Does Schmidt violate the CFA Institute Asset Manager Code of Professional Conduct with respect to his current Trezeguet board service?

   A. No.

   B. Yes, with respect to priority of client interests only.

   C. Yes, with respect to priority of client interests and participation in business relationships.

3. By agreeing to Sastre's direction, does Ronoldo violate the CFA Institute Asset Manager Code of Professional Conduct?

   A. No.

   B. Yes, only with respect to best execution.

   C. Yes, only with respect to fair and equitable trade allocation.

4. Does Zane's revision of SZR's trading process violate the CFA Institute Asset Manager Code of Professional Conduct?

   A. No.

   B. Yes, only with respect to best execution.

   C. Yes, with respect to best execution and fair, equitable trade allocation.

5. Does Schmidt violate the CFA Institute Asset Manager Code of Professional Conduct in his interaction with consultants?

   A. No.

   B. Yes, only with respect to confidentiality.

   C. Yes, only with respect to business relationships that could affect independence.

6. Does Karna's role as Chief Compliance Officer, and the process of SZR's Business Continuity Plan, respectively, conform to the requirements and recommendations of the CFA Institute Asset Manager Code of Professional Conduct?

   A. Neither Karna's role nor the Business Continuity Plan conforms.

   B. Karna's role conforms, but the Business Continuity Plan does not conform.

C. Karna's role does not conform, but the Business Continuity Plan does conform.

The following information relates to questions 7-12

Bornelli Asset Management offers traditional long-only funds as well as a variety of hedge funds for both private and institutional clients. Bornelli is a well-managed firm of more than 100 employees. Its board of directors has voted to adopt the Asset Manager Code of Professional Conduct (the Code).

Bornelli has hired Ava Campanelli as chief compliance officer with responsibility for implementing the Code. Campanelli develops a plan to evaluate the firm's current policies and procedures for compliance with the Code. Campanelli begins by reviewing three of the firm's compliance procedures:

Portfolio review	Portfolio information provided to clients is reviewed by an independent third-party.
Record retention	The firm retains records to substantiate all investment decisions for seven years. In compliance with regulatory requirements, the firm also retains copies of all emails for the same period. The firm retains its records in a combination of both hard-copy and electronic formats.
Investigation of complaints	The chief compliance officer (CCO) is responsible for investigating and documenting all complaints. The CCO reports to the chief investment officer and works with management to take appropriate disciplinary action in cases of compliance breaches.

Campanelli then evaluates the firm's business-continuity plan. Under the current plan, the technology division backs up all of the firm's computer systems and client records twice daily. The back-ups are stored in a fireproof storage facility offsite. Bornelli outsources certain emergency plans to a disaster recovery firm. The disaster recovery firm is responsible for developing and implementing plans to communicate with employees and mission-critical vendors and suppliers in the event of a facility or communication disruption. The same firm also provides plans for contacting and communicating with clients in event of an extended disruption.

For her next project, Campanelli reviews the disclosures provided to both prospective and current clients. The disclosures regarding management fees state:

Bornelli charges a 2% asset-based management fee. In addition to the management fee, clients may pay an incentive fee at the end of each year. The incentive fee is equal to 20% of the account's net investment income and net realized and unrealized capital gains for the year.

No incentive fee will be paid unless the Fund has offset all prior net realized capital losses and net investment losses with realized capital gains, unrealized appreciation, and net investment income from all securities held by the Fund.

Campanelli's evaluation of the management fee disclosures is interrupted by a more urgent matter involving a client. The client has requested monthly performance reporting of his investment in a long-short equity hedge fund. The fund's administrator argues "Our procedures call for us to provide clients with both gross- and net-of-fees returns within 30 days of the end of the quarter." He adds "Quarterly reporting is the industry standard."

The administrator complains "This client, Rossi, is overly demanding. He telephoned yesterday and requested an itemization of the fees and other costs charged to him for the past three years. He wants to know the specific management fee, the incentive fee, and the amount of commissions paid. The more time we spend answering his requests, the less time we have to research investments." Campanelli promises to look into the matter for the administrator.

The following week, Campanelli meets with Lee Bruno, manager of the firm's alternative assets fund. Bruno informs Campanelli, "The fund has a three-year lock-up period. We disclosed to all the prospective clients in writing before they invested that this is a long-term investment and that they should not focus on short-term performance results. During the lock-up period, we provide semiannual reporting. After the lock-up, we report quarterly."

Bruno informs Campanelli that whenever possible, the firm uses fair market prices to value client holdings. He adds "Of course, our fund invests in alternative assets—some of which are very difficult to value. They aren't like public equities with independent, third-party market quotations available, so we use an internal model to value client holdings." He continues, "We disclose the use of internal models for valuation purposes on all our reports."

Following her conversation with Bruno, Campanelli researches a complaint from a new client regarding the valuations of his fund's holdings. The client complains that another management firm reported much lower valuations on similar instruments. Campanelli researches the methodologies Bornelli uses for valuing fund holdings. She determines the following:

- All publicly traded US and foreign equities, including large-, mid-, small-, and micro-cap shares are valued at the last available closing price.
- The value of certain securities such as swaps are based on quotes collected from broker-dealers.
- When prices are not available from either of the above sources, valuations are based on internal models.

7. Are the three compliance procedures reviewed by Campanelli consistent with both the required and recommended standards of the CFA Institute Asset Manager Code of Professional Conduct?

   A. No, the procedures regarding record retention are inconsistent.

   B. No, the procedures regarding portfolio review are inconsistent.

   C. No, the procedures regarding investigation of complaints are inconsistent.

8. Is Bornelli's disaster recovery plan consistent with both the required and recommended standards of the Asset Manager Code?

   A. Yes.

   B. No, because the plan lacks a backup plan for monitoring, analyzing, and trading investments.

   C. No, because the plan only provides for contacting and communicating with clients during periods of extended disruption.

9. Are the firm's disclosures regarding management fees consistent with the required and recommended standards of the Asset Manager Code?

   A. Yes.

B. No, because they do not use plain language.

C. No, because they do not include the average or expected expenses or fees clients are likely to incur.

10. Are the performance reporting procedures described by the fund's administrator consistent with the required disclosure standards of the Asset Manager Code?

A. Yes.

B. No, because the AMC requires firms to report performance to all clients on a monthly basis.

C. No, because the AMC requires firms to provide performance on a monthly basis when requested by clients.

11. To comply with both the required and recommended standards of the Asset Manager Code, must Bornelli honor Rossi's telephone request regarding an itemization of fees?

A. Yes.

B. No, because the firm is not required to disclose the amount of incentive fee charged to an individual client.

C. No, because unless the firm claims compliance with the Soft Dollar Standards, it is not required to disclose the amount of commissions paid on clients' behalf.

12. Are the policies of the alternative assets fund consistent with the required and recommended standards of the Asset Manager Code?

A. Yes.

B. No, the frequency of reporting is inconsistent with the AMC.

C. No, the use of internal valuation models is inconsistent with the AMC.

SOLUTIONS

1. B is correct. Ronoldo should have disclosed his change in investment strategy to clients, allowing them to move their accounts if not in agreement. Until he disclosed a planned change in strategy, he should have continued to manage in the manner for which clients had hired him.

2. C is correct. Schmidt is on the board of a company whose stock is in microcap indexes. This is a conflict of interest, as Ronoldo's widened investment guidelines allow purchase of Trezeguet stock for the fund. As Schmidt is an insider for the company and received options that can be sold (after 24 months), this relationship should be terminated.

3. A is correct. The Sastre board requests directed trading for its discretionary account and acknowledges, in writing, that trading through the local financial advisor may limit best execution. As this is a discretionary (not pension) account, the client has the right to direct to a less-than-optimal trading venue.

4. C is correct. Zane should have pursued best execution for all clients in the fund (which is not accomplished by placing trades with the local financial advisor first versus with national brokers or electronic networks), and fairly traded for all clients. While Sastre is welcome to direct trades, Zane's change in procedures harms other clients.

5. B is correct. Schmidt violated Code A-2 by revealing Sastre's hiring of SZR and its special fee discount.

6. A is correct. Karna's qualification as compliance officer is inadequate (D-2, D-5), and taking tapes home each night is inadequate business continuity for a firm of $1.5 billion (D-6).

7. C is correct. According to the recommendations of Section D(2) of the Asset Manager Code, where possible, the CCO should be independent from the investment and operations personnel and should report directly to the CEO or the board of directors.

8. B is correct. According to the guidance provided in Section D(6) of the Asset Manager Code, the level and complexity of business-continuity planning depends on the size, nature, and complexity of the organization involved. Bornelli is a large firm with hedge fund investments and it should have alternative plans for monitoring, analyzing, and trading investments if primary systems become unavailable.

9. C is correct. According to the recommendations and guidance of Section F(4d) of the Asset Manager Code, managers must disclose to prospective clients the average or expected expenses or fees clients are likely to incur, and to existing clients the actual fees and other costs charged to them.

10. A is correct. The performance reporting procedures described by the administrator are consistent with the Asset Manager Code (AMC) which requires disclosing the "performance of clients' investments on a regular and timely basis." The AMC recommends that "managers should report to clients at least quarterly, and when possible, such reporting should be provided within 30 days after the end of the quarter." The AMC also states that "at a minimum, Managers should provide clients with gross- and net-of-fees returns." Because quarterly reporting is the

recommended minimum, managers may choose to provide more timely performance to clients.

11. A is correct. According to the recommendations of Section F(4d) of the Asset Manager Code, managers should disclose to each client the actual fees and other costs charged to them, together with itemizations of such charges, when requested by clients. The disclosure should include the specific management fee, incentive fee, and the amount of commissions paid on clients' behalf during the period.

12. B is correct. Clients must have regular performance information to evaluate their overall asset allocations and to determine whether rebalancing is necessary. This concept applies even to investment vehicles with lock-up periods. According to the Asset Manager Code, unless otherwise specified by the client, managers should report to clients at least quarterly, and when possible, within 30 days of the end of the period.

Level III Core Glossary

Absolute return benchmark A minimum target return that an investment manager is expected to beat.
Accrual taxes Taxes levied and paid on a periodic basis.
Accumulation phase Phase where the government predominantly contributes to a sovereign wealth pension reserve fund.
Active management A portfolio management approach that allows risk factor mismatches relative to a benchmark index causing potentially significant return differences between the active portfolio and the underlying benchmark.
Active return The return on a portfolio minus the return on the portfolio's benchmark.
Active risk The standard deviation of active returns.
Active risk budgeting Risk budgeting that concerns active risk (risk relative to a portfolio's benchmark).
Active share A measure of how similar a portfolio is to its benchmark. A manager who precisely replicates the benchmark will have an active share of zero; a manager with no holdings in common with the benchmark will have an active share of one.
Aggregate wealth The total value of all assets owned, encompassing personal property, financial assets, real assets, and rights.
Arithmetic attribution An attribution approach which explains the arithmetic difference between the portfolio return and its benchmark return. The single-period attribution effects sum to the excess return, however, when combining multiple periods, the sub-period attribution effects will not sum to the excess return.
Ask price The price at which a trader will sell a specified quantity of a security. Also called *ask*, *offer price*, or *offer*.
Asset-only With respect to asset allocation, an approach that focuses directly on the characteristics of the assets without explicitly modeling the liabilities.
Authority bias A behavioral bias which involves groups deferring to a group member that is a subject matter expert or in a position of authority.
Aversion to complexity A behavioral phenomenon of groups in many professional contexts, in which disproportionate attention is given to trivial issues at the expense of important but harder-to-grasp or contested topics.
Back-fill bias The distortion in index or peer group data which results when returns are reported to a database only after they are known to be good returns.
Base With respect to a foreign exchange quotation of the price of one unit of a currency, the currency referred to in "one unit of a currency."
Basis risk The possibility that the expected value of a derivative differs unexpectedly from that of the underlying.
Bear spread An option strategy that becomes more valuable when the price of the underlying asset declines, so requires buying one option and writing another with a *lower* exercise price. A put bear spread involves buying a put with a higher exercise price and selling a put with a lower exercise price. A bear spread can also be executed with calls.
Best ask The offer to sell with the lowest ask price. Also called *best offer* or *inside ask*.
Best bid The highest bid in the market.
Best offer The lowest offer (ask price) in the market.
Best-in-class An ESG implementation approach that seeks to identify the most favorable companies in an industry based on ESG considerations.
Bid price In a price quotation, the price at which the party making the quotation is willing to buy a specified quantity of an asset or security.
Bid–ask spread The ask price minus the bid price.
Buffering Establishing ranges around breakpoints that define whether a stock belongs in one index or another.
Bull spread An option strategy that becomes more valuable when the price of the underlying asset rises, so requires buying one option and writing another with a *higher* exercise price. A call bull spread involves buying a call with a lower exercise price and selling a call with a higher exercise price. A bull spread can also be executed with puts.
Business cycle Fluctuations in GDP in relation to long-term trend growth, usually lasting 9-11 years.
Calendar rebalancing Rebalancing a portfolio to target weights on a periodic basis; for example, monthly, quarterly, semiannually, or annually.
Calendar spread A strategy in which one sells an option and buys the same type of option but with different expiration dates, on the same underlying asset and with the same strike. When the investor buys the more distant (near-term) call and sells the near-term (more distant) call, it is a long (short) calendar spread.
Canada model Characterized by a high allocation to alternatives. Unlike the endowment model, however, the Canada model relies more on internally managed assets. The innovative features of the Canada model are the: a) reference portfolio, b) total portfolio approach, and c) active management.
Capital market expectations (CME) Expectations concerning the risk and return prospects of asset classes.
Capital sufficiency analysis The process of evaluating whether a client has sufficient capital resources to achieve their financial goals and objectives; it considers the client's assets, liabilities, income, expenses, risk tolerance, time horizon, and other relevant factors.
Capture ratio A measure of the manager's gain or loss relative to the gain or loss of the benchmark.
Carhart model A four factor model used in performance attribution. The four factors are: market (RMRF), size (SMB), value (HML), and momentum (WML).
Carry trade A trading strategy that involves buying a security and financing it at a rate that is lower than the yield on that security.
Cash flow matching Immunization approach that attempts to ensure that all future liability payouts are matched precisely by cash flows from bonds or fixed-income derivatives.

Cash-secured put An option strategy involving the writing of a put option and simultaneously depositing an amount of money equal to the exercise price into a designated account (this strategy is also called a fiduciary put).

Collar An option position in which the investor is long shares of stock and then buys a put with an exercise price below the current stock price and writes a call with an exercise price above the current stock price. Collars allow a shareholder to acquire downside protection through a protective put but reduce the cash outlay by writing a covered call.

Contingent immunization Hybrid approach that combines immunization with an active management approach when the asset portfolio's value exceeds the present value of the liability portfolio.

Cost basis The initial cost of acquiring an investment including expenses incurred to acquire the investment. Also referred to as simply basis.

Covered call An option strategy in which a long position in an asset is combined with a short position in a call on that asset.

Cross hedge A hedge involving a hedging instrument that is imperfectly correlated with the asset being hedged; an example is hedging a bond investment with futures on a non-identical bond.

Cross-currency basis swap A swap in which notional principals are exchanged because the goal of the transaction is to issue at a more favorable funding rate and swap the amount back to the currency of choice.

Cross-sectional consistency A feature of expectations setting which means that estimates for all classes reflect the same underlying assumptions and are generated with methodologies that reflect or preserve important relationships among the asset classes, such as strong correlations. It is the internal consistency across asset classes.

Currency overlay programs A currency overlay program is a program to manage a portfolio's currency exposures for the case in which those exposures are managed separately from the management of the portfolio itself.

Custom security-based benchmark Benchmark that is custom built to accurately reflect the investment discipline of a particular investment manager. Also called a *strategy benchmark* because it reflects a manager's particular strategy.

Decision-reversal risk The risk of reversing a chosen course of action at the point of maximum loss.

Decumulation phase Phase where the government predominantly withdraws from a sovereign wealth pension reserve fund.

Deferred taxes Taxes postponed until some future date.

Defined benefit A retirement plan in which a plan sponsor commits to paying a specified retirement benefit.

Defined benefit plan Retirement plan that is funded by the employer that guarantees a retirement benefit based on factors such as years of service, salary, and age.

Defined contribution A retirement plan in which contributions are defined but the ultimate retirement benefit is not specified or guaranteed by the plan sponsor.

Defined contribution plan Retirement plan in which the employer, employee, or both contribute to an account in which the employee bears the investment risk.

Delay costs Implicit trading costs that arise from the inability to complete desired trades immediately. Also called *slippage.*

Delta The relationship between the option price and the underlying price, which reflects the sensitivity of the price of the option to changes in the price of the underlying. Delta is a good approximation of how an option price will change for a small change in the stock.

Delta hedging Hedging that involves matching the price response of the position being hedged over a narrow range of prices.

Demand deposits Accounts that can be drawn upon regularly and without notice. This category includes checking accounts and certain savings accounts that are often accessible through online banks or automated teller machines (ATMs).

Diffusion index Reflects the proportion of the index's components that are moving in a pattern consistent with the overall index.

Dividend capture A trading strategy whereby an equity portfolio manager purchases stocks just before their ex-dividend dates, holds these stocks through the ex-dividend date to earn the right to receive the dividend, and subsequently sells the shares.

Domestic asset An asset that trades in the investor's domestic currency (or home currency).

Domestic currency The currency of the investor, i.e., the currency in which he or she typically makes consumption purchases, e.g., the Swiss franc for an investor domiciled in Switzerland.

Domestic-currency return A rate of return stated in domestic currency terms from the perspective of the investor; reflects both the foreign-currency return on an asset as well as percentage movement in the spot exchange rate between the domestic and foreign currencies.

Drawdown A percentage peak-to-trough reduction in net asset value.

Drawdown duration The total time from the start of the drawdown until the cumulative drawdown recovers to zero.

Due diligence Investigation and analysis in support of a recommendation; the failure to exercise due diligence may sometimes result in liability according to various securities laws.

Duration matching Immunization approach based on the duration of assets and liabilities. Ideally, the liabilities being matched (the liability portfolio) and the portfolio of assets (the bond portfolio) should be affected similarly by a change in interest rates.

Duration times spread Weighting of spread duration by credit spread in order to incorporate the empirical observation that spread changes for lower-rated bonds tend to be consistent on a percentage, rather than absolute, basis.

Dynamic asset allocation Dynamic asset allocation is an investment strategy premised on long-term asset allocation but employing short-term, tactical trading to maintain investment allocation targets.

Dynamic hedge A hedge requiring adjustment as the price of the hedged asset changes.

Econometrics The application of quantitative modeling and analysis grounded in economic theory to the analysis of economic data.

Economic balance sheet An extended balance sheet that includes the present values of both lifetime earnings and future consumption.

Economic indicators Economic statistics provided by government and established private organizations that contain information on an economy's recent past activity or its current or future position in the business cycle.

Effective federal funds (FFE) rate The fed funds rate actually transacted between depository institutions, not the Fed's target federal funds rate.

Effective spread Two times the difference between the execution price and the midpoint of the market quote at the time an order is entered.

Endowment model Characterized by a high allocation to alternative investments (private investments and hedge funds), significant active management, and externally managed assets.

Enhanced indexing approach Maintains a close link to the benchmark but attempts to generate a modest amount of outperformance relative to the benchmark.

Excess return Used in various senses appropriate to context: 1) The difference between the portfolio return and the benchmark return, which may be either positive or negative; 2) The return in excess of the risk-free rate, thus representing the return for bearing risk.

Exhaustive Covering or containing all possible outcomes.

Extended portfolio assets and liabilities Assets and liabilities beyond those shown on a conventional balance sheet that are relevant in making asset allocation decisions; an example of an extended asset is human capital.

Factor-model-based benchmarks Benchmarks constructed by examining a portfolio's sensitivity to a set of factors, such as the return for a broad market index, company earnings growth, industry, or financial leverage.

Family offices Private firms that offer a range of wealth management services tailored specifically for ultra-high-net-worth individuals.

Foreign assets Assets denominated in currencies other than the investor's home currency.

Foreign currency Currency that is not the currency in which an investor makes consumption purchases, e.g., the US dollar from the perspective of a Swiss investor.

Foreign-currency return The return of the foreign asset measured in foreign-currency terms.

Forward rate bias An empirically observed divergence from interest rate parity conditions that active investors seek to benefit from by borrowing in a lower-yield currency and investing in a higher-yield currency.

Funding currencies The low-yield currencies in which borrowing occurs in a carry trade.

Gamma A numerical measure of how sensitive an option's delta (the sensitivity of the derivative's price) is to a change in the value of the underlying.

General account Account holding assets to fund future liabilities from traditional life insurance and fixed annuities, the products in which the insurer bears all the risks—particularly mortality risk and longevity risk.

Gini coefficient A measure of inequality of wealth, or *i*, that ranges from 0 (perfect equality) to 1 (perfect inequality).

Goals-based With respect to asset allocation or investing, an approach that focuses on achieving an investor's goals (for example, related to supporting lifestyle needs or aspirations) based typically on constructing sub-portfolios aligned with those goals.

Goals-based investing An investment industry term for approaches to investing for individuals and families focused on aligning investments with goals (parallel to liability-driven investing for institutional investors).

Grinold–Kroner model An expression for the expected return on a share as the sum of an expected income return, an expected nominal earnings growth return, and an expected repricing return.

Groupthink A behavioral bias that occurs when a team minimizes conflict and dissent in reaching and maintaining a consensus.

Hedge ratio The proportion of an underlying that will offset the risk associated with a derivative position.

High-net-worth individuals (HNWIs) Individuals with investable assets exceeding a certain minimum level, often as low as USD1 million, but typically more.

High-water mark A measure that reflects the fund's maximum value as of a performance fee payment date net of fees.

Holdings-based attribution A "buy and hold" attribution approach which calculates the return of portfolio and benchmark components based upon the price and foreign exchange rate changes applied to daily snapshots of portfolio holdings.

Holdings-based style analysis A bottom-up style analysis that estimates the risk exposures from the actual securities held in the portfolio at a point in time.

Home bias A preference for securities listed on the exchanges of one's home country.

Home currency See *domestic currency*.

Home-country bias The favoring of domestic over non-domestic investments relative to global market value weights.

Human capital The present value of an individual's future expected labor income.

Impact investing Refers to investments made with the specific intent of generating positive, measurable social and environmental impact alongside a financial return (which differentiates it from philanthropy).

Implementation shortfall (IS) The difference between the return for a notional or paper portfolio, where all transactions are assumed to take place at the manager's decision price, and the portfolio's actual return, which reflects realized transactions, including all fees and costs.

Implied volatility The standard deviation that causes an option pricing model to give the current option price.

Implied volatility surface A three-dimensional plot, for put and call options on the same underlying asset, of days to expiration (x-axis), option strike prices (y-axis), and implied volatilities (z-axis). It simultaneously shows the volatility skew (or smile) and the term structure of implied volatility.

Inflation-linked bonds Debt instruments that link the principal and interest to inflation.

Input uncertainty Uncertainty concerning whether the inputs are correct.

Inside ask See *best ask*.

Inside bid See *best bid*.

Inside spread The spread between the best bid price and the best ask price. Also called the *market bid-ask spread, inside bid-ask spread*, or *market spread*.

Interaction effect The impact of overweighting and underweighting individual securities within sectors that are themselves overweighted or underweighted.

Intertemporal consistency A feature of expectations setting which means that estimates for an asset class over different horizons reflect the same assumptions with respect to the potential paths of returns over time. It is the internal consistency over various time horizons.

Intrinsic value The amount gained (per unit) by an option buyer if an option is exercised at any given point in time. May be referred to as the exercise value of the option.

Investable net worth The sum of liquid assets, such as savings and investment accounts, and less short-term liabilities such as credit card debt.

Investable wealth The sum of liquid assets such as savings and investment accounts.

Investment currencies The high-yielding currencies in a carry trade.

Investment policy statement (IPS) A description of a client's unique investment objectives, risk tolerance, investment time horizon, and other applicable constraints.

Investment style A natural grouping of investment disciplines that has some predictive power in explaining the future dispersion of returns across portfolios.

Key person risk The risk that results from over-reliance on an individual or individuals whose departure would negatively affect an investment manager.

Knock-in/knock-out Features of a vanilla option that is created (or ceases to exist) when the spot exchange rate touches a pre-specified level.

Latency The elapsed time between the occurrence of an event and a subsequent action that depends on that event.

Leading economic indicators Turning points that usually precede those of the overall economy; they are believed to have value for predicting the economy's future state, usually near-term.

Liability driven investing (LDI) model In the LDI model, the primary investment objective is to generate returns sufficient to cover liabilities, with a focus on maximizing expected surplus return (excess return of assets over liabilities) and managing surplus volatility.

Liability glide path A specification of desired proportions of liability-hedging assets and return-seeking assets and the duration of the liability hedge as funded status changes and contributions are made.

Liability-based mandates Mandates managed to match or cover expected liability payments (future cash outflows) with future projected cash inflows.

Liability-driven investing An investment industry term that generally encompasses asset allocation that is focused on funding an investor's liabilities in institutional contexts.

Liability-relative With respect to asset allocation, an approach that focuses directly only on funding liabilities as an investment objective.

Limit order book The book or list of limit orders to buy and sell that pertains to a security.

Limited-life foundations A type of foundation where founders seek to maintain control of spending while they (or their immediate heirs) are still alive.

Longevity risk The risk of exhausting an individual's financial resources before passing away, thereby leaving insufficient capital for living expenses and unmet needs.

Lorenz curve A measure of the cumulative percentage of wealth owned by each percentage of the population.

Macro attribution Attribution at the sponsor level.

Manager peer group See *manager universe*.

Manager universe A broad group of managers with similar investment disciplines. Also called *manager peer group*.

Marginal tax rate The highest rate of tax applied to taxable income.

Market fragmentation Trading the same instrument in multiple venues.

Market impact The effect of the trade on transaction prices. Also called *price impact*.

Micro attribution Attribution at the portfolio manager level.

Midquote price The average, or midpoint, of the prevailing bid and ask prices.

Minimum-variance hedge ratio A mathematical approach to determining the optimal cross hedging ratio.

Mission-related investing Investing aimed at causes promoting positive societal or environmental change.

Model uncertainty Uncertainty as to whether a selected model is correct.

Negative screening An ESG investment approach that consists of excluding investments in certain sectors, companies, or practices in a fund or portfolio based on specific ESG criteria.

Net worth The difference between assets and liabilities.

Non-deliverable forwards Forward contracts that are cash settled (in the non-controlled currency of the currency pair) rather than physically settled (the controlled currency is neither delivered nor received).

Nonstationarity A characteristic of series of data whose properties, such as mean and variance, are not constant through time. When analyzing historical data it means that different parts of a data series reflect different underlying statistical properties.

Norway model Characterized by an almost exclusive reliance on public equities and fixed income (the traditional 60/40 equity/bond model falls under the Norway model), with largely passively managed assets and with very little to no allocation to alternative investments.

Offer price The price at which a counterparty is willing to sell one unit of the base currency.

Opportunity cost The value that investors forgo by choosing a particular course of action; the value of something in its best alternative use.

Optional stock dividends A type of dividend in which shareholders may elect to receive either cash or new shares.

Overbought When a market has trended too far in one direction and is vulnerable to a trend reversal, or correction.

Oversold The opposite of overbought; see *overbought*.

Packeting Splitting stock positions into multiple parts.

Parameter uncertainty Uncertainty arising because a quantitative model's parameters are estimated with error.

Participant-switching life-cycle options Automatically switch DC plan members into a more conservative asset mix as their age increases. There may be several automatic de-risking switches at different age targets.

Participant/cohort option Pools the DC plan member with a cohort that has a similar target retirement date.

Passive management A buy-and-hold approach to investing in which an investor does not make portfolio changes based upon short-term expectations of changing market or security performance.

Percent-range rebalancing An approach to rebalancing that involves setting rebalancing thresholds or trigger points, stated as a percentage of the portfolio's value, around target values.

Performance attribution The process of disaggregating a portfolio's return to determine the drivers of its performance.

Personal assets Nonbusiness, on-investment assets including personal property and real property.

Personal property Property owned by individuals that are not real property and not considered investments.

Planned goals Financial objectives that can be reasonably estimated or quantified at the onset and can be achieved within an expected time horizon.

Position delta The overall or portfolio delta. For example, the position delta of a covered call, consisting of long 100 shares and short one at-the-money call, is +50 (= +100 for the shares and -50 for the short ATM call).

Positive screening An ESG investment approach that consists of including investments in sectors or companies in a fund or portfolio typically based on ESG performance relative to industry peers.

Price improvement When trade execution prices are better than quoted prices.

Private wealth management Financial planning and investment management to help individual investors, particularly high-net-worth individuals (HNWIs) and ultra-high-net-worth individuals (UHNWIs), manage their wealth.

Protective put A strategy of purchasing an underlying asset and purchasing a put on the same asset.

Pure indexing Attempts to replicate a bond index as closely as possible, targeting zero active return and zero active risk.

Put spread A strategy used to reduce the upfront cost of buying a protective put, it involves buying a put option and writing another put option.

Re-base With reference to index construction, to change the time period used as the base of the index.

Realized volatility Historical volatility, the square root of the realized variance of returns, which is a measure of the range of past price outcomes for the underlying asset.

Rebalancing In the context of asset allocation, a discipline for adjusting the portfolio to align with the strategic asset allocation.

Rebalancing range A range of values for asset class weights defined by trigger points above and below target weights, such that if the portfolio value passes through a trigger point, rebalancing occurs. Also known as a corridor.

Rebate rate The portion of the collateral earnings rate that is repaid to the security borrower by the security lender.

Reduced form models Statistical credit models that solve for the probability of default over a specific time period, using observable company-specific and market-based variables.

Regime The governing set of relationships (between variables) that stem from technological, political, legal, and regulatory environments. Changes in such environments or policy stances can be described as changes in regime.

Relative value A concept that describes the selection of the most attractive individual securities to populate the portfolio with, using ranking and comparing.

Repo rate The interest rate on a repurchase agreement.

Repurchase agreements In repurchase agreements, or repos, a security owner agrees to sell a security for a specific cash amount while simultaneously agreeing to repurchase the security at a specified future date (typically one day later) and price.

Reserve portfolio The component of an insurer's general account that is subject to specific regulatory requirements and is intended to ensure the company's ability to meet its policy liabilities. The assets in the reserve portfolio are managed conservatively and must be highly liquid and low risk.

Resistance levels Price points on dealers' order boards where one would expect to see a clustering of offers.

Return attribution A set of techniques used to identify the sources of the excess return of a portfolio against its benchmark.

Returns-based attribution An attribution approach that uses only the total portfolio returns over a period to identify the components of the investment process that have generated the returns. The Brinson–Hood–Beebower approach is a returns-based attribution approach.

Returns-based benchmarks Benchmarks constructed by examining a portfolio's sensitivity to a set of factors, such as the returns for various style indexes (e.g., small-cap value, small-cap growth, large-cap value, and large-cap growth).

Returns-based style analysis A top-down style analysis that involves estimating the sensitivities of a portfolio to security market indexes.

Reverse repos Repurchase agreements from the standpoint of the lender.

Risk attribution The analysis of the sources of risk.

Risk aversion The dislike for risk such that compensation is required in terms of higher expected returns for assuming higher risk.

Risk budgeting The establishment of objectives for individuals, groups, or divisions of an organization that takes into account the allocation of an acceptable level of risk.

Risk capacity The ability to bear financial risk.

Risk premiums Extra returns expected by investors for bearing some specified risk.

Risk reversal A strategy used to profit from the existence of an implied volatility skew and from changes in its shape over time. A combination of long (short) calls and short (long) puts on the same underlying with the same expiration is a long (short) risk reversal.

Risk tolerance The level of risk an investor is willing and able to bear.

Seagull spread An extension of the risk reversal foreign exchange option strategy that limits downside risk.

Securities lending A form of collateralized lending that may be used to generate income for portfolios.

Selective An index construction methodology that targets only those securities with certain characteristics.

Separate accounts Accounts holding assets to fund future liabilities from variable life insurance and variable annuities, the products in which customers make investment decisions from a menu of options and themselves bear investment risk.

Sharpe ratio The ratio of mean excess return to standard deviation (excess return).

Shortfall probability The probability of failing to meet a specific liability or goal.

Shrinkage estimation Estimation that involves taking a weighted average of a historical estimate of a parameter and some other parameter estimate, where the weights reflect the analyst's relative belief in the estimates.

Special dividends Dividends paid by a company that does not pay dividends on a regular schedule, or dividends that supplement regular cash dividends with an extra payment.

Spread duration The change in bond price for a given change in yield spread. Also referred to as OAS duration when the option-adjusted spread (OAS) is the yield measure used.

Static hedge A hedge that is not sensitive to changes in the price of the asset hedged.

Stock lending Securities lending involving the transfer of equities.

Stops Stop-loss orders involve leaving bids or offers away from the current market price to be filled if the market reaches those levels.

Straddle An option combination in which one buys *both* puts and calls, with the same exercise price and same expiration date, on the same underlying asset. In contrast to this long straddle, if someone *writes* both options, it is a short straddle.

Strangle A variation on a straddle in which the put and call have different exercise prices; if the put and call are held long, it is a long strangle; if they are held short, it is a short strangle.

Strategic asset allocation A long-term strategy that establishes target allocations for various asset classes and aims to optimize the balance between risk and reward by diversifying investments.

Structural models Models that specify functional relationships among variables based on economic theory. The functional form and parameters of these models are derived from the underlying theory. They may include unobservable parameters.

Support levels Price points on dealers' order boards where one would expect to see a clustering of bids.

Surplus The difference between assets and liabilities, analogous to shareholders' equity on a corporate balance sheet.

Surplus portfolio The component of an insurer's general account that is intended to realize higher expected returns than the reserve portfolio and so can assume some liquidity risk. Surplus portfolio assets are often managed aggressively with exposure to alternative assets.

Survivorship bias Relates to the inclusion of only current investment funds in a database. As such, the returns of funds that are no longer available in the marketplace (have been liquidated) are excluded from the database. Also see *backfill bias.*

Synthetic long forward position The combination of a long call and a short put with identical strike price and expiration, traded at the same time on the same underlying.

Synthetic short forward position The combination of a short call and a long put at the same strike price and maturity (traded at the same time on the same underlying).

Tactical asset allocation A proactive strategy that adjusts asset class allocations within a portfolio based on short-term market trends, economic conditions, or valuation changes to capitalize on temporary market inefficiencies or opportunities to improve returns or manage risk more effectively.

Tax drag The negative effect of taxes on an investment's net returns.

Taylor rule A rule linking a central bank's target short-term interest rate to the rate of growth of the economy and inflation.

Term deposits Interest-bearing accounts that have a specified maturity date. This category includes savings accounts and certificates of deposit (CDs). Also see *time deposits.*

Term structure of volatility The plot of implied volatility (y-axis) against option maturity (x-axis) for options with the same strike price on the same underlying. Typically, implied volatility is not constant across different maturities – rather, it is often in contango, meaning that the implied volatilities for longer-term options are higher than for near-term ones.

Thematic investing An ESG investment approach with a focus on assets relating to ESG factors or themes, such as clean energy, green technology, sustainable agriculture, gender diversity, and affordable housing.

Theta The change in a derivative instrument for a given small change in calendar time, holding everything else constant. Specifically, the theta calculation assumes nothing changes except calendar time. Theta also reflects the rate at which an option's time value decays.

Threshold-based rebalancing policy The manager rebalances the portfolio when asset class weights deviate from their target weights by a prespecified percentage regardless of timing and frequency.

Time deposits Interest-bearing accounts that have a specified maturity date. This category includes savings accounts and certificates of deposit (CDs). Also see *term deposits.*

Time value The difference between an option's premium and its intrinsic value.

Time-based rebalancing policy The manager rebalances the portfolio regularly, at a certain given time interval such as quarterly, semi-annually, or annually, regardless of any difference between prevailing asset class weights and target asset class weights.

Time-series estimation Estimators that are based on lagged values of the variable being forecast; often consist of lagged values of other selected variables.

Total factor productivity A scale factor that reflects the portion of growth unaccounted for by explicit factor inputs (e.g., capital and labor).

Total return payer Party responsible for paying the reference obligation cash flows and return to the receiver but that is also compensated by the receiver for any depreciation in the index or default losses incurred by the portfolio.

Total return receiver Receives both the cash flows from the underlying index and any appreciation in the index over the period in exchange for paying the MRR plus a predetermined spread.

Tracking risk The standard deviation of the differences between a portfolio's returns and its benchmarks returns. Also called tracking error.

Transactions-based attribution An attribution approach that captures the impact of intra-day trades and exogenous events such as a significant class action settlement.

Trigger points In the context of portfolio rebalancing, the endpoints of a rebalancing range (corridor).

Ultra-high-net-worth individuals (UHNWIs) Individuals with net worth usually exceeding USD30 million or more.

Unplanned goals Unforeseen financial needs that are difficult to quantify because either the funding need, the timing of the financial need, or both may not be estimated.

Unsmoothing An adjustment to the reported return series if serial correlation is detected. Various approaches are available to unsmooth a return series.

Variance notional The notional amount of a variance swap; it equals vega notional divided by two times the volatility strike price [i.e., (vega notional)/(2 × volatility strike)].

Vega The change in a given derivative instrument for a given small change in volatility, holding everything else constant. A sensitivity measure for options that reflects the effect of volatility.

Vega notional The trade size for a variance swap, which represents the average profit and loss of the variance swap for a 1% change in volatility from the strike.

Vesting The process of an employee becoming unconditionally entitled to, and an employer becoming obligated to pay, compensation.

Volatility clustering The tendency for large (small) swings in prices to be followed by large (small) swings of random direction.

Volatility skew The skewed plot (of implied volatility (y-axis) against strike price (x-axis) for options on the same underlying with the same expiration) that occurs when the implied volatility increases for OTM puts and decreases for OTM calls, as the strike price moves away from the current price.

Volatility smile The U-shaped plot (of implied volatility (y-axis) against strike price (x-axis) for options on the same underlying with the same expiration) that occurs when the implied volatilities priced into both OTM puts and calls trade at a premium to implied volatilities of ATM options.

Wealth The value of all the assets owned by an individual.

Wealth life cycle Stages of an individual investor's wealth in terms of human capital, financial capital, and economic net worth.

Portfolio Management Pathway Glossary

Accounting defeasement A way of extinguishing a debt obligation by setting aside sufficient high-quality securities to repay the liability. Also called *in-substance defeasance*.

Active management A portfolio management approach that allows risk factor mismatches relative to a benchmark index causing potentially significant return differences between the active portfolio and the underlying benchmark.

Active return The return on a portfolio minus the return on the portfolio's benchmark.

Active risk The standard deviation of active returns.

Active share A measure of how similar a portfolio is to its benchmark. A manager who precisely replicates the benchmark will have an active share of zero; a manager with no holdings in common with the benchmark will have an active share of one.

Agency trade A trade in which the broker is engaged to find the other side of the trade, acting as an agent. In doing so, the broker does not assume any risk for the trade.

Alpha decay In a trading context, alpha decay is the erosion or deterioration in short term alpha after the investment decision has been made.

Alternative trading systems Trading venues that function like exchanges but that do not exercise regulatory authority over their subscribers except with respect to the conduct of the subscribers' trading in their trading systems. Also called *electronic communications networks* or *multilateral trading facilities*.

Arrival price In a trading context, the arrival price is the security price at the time the order was released to the market for execution.

Asset swap spread (ASW) The spread over MRR on an interest rate swap for the remaining life of the bond that is equivalent to the bond's fixed coupon.

Asset swaps Convert a bond's fixed coupon to MRR plus (or minus) a spread.

Authorized participants (APs) A special group of institutional investors who are authorized by the ETF issuer to participate in the creation/redemption process. APs are large broker/dealers, often market makers.

Barbell A fixed-income investment strategy combining short- and long-term bond positions.

Bear flattening A decrease in the yield spread between long- and short-term maturities across the yield curve, which is largely driven by a rise in short-term bond yields-to-maturity.

Bear steepening An increase in the yield spread between long- and short-term maturities across the yield curve, which is largely driven by a rise in long-term bond yields-to-maturity.

Breadth The number of truly independent decisions made each year.

Bull flattening A decrease in the yield spread between long- and short-term maturities across the yield curve, which is largely driven by a decline in long-term bond yields-to-maturity.

Bull steepening An increase in the yield spread between long- and short-term maturities across the yield curve, which is largely driven by a decline in short-term bond yields-to-maturity.

Bullet A fixed-income investment strategy that focuses on the intermediate term (or "belly") of the yield curve.

Butterfly spread A measure of yield curve shape or curvature equal to double the intermediate yield-to-maturity less the sum of short- and long-term yields-to-maturity.

Butterfly strategy A common yield curve shape strategy that combines a long or short bullet position with a barbell portfolio in the opposite direction to capitalize on expected yield curve shape changes.

Carry trade across currencies A strategy seeking to benefit from a positive interest rate differential across currencies by combining a short position (or borrowing) in a low-yielding currency and a long position (or lending) in a high-yielding currency.

Cash drag Tracking error caused by temporarily uninvested cash.

CDS curve Plot of CDS spreads across maturities for a single reference entity or group of reference entities in an index.

Cell approach See *stratified sampling*.

Closet indexer A fund that advertises itself as being actively managed but is substantially similar to an index fund in its exposures.

Completion overlay A type of overlay that addresses an indexed portfolio that has diverged from its proper exposure.

Conditional value at risk (CVaR) Also known as expected loss The average portfolio loss over a specific time period conditional on that loss exceeding the value at risk (VaR) threshold.

Contingent immunization Hybrid approach that combines immunization with an active management approach when the asset portfolio's value exceeds the present value of the liability portfolio.

Covered interest rate parity The relationship among the spot exchange rate, the forward exchange rate, and the interest rates in two currencies that ensures that the return on a hedged (i.e., covered) foreign risk-free investment is the same as the return on a domestic risk-free investment. Also called *interest rate parity*.

Credit cycle The expansion and contraction of credit over the business cycle, which translates into asset price changes based on default and recovery expectations across maturities and rating categories.

Credit default swap (CDS) basis Yield spread on a bond, as compared to CDS spread of same tenor.

Credit loss rate The realized percentage of par value lost to default for a group of bonds equal to the bonds' default rate multiplied by the loss severity.

Credit migration The change in a bond's credit rating over a certain period.

Credit valuation adjustment (CVA) The present value of credit risk for a loan, bond, or derivative obligation.

Cross-currency basis swap A swap in which notional principals are exchanged because the goal of the transaction is to issue at a more favorable funding rate and swap the amount back to the currency of choice.

Currency overlay A type of overlay that helps hedge the returns of securities held in foreign currency back to the home country's currency.

Decision price In a trading context, the decision price is the security price at the time the investment decision was made.

Default intensity POD over a specified time period in a reduced form credit model.

Default risk See *credit risk.*

Delay cost The (trading related) cost associated with not submitting the order to the market in a timely manner.

Direct market access (DMA) Access in which market participants can transact orders directly with the order book of an exchange using a broker's exchange connectivity.

Discount margin The discount (or required) margin is the yield spread versus the MRR such that the FRN is priced at par on a rate reset date.

Duration Times Spread (DTS) Weighting of spread duration by credit spread to incorporate the empirical observation that spread changes for lower-rated bonds tend to be consistent on a percentage rather than absolute basis.

Empirical duration Estimation of the price–yield relationship using historical bond market data in statistical models.

Enhanced indexing strategy A method investors use to match an underlying market index in which the investor purchases fewer securities than the full set of index constituents but matches primary risk factors reflected in the index.

Evaluated pricing See *matrix pricing.*

Excess spread Surplus difference of yield remaining after payments to bondholders are made after expenses are made and losses are covered.

Execution cost The difference between the (trading related) cost of the real portfolio and the paper portfolio, based on shares and prices transacted.

Expected shortfall The average loss conditional on exceeding the VaR cutoff; sometimes referred to as *conditional VaR* or *expected tail loss.*

Expected tail loss See *expected shortfall.*

Forward rate bias An empirically observed divergence from interest rate parity conditions that active investors seek to benefit from by borrowing in a lower-yield currency and investing in a higher-yield currency.

Full replication approach When every issue in an index is represented in the portfolio and each portfolio position has approximately the same weight in the fund as in the index.

G-spread Yield spread in basis points between a bond's yield-to-maturity and that of an actual or interpolated government bond. It represents the return for bearing risks relative to the government bond.

Green bonds Bonds used in green finance whereby the proceeds are earmarked toward environmental-related products.

Hazard rate The probability that an event will occur, given that it has not already occurred.

I-spread (interpolated spread) Yield spread measure using swaps or constant maturity Treasury YTMs as a benchmark.

Immunization An asset/liability management approach that structures investments in bonds to match (offset) liabilities' weighted-average duration; a type of dedication strategy.

Implementation shortfall (IS) The difference between the return for a notional or paper portfolio, where all transactions are assumed to take place at the manager's decision price, and the portfolio's actual return, which reflects realized transactions, including all fees and costs.

Incremental VaR (or partial VaR) The change in the minimum portfolio loss expected to occur over a given time period at a specific confidence level resulting from increasing or decreasing a portfolio position.

Information coefficient Formally defined as the correlation between forecast return and actual return. In essence, it measures the effectiveness of investment insight.

Key rate duration Also known as partial duration, is a measure of a bond's sensitivity to a change in the benchmark yield at a specific maturity.

Liquidity budget The portfolio allocations (or weightings) considered acceptable for the liquidity categories in the liquidity classification schedule (or time-to-cash table).

Liquidity classification schedule A liquidity management classification (or table) that defines portfolio liquidity "buckets" or categories based on the estimated time necessary to convert assets in that particular category into cash.

Loss severity Portion of a bond's value (including unpaid interest) an investor loses in the event of default.

Matrix pricing An estimation process for financial instruments based on the prices of comparable instruments.

Multilateral trading facilities See *alternative trading systems.*

Negative butterfly An increase in the butterfly spread due to lower short- and long-term yields-to-maturity and a higher intermediate yield-to-maturity.

OAS duration The change in bond price for a given change in OAS.

Opportunity cost The value that investors forgo by choosing a particular course of action; the value of something in its best alternative use.

Option-adjusted spread (OAS) A generalized constant yield spread over the zero curve that incorporates bond option pricing based on assumed interest rate volatility and may be used for callable, putable, and non-callable bonds.

Options on bond futures contracts Instruments that involve the right, but not the obligation, to enter into a bond futures contract at a pre-determined strike (bond price) on a future date in exchange for an up-front premium.

Overlay A derivative position (or derivative positions) used to adjust a pre-existing portfolio closer to its objectives.

Passive investment In the fixed-income context, it is investment that seeks to mimic the prevailing characteristics of the overall investments available in terms of credit quality, type of borrower, maturity, and duration rather than express a specific market view.

Portfolio overlay An array of derivative positions managed separately from the securities portfolio to achieve overall intended portfolio characteristics.

Positive butterfly A decrease in the butterfly spread due to higher short- and long-term yields-to-maturity and a lower intermediate yield-to-maturity.

Present value of distribution of cash flows methodology Method used to address a portfolio's sensitivity to rate changes along the yield curve. This approach seeks to approximate and match the yield curve risk of an index over discrete time periods.

Principal trade A trade in which the market maker or dealer becomes a disclosed counterparty and assumes risk for the trade by transacting the security for their own account. Also called *broker risk trades.*

Probability of default The likelihood that a borrower defaults or fails to meet its obligation to make full and timely payments of principal and interest.

Program trading A strategy of buying or selling many stocks simultaneously.

Pure indexing Attempts to replicate a bond index as closely as possible, targeting zero active return and zero active risk.

Quoted margin Specified spread of a floating rate instrument over a market reference rate or benchmark.

Rebalancing overlay A type of overlay that addresses a portfolio's need to sell certain constituent securities and buy others.

Reduced form credit models Credit models that solve for default probability over a specific time period using observable company-specific variables such as financial ratios and macroeconomic variables.

Relative VaR See *ex ante tracking error.*

Request for quote (RFQ) A non-binding quote provided by a market maker or dealer to a potential buyer or seller upon request. Commonly used in fixed income markets these quotes are only valid at the time they are provided.

Scenario analysis A variation of the valuation process combining a base case with alternative outcomes, allowing the incorporation of more favorable or adverse scenarios in the valuation process.

Smart beta Involves the use of transparent, rules-based strategies as a basis for investment decisions.

Smart order routers (SOR) Smart systems used to electronically route small orders to the best markets for execution based on order type and prevailing market conditions.

Spread duration The change in bond price for a given change in yield spread. Also referred to as OAS duration when the option-adjusted spread (OAS) is the yield measure used.

Stratified sampling A sampling method that guarantees that subpopulations of interest are represented in the sample. Also called *representative sampling* or *cell approach.*

Structural credit models Credit models that apply market-based variables to estimate the value of an issuer's assets and the volatility of asset value.

Structural risk Risk that arises from portfolio design, particularly the choice of the portfolio allocations.

Surplus The difference between assets and liabilities, analogous to shareholders' equity on a corporate balance sheet.

Swaption This instrument grants a party the right, but not the obligation, to enter into an interest rate swap at a pre-determined strike (fixed swap rate) on a future date in exchange for an up-front premium.

Time-to-cash table See *liquidity classification schedule.*

Total return swap A swap in which one party agrees to pay the total return on a security. Often used as a credit derivative, in which the underlying is a bond.

Tracking error The standard deviation of the differences between a portfolio's returns and its benchmark's returns; a synonym of active risk. Also called *tracking risk.*

Tracking risk The standard deviation of the differences between a portfolio's returns and its benchmarks returns. Also called tracking error.

Trade urgency A reference to how quickly or slowly an order is executed over the trading time horizon.

Transfer coefficient The ability to translate portfolio insights into investment decisions without constraint.

Uncovered interest rate parity The proposition that the expected return on an uncovered (i.e., unhedged) foreign currency (risk-free) investment should equal the return on a comparable domestic currency investment.

Value at risk (VaR) The minimum loss that would be expected a certain percentage of the time over a certain period of time given the assumed market conditions.

Yield spread The difference in yield-to-maturity between a bond and that of a another bond.

Z-score A reduced-form statistical credit measure that uses company-specific and market-based ratios to create a composite score used to determine whether a firm is likely to default or remain solvent.

Zero-discount margin (Z-DM) A yield spread calculation for FRNs that incorporates forward MRR.

Zero-volatility spread (Z-spread) A constant spread which is estimated using the market prices of comparable bonds for issuers of similar credit quality of a bond over the benchmark rate.

Private Markets Pathway Glossary

100/10/1 rule of thumb A VC investor's rule of thumb that demonstrates the high selectivity required, as one may review 100 startup pitches, conduct due diligence on 10 of those reviewed, and select just one for investment.

Acquisition and development loan A loan used to purchase and prepare land for a specific construction use.

Agency cost of equity A principal–agent problem which arises when company managers have more information about a company than public shareholders, limiting the ability to assess performance and take corrective action.

Agreement among lenders A contractual arrangement among lenders in a unitranche debt facility which may reallocate interest and principal payments, priority of claims, or voting rights on covenant or other credit agreement changes.

Angel investors High-net-worth investors who are also often entrepreneurs that provide seed financing to startup companies.

Arbitrage spread The difference between an announced acquisition price and the post-announcement market price, which represents the potential return to a merger arbitrage strategy prior to considering transaction costs.

Asset impairment An adverse change in the market value of an asset that falls below its balance sheet carrying value.

Asset swap Converts a bond's fixed coupon to MRR plus (or minus) a spread using an interest rate swap for the remaining life of the bond.

Asset-based lending Revolving credit facility extended on a secured basis using accounts receivable, inventory, or equipment as collateral.

Bankruptcy Legal proceedings, which vary by jurisdiction, allowing a firm whose liabilities exceed its assets to restructure existing debt obligations or liquidate assets in an orderly manner.

Bond tender offer An offer from a fixed-income issuer to repurchase outstanding loans or bonds.

Brownfield investment Infrastructure investments that involve existing rather than to-be-built facilities, which may involve the privatization or repurposing of existing public assets or an expansion of existing facilities.

Build-operate-transfer (BOT) project Infrastructure project whose construction and development is conducted by private entities sponsored by a public entity and transferred to public control after a finite operating period.

Business development companies A type of closed-end investment vehicle in the United States which are publicly traded and specialize in private debt.

Buyout equity Private equity investment in a mature company with the intent to transform, divest, or acquire businesses and sell the reorganized firm at a higher price to public or private investors.

Capital structure arbitrage An investment approach that combines long or short debt, equity, and/or credit default swap positions to exploit mispricing in a single issuer's obligations.

Capitalization rate A measure of the required rate of return on a property, also known as *cap rate*.

Capitalization table A detailed summary of changes in firm value, fractional ownership dilution, and prices paid by investors or stakeholders over the course of multiple equity rounds typically shown on a fully diluted basis.

Carbon offset Investments that reduce or remove carbon dioxide and other greenhouse gases to compensate for emissions produced elsewhere to achieve reduction or net-zero emission goals.

Carried interest A performance or incentive fee applied to private market fund investments based on returns above a hurdle rate.

Catch-up clause A clause in a limited partner agreement that specifies that a general partner will receive 100% of the distributions above a prespecified hurdle *until* the GP receives the carried interest percentage (such as 20%) of the returns generated and then every excess dollar will be split between the LPs and GP based on the carried interest percentage.

CDS basis Differences in bond and CDS spreads that arise because of bond price differences from par, accrued interest, and varying contract terms.

Change of control A debt clause that requires an issuer to repurchase outstanding bonds at a fixed price at or above par if a new owner acquires a predetermined percentage of voting shares.

Change of control clause Debt provision that requires an issuer to offer to repay outstanding debt if a new owner acquires a predetermined percentage of voting shares.

Change of control provision A restrictive covenant typically included in a high-yield bond indenture that requires the issuer to offer to repurchase outstanding bonds at a fixed price (above par) if a new owner acquires a predetermined percentage of voting shares.

Circulation Zoning requirement mandating provisions for security and emergency access to buildings or facilities.

Clawback provisions Limited partnership agreement provisions that involve returning GP performance fees to LPs in cases where transactions that are initially successful later face losses.

Closed-end funds Funds with a finite life requiring an initial capital commitment with a lockup period and eventual sale of the property or properties for distribution to investors.

Collateralized loan obligations (CLOs) Investment vehicle with exposure to a portfolio of leveraged loans separated into tranches with different cash flow claims and exposure to losses based on a waterfall.

Concession agreement A contractual arrangement under which an entity (also known as a grantor) establishes terms and conditions with a developer or operator (referred to as a concessionaire) to plan, build, operate, finance, and maintain an infrastructure asset for a specific period.

Concessionaire A developer or operator that is provided the right under a concession agreement to charge user fees over an operating period to recover construction, maintenance, and operational costs and compensate investors.

Construction and development (C&D) loan Debt financing for real estate development which is committed prior to project initiation and drawn through a construction phase, accruing interest over time, and typically repaid with a mortgage loan.

Construction and development loan A loan used to provide funds during the building phase of a real estate project.

Continuation funds New private investment funds established by GPs through the sale of existing assets in another limited partnership in GP-led secondary transactions.

Contracts for difference (CfDs) Contracts used as an income stabilization measure under which the difference between a pre-agreed, fixed contractual price (or strike price) for a service or good is exchanged for the current prevailing market price (or so-called reference price).

Contractual subordination Use of contract or intercreditor agreement between senior and subordinated lenders to establish seniority ranking of debt obligations.

Conversion period The period over which a convertible bond may be exchanged for equity at a predetermined price.

Conversion price Predetermined share price at which convertible debt may be fully exchanged for common shares during the conversion period.

Conversion ratio The number of common shares a convertible bond or noteholder may receive in exchange for a specific bond par value.

Conversion value The current contingency feature value derived by comparing a convertible bond's price with its value if a bondholder were to exchange bonds for shares.

Convertible arbitrage A special situations investment approach that involves capitalizing on the perceived mispricing of the underlying risk components of a convertible bond.

Convertible debt A fixed-income instrument which combines the features of debt with equity via a contingent feature, allowing debtholders to exchange their claim for common shares at a predetermined fixed price in the future.

Convertible preferred shares (CPS) A form of preferred stock that may pay a dividend and be converted into common shares at a fixed conversion ratio, or number of common shares received for each preferred share.

Convexity The second order, usually a positive change in the price of a bond for a given change in yield, which can be negative for a callable bond such as a high-yield bond.

Covenant-lite Debt transactions involving a relatively weak set of restrictive covenants imposed on an issuer due to competitive market pressures.

Credit event An occurrence that triggers the settlement of a CDS contract, including failure to make a debt payment, debt restructuring, or a bankruptcy filing.

Credit loss rate The realized percentage of par value lost to default for a group of bonds equal to the bonds' default rate multiplied by the loss severity.

Credit valuation adjustment (CVA) The present value of credit risk for a loan, bond, or derivative obligation.

Data room A repository used to store confidential company documents that may be accessed by potential bidders who sign a non-disclosure agreement.

Debt profile A detailed breakdown of short-term and long-term liabilities by tenor, seniority, and other features, used in a private debt market strategy.

Debt service coverage ratio A ratio in which the net operating income of a real estate investment for a specific period is divided by the amount of debt service to be paid during the same time period.

Debt service reserve account (DSRA) A separate fund established to accumulate the cash flow necessary to meet debt service requirements from which cash is released when debt interest and principal payments are due.

Debt-for-equity exchange An exchange executed by distressed firms in which new shares are issued to debtholders in exchange for the extinguishment of existing debt claims.

Debtor in possession (DIP) A debtor that has filed for Chapter 11 US bankruptcy protection but remains in possession of company assets for the purpose of maintaining operations as a going concern.

Delay option Developers may increase a project's present value by postponing property construction until market conditions improve.

DIP financing Super senior debt financing obtained on a short-term basis to cover ongoing bankruptcy costs and provide funding to maintain operations as a company completes the bankruptcy process.

Direct capitalization approach A property valuation approach that divides a single year's net operating income by the cap rate to estimate a property's value.

Direct co-investment The direct purchase of an ownership stake or private debt investment with the use of one or more partners, one or more of whom may be a private fund manager.

Direct investment The purchase of an ownership stake or debt investment without the use of a partner or an investment intermediary.

Direct lending A type of senior secured leveraged loan privately issued on a floating-rate basis by non-bank lenders, usually to small and medium-sized companies.

Distressed debt Loans or bonds which face a high likelihood of non-payment or bankruptcy.

Distressed debt exchange An exchange of existing bonds for new securities from the same issuer that involve lower par values, longer maturities, and/or fewer protective financial covenants than current outstanding bonds.

Distributed to paid-in (DPI) Also referred to as the cash-on-cash return, this ratio gauges an investor's realized rate of return via the ratio of cumulative distributions to limited partners to the capital invested.

Dividend recapitalization A change in the mix of debt and equity outstanding for an existing corporate issuer which increases leverage via debt-financed dividends or share repurchases to benefit existing shareholders.

Down round Venture capital financing of an early-stage company which takes place at a share price below that of the previous financing round.

Duration The first-order, linear change in a bond's price for a given yield change in yield, which is a negative or inverse relationship.

Effective spread duration Change in a loan or bond price for a given change in yield spread, with the spread typically defined as OAS.

Empirical duration Estimation of the price–yield relationship using historical bond market data in statistical models.

Equity dividend rate A ratio in which a real estate investment's before-tax cash flow (equal to net operating income minus debt service) is divided by the difference between the investment's purchase price and the amount of debt outstanding.

Exit value of equity The expected terminal value of an early-stage firm at the end of a holding period is determined by using the required return on investment or a market multiple if the firm is expected to be profitable.

Export credit agencies (ECAs) Quasi-government entities sponsored by developed market governments to promote the export of domestic goods and services via credit insurance, political risk insurance, or subsidized or guaranteed debt financing.

Fallen angels Formerly investment-grade-rated issuers whose bonds are downgraded to high yield due to credit deterioration.

Feed crops Crops such as grain used as either raw material in food production or as an intermediate good.

Financial buyer An owner seeking to earn investment returns from an existing company without identifying or capitalizing on synergies from a controlling interest.

Financial dislocation A situation in which market prices are misaligned on an absolute or relative basis due to financial market stress, changes in liquidity, market constraints, or other industry- or company-specific factors.

Financial sponsor A private equity buyout fund which purchases a controlling stake in a firm distributed to investors in the form of limited partnerships.

First lien Also known as a priority lien, this investor protection grants a lender the right to take possession of property from a borrower which fails to repay debt.

First-out tranche Senior debt tranche in a unitranche facility which is typically at an interest rate below the blended facility rate and repaid earlier than subordinated debt claims.

Fraudulent conveyance An unlawful transfer of assets by an issuer to a third party to prevent creditors from reaching a borrower's assets, which in some cases may be voided by a court under bankruptcy law.

Free cash flow to the firm (FCFF) Free cash flow to both debt and equity holders composed of after-tax EBITDA plus tax benefits of depreciation less changes in long-term assets and working capital.

Free fall bankruptcy A situation in which an issuer enters the bankruptcy process without a reorganization plan in place.

General partners (GPs) Private fund managers responsible for sourcing and deploying capital from limited partner investors over an investment life cycle and distributing returns to those investors over a finite investment holding period.

Go-shop process Provision in a sale or merger agreement in which the seller solicits bids from potential third-party buyers for a limited period after extending the offer to an initial buyer.

Governance rights Powers extended to preferred or minority shareholders which may include board seats, special voting rights, or the ability to observe board meetings, among others.

GP-led secondary A form of private market sale in which a general partner sells a private asset from an existing portfolio into a new fund.

Grantor Another word for "settlor," who is a person who creates a trust.

Greenfield investment New "to be built" infrastructure projects and assets created to provide a specific essential service or to supply a public good.

Growth equity Private equity investment in a young company with a business model and growing revenue used to reach its total addressable market and reduce concentrated ownership of founders and initial investors.

Growth equity method Valuation approach used for private companies engaging in profitable expansion which incorporates cash flow projections over an investment horizon required to achieve a desired exit valuation and initial capital necessary to reach a targeted investor ROI.

Hard hurdle rate The minimum rate of return in a performance-based fee arrangement in which the GP earns only fees on annual returns that exceed the hurdle rate.

Heavily indebted poor countries (HIPCs) A specific group of developing countries eligible for support from the International Monetary Fund (IMF) and the World Bank.

High-water mark A measure that reflects the fund's maximum value as of a performance fee payment date net of fees.

High-yield bonds Fixed-income securities issued on a fixed-rate basis by sub-investment grade companies, which are typically subordinate to leveraged loans and include call features.

Hurdle rate A predetermined minimum rate of return an investment fund must reach before a GP receives incentive-based compensation.

Incurrence covenants Restrictive debt covenants involving financial metrics which only must be met at the time the issuer seeks to take on additional debt.

Infrastructure Company Classification Standard (TICCS) A standard developed to categorize infrastructure investments based on key characteristics affecting relative risk and return with the input of asset owners and asset managers.

Insolvency A situation in which an issuer's total liabilities exceed the market value of its assets.

Intercreditor agreement Legal contract specifying details of the priority of claims and other key terms governing separate debt claims to the same assets and legal entity.

Intermittent market reference price (IMRP) The UK market reference price for intermittently produced power determined daily based on the prior day's hourly electricity rates.

Internal rate of return (IRR) The uniform discount rate for a series of cash flows over n periods that returns a net present value of zero.

Interval funds Open-end funds with certain constraints that have no predetermined maturity date but include liquidity restrictions, such as limits on the fraction of total assets available for redemption on a periodic basis.

J-curve effect Net income over a multiyear private investment holding period characterized by negative returns in an initial phase, followed by cash flow and income growth toward the end of the holding period.

Land expectation value Value of an acre of bare land in perpetual timberland production.

Last-out tranche Junior debt tranche in a unitranche facility which is at an interest rate above the blended facility rate and repaid after senior debt claims.

LBO model Valuation approach used for buyout equity which uses expected cash flows of a target acquisition, as well as expected capital structure composition and cost, to establish the maximum price that can be paid to a seller while satisfying targeted financing returns.

Leveraged buyout (LBO) Buyout equity transaction that uses a high proportion of debt financing to make a company acquisition.

Leveraged loan Term debt extended to sub-investment-grade borrowers with a floating-rate periodic coupon based on market reference rates plus a spread that usually is secured and involves restrictive covenants.

Leveraged loans Term debt extended to sub-investment grade borrowers with a floating-rate periodic coupon based upon market reference rates plus a spread, which usually are secured and involve restrictive covenants.

Limited partner co-investment Involves the purchase of an ownership stake or private debt investment in a single investment that is managed by a private fund manager or general partner.

Limited partners (LPs) Outside investors in a private market fund who own a fractional interest in a limited, closed-end partnership managed by a general partner based on the investment commitment and other terms set out in a limited partner agreement.

Limited partnership Closed-end form of ownership frequently used in private market funds in which private market fund investors, or limited partners, commit capital that is invested, managed, and distributed by a private market fund manager, or general partner, over an investment holding period.

Liquidation preference payout Predefined distribution of cash proceeds to preferred shareholders made in full before any distributions are made to common shareholders.

Liquidity financing Private debt funds which seek to generate income by investing in a portfolio of short-term obligations in order to maintain a stable net asset value.

Loan to value (LTV) A measure of leverage used by debt investors that equals the loan amount outstanding divided by the project value.

Loan-to-value ratio A ratio in which the amount of debt outstanding on a real estate investment is divided by the current value of the investment.

Lockup agreement A provision requiring a private equity investor to retain a material interest in the shares of a new public company for a predetermined period to protect the interests of institutional investors.

Loss given default (LGD) The amount a debtholder fails to recover if a default occurs, usually expressed as a percentage of par value.

Low Carbon Contracts Company (LCCC) UK government-owned counterparty for qualified low-carbon energy contracts for difference.

Maintenance covenants Restrictive debt covenants requiring an issuer to meet certain financial metrics for each financial reporting period.

Management buyout A private sale to a strategic buyer that includes a company's existing management. The management team commits their own equity capital along with other investors as an incentive to grow the firm's cash flows and value.

Merchant payment scheme Also referred to as a commercial payment scheme, under this structure frequently used for power generation and toll road assets, an operator has the right to collect service or user fees over an operating period but remains exposed to the asset's business risk based on demand and other economic factors.

Merger arbitrage Special situations investments related to business combinations in which investors seek to capitalize on price discrepancies of securities issued by the target company.

Mezzanine debt Debt claims that are serviced after all senior debt claims, but before common shares and other forms of equity in the capital structure.

Mezzanine loan A debt claim that is serviced after all senior debt claims but before common shares and other forms of equity in the capital structure.

Multiple of invested capital A ratio in which the total value of all realized investments and residual asset values (assets that may still be awaiting sale) are divided by capital invested.

Multiple of invested capital (MOIC) Also referred to as the multiple of money or total value to paid-in, this private market performance measure incorporates both the cumulative distributions received and the net asset value of a fund as a proportion of invested capital.

Multiple of money (MOM) Also referred to as the multiple of invested capital or total value to paid-in, this private market return measure incorporates both the cumulative distributions received and the fund's net asset value as a proportion of invested capital.

Net operating income A key property income measure that ignores financing costs and taxes and is measured as NOI = Effective gross income – Operating expenses – Property maintenance allowance.

Non-disclosure agreement A legal contract specifying that any confidential information received by a prospective company buyer is used only to evaluate a possible transaction.

Non-sponsored loans Direct loans to small- or medium-sized firms which lack a controlling financial sponsor and involve greater search, due diligence, and monitoring costs.

Open-end diversified core equity (ODCE) funds Private investment funds that hold portfolios of core income-producing properties.

Open-end funds Funds which allow investors to contribute or withdraw capital freely and have no predetermined end date.

Optimal conversion point The implied equity price at which convertible preferred shareholders are better off exercising their right to convert preferred shares into common shares.

Option-adjusted spread (OAS) A generalized constant yield spread over the zero curve that incorporates bond option pricing based on assumed interest rate volatility and may be used for callable, putable, and non-callable bonds.

Own–lease A farmland investing model more common among financial investors in which an owner or lessor receives fixed rental payments for undeveloped tillable acreage under a multiyear lease agreement from a farm operator lessee who assumes all other business risks.

Own–operate A farmland investing model which involves owning land, buildings, equipment, and other assets as well as operating an agricultural business.

P90 level Probability-weighted measure of the minimum amount of electricity an average wind turbine is 90% likely to produce over an average period given changing weather conditions.

Paid-in capital (PIC) Reflects the proportion of the limited partners' total committed capital that the general partner has so far deployed, following any capital calls, to total committed capital.

Participation rights Preferred share feature which offers upside gains to investors via similar distributions to those received by common shareholders instead of a conversion to common equity.

Payment in kind (PIK) Interest paid not in cash, but via accrual, increasing the debt principal outstanding, which is then paid at maturity.

Permanent crops Agricultural crops planted for many seasons, such as orchards or vineyards, which typically generate a higher return per acre or hectare.

Post-money valuation A combination of the pre-money valuation and new equity invested.

Pre-money valuation Estimated current value of a startup company prior to new financing derived using the VC method.

Pre-seed capital Initial equity capital for a new business, most often sourced from founders and angel investors, which is used to establish the feasibility of a product or market need.

Prepackaged bankruptcy A detailed business plan and exit strategy with a new capital structure proposal that is formulated and agreed on with major creditors prior to entering the bankruptcy process.

Price step-up Change in a company's price per share over a series of financings.

Private asset investment life cycle Refers to the multiyear investment holding period common among private investments that consists of capital commitment, deployment, distribution and exit phases.

Probability of default (POD) The likelihood that a borrower fails to make full and timely payments of principal and interest according to debt terms, usually expressed in annual percentage terms.

Public market equivalent A theoretical public market investment in which private fund cash outflows are invested in a public market index while cash inflows are sold from a public market index.

Public–private partnerships (PPPs) A long-term contractual relationship between the public and private sectors involving a concession agreement or other form of compensation in exchange for delivering an essential service or public good.

Pulpwood A timber product consisting of lower-quality, small, and often thinned trees that is the primary input for paper products.

Quoted margin (QM) Spread over the market reference rate for a floating-rate loan established at the time of issuance to compensate investors for issuer credit and liquidity risk.

Ratchet provision Antidilution provision negotiated by investors in early-stage companies that partially or fully reduces the conversion price of existing options or preferred shares to the price at which new shares are issued in a subsequent financing round.

Real options Refers to the right but not the obligation to take future action. The existence of such options may affect the value of a real estate investment.

Recurring revenue financing A form of venture debt in which a private loan is offered to a startup firm with an established subscriber base in the form of a discounted upfront monthly payment of expected subscription revenue in exchange for all monthly subscriber cash flows.

Redemption rights Grant an investor the right to redeem preferred shares for cash as a form of downside protection against adverse events.

Reduced form models Statistical credit models that solve for the probability of default over a specific time period, using observable company-specific and market-based variables.

Reference price The current prevailing market price for a service or good whose difference from a pre-agreed, fixed contractual price (or strike price) determines the settlement amount in a contract for difference.

Request for proposal (RFP) Standardized document used by public entities to choose parties involved in the development, construction, operation, and financing of infrastructure projects that outlines project details, requirements, and timing, as well as assessment criteria used to award contracts to successful bidders.

Required margin Also known as discount margin. The market-determined yield spread over or under the market reference rate such that a floating-rate loan is priced at par on a rate reset date following issuance.

Reserve currencies Freely floating currencies issued by central banks in major developed markets that are widely held by external parties, including central banks.

Residual value to paid-in (RVPI) A measure of an investor's unrealized return on investment equal to the fund's net asset value as a proportion of the total invested capital.

Retained cash flow (RCF) Net cash from operating activities less dividends, and often compared to net debt as a measure of financial leverage.

Return on investment (ROI) A simple performance measure equal to the ratio or multiplier of cash flows received versus those invested that ignores the time value of money and length of an investment holding period.

Revolving credit agreement The most reliable form of a short-term bank borrowing facility, which can be drawn and repaid based upon working capital needs and in effect for multiple years on either a secured or unsecured basis. Also known as revolvers.

Row crops Agricultural crops harvested annually and rotated.

Sawtimber Top-quality timber used for construction lumber, as well as other building products, such as plywood or particleboard.

Scenario analysis A variation of the valuation process combining a base case with alternative outcomes, allowing the incorporation of more favorable or adverse scenarios in the valuation process.

Second lien An investor protection which increases the recovery rate in the event of default versus unsecured debt. A second lien loan is secured by an asset with an existing lien and will only be repaid once the first lien creditor receives payment.

Secondaries Limited partnership stakes in existing mid-cycle private market funds that are purchased and sold among LPs, which in many cases involves the fund GP as an intermediary.

Seed capital Equity investment(s) used to launch a startup company once it has a proven business idea.

Sensitivity analysis A form of analysis used to determine the impact of a change in one or more key variables affecting investment returns or valuation.

Sequencing option Dividing and executing a project in staggered phases rather than all at once, which may increase a project's risk-adjusted return by reducing exposure to market oversupply during the lease-up period.

Series financing One or more stages of equity investment in young companies which occurs after the firm is established and before it is sold or goes public.

Setback Zoning requirement mandating provisions for distance to property lines.

Social infrastructure Infrastructure investments directed toward essential government services, such as education and health care.

Soft hurdle rate The minimum rate of return in a performance-based fee arrangement in which the entire return is subject to the fee once the hurdle is exceeded.

Sovereign immunity A principle that limits legal recourse of lenders from forcing a sovereign borrower to declare bankruptcy or liquidate its assets to settle debt claims.

Special purpose entity (SPE) Also referred to as a special purpose vehicle (SPV), this legal entity is created for a specific economic purpose. In the case of a project SPV, the entity's sole purpose is to facilitate the construction, operation, and financing of an infrastructure asset over its contractual life.

Special situations An area of private capital investment that targets return by investing in stressed, distressed, or event-driven opportunities.

Specialty financing Involves forms of non-bank lending to commercial and consumer borrowers such as credit card receivables, leasing, and installment loans.

Sponsored loans Debt funding in which a private equity firm with a large equity investment in a prospective borrower directly solicits debt investors for the company.

Stabilized NOI A more permanent level of the property's earnings potential over time, as opposed to the amount of NOI observed during a specific time period that may result from temporary market cycles.

Strategic buyer An investor seeking to capitalize on synergies by extending the value creation process initiated by a GP, combining a business with another portfolio company, or taking other actions to increase firm value.

Strike price A pre-agreed, fixed contractual price per period whose difference from the current prevailing market price (or so-called reference price) determines the settlement amount in a contract for difference.

Structural credit risk models Option-based models of a firm's market value of assets over time versus its fixed obligations used to link an issuer's likelihood of default to its equity price.

Structural subordination Refers to the positioning of debt, which is issued by a legal entity, typically a holding company, which is separate and therefore one step removed from an operating company, which holds assets pledged under a security agreement to senior secured debtholders.

Stumpage fee A fee paid to timberland owners by private firms for the right to harvest timber.

Subscription lines Short-term lines of credit extended to private market funds that are secured by LP investor fund commitments prior to drawdown.

Sum-of-the-parts valuation A valuation approach that considers the value of a firm's business segments if they are sold separately.

Switching option The option to choose among alternative projects for a given plot of land or switch economic uses for an existing project, such as a mixed-use facility, which may increase value.

Take-private transaction Also referred to as a *go-private transaction*, this involves the purchase of a public company by private investors in which the target company's shares are no longer publicly traded.

Technical default A violation of the terms and conditions of a credit, loan, or bond agreement, such as the breach of a financial covenant.

Tender process Early bond repayment mechanism in which a voluntary offer is extended to bondholders by an issuer to repurchase outstanding bonds prior to maturity.

Total addressable market A measure of the industry-wide revenue potential for the company's product or service.

Total value to paid-in (TVPI) Also referred to as multiple of invested capital or multiple of money, this measure reflects the overall value to the limited partner by incorporating both the cumulative distributions received and the net asset value as a proportion of invested capital. TVPI is the sum of distributed to paid-in and residual value to paid-in.

Turnkey A type of construction project in which a general contractor agrees to deliver a project on a fully completed basis.

Unitranche debt A hybrid loan combining senior and subordinated debt in one facility, typically issued to small- or medium-sized corporate borrowers by private debt funds.

VC method Valuation method for startup companies in which the current value is determined using the expected terminal value of the firm (or exit value of equity) and the required return on investment.

Venture capital Private equity investment in a startup or early-stage company involving high risk and a high rate of failure.

Venture debt Unsecured debt from non-bank lenders offered to startup companies, often in anticipation of follow-on equity offerings, which typically involves a loan plus a warrant.

Vintage year Year in which capital is initially deployed to a specific investment or project or a private market fund, used for benchmarking purposes and to seek diversification over time in a private market allocation.

Voidable preference A situation in which an issuer grants a preference to one creditor over another in violation of a loan agreement or bond indenture, which may be reversed in bankruptcy court.

Warrant Debt feature or security granting the right to purchase additional common equity shares issued by the company at a predetermined price for a given period.

Weighted average cost of capital (WACC) The expected cost of debt and equity weighted by the proportion of each used in a company's capital structure.

Z-score A reduced-form statistical credit measure that uses company-specific and market-based ratios to create a composite score used to determine whether a firm is likely to default or remain solvent.

Zero-volatility spread (Z-spread) A constant spread which is estimated using the market prices of comparable bonds for issuers of similar credit quality of a bond over the benchmark rate.

Private Wealth Pathway Glossary

Accumulation The process of saving for retirement.

Accumulation period In a lifetime or period-certain annuity, the accumulation period is the phase during which the annuitant makes regular premium payments to build up the annuity's investment value.

Acquirer's dilemma The process of incorporating a new identity as a wealthy person into the identity that an individual already has from their formative years.

Advanced-life deferred annuity An annuity purchased in later life, providing deferred income initiated by a lump-sum payment.

Agreeableness A personality trait that describes the degree to which a person has a kind and empathic orientation to others.

Allocation effect The impact of overweighting and underweighting sectors relative to the benchmark on the return of the portfolio.

Alternative minimum tax (AMT) A special regime of taxation under which an individual calculates their taxes under two sets of rules—one being the conventional and an alternative one, usually more conservative with respect to deductions and tax credits, which is referred to as AMT. The taxable entity will pay the tax calculated under the method that results in the higher tax amount.

Anchoring A type of cognitive bias that makes individuals focus on the first idea or value they are presented with as a baseline for subsequent evaluations of a decision.

Annuity A decumulation vehicle that requires an upfront payment for a stream of periodic payments.

Anstalt A structure combining the attributes of a company and a foundation that is used in civil law jurisdictions for wealth transfer purposes.

Arithmetic active return The arithmetic difference between the return of the portfolio and the return of its benchmark.

Arm's-length transaction Both buyer and seller act independently without any preexisting relationship that may sway their decision making.

Asset structuring The process of structuring a collection of investments, business interests, or other financial holdings to maximize wealth.

Availability heuristic A type of cognitive bias that makes individuals overweight information that is readily available when making decisions.

Beneficiary A person who has beneficial ownership of trust assets and to whom the trustee is accountable.

Bequest The act of giving or leaving property to a specified person(s) through the provisions of a will.

Centralized portfolio management (CPM) A paradigm of total portfolio construction and investment operation whereby the assets of a single beneficiary are managed by multiple managers, internal or external, who act in a coordinated fashion with the goal of improving the optimality of the investment outcome. The coordination involves trading, information sharing, and aggregation that reduces turnover, taxes, and improves the risk-return profile of the overall portfolio.

Charitable incorporated organizations Legally incorporated entities established for non-profit purposes, like social welfare, education, and environmental protection, under the law of Japan.

Charitable lead trust (CLT) A US philanthropic vehicle that inverts the sequence of benefits provided by a CRT. A CLT focuses on offering an immediate income stream to charitable causes while preserving the remainder of the trust's assets for the donor's heirs.

Charitable remainder trust (CRT) A US philanthropic vehicle that provides an income stream to the donor while committing the remaining assets to a future gift to charity.

Choice overload bias This cognitive bias occurs when an individual feels paralyzed into inaction because of the variety and abundance of options.

Citizenship-based tax systems Tax their citizens regardless of their residential status.

Civil law system The elected legislatures, derived from Roman jurisprudence, that enact laws; the courts interpret and apply these laws to each particular case through their judges.

Cohabitation agreement A legal and financial framework for a relationship between two unmarried adults that defines how assets and debts will be treated during cohabitation and in the event of separation or death.

Common law system A case law system derived from the British legal tradition in which previously adjudicated cases influence pending and future cases.

Community foundation A charitable organization that makes social or educational grants for the benefit of a local community as is typically funded by public donations.

Community property Property acquired by a spouse during a marriage that is owned jointly by both spouses and is divided upon divorce, annulment, or the death of a spouse.

Community property regimes Regimes that treat marital assets as jointly owned and thus divided equally in the event of divorce.

Comprehensive wealth planning Focuses on integrated management of all of a client's financial and business affairs.

Concentrated position A holding that, due to its low tax basis and implicit large potential capital gains or personal association with the client, inhibits the development of an efficient, diversified portfolio.

Confirmation bias A type of cognitive bias that makes individuals view information that confirms beliefs they already hold as more salient.

Conscientiousness A personality trait characterizing the ability to exercise discipline and self-control to achieve goals.

Cost-push inflation Inflation triggered by an increase in the costs of production inputs, such as labor and materials, which leads businesses to raise their prices.

Credit method A method that offsets domestic tax liability with the taxes already paid to a foreign country.

Cross-Border Financial Center A financial hub that specializes in providing financial services, like banking, asset management, or investment opportunities, to clients located in different jurisdictions. Unlike OFCs, the emphasis is not necessarily on tax advantages but on serving diverse geographic markets.

Custodian A specialized financial institution responsible for safeguarding an investor's financial assets and is not typically involved in asset management activities. The custodian may offer additional services like performance analytics to assist in portfolio evaluation.

Decumulation The process of spending down savings in retirement.

Deduction method A method that reduces taxable income by the amount already paid to a foreign government.

Deemed disposition A tax event upon death, among others, in certain countries, including Canada, which treats property as if it were sold upon death and imposes a capital gains tax on the assets as if they were sold.

Deferred fixed annuity Provides an annuity payout at a future date, not immediately.

Deferred variable annuities Annuities that initiates payments at a future date, allowing contributions to an investment account whose performance affects payouts.

Demand-pull inflation Inflation triggered by increased consumer demand for goods and services, resulting in upward pressure on prices.

Digital Security Technologies and best practices employed to protect sensitive financial information and digital assets from unauthorized access, data breaches, or cyberattacks. For high-net-worth individuals, robust digital security measures are essential to safeguard not only investment portfolios but also personal data, as these clients are often prime targets for cybercriminals.

Disability A temporary or permanent impairment that substantially limits an individual's employment, employability, and human capital.

Discretionary financial goals Non-essential objectives that are desirable but not critical for maintaining one's lifestyle.

Discretionary trust A trust that provides the trustee discretion in determining what distributions may be made to a beneficiary.

Discretionary wealth The difference between the sum of explicit and implied assets less the sum of current and implied liabilities.

Disposition effect A type of cognitive bias that makes individuals unwilling to sell their possessions at a loss.

Donative intent The making of a transfer without any expectation of anything in exchange.

Donee The person receiving the gift.

Donor A person making a lifetime gift.

Donor-advised fund (DAF) A philanthropic fund that allows donors to make charitable contributions, immediately benefit from tax deductions, and subsequently recommend grants to other qualified charities over time.

Double taxation Income is taxed twice.

Dynasty trusts Trusts that can last for multiple generations, perhaps perpetually, usually created in a jurisdiction that has abolished its rule against perpetuities.

Embedded family office (EFO) A dedicated space within the family business with a small number of staff who handle the financial, legal, and tax matters of the owners.

Endowment effect A type of cognitive bias that makes individuals value an object more highly if they own it than if they did not.

Endowment life insurance A hybrid insurance product that combines features of term and whole life insurance, offering a set coverage period after which the policy matures and pays out the cash value to the policy owner if the insured has not died by that time.

Entrepreneurial personality profile A set of personality traits described in Bill Wagner's book, The Entrepreneur Next Door: Discover the Secrets to Financial Independence, that differentiate entrepreneurs from an average person.

Equivalency determination The determination by the tax authorities that a donee non-US charity is the equivalent of a US public charity.

Estate A person's assets at death.

Estate tax A tax imposed on the value of the estate of a decedent payable by the estate, not the recipient.

Excess return Used in various senses appropriate to context: 1) The difference between the portfolio return and the benchmark return, which may be either positive or negative; 2) The return in excess of the risk-free rate, thus representing the return for bearing risk.

Exemption method A method that allows for offsetting taxes; the home country relinquishes its taxation rights on foreign-source income.

Expenditure responsibility The determination by the tax authorities that a donee non-US charity will use a grant for appropriate purposes as stated in the grant agreement.

External Asset Managers (EAMs) Independent firms or individuals that manage assets on behalf of a client but use the infrastructure and services of a larger financial institution for trade execution, custody, and other operational needs. EAMs offer a personalized touch and can provide a more boutique experience than traditional asset management services.

Externally managed assets Financial and investment assets managed by a hired external manager who the client has determined can add more value to than the client themselves.

Extroversion A personality trait characterizing the degree to which an individual is comfortable in social environments.

Family advisory board A group of family members and non-family members that assist in setting a strategic direction and establishing priorities for overseeing the family's wealth.

Family constitution A formal written agreement among family members that sets out the principles, values, and guidelines by which the family will interact with its wealth, including its family business(es), investments, and philanthropic endeavors.

Family council A select group of family members who act as a representative body that makes decisions on issues concerning family wealth and family business.

Family extended balance sheet Comprehensively accounts for a client's explicit and implicit financial assets, current and future expected liabilities, and net worth.

Family foundation A platform for focused philanthropy. It unites family members toward achieving common charitable goals.

Family limited partnership (FLP) A family limited partnership is a limited partnership created by a family to pool assets. While FLPs have non-tax reasons for their creation, often interests in the FLP can be transferred to family members for estate planning purposes at a valuation discount.

Family mission statement An aspirational statement that reflects a family's shared values and commitments.

Family office A private wealth management advisory firm serving very wealthy clients.

Fideicomiso A trust-like entity that holds and manages assets for specific purposes, including charitable ones, within certain civil law jurisdictions in Latin America.

Fiduciary standard of care States that an advisor must put their clients' interests above their own over the entire course of a relationship.

Fixed annuity An annuity offering a predetermined, fixed annual income derived from an initial lump-sum investment.

Fixed trust A trust that, by its terms, provides for fixed distributions to a beneficiary.

Fondation An independent legal entity used in European civil law countries for philanthropic activities and charitable grantmaking in which founders benefit from income tax deductions for contributions, and the Fondation typically enjoys tax exempt status.

Forced heirship The regime in civil law jurisdictions that requires disposing of a portion of one's estate to one's spouse and descendants.

Forced inheritance rules Rules that establish a legal obligation to leave a portion of one's estate to certain family members, typically children or descendants.

Framing effects A type of cognitive bias that makes the way in which a choice is presented affect decisions.

Funding ratio The ratio of assets to liabilities.

Funding ratio return The ratio of funding ratio at time t to funding ratio at time $t - 1$.

Generation skipping The process of transferring capital directly to the third generation to avoid a double layer of taxation.

Generation-skipping transfer tax A tax imposed in the United States on transfers that skip a generation, which is intended to impose a tax at each generational level.

Gift tax A tax imposed on the donor of a gift based on the value of the gift.

Goals-based planning Aligns an individual's financial resources with their unique goals and circumstances, with the aim of achieving specific financial objectives.

Golden visas Visas that provide initial residency, work rights, and a path to permanent residency, and potentially citizenship, through significant investments in areas like real estate, government debt, or business ventures.

Grantor Another word for "settlor," who is a person who creates a trust.

Grantor retained annuity trust (GRAT) A trust that provides the grantor with an annuity for a period of years.

Health risk Risk that encompasses both direct and indirect costs stemming from unexpected illness or injury, affecting human capital.

Healthspan The number of years of life from birth to the onset of chronic disease or disability.

Hindsight bias A type of cognitive bias that makes individuals misremember the past in ways that make them appear to have made better and more well-informed choices.

Immediate variable annuities Annuities beginning payments immediately after a lump-sum investment, where payment amounts vary based on underlying investment performance.

Income yield The fixed annual income, expressed as a percentage of the initial annuity investment, that the annuitant receives.

Individualism versus collectivism A Hofstede cultural dimension that considers the degree to which individuals are supposed to look out for themselves versus relying on the community for support and sustenance.

Indulgence versus restraint A Hofstede cultural dimension that refers to society's willingness to accept and encourage the gratification of desires versus discouraging the gratification of desires within a relatively rigid set of norms. Another way of looking at this is the degree of permissiveness within a society.

Inflation-adjusted payments Payments that allow annuitants to counter inflation erosion by choosing payments that adjust for inflation or grow by a fixed percentage, although the latter provides a weaker protection against inflation.

Information ratio The ratio of mean active return to standard deviation (active return).

Inheritance Assets that a person receives as a beneficiary after someone's death.

Inheritance tax A tax imposed on the recipient of an inheritance.

Inheritor's dilemma The combination of financial and emotional challenges faced by individuals inheriting significant wealth. It is marked by the pressure to manage and uphold the legacy responsibly.

Institutional family office (IFO) See Professional family office (PFO).

Intentionally defective grantor trust A trust that is created in the United States whereby the gift is not part of the estate of the grantor, but the grantor continues to pay income tax on the assets in the trust.

Inter vivos trust A trust created during the settlor's lifetime.

Interaction effect The impact of overweighting and underweighting individual securities within sectors that are themselves overweighted or underweighted.

Internally managed assets Businesses in which the individual or family holds controlling or direct ownership, privately owned residential real estate, or other properties that generate value through the client's activities; human capital is an important component of internally managed assets.

Intestacy Dying without a will.

Investor visa A visa that offers temporary residency in exchange for specified investments in local businesses or industries, without guaranteeing a route to full citizenship.

Irrevocable trust A trust that cannot be changed or revoked by the settlor.

Joint life annuity An annuity that covers two annuitants, typically spouses with lifetime payments. Also called *survivor option*.

Joint tenants with right of survivorship (JTWROS) A form of ownership of property in which two or more individuals own the property together, and upon the death of one of the owners, the deceased owner's share automatically passes to the surviving owner(s).

Kinecon group A network of individuals that share both a kinship bond and economic interests.

Liability risk The risk of financial losses due to legal responsibility for property damage or personal injury.

Life annuity with period certain An annuity in which the annuitants are guaranteed a minimum number of payments even if they die prematurely, with any remaining payments going to a designated beneficiary.

Life annuity with return-of-premium An annuity that ensures that if the annuitant passes away before recouping the initial investment, the unpaid principal balance, after subtracting any fees and adjustments, is disbursed to a designated beneficiary.

Life insurance wrappers A type of financial product that allows investors to house a variety of assets, such as equities or hedge funds, within a life insurance policy coverage structure and to benefit from tax advantages on investment income generated by these assets.

Lifespan The number of years of life from birth to death.

Lifetime annuity An annuity in which annuitants can opt to receive payments for their entire lives. Also called *period-certain payments.*

Lifetime gifts Gifts made during lifetime, usually for tax purposes.

Liquidity event Converts heretofore illiquid assets into more liquid assets either in the form of cash or securities.

Liquidity premium The compensation for liquidity risk that increases in proportion to the investment's illiquidity.

Liquidity risk The risk that an investment may not be readily sold at its true value.

Logarithmic active return The natural log of 1+Arithmetic active return.

Long-term versus short-term orientation A Hofstede cultural dimension that refers to the degree to which cultures encourage delayed gratification of material, social, and emotional needs.

Longevity risk The risk of exhausting an individual's financial resources before passing away, thereby leaving insufficient capital for living expenses and unmet needs.

Loss control Strategies implemented to mitigate or prevent a loss.

Loss prevention Strategies implemented to mitigate the likelihood of incurring a loss.

Loss reduction Strategies implemented to mitigate the impact after a loss occurs.

Masculine versus feminine A Hofstede cultural dimension that defines "masculine values" as success, wealth, and personal accomplishment and "feminine values" as those that emphasize caring for others and a holistic quality of life.

Mission-related investing Investing aimed at causes promoting positive societal or environmental change.

Money scripts Function as unconscious "tapes" consisting of beliefs and attitudes about money that are informed and shaped by one's experiences as a child or a young adult.

Multi-family office Unlike a single-family office that serves one affluent family, a multi-family office (MFO) provides comprehensive wealth management services to multiple high-net-worth families. The scale allows for a diversified service offering and potential cost efficiencies.

Multi-partiality A facilitation technique in which the advisor takes the sides of all participants simultaneously, thus giving equal attention to the many identities and experiences of the dialogue participants.

Net New Business Volume The volume of new business across new and existing clients.

Net New Money New sources of revenue obtained within a specific time frame, net of cancellations and other revenue deductions. In private wealth management, it is a key measure of the effectiveness of Relationship Managers and other asset gatherers.

Neuroticism A personality trait characterizing the degree to which a person displays emotional instability.

No contest clause A provision included in an estate plan that disinherits any beneficiary who challenges the plan.

Non-discretionary financial goals Encompass necessary expenses essential for sustaining the current lifestyle.

Non-forfeiture clause Clause allowing policyholders of permanent life insurance to access a portion of their benefits even if they miss premium payments, provided this is done before the policy lapses.

Non-grantor charitable lead trust A charitable lead trust where the donor is not a remainder beneficiary.

Non-participating life insurance Insurance that offers policyholders fixed benefits that remain unaffected by the insurer's profits or performance.

Offshore Financial Centers (OFCs) Jurisdictions that provide financial services to non-residents in a way that is more regulatory-efficient or tax-efficient than the client's home jurisdiction. These centers often attract capital flows seeking tax optimization, asset protection, or enhanced confidentiality.

Offshore trust A trust established in a foreign jurisdiction, often a foreign tax haven.

Openness A personality trait characterizing the willingness to be open to new experiences.

Participating life insurance Insurance that enables policyholders to share in the insurer's profits via potential dividends above the guaranteed value.

PATRIOT Act A US law enacted in 2001 which, among other goals, was aimed at preventing the funding of terrorist activities.

Performance attribution The process of disaggregating a portfolio's return to determine the drivers of its performance.

Permanent life insurance A type of life insurance that remains in force for the insured's entire lifetime, provided the premiums are consistently paid, and offers an accumulated cash value component.

Personal umbrella liability policy Such an insurance offers specified limits and pays claims when the liability limits of the home or auto insurance are reached, thereby providing additional coverage.

Polysemy Refers to the fact that value terms can have multiple meanings to different people.

Postnuptial agreements Contracts signed after marriage that outline the division of assets, debts, and financial obligations in case of divorce or death.

Power distance index A Hofstede cultural dimension that reflects the degree to which a society accepts that power in social groups is distributed unequally.

Prenuptial agreements Contracts signed before marriage that outline the division of assets, debts, and financial obligations in case of divorce or death.

Prepaid variable forward A contract that offers the asset owner an immediate cash payment, without immediate tax consequences, from a sale.

Private grant-making foundation An independent legal entity created for charitable purposes in which the donor funds the foundation and receives a tax deduction, and the foundation must distribute at least 5% of its assets annually towards charitable endeavors.

Private Placement Life Insurance (PPLI) A form of variable universal life insurance that offers more extensive investment choices and greater flexibility compared to traditional life insurance products. Often used by high-net-worth individuals for tax optimization and estate planning, PPLI policies are not publicly available and must be purchased through private placement. The policyholder can customize the asset allocation, which may include a range of investment options often not available in standard life insurance policies.

Probability of ruin The likelihood that an investor will deplete their financial assets before meeting a specific financial obligation or goal, including sustaining spending throughout retirement.

Probate A legal proceeding to confirm the validity of a will.

Professional family office (PFO) An institutionally backed entity that offers comprehensive services to its wealthy clients (also known as an institutional family office [IFO]).

Property or wealth tax Applies to property, real estate, financial, and other assets and is usually assessed annually.

Prudent investor rule The rule of law that governs trust investing.

Publicly supported charitable organizations Charities in the United States receive at least one-third of their support from the public, such as churches, hospitals, museums, and schools.

Qualified charitable distribution An income tax-free gift of up to USD 100,000 made via a required minimum distribution from a US retirement plan.

Related-party, arm's-length transaction A business arrangement between a company and its owners or executives made on terms that are comparable to what would be offered in the open market to unrelated parties under similar circumstances.

Residence rules The time a person can spend in a country without becoming a taxable resident.

Resident An individual or entity subject to tax in a specific country based on such factors as domicile or physical residence.

Revocable trust A trust that can be changed or revoked by the settlor.

Risk acceptance The decision of assuming specific risks and a strategy to mitigate the overall financial exposure based on one's financial capacity.

Risk avoidance The decision of avoiding specific risks and a strategy to mitigate the overall likelihood of significant loss by eliminating certain risks.

Risk mitigation Strategies implemented to mitigate the severity or probability of financial loss.

Risk transfer Strategies implemented to mitigate the impact of specific risks by transferring them to an insurance company.

Robo-Advisers Automated investment platforms that use algorithms to provide financial planning services with minimal human intervention. While they often serve retail clients, they are increasingly being integrated into wealth management offerings for more affluent clients.

Rule against perpetuities A common law rule that requires trusts to terminate or vest within 21 years after the date of death of a group of individuals who were alive when the trust was created or where a fixed date for termination or vesting is required.

Selection effect The impact of overweighting and underweighting individual securities relative to the benchmark on the return of the portfolio.

Separate property The regime in which each spouse can own and control property as an individual, enabling each to dispose of property as they wish.

Separate property regimes Regimes that consider pre-marital or post-marital gifts and inheritances as individual property.

Settlor A person who creates and funds a trust, also sometimes referred to as a grantor.

Shari'a law The law of Islam.

Sharpe ratio The ratio of mean excess return to standard deviation (excess return).

Short sale against the box position A hedging strategy that shorts a security that is held long.

Single-family office (SFO) A corporate structure owned by a single family and dedicated to the management of family assets and the fulfillment of individual and tailored needs of family members.

Single-premium immediate annuity (SPIA) An annuity converting a lump-sum investment into fixed annual income for a predetermined period or lifetime.

Social desirability bias A bias in which individuals give an answer that they believe is more socially acceptable than their genuine and authentic feeling.

Socioemotional wealth (SEW) A methodology to understand how family firms make decisions regarding the disposition of their business. It takes into account the fact that family business owners are often motivated by considerations other than profit.

Source state Jurisdiction where income originates—generally where the related economic activity takes place.

Stamp duties Taxes imposed on the purchase price of assets like shares or real estate.

Stewardship of wealth Refers to the responsible management of one's wealth to ensure a positive, lasting impact. It is typically manifested by wealthy individuals through philanthropy and aligning assets with values to benefit both family and society.

Stiftung A structure similar to an institution or foundation used in civil law jurisdictions for wealth transfer purposes.

Supposedly irrelevant factors (SIFs) A factor that is supposedly irrelevant to a decision being made. In practice, however, some SIFs have an outsized influence on decision making.

Surplus The difference between assets and liabilities, analogous to shareholders' equity on a corporate balance sheet.

Tax avoidance The practice of using legal means to reduce tax liability by conforming to both the spirit and the letter of the tax codes in relevant jurisdictions.

Tax domicile Country where an individual is considered a tax resident.

Tax evasion The illegal act of reducing tax liability by deliberately misreporting or concealing information from tax authorities.

Tax haven A country or independent region with no or very low tax rates for foreign investors.

Tax lot Represents the quantity, cost basis, and date of the security for tax purposes in a particular transaction.

Tax-deferred account Investment and contributions may be made on a pretax basis, and investment returns accumulate on a tax-deferred basis until funds are withdrawn, at which time they are typically taxed at ordinary income.

Tax-exempt account Taxes may or may not be assessed on the initial investment or contribution. Investment returns are typically allowed to grow and the proceeds withdrawn without tax.

Tax-loss harvesting A strategy used by investors to reduce their tax liability in taxable accounts by creating a tax offset, and involves selling securities at a loss to offset capital gains, thereby reducing the net tax liability in that period.

Taxable account The normal tax rules of the jurisdiction apply.

Term life insurance A type of life insurance that provides coverage for a predetermined period but lacks a cash value component and becomes void if the insured individual either fails to pay the premiums or does not die within the policy term. Also called *temporary life insurance.*

Territorial tax system A country that taxes income sourced within its borders; also known as source jurisdiction.

Testamentary A provision in a will.

Testamentary documents Documents such as a will or testamentary trust that take effect at death.

Testamentary gratuitous transfer A gift by will.

Testamentary trust A trust created under a will.

Testator The person who creates a will.

Tontine A pooled decumulation vehicle that allows longevity risk to the moderated by averaging.

Transfer tax The tax imposed on the transfer of assets, including gift tax, estate tax, inheritance tax, and generation-skipping tax.

Treaty shopping The attempt by a taxpayer to leverage treaty tax advantages without engaging in genuine economic activities in either country.

Trust A structure whereby legal title to assets is held by one person (a trustee) who holds and manages the assets for the benefit of a third party or parties (the beneficiaries) who are the beneficial owners of the assets.

Trust agreement The document that sets forth the terms of a trust.

Trustee A person who has legal title to assets in the trust and who must administer the trust for the benefit of its beneficiaries.

Unanchored inflation expectations The anticipation of rising inflation rates in the future, subsequently influencing economic decision-making for consumers, manufacturers, and service providers.

Uncertainty avoidance index A Hofstede cultural dimension that considers the degree to which individuals are comfortable in ambiguous situations and tolerant of risk.

Universal life insurance A flexible type of permanent life insurance that permits adjustable premiums and offers investment options for the accumulated cash value, remaining in effect as long as premiums are paid.

Virtual family office (VFO) A legally organized business designed to manage, control, and facilitate both the financial and non-financial wealth and transactions of a family.

Wash sale An investor sells a security at a loss and buys a very similar or substantially identical stock or security within a given time period before or after the sale.

Wealth transfer tax Tax when assets are transferred from one owner to another through means other than a direct sale or purchase.

Whole life insurance A life insurance policy that provides coverage for the insured's entire lifetime, with premiums usually paid annually. See *Permanent life insurance.*

Will A legal document that becomes effective after a person's death that disposes of that person's property.

Withholding taxes Imposed by countries for non-resident investors for interest and dividend payments. Depending on the jurisdictions involved, there may be tax treaties between the sending and receiving countries, which will impact the withholding tax rate.

Worldwide tax systems Jurisdictions that tax all income no matter where it's earned.

Zeroed-out CLAT A charitable lead annuity trust with an annuity so large that the actuarial remainder value is zero.